THE BEST OF CELLARS

THE STORY OF THE CAVERN CLUB

THE BEST OF CELLARS

THE STORY OF THE CAVERN CLUB

PHIL THOMPSON

TEMPUS

This book is dedicated to Linda, Louise and Helen.
And two cave dwellers, Peter and Brian.

First published 1994 by The Bluecoat Press
This edition first published 2007

Tempus Publishing Limited
The Mill, Brimscombe Port,
Stroud, Gloucestershire, GL5 2QG
www.tempus-publishing.com

British Library Cataloguing in Publication Data.
A catalogue record for this book is available from the British Library.

ISBN 978 0 7524 4202 0

Typesetting and origination by Tempus Publishing Limited
Printed in Great Britain

CONTENTS

ACKNOWLEDGEMENTS

Thanks to: Holly Bennion, Rob Sharman, Lucy Chowns and all at Tempus Publishing.

Special thanks to: Cavern DJ Bob Wooler, Roger Baskeyfield, Johnny 'Guitar' Byrne, Ken Cochran, Frankie Connor, Tony Davis, Bob Ellis, Ralph Ellis, Mick Groves, Bill Heckle, Tommy Hughes, George James, John Lawrence, Charles Lyth, Peter Morris, Phil Munroe, Dave Percy, Alan Stratton, Alan Sytner, Brian Thompson, Steve Voce, Dave Williams, Ozzie Yue, *The Beatles Monthly* and the Cavern Club.

Grateful thanks also to Robin Bird for the use of his photographs from the Bob Bird archive and to Monty Lister for his help and assistance.

Cavern diary researched and compiled by Peter Thompson.

Opposite: Resident DJ Bob Wooler on stage at the Cavern, with actor Peter Adamson (Len Fairclough in *Coronation Street*) and two members of the Hideaways in 1964.

FOREWORD BY BOB WOOLER

RESIDENT DJ/COMPERE AT LIVERPOOL'S
WORLD FAMOUS CAVERN CLUB 1961-1967

Henry Ford is believed to have said 'History is bunk!' and in way of saying the same thing, only satirically, Oscar Wilde declared that 'the duty we owe to history is to rewrite it'.

Facile and facetious, and very quotable, these remarks may well be. But of course simplistic. All our yesterdays cannot be so glibly dismissed.

Bygone episodes of good vibrations should be cherished, especially if one has played a pivotal part in helping to create them.

Telling how it really was may well be unpalatable. But it should be done, if only through a sense of history, so that future generations will have something reliable to work on.

So many unbelievable exaggerations, embellishments and downright inventions of incidents have come about since The Beatles' Cavern was bulldozed out of existence (where was the outcry at the time?) about thirty years ago, that I now regard Mathew Street as 'Mythew Street'.

Like the cola we used to sell at the Cavern in its soft drinks days, I believe in giving researchers and writers and tourists the 'Real Thing.' They may not warm to what I reveal, being used to the cosy, rosy Fab-rications of others. But I feel impelled, for the record, to present an undistorted picture, warts and all. I let others present it warps and all.

I take the uncompromising view that if they want to hear it from the horse's mouth – halitosis and all – they know where to come. If they want to hear it from the other end of the horse, they know where to go!

The Merseybeat rock 'n' roll era of the 1950s and '60s was an exceptional time and without putting too great an emphasis on it, it must go down in pop music annals. The Beatles, of course, have ensured that.

Although many 'menus' and many venues had a hand in fashioning the fads and fabs of forty years ago, the Cavern Club, with its imperishable Beatles' connection, became its bedrock symbol. (Did you know that the group played at the club more times than at all their other Merseyside engagements put together?)

Almost all my memories of the Cavern are good ones. But there are one or two that struck a sour note. Here, for the record, is one of them. The club, like most others, had a chequered career – sometimes a rubber chequered one! It started out as a jazz scene and then progressed to beat group sounds. Or, as some jazz die-hards maintained, it *retrogressed* as a result.

But then, as everywhere in commercial entertainment, the sweetest music is made by the cash register. One of my most unpleasant recollections was when I was lambasted by a certain jazz band, who played regularly at the club and obviously had an eye to the frequency of their future bookings, who verbally lacerated me for encouraging rock 'n' roll to be played. In no uncertain terms they told me that I should be ashamed of myself for supporting such 'trashy, amateurish kids' music'. (This was particularly hurtful to me, as at heart I was a big band 'closet' fan, valuing the likes of Duke Ellington, Stan Kenton, Ella, Sinatra and the Golden Age songwriters.)

This intimidating band didn't exactly rough me up, physically that is, but they came very near to it, and I had to stomach some very nasty remarks. Thankfully, ugly incidents of this sort were overwhelmed by the harmonious ones. I only mention this now in case anyone should misguidedly think that everything was beer and skittles in those days.

I feel reassured that Phil Thompson, the author of this book, has made every effort to research the scene thoroughly, bearing in mind how the passage of time can play tricks with the memory. (Should any Cavernite reader detect any glaring errors or omissions, I'm sure the author will be glad to learn of them, via the publisher, as indeed I will.)

Yes, all in all, I can recommend this history of the world's greatest rock 'n' roll club – the Cavern, Liverpool, of course! Where else? You'll find it contains some astounding recollections!

My advice is don't just borrow this book from the library. Treat yourself to a copy instead, and keep it handy for reference. It's bound to bring back lots of feel-good memories to those who were around at the time. And for those who had (have) yet to come, they'll learn why the beat goes on, and on, and on...

Charlie and Inez Foxx along with the Spencer Davis Group at the Cavern in July 1964. Bob Wooler, Ray McFall and a young Stevie Winwood (extreme right) can also be seen.

Chapter 1

THE CAVERN JAZZ CLUB OPENS

Gerry Marsden summed up the Cavern Club in a few words: 'It stank of disinfectant and stale onions. It was hot, sweaty and oppressive.' This is universally agreed, yet the club achieved legendary status as the birthplace of the great 1960s beat scene, assuring it of a key position in popular music history.

Although famed for its role in the story of The Beatles, the history of the Cavern Club actually begins in the mid-1950s with Alan Sytner, the son of Dr Joe Sytner, a popular Liverpool dockland GP. Alan was running two jazz clubs, the 21 Jazz Club which was based in Toxteth and the West Coast Jazz Club, which was based at the Temple Restaurant on Sunday nights. Jazz at the Temple was popular, but the restaurant was not the ideal setting for a jazz club, and Alan began to look for premises where he could set up a permanent city-centre jazz Mecca for Liverpool's growing band of jazz enthusiasts. The type of club he hoped to set up was influenced by a holiday he had taken in France. Many of the Paris jazz clubs were situated on the Left Bank of the Seine, several of which were built into caves. One club in particular, Le Caveau Français, impressed Alan greatly and he hoped one day to create a similar type of club in Liverpool. Alan's search for his ideal venue led him to Mathew Street, a small alley that housed warehouses for fruit and other food products. The cellars of 10 Mathew Street were particularly suitable, with the arches having been strengthened to make sure it was sturdy enough to be used as an air-raid shelter during the war. The basement, in fact, looked like a section of subway tunnels. There were three parallel barrel vaults, each of them being about a hundred feet long and ten feet wide and joined by six-foot archways. Alan Sytner had found the premises that had the potential to be turned into Liverpool's first major jazz club.

Alan's decision to go ahead with his plans to open the Cavern upset his father, who had hoped that his son would one day follow him into the medical profession. The finance for the venture came from a £400 insurance policy that Alan received when he reached the age of twenty-one. Once the Cavern opened, however, Dr Sytner's antipathy towards his son's new profession soon faded and on occasion he would even assist in the running of the club, with Alan's mother also helping out at the refreshment bar.

Alan Sytner still took a huge financial gamble when he decided to go ahead with his plans to open the club. Once he had made his decision, improvements were made to the floors of the cellars; the brickwork, in keeping with the cave-like atmosphere he hoped to create, was painted black. A small wooden stage was constructed and large quantities of wooden chairs were purchased to give a certain amount of comfort for the jazz fans. The majority of the work was carried out by a large group of volunteers, most of whom were jazz enthusiasts from Sytner's previous clubs. Armed with paint brushes they set about converting the cellar into their own jazz venue. Although Alan Sytner was the manager and owner of the club, it was run under the guidelines set out by the National Jazz Union. The main aim of the Union was to promote and stimulate support for jazz on Merseyside. A yearly subscription rate was set at one shilling and a committee was formed to preside over the operation of the club. The decision to name the club the Cavern was obviously influenced by Sytner's visit to Le Caveau Français in Paris, but he recently admitted that in some ways it was a coincidence. He was looking for a basic name like 'Cave,' something that typified the basic nature of the club, and the name Cavern seemed to fit the bill perfectly. It is

Clockwise from top left:
Mathew Street in the 1920s. It had hardly changed when the Cavern Club opened in 1957.

Advertisement for the opening night of the Cavern Club.

The man who opened what was to become the most famous club in the world, Alan Sytner, deep in thought at an empty Cavern in January 1957. Sytner sold the club to Ray McFall in 1958 for £2,750. Alan Sytner then went on to launch one of Britain's largest BMW dealerships in Nottingham. Sytner retired to Cannes, France in the 1990s and died in January 2006.

The Dolphins Jazz Band.

The Dolphins Jazz Band performing at the first Saturday session at the Cavern on 20 January 1957.

Above left: The headline act at the opening night of the Cavern in January 1957, the Merseysippi Jazz Band. The first act to actually appear on the Cavern stage was the Wall City Jazzmen.

Above right: George Webb plays piano at a Cavern after-hours party in 1958. Webb was credited with instigating the post-war trad jazz revival in Britain.

interesting to note, however, that an article in the *Liverpool Evening Express* in August 1956 actually invited readers to send suggestions to Alan Sytner stating what they thought the club should be named.

The opening acts at the Cavern were the Merseysippi Jazz Band, the Wall City Jazzmen, the Ralph Watmough Jazz Band and the Coney Island Skiffle Group. Alan Sytner had stated in the newspaper advertisements for the Cavern's opening that the club was to be opened by jazz drummer the Earl of Wharncliffe, but Peter Morris recalls that the Earl, in fact, was never invited to the opening:

> All the publicity in the *Liverpool Echo* had mentioned the official opening by the Earl of Wharncliffe. There was no sign of the Earl on the opening night and when I asked Alan when he was coming he told me that he had just used his name for publicity purposes. It didn't stop Alan getting up onto the stage at the start of the evening and announcing that due to a family bereavement the Earl could not be present and he was to be sent a letter of condolence!

As it turned out, there could not have been a more appropriate opening act than the Merseysippi, who are still going strong forty-five years after their formation, and when it comes to the Liverpool jazz scene the band have achieved the same kind of legendary status as the Cavern Club itself.

Jazz writer Steve Voce recently said of the Merseysippi, 'People go on about Liverpool being symbolised by The Beatles and things like that. Well you can keep that sort of thing. For me Liverpool is symbolised by the Merseysippi Jazz Band.' They were originally formed in 1949 when founding members Dick Goodwin, Frank Robinson and Ken Metcalf decided to set themselves up as a jazz trio after meeting at a record collectors club in Wallasey known as the Wallasey Rhythm Club. They were soon joined by other jazz enthusiasts, but not on a permanent basis, and it was not until John Lawrence on trumpet, Frank Parr on trombone and Pete Daniels, also on trumpet, joined that they had their first permanent line-up. Londoner Pete Daniels, in fact, first heard the Merseysippi when they made their first radio broadcast for the BBC. The following day he travelled up to Merseyside to watch the band play and decided to take up their offer to become a member. With the addition of Pete, the Merseysippi now had a unique two-trumpet front line. By the time the Merseysippi performed at the Cavern opening night the band had gone through several changes in their line-up, most notably the replacement of the trombone player (former Lancashire County Cricket Club wicketkeeper Frank Parr) by Johnny Parkes. Parr had decided to take up the offer to join the Mick Mulligan Band in 1954.

When the Merseysippi took to the stage at the Cavern on the evening of Wednesday 16 January 1957, it was estimated that more than 600 people were crammed into the cellar, with over 1,000 disappointed jazz fans unable to gain entrance crowding into Mathew Street and the surrounding area. Delighted by the Cavern's initial success and fully vindicated in his gamble to take the plunge and open up Liverpool's first major jazz club, Sytner now decided to fulfil his main ambition which was to bring some of the star names in jazz to the Cavern. He decided to present traditional jazz on Fridays, Saturdays and Sundays and modern jazz on a Thursday. For modern jazz nights the club changed its name to the Club Perdido. Within a short period of time the Cavern membership was running into several thousand and by 1959 it was estimated at 25,000. Recalling the early days of the Cavern, Steve Voce had little doubt that this was a golden period for jazz enthusiasts: 'The Cavern gave us our first focal point for jazz in the city, and it was here that the gifted amateur jazzman first came into contact with the professional dance musicians who played at, say, the Grafton or Reeces' for a living, but liked to play jazz for kicks.' Always conscious of the value of publicity for the Cavern, Alan Sytner invented a story about a ghost being spotted in the ladies' toilet and the *Daily Herald* ran the story. On another occasion he hired a Cavern regular, Maureen Hayden, to act as an 'anti-smooch' girl. Maureen would go around the club checking if couples were getting too amorous and she would give them a tap on the shoulder and tell them to cool down. The newspapers got hold of the story and the *Sunday People* informed the nation of the Cavern's 'anti-smooch girl'. Those who knew him at the time remember Sytner as a tough, confident man, and it was not unknown for him to go into a rival club, where a local jazz band would be playing, and announce, 'I've come to see if you're good enough to play at the Cavern!'

Clockwise from top left:
Jazz musicians jam at an after-hours Cavern party in 1958.

An after-hours jam session at the Cavern in 1958.

An early press advertisement for the Cavern Club.

A SPOOK IN BOOTS IN THE POWDER ROOM

By Don Smith

THE basement jazz group was gettin' real c-o-o-l when "Short John" invaded the ladies' powder room.

Sure, a guy can make a mistake. But "Short John" didn't withdraw blushing.

WELL, I MEAN, WHO EVER SAW A GHOST BLUSH?

Typist Jacqueline McColl, aged 20, and Edie Moreland, 21, certainly blushed.

They were changing their office dresses for dance outfits.

Said Jacqueline: "It was horrible. A thing in black thigh-boots appeared between us.

"... to pick up our coats, wrap them around us and run out."

▢ A joke ▢

Edie, a costing clerk, added: "At first we thought it was one of the band playing a joke. Then we realised we could see through him."

Members of the Cavern Club took the cellar story about the indiscreet phantom with a pinch of salt.

That is until it was seen by 20-year-old Jean McCall.

She was straightening her stocking in the smallest room in the club.

Said Jean: "It nearly frightened me out of my nylons. He was just like a Teddy Boy—except he wore strange clothes.

"He just stood there—I ran. I'm not going back in there again."

Now ex-university student Alan Sytner, who started the club, has a problem.

It seems the jazzmen have disturbed an 18th century ghost in his silent haunts.

Could be.

Records indicate that the cellar, 20ft. below a Liverpool warehouse in Mathew-street, was once used by a slave-trading firm.

▢ Stop it ▢

But Mr. Sytner means to put an end to "Short John"—the name the jazz fans have given him.

A local psychical research group will spend all Saturday night in the ... er ... powder room. Alternative arrangements have been made for the ladies.

The group will be armed with tape-recorders and cameras.

Said Mr. Sytner: "We'll soon know if there is a 'ghost.'

"PERHAPS THE MODERN JAZZ WOKE HIM UP."

EDIE MORELAND
"We screamed."

JACQUELINE McCOLL
"It was horrible."

JEAN McCALL
"Never again."

Clockwise from top left:
Bootle-born Ron McKay, a regular performer at the Cavern. McKay later went on to become the drummer with the Acker Bilk Paramount Jazz Band.

The Merseysippi Jazz Band with the legendary Louis Armstrong.

Alan Sytner's Cavern Club achieves national exposure in the newspapers again when a ghost is spotted at the Club in 1958.

Clinton Ford performs for the girls at Butlins Holiday Camp, Pwllheli in 1959.

Chapter 2

SKIFFLE AT THE CAVERN

Apart from trad jazz, Alan Sytner also introduced skiffle nights at the Cavern. The term 'skiffle' was originally applied to the type of music played in the poorer parts of Chicago, New Orleans and other jazz centres. The music was often of an improvisational nature, with the instruments played including such items as jugs, washboards and packing cases. Skiffle was brought into prominence in the 1940s and early 1950s when revivalist groups would perform songs in the hillbilly style, with guitar and washboard being the main instruments used. Skiffle in Britain was introduced as an interval attraction in jazz clubs, most notably by Ken Colyer's band, with Chris Barber playing double bass and Ken Colyer on guitar. As early as 1949 the two of them would perform American blues and folk songs such as 'Midnight Special', while the rest of the band were taking an interval break.

By 1952 Ken Colyer and Chris Barber were still performing skiffle during the interval, but were now joined by the banjo player in the band, Lonnie Donegan, for their skiffle set. When Chris Barber took over the Colyer band in 1954, a skiffle New Orleans Joy album was recorded by Barber, with singer Beryl Bryden playing washboard. When one of the recorded tracks, 'Rock Island Line', became an unexpected hit single in 1956, it was inevitable that lead singer Lonnie Donegan would become the focal point for the record's success. Later in 1956 Donegan left the Barber band to begin a solo career and went on to achieve a long line of hit records. Speaking to *Reveille* magazine in May 1957, Lonnie revealed how he got involved in the skiffle craze:

I was a jazzman happily playing and singing with Chris Barber's jazz band. The only thing that made me leave him was an offer to tour America with the chance of visiting that shrine of jazz, New Orleans. I had been a jazzman for years. I knew all about New Orleans and the men who created jazz there. I knew all the names, the streets, the dives and the songs. I had even given myself the name of Lonnie Donegan because of Lonnie Johnson who was one of the great men of jazz. So I took a trip to America and skiffle has become my life. It springs from jazz and I am a jazzman first, last and always. Skiffle is light-hearted American folk music with a jazz slant and a very definite beat. The songs reflect the life of the southern negro of the early 1920s; they are work songs, songs of despair, hope, cynicism and love. It was first played by the poor negroes in New Orleans to raise money to pay the rent and for fun. A man who owed money to his landlord would buy beer and invite his friends to a 'rent party' for which he would charge a small admission fee. To make the party go with a swing the guests made instruments from comb and paper, stone jars and anything they could find. Words were added and that was skiffle.

The success of Donegan's brand of skiffle led to a boom in Britain, with a multitude of skiffle groups being formed overnight. Sales of guitars began to rocket as teenagers clamoured to participate in a brand of music that did not demand a great degree of musical prowess to play. If you had the ability to learn a few chords, could find yourself an old tea chest that was converted into a one-string bass, and discover someone with a sense of rhythm to play washboard, you were in business. Skiffle has been described as Britain's first do-it-yourself music and, following the lead of British innovators such as Colyer and Donegan, there was no shortage of young Merseysiders keen to participate in the brand of music which had its roots in jazz and folk.

Leftt: Liverpool's top folk act The Spinners. They began life as the Gin Mill Skiffle Group before changing their name to The Spinners. In the 1960s and '70s they were one of the most popular folk groups in the country and had their own television show. As The Spinners they made three Cavern appearances.

Below: The Gin Mill Skiffle Group performing at the Cavern in 1957. Tony Davis (centre stage) and Mick Groves (playing guitar to his right) went on to form The Spinners folk group.

One of the first on Merseyside was the Gin Mill Skiffle Group formed by future Spinners Tony Davis, Mick Groves and Tony's wife Beryl. Their first major booking was at Alan Sytner's 21 club based at the Temple Restaurant. Sytner was suitably impressed by the Gin Mill and when he opened the Cavern the group soon became residents at the jazz cellar. Mick Groves remembered:

It was a bit like the 'Yosser' character in Alan Bleasdale's *Boys From The Blackstuff*. Skiffle made us all feel 'I can do that' just like 'Yosser'! It was very basic and easy to learn. It gave you the chance to get up on stage and have a go. I think people sometimes underestimate how important Lonnie Donegan was to everyone, whether it was beat or folk music that you moved into. Lonnie was a working-class lad from Glasgow who moved into jazz, then skiffle and he certainly addressed working-class lads like me from Salford. He made us realise we could create our own music. Before skiffle I used to listen to the dance bands, who had singers like Dickie Valentine, but to me it was nothing new, it wasn't creative and skiffle gave me a chance to be creative. I started to make my own music and it gave me the opportunity to be a part of the creative process and not just an onlooker. It wasn't just a splinter faction like the punks, it was all the kids having a go, we were all creating something. Later on when the Beatles and the other beat groups came along and we moved into folk we were creating something, we didn't know it was new, but we were definitely creating something, and Lonnie Donegan definitely gave us the impetus to participate

in this creative process. In the early days of the Spinners, all the things that were said about Merseybeat were being said about us. The music of the early Spinners was described as raw and it came from the same black roots as beat music. It all had links with the blues.

Tommy Hughes of The Swinging Blue Genes got his cousin, cartoonist Bill Tidy, to design this calling card for the group in the late 1950s.

Liverpool skiffle groups such as the Gin Mill and Ron McKay were soon attracting audiences of over 400 to the weekly all-skiffle sessions at the Cavern, the Gin Mill always opening with their signature tune 'Down By The Riverside'. Ron McKay's group were top of the bill on the historic day of 7 August 1957 when John Lennon's Quarrymen along with the Demon Five, the Deltones and Dark Town skiffle groups played as support acts. It has to be remembered that the Cavern was very much a jazz club and skiffle was only tolerated because of its jazz origins. Alan Sytner recently confirmed that when Lennon began to sing Elvis material he had a note sent to him, telling the young rocker in no uncertain terms to 'Cut out the bloody rock!' Paul McCartney was not available to play at the Cavern that historic night, making his Cavern debut with the Quarrymen on the 24 January 1958, but Alan recently received a message from Paul that read, 'Dear Alan, I'm still playing that bloody rock!'

Skiffle at the Cavern proved such a success that Alan Sytner decided to hold a skiffle festival at the club and this took place on 26 June 1957. Twenty local skiffle groups turned up to perform at the club and each group brought with them their own group of fans from whatever youth club or school they originated from. This factor alone swelled the attendance by close on 500 extra fans, many of whom were to become Cavern regulars of the future.

Similar to Mick Groves, Paul McCartney was also soon under the spell of Lonnie Donegan and when Lonnie arrived in Liverpool in 1956 to play at the Empire Theatre, Paul and a group of his schoolmates caught a bus into the city centre during their lunch hour to try and catch a glimpse of Lonnie as he arrived at the theatre. When Paul and his friends eventually got to see Lonnie as he made his way into the theatre's stage door, the skiffle star went up even further in Paul's esteem as he witnessed the courteous way that Lonnie treated his fans crowding around the stage door. Paul McCartney, in fact, along with George Harrison, was at one time a member of the Cavern-based Lonnie Donegan Fan Club, the secretary of which was Mick Groves. There can be little doubt that it was skiffle and Lonnie Donegan that laid the foundations for Merseybeat and the beat boom that was to sweep the nation in the 1960s. It was also out of skiffle that the blues boom grew; the movement that went some way to restoring the reputation of and gaining recognition for the great American originals who were such an influence on their young white devotees.

Above left: Johnny Parkes of the Merseysippi Jazz Band playing at the Cavern in 1958.

Above *right:* The Merseysippi Jazz Band in action at the Cavern in 1958.

With the evening sessions packed to capacity, Alan Sytner was confident that there would probably be sufficient interest to begin lunchtime jazz sessions at the club, which he hoped would attract city-centre workers and students to the Cavern during their lunchtime break. The first session took place on Wednesday 30 January 1957 and the opening lunchtime acts were the Architects Jazz Band and the Ron McKay Skiffle Group. Cavern favourites the Merseysippi Jazz Band also made the occasional lunchtime appearance, but the lunchtime jazz sessions usually consisted of performances by jazz musicians from an assortment of Merseyside bands who played under the name of the Don Lowes Dixielanders. They played together only at Cavern lunchtime sessions and on their Cavern debut the line-up was: Don Lowes pianist, a member of a leading dance band on Merseyside, Hugh Potter

bassist, a member of the Liverpool University Jazz Band, Trevor Carlisle, a drummer with the Merseysippi Jazz Band, John Elder trumpet, a member of the Red Carter Jazz Band, Artie Wiliams clarinet, who had his own jazz band in Ellesmere Port, Johnny Parkes from the Merseysippi and Pete Shaw from the Ralph Watmough Jazz Band who took turns on trombone, and Ron Mckay vocalist, who had his own skiffle group. Don Lowes told the *Liverpool Echo* what he hoped the informal lunchtime sessions would achieve:

Policy of the group is trad and we are especially interested in reviving little known early jazz tunes. One number we have is 'Honey Babe', an early Jelly Roll Morton number. We are also working on 'Blueberry Rhyme', a James P. Johnson original. Johnny Parkes, who participated in these lunchtime

Above left: The Merseysippi Jazz Band at the Cavern in 1958. Notice the modern art-style mural on the wall at the back of the Cavern stage. The practice of signing the wall did not begin until the beat groups started to play at the club in 1960.

Above right: The Merseysippi Jazz Band at the Cavern 1958.

sessions, recently admitted that although there was initially a lot of interest, it did fall away and after a few months, lunchtime jazz sessions at the Cavern generally consisted of performances by whoever bothered to turn up.

These sessions were, however, particularly popular with Mick Groves, who was a Liverpool school teacher during this period:

I always looked forward to the summer holidays because it gave me the opportunity to get down to the Cavern for the lunchtime sessions. It was often a source of amusement to me years later when some of my older pupils would arrive back at school after a lunchtime session watching The Beatles. They would rave about the place, probably thinking they had invented the Cavern and not realising that I was doing exactly the same thing as them a few years previous. I felt the same about the early Cavern scene as they did about the beat period.

Refreshments at the Cavern for the lunchtime sessions would consist of soft drinks and snacks, the club being unlicensed, but Mick Groves remembered that once the 12-2p.m. sessions had ended and the club began to empty out,

Alan Sytner would produce the Merrydown cider which went down well after a couple of hours spent in the, at times, stifling heat of the basement club. Although the Cavern was an unlicensed club, the general consensus of those who appeared there and from the fans who attended Cavern sessions, from jazz through to beat, was that very few decided to smuggle their own drink into the club during the late 1950s and early '60s. Mick Groves reflected:

I suppose some may have taken their own drink in but you never noticed it much. It was a young audience and to buy bottles of spirits was not cheap. They were not the days of supermarkets and off-licences and basically it wasn't worth the bother. It certainly wasn't smuggled in on the same scale as the Troubadour Club in London, which was another popular club that was unlicensed. At the Troubadour Club everyone took a half bottle of scotch into the place; the 'in' drink at the time being scotch and coke. At the Cavern you got high on the atmosphere and the music. If I did take a bottle of pale ale in with me it would last me the night. Nowadays everyone seems to want stimulants, but the Cavern was stimulating enough.

Chapter 3

RIVERBOAT SHUFFLE

Another innovation that the Cavern can take credit for was the Riverboat Shuffle on the Mersey. These were mainly jazz-oriented cruises aboard the Royal Iris ferry boat, and hark back to the jazz days of the club. They took place once or twice a year and one that Bob Wooler particularly remembers took place in the summer of 1962:

It was a really good night, and I'm sure everybody aboard had a marvellous time. The Beatles were on the bill and sharing honours with them was

Mr Acker Bilk and his Paramount Jazz Band. I told him that I often played his 'Creole Jazz' record at the Cavern lunchtimes, as it was one of my favourites. I was made up when he played the tune especially for me.

Bob goes on to say that Acker was very generous with the scotch, when they were ensconced in his cabin-cum-bedroom. 'By the end of the cruise,' Bob confesses, 'I didn't know whether the boat was rockin' and rollin' or me. It was certainly a night to remember alright.'

Scenes from the first Riverboat Shuffle in June 1957.

Clinton Ford performing at a jazz cruise in June 1957

Clinton Ford singing with the Merseysippi Jazz Band at the first Riverboat Shuffle jazz cruise in June 1957.

Above left: Cavern Club owner Alan Sytner with a friend during the first Riverboat Shuffle in June 1957.

Above right: Scene from the first Riverboat Shuffle in June 1957.

Right: Scene from the first Riverboat Shuffle in June 1957.

Chapter 4

JAZZ GREATS AT THE CAVERN

One of Alan Sytner's main ambitions for the Cavern was to bring some of the national jazz attractions to the club and, after its initial success, he felt he was now in a position to book some of jazz's top names. One of Sytner's first major bookings was Sister Rosetta Tharpe, the black American gospel singer, who was regarded as second only to Mahalia Jackson in instigating white interest in black gospel music. Sister Rosetta was touring Britain at the time and after appearing in Liverpool she asked to be taken to the Cavern to see the club where the Merseysippi Jazz Band played. Sister Rosetta had been backed by the Merseysippi during her Manchester performance and had obviously been impressed by them. She was suitably impressed with the club and, after the club members had gone home, participated in one of the legendary impromptu Cavern parties. From all accounts, the behind-closed-doors jam session went on until the following morning and she was so impressed with the hospitality shown to her and her husband that she decided to cancel a visit to London and stay in Liverpool for the weekend, declaring, 'Monte Carlo and Liverpool have provided the highlights of my European trip.'

Alan Sytner was delighted when Sister Rosetta agreed to return to Liverpool the following week to appear before the paying customers. Steve Voce was present at Sister Rosetta Tharpe's Cavern Club performance, which was, incidentally, her only club performance during her British tour, and recalls that her opening words as she stepped onto the Cavern stage were: 'You might wonder what a woman of God like me is doing in a place like this, well our Lord Jesus went down into the highways and the byways, and if it's good enough for him it's good enough for me.' After the show, during which she was backed by the Wall City Jazzmen, Steve went back with Sister Rosetta and her husband, Lazy Daddy, to the Adelphi Hotel where they were staying. After treating him to a few brandies, Sister Rosetta bade Steve farewell with a smacking kiss on the cheek and told him, 'Don't take any wooden nickels, Daddy!' Lazy Daddy, who enjoyed a drink or two, was, Steve recalls, unique amongst Americans:

> In those days the pub opening hours were horrendously complicated and all pubs shut at 10p.m. Lazy Daddy had come over on the *Queen Mary*, their first visit to Europe. The licensing laws totally baffled all Americans except Lazy Daddy, who had a complete working knowledge of opening hours twenty minutes after stepping off the boat.

Apart from Sister Rosetta Tharpe, a look at other leading American musicians who found their way to the Cavern to attend parties reads like a 'who's who' of jazz. The list included: Jimmy Rushing, Champion Jack Dupree, Zoot Sims, Earl Hines, George Wetling, Harold Baker and some of the Duke Ellington's band after they had appeared at Liverpool University. Practically every top British jazz musician played the Cavern during the 1950s and early 1960s, including Ken Colyer, Johnny Dankworth, Kenny Ball, Terry Lightfoot, Alex Welsh, George Chisholm, Tubby Hayes, Ronnie Scott, Acker Bilk and Humphrey Lyttelton.

Humphrey Lyttelton was a particular favourite at the Cavern during the trad boom of the 1950s and in March 1959 he was top of the bill at the club's Springtime Jazz Festival. Hundreds were locked out as 600 people packed into the Cavern to listen to Lyttelton's band and the Merseysippi. Don Smith

Far left: The Merseysippi Jazz Band seen here backing Big Bill Broonzy at the Temple Jazz Club, Liverpool in 1957. Broonzy also appeared at the Cavern in 1957.

Left: From left to right: Jazz singer Ottilie Patterson, writer Steve Voce and Sister Rosetta Thorpe. Sister Rosetta wowed Cavern regulars with her dynamic performance at the club.

reported in the trad jazz vernacular of the period on the night's activities for the *Daily Herald:*

It was hot. It was cool. It was cramped. It was gone. It was – man! – it WAS jazz. It went off like a bomb – this city youngster's answer to the strictly-square flickering screen at home. For more than six hundred guys and girls packed into the Cavern Club, Liverpool, for the city's first Springtime Jazz Festival. Yes it was the coolest – and the hottest – night of the year, as Humphrey Lyttelton and his gang vied with Merseyside's own semi professional jazz band – the Merseysippi outfit. There was little stompin! There just wasn't room, and more than two hundred were turned away when the cellar club got to the stage where fans were trying to listen on the stairway to the street. It was all worth hearing. Humph would be worth listening to even if you were a foot under water – as one man said. He made the rafters ring with an out-of-this-world version of Duke Ellington's 'Caravan'. Then he followed up with 'Bodega', a saxophone feature which also introduced 'Southern Sunset', a new number by Sydney Bechet, the man who wrote 'Petit Fleur', the jazz number which had swept America and is now heading towards the top of Britain's top ten. Every now and again the Blue Genes skiffle group came on the little concrete stage to give the big boys a rest. Then Humph and his seven merry men went on playing right through the night – long after the club members had left at midnight. They do it just for fun and

because they love jazz. With them were the Merseysippi band, and dawn wasn't far off the streets when they finished. It was a great night for cool cats... Even if it was in a cellar beneath an old cheese warehouse.

Don Smith's mention of the Bluegenes was probably the first publicity that the group had ever received in the national press, but within a few years the group, who appeared at the Cavern on well over 300 occasions, would be hitting the headlines with a string of hit records. Tommy Hughes, who was in the original Bluegenes line-up, recalled their Cavern debut:

Bruce McCaskill, who formed the group and also sorted out bookings for us, was very excited at getting us a gig at the newly-opened Cavern. We went down well at the Cavern because we were basically a mixture of trad jazz and skiffle. We would watch what the jazz bands played and then copy what they did. We would put all our energy into the performance and were soon being billed as the Ravin' Bluegenes.

At the Cavern we would play during the interval while the jazz musicians nipped out for a pint at the nearby Beaconsfield or the White Star. When they arrived back at the club we would then go for a pint ourselves. The Cavern was so hot and humid that you had to take the opportunity to get some liquid refreshment when you got the chance. There was always a good, easy-going atmosphere at the

American blues great Sonny Terry
who made two appearances at the
Cavern.

our proudest moment at the Cavern was when it was announced from the Cavern stage that the Bluegenes were about to embark on a tour of the East Coast. We were probably the first Liverpool group to get a booking outside the Merseyside area and we felt the big time was not far away. When we arrived at Cleethorpes we found out that we had, in fact, only been booked for one performance at this small social club and we were expected to go out and tout for further bookings ourselves. I often laugh when I think about the digs that had been arranged for us. We had to stay in the social club manager's house. It was a tiny place with just two bedrooms. In the end, the six of us had to sleep in one bed. This was the Bluegenes' first taste of stardom!

Apart from traditional jazz, modern jazz and skiffle, the Cavern also boasted performances at the club by blues greats such as Brownie McGee and Sonny Terry and the legendary Big Bill Broonzy. Broonzy appeared at the club in 1957 and a newspaper cutting from the period described his Cavern performance:

Big Bill Broonzy gave a superb demonstration of blues singing when he appeared at the Cavern the other night. He is one of those artists who, by force of personality, can hold an audience entranced even when he is little more than whispering. He showed that volume is not an important factor in singing. He sang such a badly abused number as 'Midnight Special', with refreshing restraint. Broonzy is one of the old-time singers who believed the guitar should be used to enhance a song and not to drown it.

Mick Groves witnessed Broonzy's performance that night and described him as absolutely brilliant:

I actually met him a few days earlier when he appeared at the Bodega Club, Manchester. After the show I was fortunate to sit and have a chat with him in the dressing room. As we talked about the blues I remember saying to him, 'I'm a young white kid from Salford, I'll never be able to sing the blues.' He turned to me and replied, 'Oh no, don't say that. Blues comes in all kinds of packages. Hey! Woody Guthrie sings the blues.' I'd never heard of Woody Guthrie at that stage and remember saying to him 'Who's Woody Guthrie?' Bill just smiled.

Mick's partner in the Spinners, Tony Davis, who is 6ft 7in tall, recalls Bill looking up at him (Bill was 6ft 3in) and saying, 'From now on they better call me Little Bill Broonzy!' Johnny Parkes of the Merseysippi also remembers chatting to Broonzy after his Cavern performance and feeling honoured when Broonzy complimented him on his trombone playing by saying, 'The way you play that trombone I'm sure you've got blue blood in your veins!'

Cavern during the days when the club was frequented by the student and beatnik types. But towards the late 1950s it did start to get a little rough when it was going through the transition from jazz to beat. I remember one night we were halfway through our set when one of the local gangs took over the front seats near the stage. They started to mess about with our amplification system and one of them pulled the plug from the wall bringing the proceedings to an abrupt halt. Ray Ennis told them to cut it out and after issuing a few threats, telling us what they were going to do to us once they got us outside, they left the club. We thought no more of it until one of the Cavern regulars informed us that they were one of the most notorious gangs in Liverpool and would not think twice about using hatchets and other weapons on us. For the rest of the evening we were terrified and we decided to wait until the early hours of the morning before leaving the club. I'll always remember the trepidation I felt as I climbed the Cavern steps and peered out into a dark, murky Mathew Street and the feeling of relief when I found that there was no gang lurking in the shadows waiting to give us a good hiding.

In general, the atmosphere at the Cavern was good and I remember one occasion when Alan Sytner introduced bingo sessions at the club. You never really knew what to expect when you turned up there for a gig. Probably

Steve Voce, recalling Broonzy at the Cavern, remembers someone handing Bill a bottle of whisky before the show began. He proceeded to finish this off within half an hour and then began to prepare for the show. Steve asked him would it be okay to tape record his performance. Bill told him that throughout his career he had been ripped off by people who had recorded him and then put out the performance on record without any royalties being paid to him. He said he could record the show but he wanted a piece of paper signed by Steve stating that the recording was not to be reproduced for profit. Steve agreed to do this but they couldn't find a piece of paper to write the agreement on. Bill then proceeded to tear off the label from the whisky bottle and Steve duly wrote on it an agreement that the tape recording would not be released as a record. Steve thought no more of it as he watched Bill stuff the paper into his pocket. After Broonzy's spellbinding performance the club was emptying out when Steve happened to glance at the stage floor of the club. There amongst the debris was the scrumpled whisky label on which the agreement had been drawn up.

Broonzy's whisky-drinking exploits on his tour of Britain were legendary and on another occasion Steve Voce remembered being in a transport cafe with Bill and he accompanied him to the counter. Bill began to survey the menu, which was on the wall behind the counter. After a short period Broonzy asked the assistant, 'You've got egg and chips, sausage and chips, pie and chips, fish and chips; is everything in this place with chips?' The puzzled assistant said it was. 'In that case,' replied Broonzy, 'I'll have a double scotch and chips!'

George Melly in his book *Owning Up* recalls Broonzy staying at his parents' Liverpool home after one of his performances:

He told my parents that this was the first house in England that he'd ever stayed in where you didn't have to put money in the meter for the gas fire. At breakfast Broonzy amazed my parents when he got through two plates of Cornflakes, two helpings of bacon and eggs, and about a loaf and a half of toast.

Aside from his eating habits, it's generally agreed by those who witnessed Broonzy's performances that he was a blues great, who was a major influence on the British R&B performers of the 1960s such as Alexis Korner and Eric Clapton.

George Melly had fond Cavern memories from his days playing at the club as a vocalist with the Mick Mulligan Band. During the interval he would dash to a nearby pub with Mick and the rest of the band for liquid refreshments and to get some respite from the humid, steamy atmosphere of the club. The sight that greeted them when they arrived at the Cavern entrance always stayed with him: 'We could see clouds of steam billowing out from the door at the top of the steep stone steps which led down to the Cavern. It looked as if it must be on fire.'

Although the club was usually packed out most nights, the Cavern was, in fact, one of the first jazz clubs where you would get a section of the audience determined to dance. Mick Groves remembers:

Mainly they would either sit or stand and listen to the music, but there was an element who began to dance. The dance that became known as The Cavern Stomp during the beat period at the club, actually originated at the trad and skiffle sessions during the Cavern's formative years.

Towards the end of 1958 the popularity of the Cavern began to decline and although it was still possible to pack the club out for a big name from the jazz world such as Humphrey Lyttelton, keeping the club open four nights a week was becoming an increasingly unviable commercial enterprise. Alan Sytner's taste in jazz during this period had moved from trad to modern, but the Thursday evening modern sessions had never had the mass appeal that trad enjoyed. This was an acceptable situation while enough finance was being raised from the weekend trad sessions to subsidise the Club Perdido nights, but even the trad fans were now moving their loyalty to the newly opened Mardi Gras Jazz Club which had the added attraction of being licensed to sell alcohol. The Cavern at this stage was also beginning to attract some teenagers who would frequent the city centre at night looking for trouble. The Merseysippi's John Lawrence remembers that this was one of the main reasons why the band decided to leave the Cavern and take up an offer to become resident at the Mardi Gras:

The Cavern was beginning to get a little rough by 1959. There were even reports in the Liverpool Echo about 'Teddy Boys' fighting at the Cavern. I remember one night an almighty fight broke out when we were on stage performing. One young lad picked up a chair and was about to smash someone over the head with it. As he lifted it above his head I stood behind him and grabbed it, telling him not to be silly. Generally though, the atmosphere at the Cavern was good but you were never certain whether you would get a packed house or a small turnout. Some of the modern jazz nights would only bring in about fifty people.

It has to be remembered that Alan Sytner's reason for opening the Cavern was to present traditional and modern jazz for local fans because he, like them, was a jazz enthusiast and he did not do it with the sole intention of making vast profits out of the venture. Profits that were made were used to bring top attractions to the Cavern; the first time that most of them had ever played at a Liverpool club.

Chapter 5

RAY McFALL BECOMES THE NEW OWNER

During 1958 Alan Sytner married and moved to London, yet he was still attempting to run the Liverpool club. For a period, Alan's father attempted to help his son out at the Liverpool end of the operation, but eventually Alan took the decision to sell up his ownership of the club. He knew that it was virtually impossible to run the Cavern from his London base and he also had ambitions of moving into the London jazz club scene, so he set out to find a buyer for the club. Various people were sounded out, mainly enthusiasts from the Liverpool jazz scene. Eventually, Ray McFall, a thirty-two-year-old accountant, who was already working at the club as a cashier a few nights a week, was successful with his offer to buy the Cavern for £2,750.

Ray McFall, who had known Alan Sytner for a number of years and was a confirmed trad fan, was determined to carry on with Alan's dream to make the Cavern the top jazz club outside of London. McFall's experience as an accountant was certainly going to be a crucial factor if he was to be successful in turning the club into a viable concern. For his opening night (Saturday 3 October 1959), he decided to start with a bang with Mr Acker Bilk and his Paramount Jazz Band, plus the leading blues partnership Sonny Terry and Brownie McGee packing the place out. A number of bookings that Sytner had already organised were also honoured by McFall, the most notable perhaps being the booking of the Tubby Hayes Quartet for a series of modern jazz nights. Tenor saxophonist Hayes is regarded by many as the finest talent to emerge in the British jazz world.

Ray McFall, after the success of the Springtime Jazz Festival of March 1959 which saw Humphrey Lyttelton packing the place out, decided to hold the Liverpool Jazz Festival in January 1960. In the programme notes for the festival

Ray McFall stated: 'By comparison with the Newport Festival ours will be a very modest attempt indeed, but my earnest desire is to organise bigger and better ones in the future, and really put Liverpool on the map as the leading jazz centre in the country, outside of London.' McFall presented a strong, predominantly trad jazz line-up, but financially it was not a success. The week's festivities began on Sunday 10 January with Acker Bilk top of the bill. Cavern members were treated to Terry Lightfoot, Alex Welsh, the Saints Jazz Band, Peter Haslam's Collegians, Ken Colyer and Micky Ashman whilst the modern jazz fans had Ronnie Scott, Bert Courtley, Peter King and the Eddie Thompson Trio to enjoy. Country music fans were catered for by Johnny Goode and his Country Kinfolk and Hank Walters and the Dusty Road Ramblers. The Bluegenes were also on the bill, using the name Swinging Blue Genes on this occasion. The group were in later years to hit the heights in the pop world as the Swinging Blue Jeans with their versions of rock classics 'Hippy Hippy Shake' and 'Good Golly Miss Molly'; but at the time of the Liverpool Jazz Festival they were playing what has been described as a 'unique blend of trad and skiffle' that was acceptable to the predominantly trad jazz enthusiasts at the Cavern.

Rory Storm and the Hurricanes, on the other hand, were by this time on the verge of becoming an out-and-out rock 'n' roll outfit and when they broke into their rock repertoire they were promptly met with hostility by the jazz fans. Some of the audience began to hurl missiles at the group. Johnny Guitar remembered the occasion:

> We started with a few skiffle numbers, songs like 'Cumberland Gap'. We then said, 'Sod it!' and began to play 'Whole Lotta Shakin' Goin' On'. The jazz fraternity

Top left: The Swinging Blue Genes in 1959. At this stage in their career they were still a trad jazz-style group. They never looked back after dropping traditional jazz for beat music and changing their name from The Blue Genes to The Blue Jeans in the early 1960s.

Above: The Swinging Blue Jeans who had a massive hit with 'The Hippy Hippy Shake' in 1963. The Cavern favourites went on to achieve national fame.

Left: The Swinging Blue Jeans at the Lybro factory in Liverpool in 1963. Lybro produced thousands of pairs of blue jeans during the heyday of Merseybeat.

Above left: The Swinging Blue Jeans.

Above right: Rory Storm and the Hurricanes.

went mad and started throwing pennies at us. If anyone remembers the old copper pennies they can verify that they didn't half hurt if one of them hit you on the head. Rory was very defiant and the way we answered them was to keep playing, but the boos grew louder and louder. After the show Ray McFall fined us six shillings (a gesture that soured the group's relationship with McFall). After we finished playing we picked up all the coins that were thrown at us and I'm certain that we got more money from the floor of the stage than McFall paid us.

Although Rory and his group played the Cavern on many more occasions, the group had little time for Ray McFall. Johnny Guitar recalls:

I was never keen on Ray McFall and didn't like the way he would charge us to enter the club when we visited the Cavern on our nights off. I often used to enter the doorway to the club and pretend to be looking at a poster on the wall or something. When McFall's attention was distracted I'd nip down the stairs without paying. I always got a kick doing this. I formed the impression that when it came to rock music McFall didn't have much idea. He was kind of stumbling through it all without having much idea what was going on.

Dave Williams, however, who was a member of the Wirral group Dale Roberts and the Jaywalkers, who appeared with The Beatles on their Cavern night-time debut, remembers McFall as a reasonable man who was always fair in his dealings with them. When asked about the McFall policy of charging group members entrance money when attending Cavern sessions, Dave reasoned: 'There were hundreds of group members on Merseyside and if he allowed one in for nothing then he would have to have let all of us in for nothing, which would have cost him a fortune.' In support of Ray McFall, it should be noted that Alan Williams, the manager of the Blue Angel Club, also had the same policy and even charged the legendary Judy Garland entrance fees when she turned up at the nightclub with her husband after appearing at a Manchester venue.

Chapter 6

THE BEGINNING OF BEAT AT THE CAVERN

Despite the Cavern members' and the manager Ray McFall's antipathy towards rock 'n' roll, it seemed inevitable that beat music would eventually replace jazz as the staple musical diet of the club. The Cavern was unlicensed and most of the teenagers who frequented the club during its early years were now keen to find pastures new, preferably a place where you could get something a little stronger than a coke if you wanted a drink. The opening of the Mardi Gras obviously took some of the Cavern's maturing clientele, but the Cavern was always going to be a predominantly teenage club, and Merseyside's new generation of teenagers wanted rock, not jazz. Ray McFall had the dilemma of still wanting to provide his preferred musical fare, trad jazz, but he also wanted the Cavern to be a viable business concern.

The influence of skiffle had obviously been a key factor in instilling the confidence in the local teenagers that they could provide their own music, but an outlet in Liverpool city centre was now needed to give the blossoming beat groups of Merseyside a place where their music could bear fruition. There were many dance halls around Merseyside where beat could be heard, but most of these venues were municipally owned, such as the Grosvenor Ballroom, Wallasey, New Brighton Tower Ballroom, Aintree Institute, Litherland Town Hall and an endless assortment of halls and social clubs, but none of these venues were regarded as the teenagers' own place. The Cavern, however, had the potential to become just that. Mick Groves' endearing memory of the Cavern is that it was 'a club run by men in suits, but owned by the kids. Without the atmosphere that the Cavern teenagers generated, the place would have been another run-of-the-mill club.'

Within a year of taking over the club McFall knew that urgent action was needed to turn the club's fortunes around. He had lost several thousands financially during the first year and on the advice of those involved in the beat scene decided to give rock music at the club a try. His decision did not please the jazz fraternity and as Steve Voce recalls, it often had the effect of driving them out of the club to escape what was to them 'amplified noise!'

> I can remember before the advent of beat music at the Cavern, that the Beatles used to appear when the jazz group took an interval, and we all used to run like hell down the road to escape the noise. We thought them a passing fad of electric insanity. Little did we dream that they would have us all, metaphorically at least, on the bread line within a space of months.

One jazz enthusiast, however, who probably wished that he'd never rushed out of the Cavern when The Beatles came on stage was Alan Graham. Alan would help out at the club and would often bring along his tape to record the jazz bands' performances. However, when The Beatles came on stage he would switch his tape off or if he accidentally left the tape recording, he'd wipe their part of the show off the night's recording. Today, a recording of The Beatles playing at the Cavern would be a highly prized item indeed.

After much thought, Ray McFall decided that he would attempt to get the best of all worlds and hold beat on a Wednesday, modern jazz on a Thursday and keep Friday, Saturday and Sunday for the traditional jazz followers. The first official all-beat night was to be held on 25 May 1960, with Rory Storm and the Hurricanes and Cass and the Cassanovas providing the night's entertainment. The majority of the club's jazz membership kept well away from the club on what turned out to be, with hindsight, an historical evening in the Cavern's history. But McFall's

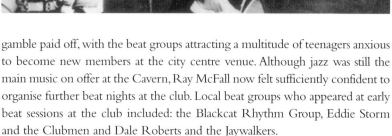

gamble paid off, with the beat groups attracting a multitude of teenagers anxious to become new members at the city centre venue. Although jazz was still the main music on offer at the Cavern, Ray McFall now felt sufficiently confident to organise further beat nights at the club. Local beat groups who appeared at early beat sessions at the club included: the Blackcat Rhythm Group, Eddie Storm and the Clubmen and Dale Roberts and the Jaywalkers.

The first major name from the pop world to appear at the club was Emile Ford, who played the Cavern in November 1960 with Cass and the Cassanovas and Gerry and the Pacemakers on the same bill. Emile Ford was the first black British pop star and was another product of the London skiffle clubs that produced so many of the early British stars of pop. Backed by the Checkmates, he had a million-seller with his 1959 hit 'What Do You Want To Make Those Eyes At Me For?' and he followed up with further top-twenty hits such as: 'On A Slow Boat To China', 'You'll Never Know What You're Missing' and 'Counting Teardrops'.

The first Merseyside pop star to play the Cavern was Birkenhead's Chris Morris, who found national fame after changing his name to Lance Fortune and had a top ten hit with 'Be Mine'. He was backed at the Cavern by The Jaywalkers, a group who were to find local fame with Dale Roberts as their frontman. Apart from the Wednesday night beat sessions, McFall also decided in October 1960 to hold lunchtime beat sessions at the club, with popular records of the day providing the entertainment. By the end of the year the lunchtime sessions were being held on a regular basis, with a mixture of records and live groups providing the entertainment. Slowly but surely, jazz was losing its grip at the Cavern.

Top left: Colin Manley and Don Andrew of The Remo Quartet. The group later changed their name to The Remo Four and became part of the Brian Epstein stable.

Top right: Lance Fortune backed by The Jaywalkers at the Cavern in 1960. He had a huge hit with 'Be Mine'.

Above: Cavern regulars Dale Roberts with The Jaywalkers. They appeared on the same bill when The Beatles made their evening debut at the club in March 1961.

Clockwise from top left:
Emile Ford, who was the first major pop name to appear at the Cavern Club. Ford had many top-ten hits and his Cavern appearance came in November 1960.

Emile Ford.

Lance Fortune who was the first Merseyside pop star to appear at the Cavern.

Lance Fortune at the Cavern backed by The Jaywalkers in 1960.

Chapter 7

THE BEATLES LEGEND BEGINS

When it comes to the history of beat at the Cavern, 1961 was the year when it began to become more and more predominant as the club's musical fare. Club stalwarts the Bluegenes were invited by Ray McFall to host Tuesday night beat sessions with guest appearances also on offer featuring mainly local groups. The Bluegenes' Guest Night on Tuesday 21 March saw The Beatles making their first evening performance at the club. Also on the bill were Dale Roberts and the Jaywalkers and the Remo Quartet. If the history of traditional jazz at the Cavern is intrinsically linked with the Merseysippi Jazz Band, and skiffle with the Bluegenes, then the history of the beat at the Cavern is synonymous with four local lads known as The Beatles. Their Cavern debut had actually taken place a month earlier at a Tuesday lunchtime session on 21 February and they had made another seven lunchtime appearances before their night-time debut. The Beatles' Cavern debut was in fact the only time that Stuart Sutcliffe ever played at the venue.

Remembering how hard it was for a beat group to get a booking at the Cavern, Gerry Marsden described in his book *I'll Never Walk Alone* how Gerry and the Pacemakers and The Beatles finally persuaded Ray McFall to give them a chance:

The Cavern was a stronghold of jazz bands, some of which came from London. This frustrated us. Paul McCartney and I often approached the club manager Ray McFall, on behalf of our bands, asking for dates there – it would be prestigious to play right in the centre of town. But he refused us for what seemed like months. 'Can we work here?' we'd ask when we wandered over there. 'No, it's a jazz club and we don't want rock 'n' roll, it's crap' he'd say.

Well, we persisted. Finally, he agreed to try us out at lunchtime sessions, to catch the young workers who popped in for a soup, a cheese roll and a soft drink between noon and two o'clock. We alternated two or three days a week with The Beatles – and the results were amazing. The place was packed. It wasn't long before Ray McFall realised there was a huge following for the pop groups and he put us and The Beatles on at nights. This was the start of the revolution; people flocked to the Cavern, but they came for rock 'n' roll instead of jazz!

One of the first groups to play the lunchtime sessions was the Big Three and the impact they made is remembered to this day. In an interview by Adrian Jones for *Marcher Gold*, Pete Best recalled attending an early Cavern lunchtime session to watch the Big Three perform. Pete and the rest of The Beatles were astonished by what they saw. He told Adrian:

One of the first sessions that The Beatles attended at the Cavern was when we went to the club one lunchtime to see the Big Three. It was the first time I'd seen their drummer Johnny Hutch perform. The following lunchtime we were playing ourselves and it was the first time Johnny had seen me on drums. It was obvious that we had two different drumming styles. The Big Three were very influential and a lot of the other Liverpool bands took to them. They were only a trio but the sound they knocked out was incredible. It was a very full sound with Johnny Hutch a great drummer, Johnny Gus great on bass and vocals and guitarist Adrian Lord completing a powerful line-up. When Brian Griffiths took over from Adrian he was a great replacement.

Paul McCartney and George Harrison belt out another Beatles' number during a 1960s concert.

Gerry Marsden sings for the lads at Port Sunlight Boys' Club on the Wirral, 1963..

Their amplifiers and speakers were nicknamed 'coffins!' Adrian had made them himself. Myself and the rest of The Beatles were amazed when we first saw them at that lunchtime session. In those days, groups had small amps and speakers, but the sounds coming out of the Big Three's equipment pinned your ears to the back of the Cavern. It was as simple as that. When Paul saw them he turned to me and said 'I've got to have one of those amps for the bass.' We had a word with Adrian and shortly after, Paul was fixed up with one. Taking all of these things into consideration; the way they built their own amps, the way they played and the material they performed; all of this contributed to them being a great live band. The records they made never did justice to their great stage sound. It was a powerhouse sound that was never captured on their records.

It is interesting that only four bass players on Merseyside acquired 'coffins', these being Johnny Gus, Paul McCartney, Tony Jackson of the Searchers and Alan Stratton of the Blackcats and later the Kansas City Five.

With Paul acquiring his own 'coffin', The Beatles were now capable themselves of pinning back the ears of those who witnessed their lunchtime and late evening sessions at the Cavern. Apart from having the ability to blast out rock with the best of them, The Beatles were also capable of switching to a ballad or whatever other form of pop took their fancy. They also had the ability to come up with material that the other groups were not playing and, in many instances, would not have dared to attempt. Their repertoire ranged from 'Shakin' All Over' and 'Whole Lotta Shakin' Goin' On' to 'The Sheik Of Araby', and 'Till There Was You'. They would attempt anything that took

their fancy and Pete Best recalled that their sheer versatility gave them the edge on most of their peers:

> We played a lot of Carl Perkins and not many Liverpool groups were playing his stuff at the time. The Beatles stood out because of the tremendous harmonies of John, Paul and George. They tried to get as close as possible to the Everly Brothers' type of harmony and the key factor was the fact that they had the confidence to try and perform in that style because they had the vocal abilities. Right from the beginning they were showing the potential to be way ahead, vocally at least, of all the other Liverpool groups.

Paul McCartney, remembering how The Beatles would practise for hours to achieve their proficiency at harmonising, recalled: 'We learnt three-part harmony from singing "To Know Him Is To Love Him". That was the first three part we ever did and learned that in my Dad's house in Liverpool.' A key element of The Beatles' act, however, was their ability to impersonate most of the top rock entertainers of the period. With this in mind, Pete Best remarked:

> It has to be remembered that there were a lot of good singers around Liverpool at the time, but none had the ability that Paul had to impersonate Little Richard, or John doing Gene Vincent, or the three of them doing the Everlys' or Carl Perkins' numbers. As they matured, their vocal ability improved, and the long hours we played on stage in Germany, often playing eight hours a night was certainly instrumental in our improvement. Before The Beatles went to Hamburg they had not developed as a dynamite package. People in Liverpool would have said 'The Beatles, we've seen them, they're not much cop.' But after playing this powerhouse music for six, seven and eight hour stints a night, we really gelled and compacted. Cass and the Cassanovas, Derry and the Seniors and all the Liverpool bands were rated ahead of us, but after Hamburg people were saying, 'My God! You've gotta' see this lot!' After Hamburg The Beatles were special, they had sexual appeal, musical appeal and charisma. The antics we got up to on stage all added to this.

Gerry Marsden recalled in Ray Coleman's book, *John Lennon*, the effect that seeing The Beatles at the Cavern after their return from Germany had on him: 'I couldn't believe how good they were. The energy, the way they shaped up to the microphone together, John standing there, couldn't give a shit. He simply stood there with this attitude – I'm going to have a bloody good time, hope you'll join me.' The famous Lennon stance on stage has been put down to the influence of Tony Sheridan, with whom The Beatles became friendly

The Big Three strut their stuff at a Liverpool venue in 1964. The Big Three had a reputation as one of the great Cavern acts.

Bob Wooler chats to The Big Three (Faron, centre, is now in the group) at a Cavern show in 1964. Bob Wooler was practically 'Mr Cavern' and was a central figure in the Merseybeat music boom of the early 1960s.

in Hamburg. Tony Jackson of the Searchers told BBC Radio Merseyside's Spencer Leigh in *On The Beat* that Sheridan influenced practically all the Liverpool groups who went to Germany. He told Spencer about the man nicknamed the 'Teacher' by Liverpool groups:

> Tony Sheridan was a great influence but was very unpredictable. He once smashed a £300 Martin guitar because he played the wrong lick on it. The audience sat there open mouthed as Sheridan threw his guitar on the floor, picked up the mike stand and shoved it through the guitar (pre-empting The Who's Pete Townsend by two or three years). This was one aspect of Tony Sheridan's performance that Lennon, as far as I know, did not copy!

Apart from Gerry Marsden, Paul McCartney, and Pete Best's mother, Mona, another Merseysider who was pushing for bookings for The Beatles and other Merseyside groups at the Cavern was Bob Wooler. It was Bob Wooler that Ray McFall turned to in 1960 to present the lunchtime sessions at the Cavern, and when McFall began to search for local groups to perform at these sessions, Bob strongly recommended The Beatles. Unlike most of the groups, The Beatles did not have daytime employment and would be available most days. He recalled:

> Eventually McFall agreed to give them a go, and they made their first appearance as The Beatles on Tuesday 21 February 1961. Ray paid them the standard lunchtime fee of £1 per man; there were five Beatles then, plus £1 for the driver, Neil Aspinall, a total of £6 in all. Two-and-a-half years later, on Saturday 3 August 1963, they made their final appearance at the club. Their fee, for what turned out to be their farewell Cavern engagement, was £300, which, at the time, was quite a princely sum.

He calculates that he hosted close on 400 Beatles' shows, most of which were at the Cavern, whilst they were on Merseyside in the early sixties.

Within a short space of time The Beatles were drawing large crowds to the Cavern and they soon established a rapport with the girls who crowded round the tiny Cavern stage. Some of these fans would shout or pass requests to the group, and when Paul McCartney was interviewed as the guest castaway on *Desert Island Discs*, he spoke with affection about his Cavern days and recalled their first unofficial fan club:

> I remember they gave themselves names such as 'The Cement Mixers' or 'The Wooden Tops'. There were two of them called Chris and Val and they would shout 'Sing "Searchin" Paul, sing "Searchin".'

John Lennon nicknamed some of these fans the 'Beatletts'. While The Beatles were performing, the 'Beatletts' would run errands for the group, fetching them cokes from the snack bar or a cheese sandwich for John. By this time The Beatles were highly popular at the Cavern with both sexes, but the group never forgot their small group of female admirers. If they had any spare tickets it was the 'Beatletts' who got them and they would often give them a lift home in the back of their van. If the group spotted them in the city centre they would buy them a soft drink or a coffee. Even more endearing to the fans was the fact that when they had finished their performance, The Beatles would sit with their fans and chat.

Paddy Delaney, who was the doorman at the Cavern, recalled the first time he saw The Beatles arriving at the Cavern in Geoffrey Giuliano's book: *Dark Horse – The Secret Life Of George Harrison*:

> The first Beatle I ever saw was George Harrison. He was very scruffy and hungry looking. I remember him ambling down the middle of the street, and for a minute I didn't think he was coming in. I stopped him at the door and asked him if he was a member. Of course I knew he wasn't and he said no, he was with The Beatles. Now, we'd heard a lot about The Beatles over the previous weeks, and I knew they were on that particular night, so I let him in even though he was wearing blue jeans, which were strictly banned from the club. About fifteen minutes later, Paul McCartney tumbled down the street with John Lennon in close pursuit. Paul was carrying his bass guitar, and John had his hands dug deep in his pockets. I had an idea they were with George because they all had the same sort of hairstyle. It wasn't quite a Beatles haircut then, but it was well past their collars. A little while after they strolled in, a taxi pulled up in front of the club and out came Pete Best. He was carrying The Beatles' first sound system, which consisted of two cheap chipboard speakers and a beat-up looking amplifier. He also had a set of old drums, which he unloaded and took down the stairs. This is how The Beatles first arrived at the Cavern.

Billy J. Kramer, recalling the first Beatles performance he witnessed after their return from Germany, admitted:

> I was freaked out by the whole band when I saw them at the Cavern. They'd come back from Hamburg and Stu had left. McCartney was playing bass and they were into leather. It was a lot slicker, the space between numbers had tightened up a lot and the vocal backings and everything, the whole thing flowed better.

The Beatles were soon Cavern favourites, not only with the fans, but also with their peers.

Jim Mawer of the Kubiks told Richard Buskin of *The Beatles Monthly* in 1962 about the first time he saw The Beatles at the Cavern:

> The whole place smelled of some kind of disinfectant, sweat would be dripping off the walls and many of the kids would be stomping. The Beatles used to mingle with everyone else and chat around. Paul was the really talkative one, he really loved it all. John was the joker, always mocking someone, and gave me the impression of being a really hard nut. I asked him for a coke at a gig a few months back and he obliged by pouring one over my head! You'd see John play his gold Rickenbacker leaning against an old piano at the side of the stage. Paul would sometimes take the microphone off its stand for a number like 'What'd I Say'. He'd sometimes give the mike to the kids at the front to let them join in the singing. In those days he had an old Rossetti guitar which he wore upside down, often without appearing to plug it in, and he used to do all of that posing with it. Paul was more like a featured singer then, almost like Cliff and the Drifters.

By spring of 1961 The Beatles were playing at the Cavern three or four lunchtimes a week, with Gerry and the Pacemakers also performing there on alternate days to The Beatles. The Beatles were still happy to pass the time in the company of the Cavern regulars when they were not appearing on stage. It was obvious that a strong bond was developing between The Beatles and their fans. In George Tremlett's book *John Lennon*, George Harrison's brother Harry recalled the type of spontaneous gesture which helped to develop this bond, which was deeper than just a musical appreciation of the group:

> The Beatles were booked for a bank holiday appearance at the Cavern and the fans started queuing days in advance, which was an extraordinary thing when you think that they were just a local group who were hardly known outside Liverpool and Hamburg. When they heard about this queue forming they all piled into the van and went down to the Cavern. They counted up how many girls were waiting, and then drove to the midnight cafe at the Pier Head. They then proceeded to buy a pile of pies and sandwiches, which they took back to the Cavern and handed to the girls in the queue.

Cavern doorman Paddy Delaney also revealed that if any Beatles fans were outside the club without enough money to get in it was not unknown for the group to slip him the money on the quiet and tell him to let them in but not

Arguably the greatest group in the history of the world, The Beatles. They appeared at the Cavern an estimated 274 times, but the true figure could well be higher.

to tell them who had paid. George Harrison told Hunter Davies of his fond memories of the Cavern when he was interviewed for his book *The Beatles*:

> We probably loved the Cavern best of anything. It was fantastic. We never lost our identification with the audience all the time, we never rehearsed anything, not like the other groups, who kept on copying the Shadows. We were playing to our own fans who were just like us. They would come in the lunchtimes to hear us and bring their sandwiches to eat. We would do the same, eating our lunch as we played. It was spontaneous. Everything just happened.

George's mention of the Shadows leads to the story of one of the most infamous nights in the history of the club. Ray McFall booked them to appear at the Cavern in January 1961. With massive-selling hits such as 'Apache' and 'FBI', the Shadows were undoubtedly Britain's top group in the years between the demise of skiffle and the rise of Merseybeat and R&B. It was with great anticipation that the Cavern regulars awaited the debut of the group at the club. Unfortunately, Jet Harris, the innovative but at times enigmatic bass guitarist with the group, decided to loosen up for the show by sharing a half-bottle of brandy with Peter Gormley, the group's manager, in the Cavern toilets. By the time the group were ready to take the stage, Jet was slightly the worse for wear. Bruce Welch, remembering

the night in his book *Rock 'n' Roll I Gave You The Best Years Of My Life*, recalled:

Jet was well gone when we went on stage and it was a miracle he could play a correct note. He was coping well until it came to the famous Shadows 'Walk'. Jet ended up walking off the stage and fell into the audience. I recall telling them Jet's not very well and before I could finish someone in the crowd shouted back, 'we know mate – he's pissed!'

After struggling on for a few more numbers the group decided to make their exit with the audience totally bemused by it all.

Opposite: The Shadows, pictured in 1963. John Rostill, second from the left, was now the group's bass player. When The Shadows played their one and only Cavern date in January 1961, the legendary Jeta Harris was bass player with the group. After downing a half-bottle of brandy before the show, Jet fell into the audience while attempting to do the famous Shadows walk.

Chapter 8

BRIAN EPSTEIN VISITS THE CAVERN

Thursday 9 November 1961 was to prove a momentous day for The Beatles and the pop world in general. This was the day that Brian Epstein saw The Beatles perform at the Cavern for the first time. The reasons behind the twenty-seven-year-old's visit to the club have been well documented elsewhere, but after he saw them on that Cavern stage their lives would never be the same again. Writing about his first experience of The Beatles and the Cavern in *A Cellarful Of Noise*, he admitted that he was captivated by The Beatles (if not the Cavern) from the start:

> I arrived at the greasy steps leading to the vast cellar and descended gingerly past a surging crowd of beat fans to a desk where a large man sat examining membership cards. He knew my name and he nodded to an opening in the wall which led into the central of three tunnels which make up the rambling Cavern. Inside the club it was dark, damp and smelly and I regretted my decision to come. I started to talk to one of the girls. 'Hey,' she hissed, 'The Beatles are going on now!' And there on the platform at the end of the cellar's middle tunnel stood the four boys. Then I eased myself towards the stage, past rapt young faces and jigging bodies and for the first time I saw The Beatles properly. I had never seen anything like The Beatles on any stage. They smoked as they played and ate and talked and pretended to hit each other. They turned their backs on the audience and shouted at them and laughed at private jokes. But they gave a captivating and honest show and they had considerable magnetism. There was some indefinable charm there. They were extremely amusing and in a rough, 'take it or leave it' way, very attractive.

It was not until 24 January 1962 that Brian Epstein officially became The Beatles' manager, but from the moment he first saw them at the Cavern he began to plan the strategy that would turn them into the biggest act in the popular music world. He lost little time in smartening them up, demanding that they were punctual for dates, no more eating on stage, no more swearing and fooling about and they definitely had to stop sticking their chewing gum on their amps at the Cavern before the show began. By March he had also, much to Lennon's disgust, put them into suits. After kitting them out with suits from Birkenhead tailor Beno Dorn, Epstein accompanied them to the Heswall Jazz Club to oversee his prodigies. The club was run by Bob Ellis and one particular action of Brian Epstein's still sticks out in Bob's memory of the night: 'With The Beatles in full flow Epstein looked down at his wrist watch and then raised his arm to signal to The Beatles to stop playing. They had fulfilled the allotted time they had been paid for (£30) and Epstein signalled to them that their time was up.' Bob Ellis still finds it hard to believe that The Beatles actually stopped playing halfway through a number on instruction from their manager, but in unison all four Beatles did! The days of leather-clad rockers playing for fun and for little monetary gain were soon to become a fading memory.

The general school of thought among Beatleologists is that it was on Brian Epstein's orders that the leather outfits had to go. But when interviewed in 1963 for the BBC documentary *The Mersey Sound*, The Beatles maintained it was a joint decision between themselves and their manager. Paul McCartney said:

> The leather gear was a bit old hat and we decided that we looked a bit ridiculous dressed in all-leather. We got the impression some people were

Above left: Brian Epstein, The Beatles' manager who took them to fame and fortune. Epstein first saw The Beatles at the Cavern on the 9 November 1961. He knew them from their visits to his shop, North End Music Stores (NEMS) in Liverpool's Great Charlotte Street. Once he saw them at the Cavern he was hooked and a month later became their manager. Paul McCartney once said of Brian Epstein, 'If anyone was the fifth Beatle it was Brian. Brian was very honest. He was an honourable businessman.'

Above right: George Harrison chats with Beatles' manager Brian Epstein. It was actually George that Epstein left a message with in the Cavern bandroom at the beginning of December 1961, to invite the band to a meeting to discuss him becoming the group's manager.

laughing at us and we looked like a gang of idiots. So Brian Epstein suggested we wear ordinary suits. So we got rid of the leather gear; I got my leather trousers pinched anyway so that made up our minds for us.

One occasion, however, when The Beatles did revert to their leather outfits for a show, and perhaps to show affinity with their hero, was when Gene Vincent played at the Cavern in July 1962. Sharing the bill were the Bluegenes and Sounds Incorporated who backed Gene. The classic Gene Vincent track 'Be Bop A Lula' was the first record that Paul McCartney had ever bought and he and the rest of The Beatles had got to know Gene

when they were appearing in Hamburg. Paul, recalling his Hamburg days when interviewed by Spencer Leigh, remembered that Gene would sit at a table in the Hamburg club he was appearing at with a full bottle of scotch whisky in front of him:

He'd invite us to join him for a drink. Gene was an ex-marine and he was always offering to knock me out by touching my two pressure points. 'You'll only be unconscious for a few minutes,' he'd say. I always resisted his offer. Gene was like a lot of stars, he put on a front but he was okay underneath it.

Above middle: A Brian Epstein presentation at Liverpool's Odeon Cinema in 1964.

Above *right:* A 1969 shot of The Hollies taken when Terry Silvester (sitting) took the place of Graham Nash in the group. The Manchester group made nineteen appearances at the Cavern during the club's heyday as a beat venue in the early 1960s. 'Allan Clarke gave me a right rollicking for having having the audacity to describe them on the bill as "Manchester's Beatles",' recalled Bob Wooler.

Liverpool's Johnny Gentle, however, who appeared with Gene Vincent and Eddie Cochran on the ill-fated 1960 tour which ended with Cochran losing his life in a car crash, had nothing but negative memories of Vincent. When interviewed by Spencer Leigh he revealed:

Gene was a weirdo, I was not very impressed with him at all, and he was a guy I could not have been friends with. I remember arriving back at my London flat, which I shared with a girlfriend. Other stars from the Larry Parnes stable had flats in the same block, including Billy Fury, Joe Brown, Gerry Dorsey, The Dallas Boys and any American artists who were touring with Parnes' acts at the time. We all shared these flats. Gene Vincent had met these two young girls in Bedford and they were overwhelmed by him, the big rock star from America. Gene brought them back to the flat he was using and after a period

of time we heard them crying outside our flat. My girlfriend opened the door and asked them what was wrong. Apparently, Gene had had his way with them and then slung them out in the middle of the night with nowhere to go. We let them in and they spent the night at our flat. The girls just couldn't believe that Vincent, the rock star they idolised, could treat them so callously; their dreams were shattered.

As a performer, however, Gentle had nothing but praise for Vincent: 'He would limp onto the stage and would create a marvellous impact.' Interviewed in the 1970s, John Lennon recalled Gene at the Cavern:

Brian Epstein used to bring over rock stars who weren't making it any more – no reflection on them, but they were coming over to England for that reason

Above left: George Harrison's favourite guitarist, Joe Brown, who was a national star when he appeared at the Cavern in July 1962.

Above middle: Joe Brown pictured here with Billy Fury. Liverpool-born Fury was destined never to appear at the Cavern.

Above right: Freddie Garrity of Freddie and The Dreamers. The Manchester group were a popular attraction at the Cavern and made fourteen appearances at the club in the early 1960s. The group had many chart hits including 'I'm Telling You Now' and 'If You've Got To Make A Fool of Somebody'.

– and he would put us on the bill with them as second billing. We'd use them to draw the crowd and then they'd see us. So we met Gene Vincent backstage, hah! It was a toilet – and we were thrilled. It's hard for people to realise how thrilled the four of us were just to see any great rock and roller in the flesh.

By 1962 the responsibility for the beat side of things at the club rested solely with Bob Wooler, with Ray McFall hiring the jazz acts. In addition to hosting the lunchtime sessions in the role of DJ/compère, Bob was eventually asked by Ray to do all the sessions at the Cavern – lunchtimes, evenings and all-nighters – more sessions per week than at any other venue on Merseyside. This Bob did, relinquishing his evening deejaying at various jive halls around Merseyside.

Bob was now prepared to look further afield for beat attractions for the Cavern, and apart from Gene Vincent, other top acts brought to the club in 1962 included: Bruce Channel, Johnny Kidd and the Pirates, Mike Berry and the Outlaws, Joe Brown and the Bruvvers and the Tornadoes. Acts from Manchester were also starting to appear at the club. Among these were Pete McLaine and the Dakotas, Freddie and the Dreamers and the Hollies. Another Manchester group, Peter Novack and the Heartbeats (later Herman's Hermits), would on several occasions get bookings to appear at the club.

Herman (Peter Noone) was well known around the Cavern, even before his group got bookings there. Roadrunner Dave Percy recalled that he was forever hanging around the groups and on occasion they would have to reprimand him for messing about with their equipment. Remembering the Manchester groups at the Cavern, Cilla Black acknowledges that they showed a lot of nerve appearing at the Liverpool city-centre venue, 'They were brave because there was rivalry between Manchester and Liverpool even in those days of the early sixties. But we totally accepted them and Manchester groups such as the Hollies and Freddie and the Dreamers were incredibly brave to come and sing at the Cavern.'

Chapter 9

MERSEYBEAT TAKES A HOLD...

By mid-1961 several other Merseyside groups had made their Cavern debut, the most notable being Kingsize Taylor and the Dominoes, with Cilla Black joining them for a few numbers, the Four Jays, who were to have many chart successes in later years as the Fourmost, and the Searchers, who by now had left Johnny Sandon and changed from C&W to beat. By July The Beatles had become Wednesday evening residents, as well as lunchtime favourites, and were now commanding a large following, made up not just of Liverpool Cavern regulars, but increasingly from areas on the outskirts of Merseyside such as Wirral, St Helens, and Widnes. The Beatles, along with other local groups, were also appearing on Cavern bills that included traditional jazz bands and were still regarded as an interval act when they played on a jazz/beat night. Being an 'interval act' was a source of irritation to The Beatles and many of the other beat group members and it led to a certain amount of resentment.

George Melly who had played the Cavern many times with the Mick Mulligan Band recalled meeting John Lennon, who had had a drink or two, in the mid-1960s when the group were rapidly becoming the pop music phenomenon of the century. 'You lot kept us from getting into the Cavern and other places much earlier. All that jazz crap held us back,' Lennon told Melly. After being told to stop playing rock years earlier by Alan Sytner, when the Quarrymen appeared at the Cavern for the first time, Lennon obviously took great delight in The Beatles being one of the main reasons that jazz was driven out of the club. Although most trad fans appreciated a certain amount of blues music, as the success of artists such as Big Bill Broonzy suggests, it had to be old and rural. Chris Barber, trad jazz band leader and a champion of 'true blues', on one occasion banned the Rolling Stones from London's Marquee Club. He considered them 'unauthentic', and Mick Jagger and Keith Richards, like John Lennon and a lot of other beat musicians on Merseyside, grew to dislike trad jazz and everything that went with it. It has to be remembered, however, that John Lennon's antipathy towards trad jazz was reciprocated by many of trad jazz's exponents such as Humphrey Lyttelton, who once withdrew from a BBC staged Albert Hall concert because the majority of the acts on the bill were rock groups.

One aspect of the British jazz scene, however, that the early Beatles, either consciously or subconsciously, appear to have been influenced by was the informal atmosphere that the jazz musicians preferred to work in when they were performing. It was commonplace to see jazz bands drinking (usually soft drinks at the Cavern) and smoking whilst on stage. Just as years later when Brian Epstein would insist that The Beatles would have to cut out the eating, drinking, smoking, swearing and general fooling about on stage, some visiting American musicians were completely taken aback by what they regarded as unprofessional behaviour. John Barnes recalled one such occasion in Jim Godbolt's book *A History of Jazz in Britain 1950-1970*. Barnes remembered the time when he was a member of a group of British musicians accompanying the great American jazz pianist Earl Hines:

After a gig at the Manchester Sports Guild with Earl Hines, he requested that the band assemble in the secretary's office. Just the band. No one else. We had no idea what to expect. Were we that inadequate for the job? We were totally mystified. The reason we had been called soon became clear. Nothing to do with our music. In fact, Earl went to great pains to say how much he enjoyed

The Fourmost with Miss USA in 1964.

The Fourmost, who were known as The Four Jays when they first performed at the Cavern. The Fourmost joined Brian Epstein's stable and had several top-ten hits.

Gerry Marsden receives two smackers from his adoring admirers in 1963.

working with us, but he objected strongly to us drinking and smoking on stage. 'It's so unprofessional,' he said. We were flabbergasted. It's something we had always done at clubs; in a way it was part of our style. But bowing to the master's admonitions, we didn't drink or smoke on the stand for the rest of the tour. Once the tour with Hines finished, we, of course, reverted to type.

Unlike their jazz counterparts, once Epstein had sanitised The Beatles they stayed that way as a live act for the rest of their performing career.

Throughout 1962, beat maintained a strong grip at the Cavern, and Gerry and the Pacemakers and The Beatles were pulling in large attendances for their lunchtime appearances. Despite their popularity at the Cavern, Gerry Marsden revealed in his autobiography that it was never his favourite venue:

It was a nightmare to get in and out of, struggling down the stairs from Mathew Street to the cellar with all our gear was tough, but it was the only entrance because there was no backstage – and no backstage toilet, either. I shudder to think of the effect of a fire down there, had there ever been one.

The damp and condensation at the Cavern would run down the walls and would often cause the groups' equipment to fuse. Paul McCartney, recalling one of these occasions in a radio interview, said: 'Our equipment would often go on the blink and we would carry on strumming our guitars and singing popular television adverts of the day until our equipment was repaired.' Keef Hartley, who at the time was drummer with Rory Storm and the Hurricanes, told *The Beatles Monthly* in 1962 about the power cuts at the Cavern:

Electricity isn't the best thing happening at the Cavern, and often the amps pack up or everything just goes out. When that happens to The Beatles, John is liable to jump on the piano and – instant Lennon – go into a talent show host routine, introducing McCartney with crazy, outlandish humour. It's that kind of thing that I'm sure is a great advantage to them, because in the early days, people who went to the Cavern must have been entertained as much by the wit as by the music. Whenever something goes wrong, The Beatles are able to keep the show going.

The Beatles' training in Hamburg had obviously given them the ability to handle any situation that cropped up. A fan recalls how on one occasion when they were playing across the Mersey at the Majestic Ballroom, Birkenhead, The Beatles were quick to react to another equipment failure:

After playing for a few minutes a power cut brought their performance to an abrupt halt. After exchanging a few words between themselves they broke into a new song strumming their non-amplified guitars and singing at the top of their voices to make themselves heard. I think it must have been The Beatles' one and only unplugged stage show in their entire career. They still managed to sound pretty good though!

Cavern favourite Gerry Marsden. Gerry and the Pacemakers were a popular attraction at the club in the early 1960s and made nearly 200 appearances at the venue.

Chapter 10

THE BEATLES, KINGS OF THE CAVERN

Back at the Cavern, The Beatles were now the undisputed local favourites and had easily topped the *Mersey Beat* newspaper's readers' poll. The screaming and fan adulation had now started to grow, but The Beatles' early fans were never the ones who instigated this. According to them it was the girls from the outlying areas of Merseyside who began the hysterical fan behaviour. Ringo Starr's first wife, Maureen Cox, who was a Cavern regular, told Hunter Davies that the fanaticism of some of The Beatles' Cavern fans was at times a little frightening:

> They used to hang round the Cavern all day long just on the off chance of seeing The Beatles. They'd come out of the lunchtime session and just stand outside all afternoon, queuing up for the evening. The object was to get as near to the front of the stage as possible, so that they could see The Beatles and be seen by them. I never joined the queue till about two or three hours before the Cavern opened. It frightened me. There would be fights and rows amongst the girls. When the doors opened the first ones would tear in, knocking each other over. They'd keep their rollers in and jeans on for the first groups. Then when it got time for The Beatles to come on, they would go off in turns to the ladies with their little cases to get changed and made up. When The Beatles came on they'd all look smashing, as if they'd just arrived.

Ringo, who was to join The Beatles in such acrimonious circumstances later in 1962, had, in fact, played with The Beatles at the Cavern before becoming an official Beatle on 18 August. He told George Tremlett:

> One day their drummer, Pete Best, went sick. A car came for me and the driver asked if I would play the drums for The Beatles at a lunchtime session down at the Cavern. What a laugh it turned out to be. We knew the same numbers, but did them differently and I didn't fit in at all well on that first session.

It was not unusual at the Cavern to see members of other groups fill in for their outfit if one of their members could not make it, or fell ill. Paul McCartney, who would sometimes take over on drums when Pete Best sang 'Wooden Heart', was always keen to display his drumming prowess, and once played an evening session with Birkenhead group the Landsliders. On another occasion Gerry Marsden filled in for John Lennon, standing on an orange box because the mike was too high for him. This was during the period when Brian Epstein had taken over as The Beatles' manager and by all accounts he blew his top when he found out.

The camaraderie between the groups was very strong during the early days and Tony Jackson of the Searchers told Spencer Leigh how they would get together in the pub near the Cavern and exchange song lyrics:

> Many times we would sit in The Grapes and exchange lyrics of current favourites with other groups. If John and Paul wanted the words to, say, 'Some Other Guy', I'd write them down, and if I needed something they'd write them out for me. That's what we all did; there was a lot of friendship between the groups.

Cilla Black, who began life as Priscilla White. A misprint in the *Mersey Beat* music paper christened her Cilla Black and she liked the sound of it. Cilla would get up and do a guest spot if groups such as Rory Storm and the Hurricanes, the Big Three or Kingsize Taylor and the Dominoes gave her the opportunity. She usually sang Peggy Lee's 'Fever'. Brian Epstein spotted her singing in the Blue Angel club and signed her up for his growing stable of Merseyside acts. At the Cavern, Cilla Black sang on the odd occasion with local groups and, according to legend, did the occasional stint working in the cloakroom and snack bar, but this has never been confirmed by Cilla. She was never known to have made a paid appearance at the club.

Learning the lyrics to new songs was always a full-time occupation for the Merseyside groups. Dave Williams of Dale Roberts and the Jaywalkers recalled:

We would sometimes buy a record as soon as it came out, learn the words and music that day and play it on stage the following night. There was a lot of prestige involved in being the first group to play a new song on stage. On other occasions members of groups would sit in coffee bars that had juke boxes and write down the lyrics as the records played. This was a lot less expensive than buying the record itself.

Cilla Black, after her Cavern debut singing a few numbers with Kingsize Taylor and the Dominoes, now had the taste for performing and was happy to take the stage with any of the groups who'd let her join them. Cilla was another who'd taken to learning new hits of the day as quickly as possible. Interviewed on BBC radio she recalled:

I would go into Brian Epstein's city centre shop NEMS and ask to hear a certain record in one of the record booths. I knew shorthand from studying at Anfield Commercial College and would quickly write down the words to the song. I was a fast learner, so I also learnt the tune quickly as well. I would rarely buy the record and Brian Epstein or one of his assistants were always throwing me out of the shop. He must have known me before he saw me sing and became my manager.

Apart from singing at the Cavern, Cilla Black would also accompany groups to bookings outside the city centre and on one occasion she travelled across the Mersey to play at the Birkenhead YMCA with the Big Three. Dances at this venue were organised by Charles Tranter who gave Cilla Black an unusual payment:

Cilla turned up with the Big Three, who were very popular at the club, but unfortunately I only had enough club funds to pay the group. After giving a rousing performance as guest singer with them I decided that Cilla deserved some reward for her endeavours. I quickly dashed out of the place and made my way back to my house which was just a short distance from the dance hall. I then quickly picked a bunch of sweet peas from the garden and ran back to the hall. Cilla gratefully accepted what was probably the most unusual payment of her long career!

One of Brian Epstein's first aims when he became The Beatles' manager was to secure a recording contract for them. The story of how Decca turned them down after giving them a recording test has been well documented, but the tale about the man who missed out on signing them because he couldn't be bothered queuing up in the rain outside the Cavern is perhaps not so well known. Dick Rowe, Decca's A&R manager, was approached by Brian

Epstein to try and obtain a recording contract with his company. Bearing in mind the strong recommendation that had been given by his assistant Mike Smith, who had seen The Beatles in all their glory performing live at the Cavern, Rowe decided to travel up to Merseyside to check them out at the Cavern himself. After settling in at his Liverpool hotel, Rowe took a taxi to Mathew Street and began to walk down to the Cavern Club. There was a huge crowd gathered outside the club and on top of this it began to rain heavily. After queuing for a while amongst the jostling teenagers and by this time soaked to the skin, Dick Rowe decided he could take no more and made his escape back to the warmth of his hotel. Rowe could have asked Brian Epstein to arrange immediate entry to the club for him on his arrival but he wanted to visit the club incognito, to see The Beatles for himself. It's highly likely that if he had stuck it out and managed to witness The Beatles' dynamic style for himself then Decca and not EMI would have signed them. It is also interesting to remember that Decca turned down Jimi Hendrix in 1966 with the words, 'Sorry, he hasn't got anything to offer'!

By the end of August 1962 The Beatles had replaced Pete Best in the group with Ringo Starr, with Best making his last appearance at a night-time session on 15 August 1962, and it was the new line-up that Granada Television captured for posterity when they sent a film crew to the Cavern to film the group performing at a lunchtime session on 22 August. They were filmed singing 'Some Other Guy' and 'Kansas City'. With the fame of the group spreading almost daily, members of their families had taken to seeing for themselves The Beatles at the Cavern. John Lennon's sister, Julia Baird, had been waiting with great anticipation for a chance to visit the club to see John and The Beatles performing. In her book, *John Lennon My Brother*, she gave a vivid account of her first Cavern visit:

> I was fifteen years old, and big enough to go into Liverpool with four or five friends from school to see John at the Cavern in Mathew Street. The din was unbelievable. The walls were dripping with damp which ran down the walls in steaming black rivulets. There was hardly any light and you had to grope your way to the so-called bar where the strongest drink they served was coke. Everyone was dressed in black. We wore black eye make-up with pan-stick foundation. Black polo-necks and dyed black jeans were the order of the day (they didn't make black jeans then). The more like a corpse you looked the better. We had to apply the final dramatic touches around the corner out of sight. You were supposed to be eighteen, and a couple of times I was told I couldn't go in unless I went back for my birth certificate. But most of the time, if you applied your make-up expertly enough, the doorman would be totally confused by your appearance and let you in.

George Harrison's mother, who was always a great champion of George and The Beatles, would often call into the Cavern to watch the group. On one occasion she remembered John's Aunt Mimi storming into the club, determined to pull John out by his ear: 'Aren't they great?' shouted George's mother, trying hard to make herself heard above the music. Mimi turned to her and retorted, 'I'm glad someone thinks so!'

Paul McCartney's father, who worked in Liverpool city centre near to the Cavern, would often pop into the club at lunchtime to see Paul. He told Hunter Davies: 'They should have been paid danger money to go down there. It reeked of perspiration. When Paul used to come home from the Cavern I would wring his shirt out in the sink and the sweat would pour out.' Jim McCartney would often have to fight his way through the fans at the lunchtime session to give Paul a bag with chops or sausages in it for their evening meal before he went back to work. 'Now don't forget son, put this on regulo 450 on the electric oven when you get home,' Jim would tell Paul before making his way back to work in the Cotton Exchange.

John Lennon's Aunt Mimi, however, was totally opposed to her nephew spending so much of his time there. She told George Harrison of the *Liverpool Echo* about her first visit to the Cavern:

> I was determined John should succeed as an artist and I paid for him to go to the College of Art. I knew that he and young Paul and George were playing together as a group for they used to rehearse in my house until I cleared out a woodshed in the garden and let them have that instead. But what I didn't know was that John was playing truant from the art school. Until one day a friend phoned me and said, 'Do you know where John is right now?' I said, 'Yes, he's at school.' She laughed and said, 'He isn't, you know. He's playing his guitar with a band at the Cavern Club here in Liverpool. Come on down and I'll show you.' So off I went to find out the truth. I had never been to the Cavern in my life and you can imagine how the doorman's eyes popped when two middle-aged, respectable ladies walked in and I said, 'I want to see John Lennon.' He took us round to the back of the stage, and if I got a shock at my first experience of the smoky little Cavern, with its stone arches and dim lights, it was nothing to the shock John got when he saw me. I raved at him, while Paul and George were trying to look as if they weren't there.

Although they were now the undisputed kings of Merseyside, John Lennon's Aunt Mimi, and to a lesser extent other members of The Beatles' families, probably doubted that their boys would ever really make an impact on the pop world on a national scale. One man who had no doubts at all, however, was Brian Epstein and throughout the rest of 1963 he set about achieving

George Harrison's mother Louise with *Coronation Street* star Peter Adamson and Cavern favourites the Hideaways in 1964. Louise still attended the Cavern sessions after the Beatles had departed the scene and would encourage the up and coming groups. The Hideaways made over 200 appearances at the club.

a level of success for The Beatles that would lead to the group leaving the Cavern behind forever. By the start of 1963 The Beatles' appearances at the Cavern were becoming less frequent and their final lunchtime date at the club was on 4 February. They had appeared 152 times at the Cavern's lunchtime sessions and many who witnessed the group going through their paces during these 12-2.15 spots claim that to have seen The Beatles at their brilliant, innovative best, then you would have to have been in the Mathew Street cellar to see them performing at these lunchtime shows. In later years the group themselves often said that they were at their best as a live act during their Cavern period and it was at the lunchtime sessions that they could really let their hair down. To the non-Beatles fans, it may seem pretty irrelevant, but it is doubtful whether there are many followers of the group who wouldn't have given their hind teeth to have seen John Lennon take a bite on his cheese buttie, tell the office workers out there with the suits on to shut up, and then break into a rasping version of 'Sweet Little Sixteen'. It's easy to understand what those who were fortunate to witness these shows mean when they say that after The Beatles left the Cavern they were never the same again.

Throughout the remainder of 1963 The Beatles were beginning to make their mark nationwide and would only play the odd date at the club. Their final Cavern performance was on 3 August 1963. Also on the bill were: The Escorts, The Sapphires, The Merseybeats, Johnny Ringo and the Colts and

George Harrison's favourite R&B group The Roadrunners. Tickets for the show sold out within thirty minutes of going on sale, and Brian Epstein stipulated that there was to be no overcrowding. With Brian Epstein's orders in mind, Ray McFall decided to allow only 500 into the club at a cost of ten shillings a ticket. As it turned out, McFall actually lost on the night. It's easy to understand why when you consider that The Beatles' fee alone was £300, whilst the support groups and club staff also had to be paid. Obviously, booking the group, who were now the hottest property in British pop, was good for the prestige of the club, but if someone had suggested to McFall a few years earlier, when he first booked them to appear at the club for a fee of £5, that a few years later booking them would have put him out of pocket, he would have probably laughed at the idea.

After the show which, according to those who witnessed it, was definitely not The Beatles at their best, Brian Epstein told Ray McFall and Bob Wooler that they would be back. But he knew deep down that they would never return to the Cavern. John Lennon for one felt that, after an estimated 274 appearances, The Beatles had outgrown the place, and he now had his sights set on conquering pastures new.

Chapter 11

CLAPTON, THE STONES AND THE BLUES GREATS AT THE CAVERN

Brian Epstein's decision to end The Beatles' reign at the Cavern may have been the end of an era for Merseyside beat fans, but there were to be many more memorable nights (and lunchtimes) at the club. Tuesday 5 November 1963 saw The Rolling Stones appearing at the Cavern for the first time. Appearing with them were Wirral group The Roadrunners, who were Cavern regulars during this period and were once paid this glowing tribute by *Mersey Beat* editor Bill Harry in an edition of the paper: 'They are considered to be the finest group of their kind in the country. Their rhythm and blues style is unique and they deserve a recording contract.' Lead guitar and vocalist with The Roadrunners during the early years of the group's formation was Dave Percy, who can recall the heady days of sharing Cavern billing with future rock music legends such as The Beatles, the Rolling Stones and The Yardbirds:

> When we played at the Cavern with The Rolling Stones one of our amps developed a fault when we were setting up our gear. We asked The Stones if we could borrow some of their gear. At that time The Stones had probably the best equipment on the market and it was with a certain amount of reluctance that they gave us permission to borrow one of their amplifiers. All went well until we were half-way through the song 'Roadrunner', when smoke started to billow from the borrowed amp. In the nick of time we managed to stop it bursting into flames but The Stones, who had been watching us from the side of the stage, were definitely not happy blokes at that moment in time!

However, once the Stones had sorted out their equipment and began to play, Dave recalls they had a wonderful crisp and clear sound: 'Their superior equipment, coupled with their wonderful talent, definitely gave them the edge over most of the other rock 'n' roll groups of the period.'

According to Bob Wooler, the Rolling Stones' fee for playing the Cavern was £70 and it was with some trepidation that the Stones stepped onto the Cavern stage, the hallowed home ground of The Beatles, but these worries soon evaporated when the Cavern crowd, urged on by Bob Wooler, gave the visiting Londoners a great reception. Mick Jagger said afterwards: 'Was it hot! We almost sweated away. They've had so many big groups at the Cavern that you've got to prove yourself. They asked us back, so they must have liked us.' Bill Wyman, recalling his Cavern debut in his autobiography, said:

> While some people were busy building a wall, metaphorically, dividing the north from the south in pop music, we found no barriers whatsoever from Merseyside fans. Walking around the city we were stopped and chatted to by friendly Liverpudlians. In the evening our show at the Cavern was fantastic, with a marvellous crowd. Two thousand fans queued to get in and twenty-five teenagers collapsed from the heat inside the dark, steaming cellar.

When they returned to Merseyside to play New Brighton Tower Ballroom a few months later their fee was £800.

One man, however, who was not impressed with his first taste of the Liverpool music scene was Ian Stewart, the Rolling Stones' road manager and one-time group member. He recalled:

Clockwise from above:

The Rolling Stones were paid just £70 for their one and only Cavern appearance on 5 November 1963 which packed the club out. Admission prices were a bit steep for Cavern regulars at 4s 6d! Bill Wyman described their Cavern appearance as 'fantastic, with a marvellous crowd'.

The Rolling Stones on stage at New Brighton Tower Ballroom in August 1964. The show was a Cavern presentation for Rael-Brook. Cavern DJ Bob Wooler presented the show.

Bob Wooler booked The Rolling Stones twice for shows across the Mersey at New Brighton Tower. Their first was in August 1963 as part of a 'Southern Sounds' presentation. A year later Wooler booked them again for the same venue. This time the show was a Cavern presentation. It is interesting to note that their fee had risen from £70 in 1963 to £800 in 1964.

I was so disappointed when I first went to Liverpool because we'd heard so much about Liverpool, the great place for R&B, all these fantastic groups, but the truth was that all the groups we heard were terrible, absolutely awful. One group, however, called The Chants, which nobody had ever heard of, were brilliant, wonderful singers, but they never got anywhere – it was just Beatles, Beatles and more Beatles. To me, The Hollies were better than The Beatles. They had a good drummer and they had some sort of feel to them.

To put Stewart's comments into context, however, he also stated that he never liked The Who because they had such a bad drummer (Keith Moon, arguably the greatest rock drummer of all time) whilst the Rolling Stones, in his opinion, would never make it: 'With Mick's thin voice and the musicians we had, I never dreamed we'd catch on. Never, never, never.'

1964 was a golden year for Cavern regulars with Bob Wooler using his entrepreneurial skills to the full to bring some of the greats of the R&B scene, such as Sonny Boy Williamson and John Lee Hooker to the Cavern. There was also an appearance by a young Londoner who today is generally acknowledged as the world's premier rock guitarist. Eric Clapton made his Cavern debut during the early part of 1964. Together with fellow Yardbirds Keith Relf, Chris Dreja, Paul Samwell-Smith and Jim McCarty, they set off on one of their first trips away from London to fulfil a Wednesday lunchtime booking at the Cavern. Chris Dreja described their Cavern appearance as one of their most amazing gigs during the whole of their career. The group set off at 8p.m. to play the lunchtime session at the Cavern the following day. Thick fog on the M1 led to a fifteen-hour crawl up the motorway and a tired and weary group arrived at the Cavern ten minutes before they were due on stage. Dreja remembers the club as:

Like a sewer – no changing facilities and the whole place seemed so foreign we could have been in Australia. We were a bit in awe of the Cavern legend but it was a bit of a memorial to us of past greatness, even then. There were thousands of groups' names on the wall, most of them we'd never heard of like Faron's Flamingos.

The Yardbirds' set included material such as: 'Too Much Monkey Business', 'Smokestack Lightning', 'Boom Boom' and 'Baby What's Wrong'. At the time, The Yardbirds were an out-and-out R&B outfit (Clapton left the group when they moved more into the pop mainstream market early in 1965) and fans at the Cavern gave them a fairly mixed reception. Dreja put the muted response to the group down to the fans being unfamiliar with The Yardbirds' R&B material. This seems unlikely, however, as among the most popular Cavern regulars during this period were The Roadrunners, a group whose music could also be described as purist R&B.

Popular Wirral R&B group The Roadrunners, who always went down well at the Cavern. George Harrison considered them to be on a par with the Rolling Stones as an R&B group.

The Roadrunners on the stage at Birkenhead Tech College in 1963.

Little Richard with The Roadrunners. This photograph was taken at Birkenhead's Plaza picture house in 1964.

The Roadrunners perform at a 1964 concert in Liverpool's Hope Hall.

After their Liverpool debut and a tour of some of the city's pubs and night spots, the group retired to the accommodation that they had been fixed up with in the city centre. This was to provide another unfavourable experience. Yardbirds' drummer Jim McCarty recalls, 'We stayed in this dreadful hotel with those horrible things in the beds that make you scratch all night. They had newspapers instead of tablecloths and the guy would cook and serve you breakfast wearing a dressing gown and pyjama bottoms!' After performing at the Cavern the following day, the group were packing their equipment into their transit van when Derry Wilkie, a popular local musician and friend of The Beatles, jumped into the back of the van and informed Clapton and the others that Paul McCartney had sent him down to the Cavern to check them out. The Yardbirds, however, had been made fully aware, even before Derry Wilkie's disclosure, by the many local musicians they had met during their two days in Liverpool, that the London music scene was one of the main topics of interest among Merseyside group members looking for new horizons away from the fading Liverpool scene. When Eric Clapton returned to the Cavern in the summer of 1965 he was by now widely recognised as one of Britain's premier blues guitarists. His decision to join John Mayall's Bluesbreakers meant that his guitar playing could now flourish and those who were lucky enough to witness his Cavern performance that night knew they were listening to a future great of the rock world.

June of 1964 saw the Cavern presenting an American Rhythm and Blues Night. Topping the bill were the great John Lee Hooker and John Mayall's Bluesbreakers and it was estimated that nearly 1,000 people crammed into the club. Later in the year other blues legends such as Howlin' Wolf, Mose Allison, Memphis Slim, Jimmy Witherspoon and Little Walter also played at the Cavern. Away from the Cavern The Beatles and other Merseyside groups were now taking the nation, and in the case of The Beatles, the world, by storm. The Cavern was now probably the most famous beat club in the world and Ray McFall was inundated with requests from around the globe to allow camera and radio crews into the club to document brief potted histories of the famous Liverpool cellar. Celebrities who were visiting Liverpool would make their way to Mathew Street to catch a glimpse of the club. American beat poet Allen Ginsberg couldn't resist a visit to the club during his 1964 English visit and he pronounced Liverpool 'The centre of the consciousness of the human universe'. At the Cavern, Ginsberg was struck by 'the beautiful boys with their golden archangelic hair'. Timex Watches filmed an advertisement for their products, using the music of Cavern favourites the Hideaways and the club as a backdrop for their advert. Radio Luxembourg began a weekly series, *Sunday Night at the Cavern*, hosted by Bob Wooler and featuring Cavern regulars such as The Roadrunners, The Clayton Squares,

Above left: John Mayall relaxing backstage before performing with John Lee Hooker in 1964.

Above right: Popular Merseyside group The Kubas, who made twenty-six appearances at the Cavern Club in the mid-1960s and an extra gig at the club when the spelling of their name was changed to the Koobas. They appeared on The Beatles' last British tour in 1965. Paul McCartney played drums for them during their performance of 'Dizzy Miss Lizzy' at the Liverpool Empire on the 5 December 1965.

Top right: The Kubas.

The Hideaways and The Kubas. Two record companies, Decca and Oriole, determined to try and capture the unique Cavern atmosphere, recorded a variety of local groups for LP release.

Bob Wooler was hard-pushed to cope with all that was going on, so Ray agreed to him having a deputy DJ to host some of the sessions. Wooler's choice was Billy Butler, who at the time was still fronting his group, The Tuxedos. From 1964 onwards, BB, as Billy became known, hosted some of the Cavern's sessions, in particular the all-nighters. Later he ran the Mardi Gras Club in Mount Pleasant, Liverpool, with his partner Chris Wharton who, in the late 1960s, ran the Cavern Agency, which Ray McFall decided to start up for groups. Ray's first signings were The Kubas, The Michael Allen Group, and The Hideaways, with great things especially predicted for The Kubas, who a few years later (with their name changed to The Koobas) signed up with Brian Epstein and appeared on The Beatles' last UK tour.

Chapter 12

THE CAVERN CLOSES FOR THE FIRST TIME

Although the Cavern was still thriving, the warning signs were showing for the decline of the beat scene on Merseyside. After the incredible peak of 1963 and early 1964, it was beginning to show signs of waning and the number of teenagers forming groups had certainly declined. In spite of this, Ray McFall was optimistic that the Cavern would continue to flourish and he decided to make certain improvements at the club, even to build a new stage. The aid stage was in fact sold in small pieces at a cost of 5s a piece, the proceeds going to Oxfam. As well as the new stage, Ray McFall in February decided to install recording facilities at the Cavern. They were known as 'Cavern Sound Recording Studio' and the intention was to provide demo recording facilities for local groups, with hopes eventually to release commercially successful records.

Although Cavern Sound did have success for a brief period with an LP entitled 'Ee Aye Addio' – a tribute album to the Liverpool FC FA Cup-winning team – in general, the venture did not prove to be a success and McFall acknowledged that he should have researched the idea and sought professional advice before going ahead with the project. McFall lost out financially with Cavern Sounds and was also hit financially when he gave support to the ailing *Mersey Beat* newspaper. Despite these setbacks McFall still brought top-notch entertainers to the club. Wednesday 31 March 1965 saw an incredible line-up at the club. On stage that night at the Cavern were: Gene Vincent, Sandie Shaw, Petula Clark, Manfred Mann, The Kinks and local favourites The Clayton Squares. The show was broadcast live on French television yet was never seen in Britain. Towards the end of the year, on Sunday 31 October, future rock legends The Who made their one and only appearance on the Cavern stage.

Early in 1966 Elton John, who at the time was a member of Bluesology, performed at the Cavern with R&B singer Doris Troy. Speaking about his appearance at the Cavern in later years, Elton said that playing the club was probably the highlight of his days with Bluesology, but he concluded that 'the gig was marred by the toilets overflowing and threatening to damage our equipment!' The toilets at the club, as Elton pointed out, had always been a problem, and Ray McFall was told by sanitation inspectors that the club would have to close unless he could come up with the cost of installing new toilets and a proper drainage system at the Cavern. The cost, said to be £3,000-plus, was out of McFall's financial reach and he knew that unless money could be found quickly the club would have to shut.

When the news reached local musicians, a marathon twelve-hour benefit concert was organised in an attempt to keep the club solvent. A galaxy of local musicians decided to play at the club for no fee and twenty-four groups appeared on stage, including The Spinners, The Scaffold and The Undertakers, all of whom had fond memories of the club's great days. It was estimated that nearly £700 was raised, with thousands of teenagers visiting the club during the day to pay their seven shillings to enter. But despite the obvious affection felt for the club by many, sufficient finance could not be found and the bailiffs entered the premises in late February 1966 to officially close the Cavern. Ray McFall's debts were estimated at £10,000. *The Liverpool Echo*, reporting on the bankruptcy hearing, stated, 'Cavern owner Andrew Ray McFall said he had been throwing money about like confetti at his public examination in bankruptcy in Liverpool today.' After witnessing the phenomenal success of Brian Epstein with The Beatles and his stable of Liverpool artists, McFall may

Top left: Members of The Scaffold and The Liverpool Scene at an impromptu jam session in 1968. The Scaffold – Roger McGough, John Gorman and Mike McGear (McCartney) – made four appearances at the Cavern. They had chart hits in the mid-1960s with 'Lilly The Pink' and 'Thank You Very Much'.

Left: After The Who had hits with 'I Can't Explain' and 'Anyway Anyhow Anywhere', and made sensational appearances on television's *Ready, Steady, Go*, Bob Wooler seized the opportunity to book them for the Cavern. The Who performed for the Cavern faithful on the 31 October 1965. Although The Who would go on to become the greatest live act in the history of rock music, according to Wooler they failed to set the place on fire during their only Cavern performance: 'The Who were ultra-cool mods and were determined to show that they were not in awe of the famous Cavern Club.'

Above: Elton John, who appeared at the Cavern in February 1966 as a member of Bluesology. Bluesology backed visiting American stars such as Major Lance, Patti LaBelle and Doris Troy. Elton's Cavern gig is ingrained in his memory because apparently the notoriously accident-prone Cavern toilets overflowed and soaked Elton and the other musicians sitting in the bandroom.

FROM

THE CAVERN - LIVERPOOL

"The Birthplace of THE BEATLES"

COMES THIS GENUINE PIECE OF THE

CAVERN CLUB STAGE ON WHICH

THE BEATLES

PERFORMED 292 TIMES DURING THE PERIOD

1961 TO 1963

have felt that he was in a position to emulate Epstein and take a slice of the pop music cake for himself. The Cavern was now, after all, the most famous beat club in the world. But, just as Epstein could never have visualised how big The Beatles were going to become, Ray McFall, when he took over the Cavern in 1959, had no idea that he was purchasing a basement club that was destined to become world famous. He may have been an accountant, but the ability to handle financial matters does not necessarily guarantee that one has the entrepreneurial skills needed to cash in when you suddenly have a hot property on your hands. McFall, with the assistance of Bob Wooler, tried as best he could to take advantage of the sudden fame of the Cavern but this glory that the Cavern basked in was, after all, only a reflected glory because of the club's links with The Beatles.

There were various factors behind the financial trouble McFall found himself in. The failure of his business ventures such as Cavern Sounds contributed to the general problems but, above all, McFall may have failed to read the signs that by late 1964 and early 1965 were patently obvious. Interest in beat music on Merseyside, after a couple of peak years, was now on the decline. Major venues such as the Majestic Ballroom, Birkenhead, where The Beatles and, more recently, the Rolling Stones and Gene Vincent had

appeared, had closed by the end of 1964. Other venues around Merseyside had now stopped having beat nights, or had closed altogether. The *Birkenhead News* entertainment page of October 1964 featured a story headlined, 'Is Merseyside on the Wane as a Top Beat Centre?' It cited the closure of the Majestic and the fact that many local groups had either disbanded or had to travel to the Continent to find work. Cavern DJ Bob Wooler was reported as saying, 'Merseyside is still the top beat area in Britain', but Mike Hart of The Roadrunners concluded, 'It's difficult for even established groups to get bookings and the trend seems to be turning towards Manchester and London.' To open up recording facilities at the Cavern under these circumstances was probably not the best idea. Perhaps the most accurate reason for the club's decline, therefore, is the theory suggested by many of those involved in the scene at the time; namely that the Cavern's days as a flourishing beat club were numbered once The Beatles had departed the scene.

Even without its reputation as the home of The Beatles, the club would undoubtedly still have been of historical importance on a local level, but it would never have attained the legendary worldwide status that it can now boast because of its links with the group who developed into the greatest popular musicians of the century.

Chapter 13

THE CAVERN REOPENS

After the closure of the Cavern an appeal fund was set up. This was the brainchild of Bob Wooler who not only thought it would be a good idea to establish a kind of Cavern co-operative with groups throughout the UK buying shares, but, as Bob put it:

I not only devised the scheme to get the Cavern open again, but I have to come clean and say I felt it would prove to be a good publicity stunt if The Hideaways were identified with the idea. After all, they were one of the last groups to play the Cavern. The Cryin' Shames, who were also on the bill on that last all-nighter, maintain that they were the last group who were playing on stage when the police eventually got into the club to close it down. Billy Butler held the fort throughout the night and I took over at 7 o'clock on that bleak Monday morning and witnessed the club's death throes. I also witnessed the very last group to play on stage – but I won't reveal who it actually was!

Speaking about the appeal fund and the closure of the Cavern, bass guitarist with The Hideaways, John Shell (who tragically lost his life during the Vietnam War), told *The Beat* magazine:

When we came off stage we were told that the Cavern – God rest its soul – was closing and the marathon was going on all night for as long as it could stay open, with the groups playing for nothing. We went back on stage about ten o'clock the next morning and played till one o'clock. Meanwhile, at eleven o'clock the police and bailiffs arrived to close the club down. We managed to lock them out for about two hours, but by one o'clock they had made their way into the club and the Cavern was closed.

The appeal fund was set up under the name of the New Cavern Ltd and supporters of the appeal were invited to buy shares in the company in denominations of £1 per share. Frank Taylor, who dealt with Ray McFall's bankruptcy, estimated that only £1,500 was raised and offers were invited from parties who were interested in purchasing the ownership of the club. An offer of £5,500 was made by Joe Davey, who owned the popular Joe's Cafe, and Alf Geoghegan. With no one else offering anywhere near this figure, they secured the club for that amount.

The Cavern was officially reopened on 23 July 1966 by the then Prime Minister, Harold Wilson. Wilson had always taken a keen interest in the beat music scene on Merseyside and, after being presented with a petition by a group of Cavern supporters, the Prime Minister gladly offered his support. At the reopening, Mr Wilson was presented with a wooden pipe crafted from a piece of the original Cavern stage. Labour MP Bessie Braddock, Ken Dodd, the players from Everton and Liverpool football clubs and numerous celebrities and musicians attended the ceremony. There was also a telegram sent by Brian Epstein on behalf of himself and The Beatles, wishing the club a successful future.

Joe and Alf lost no time in developing and improving the club, and a licensed bar, a boutique and, above all, better sanitation were all part of the new refurbishment at the club. Frankie Connor, a member of The Hideaways, the group who had fought so hard for the survival of the Cavern, recalls that,

Left: Prime Minister Harold Wilson, who reopened the Cavern on 23 July 1966. This photograph was taken at Wilson's former school, Wirral Grammar, where he was addressing the pupils during a mid 1960s visit.

Opposite: Ben E. King backstage at the Cavern in December 1966. His version of 'Stand By Me' remains a classic to this day.

although Joe Davey and Alf Geoghegan tried hard to restore the club to its former glory, the Cavern never really recaptured the magical atmosphere that was once so evident:

> The club was now licensed and to me it had lost its innocence. The Hideaways were a teenage group, but when the club reopened it seemed more grown up. It was now similar to other Liverpool night clubs such as the Mardi Gras or the Downbeat Club. Most of the same kids were still coming, but the club had definitely lost something. It was now much bigger with the improvements and the extensions that had been added and it certainly smelt better; more hygienic. Joe Davey was a more friendly man to deal with than Ray McFall. Ray was always polite, but very aloof – he was never a friendly man. Joe and Alf were different people altogether. Every group in Liverpool went to Joe's Cafe when Joe Davey was running it. Group members were supplied with food at reduced rates. I often felt that if someone like Bob Wooler, who was a wonderful entrepreneur, had owned the Cavern instead of being an employee, it would never have closed. Nothing against Ray McFall, but I didn't really feel that his heart was in it and I think it was all a matter of one pound notes and pennies with him.

The Hideaways continued to play at the Cavern until the late 1960s and Frankie Connor witnessed what was probably the last visit to the Cavern by one of The Beatles:

> It was the early months of 1968. We would sometimes rehearse in the upstairs part of the club during the afternoon and I remember Paul McCartney turning up as we were participating in one of these practice sessions. It was about 2.30 in the afternoon and Paul walked in with Jane Asher. 'Alright lads,' said Paul as he wandered about the place. We were all surprised to see one of The Beatles back at the Cavern. After chatting for a brief period he made his farewells and left.

The new owners of the Cavern lost no time in bringing some of the major names of the pop world to the club, and in November of 1966 Ben E. King performed at the Cavern for the second time. Interviewed recently on BBC Radio Merseyside's *Linda McDermot Show*, Bob Wooler revealed that after Ben E. King had appeared at the Cavern he took him to Allan Williams' Blue Angel Club, where the great American singer performed for free. Bob recalled:

> I was very annoyed by one incident. Ben E. King had appeared at the Cavern and I took him back to the Blue Angel. Ben liked the atmosphere and the next thing he's on stage with the resident group, singing. I went up to Allan Williams and asked him how much he was paying him for the show? Allan replied, 'I'm not paying him anything.' I told him we'd just paid £125 for him at the Cavern and you're getting him for free! Allan Williams replied, 'Well, I let him in for free. I didn't charge him entrance money!'

Although the Cavern was still a popular club to hear live music, some of the musicians who appeared there during the mid-1960s claim that the club was now becoming an increasingly violent venue to perform at. Phil Munroe was the vocalist with Birkenhead group The Prowlers, who played at the Cavern on numerous occasions before and after the club reopened:

> Although I loved every minute of my time at the Cavern, the club was definitely not the rose garden that some people say it was. There used to be a lot of animosity when groups from Birkenhead got bookings ahead of Liverpool groups. We were once told by a member of one of the Liverpool groups, 'You lot should stay in Birkenhead because the Cavern is for Liverpool groups.' I told him we deserved to play there because we used to bring coach loads of our fans over the Mersey with us to watch us at the Cavern. What spoilt the Cavern was when the club began to be plagued by troublemakers. We were once attacked as we loaded our gear into the van after a Cavern gig. I had to fend the gang off with a hammer that was kept inside the bass drum to secure the drum to the floor of the stage. Outside the Cavern you stood the chance of getting attacked by the people who couldn't get into the club. Inside you might get attacked by gangs inside the place. There was a hell of a lot of booze brought into the club. You'd see empty spirit bottles scattered around the place. I felt sorry for Paddy the bouncer. He was a hard lad, but he couldn't keep up with the fights that would break out in different parts of the club. He would have trouble containing it. A fight broke out one night in front of the stage and someone lunged at our bass guitarist Ian McDonald. I hit his attacker with the bass of the mike stand. The whole show

Ben E. King.

> then ground to a halt while order was restored. We'd only just started playing when another fight broke out involving some sailors who were in the club. This was the last straw and I lost my temper and began to smash up the stage. I got barred from the club for this – but not for long. Anyone who says that they never witnessed any violence at the Cavern couldn't have been there the same time as me. I'd go as far as to say that the Cavern began to lose money because people stopped going there due to the fights at the club. Despite all the trouble I loved the place and was never in a hurry to leave, even after we had finished our set. To me the Cavern was hallowed ground and I'd sit and watch the other groups or chat to people even when the rest of the band had packed up and gone home.

John Donaldson of The Hideaways also felt that the spirit that had been a feature of the Cavern before its closure was not so prevalent since the club's

Legendary American group The Drifters who appeared at the Cavern in January 1966.

reopening. Reflecting on his Cavern days in an interview with the *Liverpool Echo* in 1973, John commented:

> The Cavern was the same when it reopened, only a little sprucer, but the attitude of the people in the groups was changing. It was becoming less fun. Everyone was more posey. There wasn't the same friendliness. You didn't lend each other equipment any more and sit around showing each other the different bits you had learned the week before.

Despite the better facilities available at the Cavern, the general opinion of both the musicians and fans that frequented the club was that it had lost the originality and uniqueness that set it apart from other Liverpool city-centre clubs. Ray McFall had always maintained that once you started tinkering with the sparseness and bare decor of the Cavern then you ran the risk of destroying the unique, informal atmosphere of the club; the reaction of the Cavern regulars to the refurbished Cavern confirmed his fears. Many chose to frequent other city-centre clubs but, as they moved on, a new group of youngsters took their place and, by the late 1960s, the Cavern had not only a new audience but also a new owner. Liverpool businessman Roy Adams took over the management of the club. Jack Smith was a Cavern regular during the late 1960s and his memories of his first visit to the club in 1969 gives

one an idea of the changing scene at the Cavern as the end of the decade approached:

> I was very pissed off with the soul scene at the Mardi Gras club that was becoming rather thuggish, and I decided to become a member of the Cavern Club. With my flared trousers and locks creeping over my ears I queued with my mates in freezing conditions in January 1969 to get into the club. I had heard from various sources, notably work-mates older than me, about the slippery steps and the gloom on entering the club. But it was different from what I had been told. As I paid my entrance fee, watched over by Paddy Delaney, I was struck by the warm air wafting out from the doorway and the old entrance with the slippery steps that once led directly into the cellar had now been closed. As I walked into the club I was distraught when I saw that the place was full of mods – the very people that had driven me out of the Mardi Gras. However, it was soon pointed out to me that the place to be was across the floor and down the stairs that led to the basement. Across the floor I stumbled, to glares from the mods, and descended into a bohemian basement of tranquillity and wonderful strangeness. The DJ, Billy Butler, was playing the terrific sounds of The Doors, the Stones, Procul Harum and the Velvet Underground. There were also incredibly sensual women and two live bands, from London no less! One look around and I was hooked. The pungent smell of incense burning and the aroma of smouldering reefers was evident. There was still the original stage, with the graffiti on the wall and rows of chairs in front of the stage, but I don't think any of us even gave a thought to the old days. The Beatles had been and gone at the Cavern, but just like in their days at the club, the walls still felt slimy. There was a pungent, fruity, stale smell and clinging damp that permeated down to your socks. I can remember my mum barging in to my bedroom on a Sunday morning, throwing open the windows and regaling me with her usual, 'You've been to that smelly cellar again – pooh!'

Chapter 14

THE CAVERN CLOSES

Although the halcyon days of The Beatles at the Cavern were now a fading memory, the beginning of the 1970s saw the club continuing to provide a good standard of musical fare. Roy Adams continued the Cavern tradition of bringing top acts from outside the Merseyside area to the club. Focus, Thin Lizzy, Vinegar Joe, Status Quo, Gary Glitter, Wishbone Ash, Supertramp and Judas Priest were just some of the top names to appear at the club in the early-1970s. John Unsworth was a Cavern regular during this period and would attend the club five nights a week. He told me:

The floor of the Cavern seemed to be an inch deep in sweat – I dread to think what it really was that we were paddling around in – but I enjoyed every minute of my time at the club. Admittedly there were drugs like LSD and cannabis floating around but no more than at any other club during this period. The majority of Cavern members were there for the excellent music and we were rarely disappointed. As soon as the doors to the club opened there would be a mad scramble down the stairs to get a good seat in front of the stage. The seats there were just like church pews and were soon filled up. The DJs were backstage and you couldn't see them but you could tell who they were by the way they introduced the bands. At the stage entrance all the groupies would hang out and these girls could tell you anything you wanted to know about the bands that played at the Cavern. There were coach trips organised to pop festivals and all the Cavern members knew each other. It was really just like one big family. The cafe at the club was the place to chat because it was the furthest place away from the music. I remember that Molly the cook did great egg and chips. Most of the bands at the club were top quality musicians, but during the week days you would get some novices trying to make a name for themselves. I remember one local group who would try to play numbers like 'Johnny B Goode', but the lead guitarist couldn't play a note and they would get laughed at and booed off the stage. I remember one night the vocalist threw his microphone at the crowd and it hit my mate on the head. He threw it back at him and hit the singer right in the face. There was one local band who were very good called The Klubbs who were on most nights. Everyone looked forward to hearing them and they always gave a good show. They later changed their name to Strife. When the original Cavern closed and moved across the road to the other side of Mathew Street most of the regulars moved elsewhere because there just wasn't the same atmosphere there.

The decision to close the Cavern was actually forced on Roy Adams by British Rail who needed the land as part of the extension programme for the Liverpool underground rail loop. The site of the Cavern Club was needed for the construction of an extraction duct and after the plan was approved by the Liverpool Corporation, Roy Adams was left with little option but to close the club, which he duly did on 27 May 1973. Roy Adams resigned himself to the fact that the £10,000 he had ploughed into the club would have to be written off. Unlike in 1966, when the closure of the Cavern prompted uproar and protest, this time there was hardly a whimper of disapproval. Perhaps the fact that the club was to reopen across Mathew Street in new premises softened the blow for those who regarded 10 Mathew Street as hallowed ground; a shrine to The Beatles and the Merseybeat explosion of the 1960s. But, in general, the news that the Cavern was to be demolished was met with apathy by the majority of the Merseyside public.

The final night at the Cavern consisted of appearances by popular Merseyside groups of the time such as Supercharge and Strife, but the guests of honour were an unknown American group called The Yardleys. The Yardleys had written to Roy Adams after hearing the news that the Cavern was to close and had begged to be allowed to play at the club. The New York-based group were overjoyed when they received the news that they were to be allowed to fulfil their lifetime ambition on the club's final night. Paul McCartney also expressed an interest in seeing the Cavern for a final time, 'To kiss the old Cavern goodbye.' But on the night of the Cavern's closure Paul was appearing with his group Wings at the Odeon Cinema, Hammersmith and was unable to pay his last respects to his favourite venue.

When the news of the club's closure reached Ray McFall he was asked what had made the club so special. He replied:

> It was very loud and hot and humid. It wasn't just a club, it was something to do with the cellar idea. Going down below ground was a bit like people of old getting away from authority in the catacombs. The Cavern became a hideaway, an escape. It was the sort of place that adults would never go to and that was what the teenagers wanted. They wanted a place they could call their own and where they could hear their own kind of music and meet their own age group. The Cavern was that place.

Aware of the potential of the site of the club as a tourist attraction, Roy Adams told the *Liverpool Echo*, 'I would like to see part of the cellar preserved as a tourist attraction. I think it could be done, and would be worth the effort.' Unfortunately, Roy Adams' idea to preserve the Cavern cellar did not materialise and the club that writer Alfred Green once described as 'perhaps the only hole in the ground to put a city on the map of world entertainment' was reduced to a mountain of rubble when the bulldozers moved in shortly after its closure.

Chapter 15

THE NEW CAVERN CLUB

In the summer of 1982 the local media on Merseyside excitedly reported that plans had been unveiled for a £7 million redevelopment deal that could include the reopening of the original Cavern club. The project was to be financed by Royal Life Insurance and the architect was Liverpool man David Backhouse. The scheme was managed by Liverpool firm Merseypride. The head of Merseypride, Ted Spencer, was confident that the Cavern club was intact beneath the NCP car park. After securing the land from British Rail, the excavation of the land covering the remains of the Cavern could proceed. The exercise to unearth what was described by the local press as Liverpool's own Tutankhamun's tomb began in October of 1982.

It was soon revealed, however, that although the arches were still intact, the famous barrel ceilings had totally collapsed. David Backhouse told the *Liverpool Echo*:

> There isn't much left of the club now. Most of it was destroyed when it was turned into a car park. More of the arches will be exposed as we carry on but there is nothing of interest to souvenir hunters. I understand everything worth keeping was taken when the club closed in 1973.

Despite the disappointment of finding out that it would not be the original Cavern, Backhouse continued with the development plan and by spring of 1984 the Cavern Walks was completed. The highlight of the complex for music fans was undoubtedly the new Cavern club, constructed on the same side of the road as the original club and within yards of where the Cavern once stood. It was estimated that over 15,000 bricks from the original cellar were used in the club's construction. Prior to the opening ceremony, scores of musicians from the beat days at the Cavern arrived at the club to sign the wall at the back of the stage, a tradition that dates back to the early years. Among those who turned up to give the new Cavern their seal of approval were the Swinging Blue Genes, Billy J. Kramer, The Merseybeats, The Roadrunners, Adrian Henri, Mike McCartney and members of numerous other beat groups from the Merseybeat days.

Billy J. Kramer was clearly impressed with the recreated Cavern, which in many ways is identical to the old one, and he remarked: 'The dressing rooms are luxurious compared with what they used to be – I couldn't believe it. In the old club it was like trying to change in a telephone box. They've done a great job, but it is not exactly like the old club – it's too clean!' Ray Ennis of the Swinging Blue Genes was also impressed: 'The only thing missing is the smell.'

Two of Merseyside's most famous poets, Adrian Henri (left) and Roger McGough. Together with Brian Pattern they released a collection of poetry *The Mersey Sound* that sold by the thousand in the late 1960s. Born across the Mersey in Birkenhead, Adrian Henri was also an acclaimed artist and frontman for The Liverpool Scene. The group consisted of Adrian Henri, Mike Hart, Andy Roberts, Percy Jones and Brian Dodson. They appeared at the Cavern five times and were also on the bill at the 1969 Isle of Wight Festival with Bob Dylan. Henri organised the Black & White Show Against Apartheid at the Cavern in February 1965.

Chapter 16

CAVERN MEMORIES

These Cavern memories were compiled from letters sent in by Cavern regulars from the 1957-1973 period.

As Bob Wooler has pointed out in his introduction, the passing of time, in some cases up to fifty can lead to myths being perpetuated and the reality of what took place becoming blurred.

Nevertheless, the memories included here have been reproduced with the information left as the writers recollect.

1957

The bands' pay at the Cavern during the Alan Sytner period at the club was determined by the attendance. For my first Cavern appearance I was paid the princely sum of £1 but, a few weeks later, high attendance figures pushed up my earnings to the £3 mark. For a lunchtime session in 1957 I was paid on average £1.30, which gives an idea of the number of people attending lunchtime sessions during the trad jazz days at the club.

When The Beatles made their Cavern debut in February 1961 at a lunchtime session they were paid £1 each. Ray McFall paid the groups a set fee, regardless of whether the attendance was high or low.
Johnny Parkes, The Merseysippi Jazz Band

There was a whole gang of us, girls in their late teens or early twenties, all in work, and spending our leisure time between the Philharmonic, the theatres and cinemas and the dance halls – Reece's was the favourite, closely followed by the Rialto. I recall that in 1957, I went to see *Look Back in Anger*

at the theatre in London Road which eventually became the Everyman, Gerry Mulligan at the Philharmonic and a twenty-one-year-old Richard Briers who was wowing audiences at the Playhouse with his magnificent performances.

The Cavern, however, was something else. The opening night was advertised in the *Liverpool Echo*, and we arrived to find a long queue which swiftly became even longer. We only just managed to get in.

A club in a cellar, which until then we'd only thought of for storing coal, along with bare brick walls and bare wooden tables, seemed, for Liverpool, to be incredibly avant-garde and cosmopolitan. We were duly impressed and from then on went frequently, feeling rather like Existentialists, dressing accordingly in black with too much eye make-up and no lipstick. I can remember nothing at all about the groups which played; the music was merely the background to conversation. There was no violence and no alcohol, soft drinks only.

In October 1957 I got married and left Liverpool forever.
Maureen Lee

I was a member of a group called The Deltones. We played on a number of occasions at the Cavern which at that time was run by a man named Alan Sytner. The music played at that time was strictly traditional jazz and skiffle. The Merseysippi Jazz Band was the main attraction and visiting bands such as the Wall City Jazzmen, the Second City Jazzmen and the Manchester Saints all played there on a regular basis. We were booked as one of the skiffle groups to play in between spots.

Johnny Parkes
(Merseysippi) and his
wife.

It occurred to me that it has never been put on record who actually started rock and roll at the Cavern and the following recollection may be of interest to you.

As a group we were never keen on skiffle and were only happy playing rock and pop music. The group members were as follows: Alan Willey and Tony Ormisher (electric guitars and vocal) Fred Pennuck (drums) and myself (rhythm and vocal). During our last appearance at the Cavern, bored as always with playing skiffle, we decided to play some rock 'n' roll. I was pulled sideways off stage by my guitar lead and pounced on by an indignant Alan Sytner who made it quite clear that 'This is a trad jazz club and if you play any more of that rubbish' (despite the fact that the rock number had gone down with great success) 'you will never play the Cavern again.' He was absolutely right because we had decided to finish the rest of our spot with rock and pop numbers, so we never played the Cavern again!
Charles Lyth, The Deltones

1957-58

I was a member of the Cavern Club in the early days, when it was a jazz club. I used to go often in 1957 and 1958, usually with my brother or one or two of his friends. We preferred the Thursday night sessions, which were 'modern' jazz. The pianist Joe Palin with a small group was a regular, as was, for a time, Alan Branscombe. Those people are, or were until recently, still playing somewhere. The best of British modern jazz appeared at these Thursday night sessions. The Jazz Couriers were the most outstanding of those, headed by Tubby Hayes and Ronnie Scott, both playing tenor saxophones. Tubby also played vibes; this was a high experience of my life, witnessing these two at the peak of their creative vigour. As a receptive twenty-year-old this music was etched into my soul. How lucky I was to have been there. Dare I say nobody plays like that now? I don't remember any amplification yet the music was plenty loud enough. I can rarely abide for long the amplified live music we get today.

We sometimes went to the Cavern on Sunday nights too. We were keen cyclists and would, after a strenuous race or a hard ride up and down the hills of Wales all day, and sometimes both, have a bath and a quick meal and soon be on the bus to Rock Ferry (from Bromborough), for the train to Liverpool. I could have negotiated the route from James Street Station to Mathew Street blindfolded. On Sunday nights it was traditional jazz. I remember seeing Acker Bilk perform there.

Dancing was popular in the club and it worked very well, even to most of the modern jazz – although we were so entranced by the playing of the top 'modern' bands that we usually preferred to be seated and concentrate on the music when they were on the stand. No alcohol was allowed but we sometimes would get a pass-out and go to the 'Grapes' or the 'White Star' for a beer. I never went to the Cavern much after 1958, having been called up for National Service in early 1959. Once in 1962 or 1963 I gave up queuing when The Beatles were on and never saw them or any other beat group there. A brief diary entry I made for Thursday 31 October 1957 reads: 'Saw Harry Klein (Baritone Sax) at the Cavern.' The Cavern used to be referred to by some at one time as 'the cave', but I don't think we used that term much in the early days.
Neil Hanson

Clinton Ford, who was back at the Cavern after appearing at Butlins Pwllheli for the summer season, was a bit short on funds and could only afford one big meal a week. He told Alan Sytner about his plight and Sytner told him that if Clinton could eat him under the table than he would pay for the meal. They made their way to a restaurant in Liverpool's Chinatown district and began to gorge themselves fit to burst. Neither of them could eat another mouthful and it looked like Clinton had lost the bet. He won the day, however, when he raised his hand and asked the waiter for another bowl of noodles which he somehow managed to eat.
John Lawrence, The Merseysippi Jazz Band

1957-62

Quite a few of us in my age group went to the Cavern Club in Mathew Street, Liverpool, around 1957-62. I first knew the Cavern as the West Coast Jazz Club where jazz groups of the modern jazz and traditional schools would play and you went on the night according to your taste in jazz. There were about six of us who were a hardcore of modernists, as we were known in those days. We all wore a uniform of dark Ivy League suits. Ivy League is a full drape, three button, single-breasted jacket with high narrow lapels and a single rear vent. The trousers had a tapered eighteen inch bottom and no turn-ups with a non-pleated waistband. The suits were worn with black winkle-pickers or Cuban heel elasticated side boots, a tabbersnap or button down shirt with long sleeves peeping below the suit jacket sleeves and a narrowed 'old boys' school tie, half an inch wide. A short crew-cut (flat top) hairstyle finished the look – we thought we were very smart.

As jazz progressed to more sophisticated places like the Liverpool Philharmonic Hall (modern jazz), pop music or rock 'n' roll had also become more sophisticated and venues to showcase rock and pop bands had to be found. The Cavern was actually based on 'Le Caveau' in Paris which was a discotheque, playing jazz records on a 'dansette hi-fi' gramophone, quite literally. It was a place where people could meet, chat and listen to jazz music or even dance and smooch; it was very atmospheric.

But back to Liverpool. The jazz side of things seemed to die a natural death at the Cavern. That's when pop music came on the scene through The Beatles. We, my girlfriend and I (now my wife), saw an ad in the *Liverpool Echo* personal column which read 'The Beatles are coming' or words to that effect – 'watch this space'. So we watched and sure enough the date came up and we got in the car (my first: a Vauxhall Velox, 2.4 litres, leather seats, very posh). Anyway, we parked the car in Victoria Street quite easily which was very handy for no.10 Mathew Street. As we sat momentarily bracing ourselves for the rigours of the evening, we looked up, and there they were, the Fab Four, as they were to become known, a long way off. John, Paul, George and Pete (Ringo was still with Rory Storm and the Hurricanes) were crossing the road from a pub off Dale Street, making their way to the Cavern. So we made our way to no.10 Mathew Street, tacked on the back of the queue and gradually made our way down the narrow, steep steps into the Cavern, turning left at the bottom and arriving at the table at which you paid your entrance fee, 5s old money, approximately. If we were lucky, one of The Beatles would be on the table watching us all trail in with a welcoming grin.

Clinton Ford, a Cavern regular with the Merseysippi Jazz Band in the late 1950s and early '60s. Seen here performing at the Royal Albert Hall.

The Cavern was set out in three long archways like a wine cellar. The first arch to the right as you entered was a dance area with a cloakroom at the bandstand end with chairs down each side. The middle archway was all seating to back level with the entrance, then a clear space for you to move around and at the rear of this area were the toilets, gents and ladies. They said the ladies was haunted by a slave overseer dressed in eighteenth-century gear, although I never saw him and neither did my girlfriend. At the end of the third archway was another cloakroom and at the other end was the bandroom where the boys would gather before bursting onto the Cavern stage. Oh yes, in this cloakroom was Priscilla White, who would hang up my lovely white mac and trilby which I would wear – you see I was one of a rare breed who loved jazz and rock and pop, in fact all types of music. In the dance area the Cavern Stomp developed, which was a dance basically like pogoing up and down and wiggling your shoulders a bit like the Masai Tribes of Kenya.

When we saw The Beatles that night the first thing that impressed me was their leather gear; jackets and trousers. Bob Wooler was the resident compère/DJ and when he announced 'Ladies and gentlemen the Cavern Club proudly presents The Beatles!' the place went nuts. They were good, in fact bloody fabulous. The first two or three tunes were mostly Motown covers or own compositions; their opening number was usually 'Some Other Guy' – superb.

After their third number the jackets would come off and although they looked 'cool' they were decidedly 'hot'. We saw them quite a few times and then all of a sudden, Pete Best did not appear and who should appear but Ringo Starr, from Rory Storm's Hurricanes. He was quite good, solid and a personality in himself because he used to have his own spot in Rory's set called Ringo's Starr Time. Apparently the reason for Pete Best's demise was that he was more popular than John, Paul and George and I think Epstein wasn't going to have a low-down drummer (we are still treated like the lowest of the low) who was more popular than the front men, so out he went.

The ventilation in the Cavern was literally one little skylight in the band end cloakroom and the entrance stairwell, so with a couple of hundred people (so it seemed) dancing and going into raptures over groups, the walls were literally streaming with condensation.

As The Beatles became more famous, recording and touring meant that they wouldn't appear at the Cavern, so the lesser known groups got a look in; groups like The Big Three, the Remo Four, Swinging Blue Genes, Billy J. Kramer, Johnny Sandon, Gerry and the Pacemakers and Kingsize Taylor and The Dominoes. They were our favourites and still are to this day – we still play their singles. Then came the international stars such as Bee Bumble and the Stingers (bit of a let down) and Gene Vincent with Sounds Incorporated. We later saw The Beatles at the Tower, New Brighton with Little Richard who also appeared with Sounds Incorporated.

Now we are getting to 1963 when The Beatles were famous and all the little groups were getting known and having records played on *Ready, Steady, Go.*

I was a drummer in a band similar to Sounds Incorporated called The Saxons since we had two tenor saxophonists in the line-up. We entered a rock contest at the Philharmonic Hall and we were up against bands like The Merseybeats, The Mojos, Derry Wilkie and The Pressmen (our main competition). When we had finished our spot, we were asked to return the next day for the semi-finals. That day we did our spot and went to the back of the hall to listen to the competition. Who should be there but George Harrison and Ringo Starr. We chatted and asked them how we sounded from the back. They said that they thought we were the best band on the day – I bet they said that to all the bands! We got to be stand-by band but were never called. We might have got somewhere, but who knows? *Alan W. Rogers, The Saxons*

1959

It was in late 1959 that an advert appeared in the *Echo* for a grand skiffle contest at the Cavern. It was for the Lonnie Donegan skiffle trophy and the prize was a chance to appear on the *6.5 Special* TV programme.

The Atlantics were an up and coming group and we were trying to establish a reputation. We used to enter every skiffle and talent contest that was held in the area. After contacting the Cavern to enter our group in the contest we made the journey to the Cavern by bus and ferry. Whilst crossing the river on the ferry we had a practice session on the top deck of the *Royal Daffodil* and after about five minutes of good solid skiffle music the captain of the vessel appeared. We thought, 'great! We have another admirer', but to our dismay he bellowed the following words: 'If you lot don't stop that racket on my boat I'll have the lot of you thrown overboard.' So, we all suddenly went quiet and sheepishly packed our instruments up and made our was down to the lower deck to disembark, finally walking up from the Pier Head to Mathew Street, carrying two guitars, one amplifier, one tea chest bass, and a set of drums. Very few groups had their own transport in those days, but public transport was good and we were all doing it for fun and the love of music, not for the money.

Mathew Street was about seven minutes walk from the Pier Head and was a dark and narrow road which had tall warehouses on each side, which at night were quite foreboding. We eventually found the club halfway down on the right-hand side. There was no bright neon light or anything to make the club noticeable, just a narrow front door leading to a steep, downward flight of steps into the basement of this old warehouse. When we got down into the cellar it was really dark except for the odd light or two and it was like being in a long, dark tunnel. As our eyes got used to the dark, we could see a sort of makeshift stage at one end and a sort of bar and cloakroom at the other end. The only drinks available were non-alcoholic soft drinks; orange juice, tango, coke and the like. As the club filled with people, the air down there – what there was of it – filled with tobacco smoke, because everybody smoked in those days. Looking upwards, we could make out the fine, arched brick ceilings which only seemed to be a couple of feet above our heads.

As this was our first appearance at the Cavern, we did not know what to expect. Not all clubs even had a microphone, so we used to take our own just in case and we could only afford one microphone and a small amp. The stage was barely big enough to hold one group, as we found out when we came to assemble our gear, especially the drum kit. Within about half an hour of us arriving, another six or so groups arrived and the place was really beginning to fill up with the teenagers eagerly awaiting the first group to play so that they could dance. Each group in those days had a following, usually between ten and thirty girls, who followed the groups everywhere they played. The tables at the sides of the club soon filled and the stone-flagged floor was crammed tight with eager dancers. The groups, meanwhile, were trying to assemble their gear amongst the mayhem as near to the stage as possible. The groups for the skiffle contest were chosen at random and the first group squeezed themselves and their instruments through the crowd and up onto the stage. Soon the air was electrified to the sounds of the old railroad songs of skiffle and the Old West. Each group did twenty minutes or so and it went on like that until midnight and the kids were shouting for more. All of the groups were good and had their own styles and some even wrote their own songs. Some teenagers actually fainted because after about two hours of solid dancing the cellar got that hot that everyone was sweating and the condensation could be seen on the ceilings. There was no ventilation in there, no emergency lighting, no fire extinguishers, or even a fire exit. There was only one way in and one way out, and that was up the narrow stairs. People used to line the stairs from bottom to top, smoking and trying to get some air in from Mathew Street. The stairs were the coolest place to be.

I can remember some of the groups we played alongside at the Cavern: The Bluegenes, Hank Walters and The Dusty Road Ramblers, the Red Devils etc. – a few groups still used a washboard and a tea chest bass. We, The Atlantics, only ever wrote one song which we performed regularly called 'The Eighth Wonder'. It was all about the Mersey Tunnel and the Irishmen who built it. We also cut a record at Frank Phillips' Recording Studio at 38 Kensington, Liverpool and during one of our practice sessions in 1960 we recorded twenty-four songs non-stop onto a reel-to-reel recorder. The recording has survived to this day.

The Atlantics had been going for quite some time before appearing at the Cavern, and we had all saved hard to change our old drums and guitars to new and better instruments. Our lead singer, Ron Higginson, bought a German-made Framus and I bought a German Hofner President semi-acoustic guitar, and also a Selmer amplifier. We both still have and play these original instruments today. These were bought from our friend Jim Gretty of Hessy's Music Shop in Whitechapel, who was also a musician. The shop stocked everything any band could ever need, including a good selection of sheet music. After a couple of sessions at the Cavern I was approached by the entertainments secretary of another Liverpool jazz club, 'The Unicorn' in Duke Street, and The Atlantics were booked for six months playing there two to three nights a week. The club was billed in the local papers as 'The Most Swinging Club in Town' and we used to support such famous names as the Temperance Seven, Cuddly Duddly, Ray Ellington and Jim Gretty's Feetwarmers. The Cavern really only had local bands at first, but there was never a shortage of groups to appear at the Cavern and most of them followed the usual tradition of writing the group's name on the wall somewhere near or at the back of the stage. We were no exception and our name went on the wall at the back of the stage.

John Lomax, The Atlantics Skiffle Group

1960-62

I was a tenor sax player in The Delacardoes in the late 1950s/early 1960s and we went to the Cavern regularly, not just for entertainment but to check up on the competition! I think our first visit was in 1960 and we always used to drink at the White Star or Rigby's in Dale Street first, because the Cavern then, as you know, was dry.

Paul McCartney once reminded people of something that is often forgotten – that lots of blokes went to the club in suits, not in leather jackets and jeans, as the popular idea has it. In 1961 our suits were Italian: three-button jacket and narrow trousers with no turn-ups, plus matching horizontally-striped ties.

There were three of us and we'd take it in turn to 'split up' a couple of girls who were jiving together – sometimes they'd refuse but usually they'd agree to at least one dance. Everyone who went remembers the 'Cavern smell' – that peculiar aroma of mould, damp, sweat, BO, the smell of urine from the gents' toilet and the acrid fumes of hot dogs, hamburgers and frying onions.

One particularly crowded Saturday night so many people were using the urinals (which were long troughs) that they overflowed and streams of urine flowed down the slope from the entrance of the gents' toilet. People coming in were literally paddling in piss.

You never bothered about such unhygienic conditions because the atmosphere was so exciting. Our favourite group was probably the Remo Four. We liked them because they were smartly dressed, well-practised and with an all-Fender line-up; they also played a lot of our favourite instrumentals, e.g. 'Trambone' by Chet Atkins and 'Quite a Party' by the Fireballs.

Gerry and the Pacemakers were very professional, too, but really, Gerry was the draw and not the rest of his musicians. His cheeky, lively personality scored with both males and females. He did a very good version of 'Pretend' and the highly unusual 'Nature Boy' (a very hard song to sing – I never heard any other group attempt it). His voice, however, did have a tendency to hoarseness. His piano player was very good, too, and I recall his doing a good version of 'Beachcomber', an obscure Bobby Darin instrumental track.

As a sax player, I remember Howie Casey very well and often button-holed him in the club to ask what mouthpiece reeds he used. He was very kind and patient in answering my questions but I think he got fed up with my constant queries in the end! He amused me once by throwing a snatch of 'Entry of the Gladiators' into one of his sax solos.

We never rated The Beatles! We considered them scruffy, arrogant and unprofessional!

Bob Wooler described the Bluegenes as unique and that is true. I remember them playing 'Sucu Sucu' (the Laurie Johnson number) in 1961 and the lead singer had got hold of a huge Mexican hat from somewhere (the sort that looks like an enormous multi-coloured ice-cream cone) and he was capering around the stage with it.

I've only mentioned a few groups as although we saw most of the main ones only a few stuck in our minds.

Even when beat groups dominated the scene there would still be nights at the Cavern at which a jazz band played on the same bill, e.g. the Red River Jazz Band and Gerry and the Pacemakers. The snag with this was that if you started jiving to a jazz number you might have to carry on for ten minutes (because everyone in the band had to have a solo)!

I saw jazz tenor sax star Zoot Sims at the Cavern in 1961 and paid £1 for the privilege – the most I'd ever paid to see anyone! A jazz-loving friend told me afterwards that he was an alcoholic and had to be lifted onto the stage but I can't say that it seemed to affect his playing.

The last time I went to the club was in early 1962. It was one of the Tuesday night Bluegenes' guest nights and their guests were The Beatles. I knew how popular they were becoming so I thought I'd have another look at them but I realised that if I got in too late the place might be too jammed. I had a few drinks and came in about 9p.m. There was a crowd about six-deep filling every archway and vantage-point. I'd paid to see them and all I got to see was the Cuban heel of McCartney's left boot! I realised then that they were unstoppable.

I stopped going to the Cavern after that for two reasons. Firstly, the leader of our group persuaded us that our future lay in London, not Liverpool, so we moved there in May 1962. What a boob! Secondly, I was now twenty-two years old and the crowd at the Cavern seemed to be getting too young for me. And anyway, the place was too damned popular!

Neil Foster, The Delacardoes

1960-63

I was an avid visitor of the Cavern during 1960-63 and I still have some lovely memories of it.

My friend Gillian and I would rush home from work, buy the *Liverpool Echo* and see who was performing that night at the Cavern. If it was one of our favourite groups, we would don our best clothes and head straight down there. We averaged about three times a week at the Cavern.

Some of the groups were brilliant, especially The Beatles, who we loved. I remember Pete Best being the drummer before Ringo Starr came on the scene.

Some of the other groups that come to mind are: the Swinging Blue Genes, Billy J. Kramer, the Fourmost, the Searchers and Rory Storm and the Hurricanes. We also loved listening to the traditional jazz, which gave the Cavern a very vibrant atmosphere.

I think we liked the Cavern so much because it had a character all of its own. It had a distinctive smell of rotten fruit – I believe it was a fruit warehouse above.

We made many friends with the regulars who used to frequent the Cavern – my friend Gillian met her husband there. Gillian and I used to dance practically the whole time we were there – how could one sit down with all that marvellous music beating out? We also had a go at the Cavern Stomp (a way out dance the beatniks used to do).

The perspiration used to pour off us – we used to get some funny looks on the bus home. I'm sure people thought we had been swimming in the Mersey – our hair used to be dripping wet and our clothes could be wrung out.

I don't think anything can beat those years of the sixties, and I still love the sixties music. I still like to have a jive now and again. I am so glad that I was a part of that era, and it is nice to look back on those wonderful memories of when I was a teenager.

Joyce Grainger

My recollections of the Cavern go back to a period between 1960 and 1963, although my first encounter with the place occurred in 1958.

Being a young fan of Lonnie Donegan I joined his fan club and duly received my membership card with the address of my nearest 'fan club meeting' venue. This turned out to be a get-together for members, held once a month, at the Cavern Club in Mathew Street. Being quite young and naive (I was fourteen and lived in a small town twelve miles away), I set off for the big city to attend one of these meetings. When I arrived at what appeared to be a 'hole in the wall' leading to some underground cave, it looked so awesome I turned around and headed for home.

Little did I realise that one day I would be performing, on stage, at that very place. At the age of sixteen I was music mad, just like every teenager of the day, and was determined to become a pop star. I had started work and saved my wages until I had enough money to buy a guitar. Within a few months, four friends and I had got a group together and played, for free, at parties and the local youth club. Soon we were playing for local dances and then progressed to playing in other towns around our area.

Having read the *Liverpool Echo* and seen all the venues that had groups playing at them, we decided to try our luck. The singer in the group and I took a trip to Liverpool one night with the intention of visiting all of these clubs and asking if we could have a booking there. Arriving on the train, I remembered that the Cavern Club was quite near to the station, so that was to be our first port of call. Outside the Cavern was a huge doorman who, as we walked up to him, asked, 'Are you members?' We explained that we were members of a group who wished to play there and asked if we could talk to the compère. Without hesitation, we were accompanied through a steaming, sweaty sea of bodies to the dressing room and introduced to a man called Bob Wooler. Having said who we were and what we wanted, Bob told us to come the following week when he would allow us to sing three songs on stage and he would be quite frank as to whether we were any good for the club. That was all we needed so we excitedly went home and informed the rest of the group. The next week when we arrived for our audition the poster outside read, 'Tonight at the Cavern, the Bluegenes' Guest Night'. So for the first time Dee Young and the Pontiacs, as we had called our group, took to the stage of the Cavern. We nervously sang our three songs and then came off to face Bob Wooler. His first words were 'Have you got a diary? I've got some dates for you'. Naturally we were thrilled and, starting the following week, we played the first of many dates at the Cavern Club.

I will always remember the first gig; we played as the 'guests' on The Beatles Guest Night, although we had never heard of The Beatles. On arriving at the Cavern at about seven o'clock, we opened the van door to get our gear out. The first thing to hit us was the overpowering smell of disinfectant coming from the entrance door. Upon entering, we were faced with narrow stone steps leading down to the Cavern itself. Being empty at that time it looked quite big, with the three 'tunnels' from end to end, and archways along the two middle walls. The dressing room was a boarded-off section to the left of the stage which itself was very small and hardly big enough for a group. When the audience arrived and the place got full there was no room to swing a cat and condensation ran down the walls. The gents' toilets, which were situated near the bottom of the entrance steps, were always awash with urine because the outlet pipe seemed to be constantly blocked.

When one group had finished, the next one due on stage were given the time taken to play two single records to get all their equipment on and set up. Very often we were announced by the compère as our amplifiers were still being plugged in. The stage was very small and hardly big enough to hold all the group's gear, never mind the players as well. The view from the stage was of about twelve rows of seats, maybe six wide, stretching from the front of the stage backwards down the centre 'tunnel'. The rest of the floor area was open for dancing, apart from a cloak room, the toilets and a small hatch selling soft drinks (no alcohol).

The heat in the club was intense but on stage it was unbearable; every group came off drenched in sweat. It was different in the winter. When we arrived early, so as to get our equipment in the dressing room, the club was always freezing and many was the time we nipped round to Yates' Wine Lodge for a 1s 6d glass of Australian white wine, just to get warmed up. On the night we first played at The Beatles Guest Night, I remember sitting listening to them and thinking 'this group is different'. Most of the other groups copied Cliff Richard and The Shadows or Shane Fenton while The Beatles chose songs such as 'Besame Mucho' and ''Till There Was You', which no-one else would dare tackle. They were very inventive.

Bob Wooler was keen to give encouragement to all new groups and he was always helpful sorting out their problems. If one band had a faulty amplifier he wouldn't hesitate to ask one of the other bands for a loan. One night he asked us if we would mind backing a girl from the audience who wanted to get up and sing a song. She wanted to audition. We were naturally impressed with this until we found out later that all the other groups had said 'no'. The girl wanted to sing 'Fever', the Peggy Lee song, and when she started to sing everyone walked away off the floor. She sounded awful and it was embarrassing for us, but she eventually made it later in life as a professional singer, her name was Cilla White.

One of the groups which was popular was the Bluegenes whose music was jazz based. I remember them playing one song in which every member swapped instruments at the end of every verse until they had all played each other's instrument. Those days they had a banjo player in their line-up and I do remember two of them playing penny whistles in one of the songs in their act.

Other groups we played with included The Pacemakers, The Searchers, Billy Butler and The Tuxedos, the Big Three and many more. Bob Wooler once remarked that there were about 350 groups in the Liverpool area – I do know that up to ten groups a night appeared at the Cavern when the all-night sessions were held. They happened usually on a Saturday night, finishing early Sunday morning. On odd occasions at the Cavern, when we were packing up our gear, someone would crack off playing a guitar and soon a jam session would be underway with members of different bands all together. The atmosphere in the Cavern was exciting and the setting was unique, unlike any other club we played at. Looking back though, I shudder now to think what would have happened if a fire had broken out with the place having just the one narrow entrance/exit.

One of the lads in our group bought an Elizabethan reel-to-reel tape recorder and early one night before anyone else had arrived in the Cavern, we rigged it up in the dressing room and with the lad holding just the simple, cheap microphone in his hand, we recorded three instrumentals on to the tape. I still have a copy of this recording, nearly thirty years later, and although the lad didn't know how to operate the sound levels properly, the music sounds quite impressive even today.

There was always a bit of friendly rivalry between groups, such as who had the best guitars or who wore the flashiest outfits. We had a manager – he was a guy who owned a car, so we said he could be manager if he would run us to the gigs in his Morris Traveller – and he came to us one night at the Cavern and asked what the chords were to the song 'Can't Help Falling in Love' by Elvis Presley. When we asked why, he said that he had been talking to Billy J. Kramer and that Billy had asked for a copy of the chords. We sussed that Billy had heard us play it earlier and wanted to sing it himself. Having spent time practising and learning the words we weren't going to give away all our efforts for free, so we wrote down a lot of nonsense chords and sent them back. We never heard him sing the song.

In those days the groups used the club's own PA system and our amplifiers consisted of Truvoice 15 watts, into which we had two guitars plugged, and one Selmer 30 watt for the bass guitar. The size and shape of the Cavern helped to carry the sound so no huge amplification system was needed. Our act consisted of starting with an instrumental, after which the singer would come bounding on for the first song. One night he came running on and grabbed the mike but as he brought it upwards to his mouth, the mike touched his lip and there was a huge spark which caused him to drop it. The cause was something to do with water getting into the PA system which then was not earthed. Little did we know that later, in the pop scene, musicians would lose their lives due to faulty earthing.

We struck up quite a friendship with the doorman at the Cavern, Paddy Delaney. He was willing to help carry equipment down those narrow steps and always kept an eye on our van which was parked outside. The owner of the Cavern was Ray McFall; we had heard of him but never got to meet him. We did see Brian Epstein at the Cavern on several occasions and when he was there each group tried to sound better that night in the hope of being 'discovered'.

Michael Tromp, Dee Young and the Pontiacs

I certainly have memories of the Cavern. I, along with my friend, used to go there from 1960 to 1963; we rubbed shoulders with The Beatles as they drank coke at the 'bar'. They used to wear leather jackets which dripped with sweat, like the walls in that place. I remember Cilla Black used to take the coats and if you wanted money out of your pocket during the night, she would say, 'You'll have to take your coat, take the money, then pay again to put your coat back in the cloakroom.' She certainly wasn't the sparkling personality she is today!

I'll always remember the night Ringo Starr replaced Pete Best on drums. All the girls fancied Pete so there was bedlam when he was dropped. I also remember Stu Sutcliffe – he was very quiet and always wore dark glasses. When The Beatles came on everyone ran to the stage. When they played, the place vibrated; it was marvellous.

I remember the tiny toilets; it took ages to get into the toilets when the club was packed, so we used to 'hang on' in case we missed a certain song or a dance. I also remember queuing outside to get in; Bob Wooler used to walk up and down looking at everyone and if there was anyone he didn't like the look of he chased them! I remember the groups arriving and struggling down that winding, narrow staircase with all their gear! Bobby Willis, now Cilla Black's husband, used to help all the groups with their gear.

We couldn't jive in the Cavern like we used to in the Orrell or Iron Door, there just wasn't enough room, so the 'Cavern Stomp' was invented as it took very little room to do! I remember the all-night sessions – my friend and I would tell our parents that we were staying the night at each other's houses. Our mothers thought that the Cavern was a den of vice anyway, so we tried not to let on that we were going there, until we were caught out when a lad who lived near my friend 'snitched'. When The Beatles became famous, however, the Cavern was suddenly a 'good' place.

These are a few of my memories of the Cavern; they were marvellous times.

Carole Ferber

1961-63

I lived in Liverpool through the sixties. We visited the Cavern regularly during The Beatles, Hollies and Manfred Mann era. I had the good fortune to see them all. Dancing the Cavern Stomp was brilliant due to the confined space we had, also we were perfectly happy drinking coke – no alcohol there. I remember talking to Manfred Mann's group outside the Cavern.

I had the good fortune of living in the next road to George Harrison in Hunts Cross. It was great fun going round in the school holidays to see him. His mum used to ask us in and call him. He would come down the stairs pulling on a denim shirt or a black polo neck over his long ruffled hair, bleary eyed but always willing to have a chat. When they lived in Speke before they moved to Hunts Cross his dad was a bus driver and his mum worked at Waterworths fruit and veg shop.

My school friend lived next door to Ringo (known as Ritchie to his local mates and family) in Admiral Grove, Dingle. Paul McCartney's mum had been a midwife; she should have delivered my sister-in-law when she was born (but didn't due to complications).

My husband was at school with Paul and George at the Liverpool Institute. George used to fall asleep in the corner due to his late nights, and the teachers gave up waking him. Gerry Marsden's wife to be, Pauline, lived around the corner from us in Hunts Cross. It was great fun listening to her on the bus telling of her future plans with Gerry.

Ann Parry

I used to go to the Cavern around 1961-1963. My main memory was getting Paul McCartney's autograph outside after one of the shows. I can still remember apologising for not having a pen with me. Paul said, 'That's OK, I'll borrow John's', meaning John Lennon who was standing alongside him, also signing autographs. My friend was queuing for John's autograph – he was her favourite while Paul was mine. Of course, we would have liked to have had both autographs but in those days we got the bus home and would have missed it had we queued for both autographs.

We also saw Gerry and the Pacemakers and a lot of others who were on around that time.

Although we loved the Cavern I can remember hating the smell which hit you as you first went in down the steps!

Evelyn Owen

I worked around the corner from the Cavern in a place called 'Dan Wuille & Co.' (Fruit/Veg Wholesalers and Importers). It was known as Dan Woollies. I was sixteen or seventeen at the time (1960/61) and used to spend every lunchtime at the Cavern instead of buying lunch. I think it used to cost 1s to get in!

I knew most of the lads in the groups and the regulars who went there. I particularly remember a lad called Denny Flynn, who sadly died while still quite young. He was very popular with everyone at the Cavern. I used to be made up when he got me up to dance as he was a brilliant dancer.

Bob Wooler was loved almost as much as the groups. I remember on Friday lunchtimes we were allowed to take our records in and Bob would play them during the breaks. I particularly remember taking one in called 'Winkle Picker Stomp' which hardly anyone had heard of but which went down very well. Another favourite I took in was one called 'On the Rebound' – they were both 'brill' records to dance to!

Rory Storm was, of course, the great showman. I was quite friendly with Ringo as he lived near me up North Hill Street and Gerry also lived near us in the Dingle.

A first that happened at the Cavern, but which I hardly ever see mentioned anywhere, was when The Chants made their debut there. Who backed them and encouraged them that night? None other than The Beatles! I was there that night because my cousin, Eddie Amos (now of the Real Thing) asked me to make sure I was there for them, seeing as I knew everybody there. I must say, The Chants went down a bomb and then went on to bigger things in their own right.

Then of course there was Cilla! She was always there and I think she sang with most of the groups who played there. Her most famous rendition was 'Fever', the old Peggy Lee song.

I also remember the 'all-nighters' at the Cavern. In those days we were quite safe staying out all night and then walking home if we felt like it. My friends and I often got a lift in Gerry's van, seeing as he lived up our way. (I can even remember him giving us a lift from the Tower Ballroom in New Brighton so that we wouldn't have to leave early to catch the last train.)

To think we were able to enjoy ourselves and be happy in those days just with coffee and soft drinks in the clubs. I suppose we'd be called 'sissies' today! I still bump into some of the group members from those days but often wonder what happened to the others and whether they are still performers.

Ah! Happy days! (Although, if you think about it, we must have been mad, down in those cellars with the water – or was it sweat? – running down the walls.) I wouldn't change my time in the sixties for anything – the Cavern, the Iron Door, the Blue Angel – they were the best times ever!

Rita Martelli

I'm reminded of just how evocative smells can be by closing my eyes and seeing myself as a teenager going to the Cavern for those wonderful lunchtime sessions in the early sixties. Rotting vegetables from the nearby market, disinfectant, cigarette smoke, hot bodies and something not quite definable combined to make the sweet aroma which greeted us halfway along Mathew Street as we headed for the narrow staircase taking us to our own little corner of paradise.

The Beatles played lunchtimes on Monday, Wednesday and Friday. We arrived early enough to secure a seat on the front or second row because seeing and being seen were of equal importance. After all, we each planned to marry our favourite Beatle one day, so they had to be aware of our enduring and adoring presence. It was agony tearing ourselves away to return to college or work, knowing they would be on for another hour or so.

Nobody screamed, shouted or danced while The Beatles played, merely sat in silent rapture. Scraps of paper with requests – 'John, sing "Memphis" for Val, Sue and Rosie' were passed to the stage and to hear our names falling from their lips was joy beyond measure. On the days that Paul announced they were going to do another new song, 'one wot we writ ourselves', did we know we were present at a unique, magical moment in the history of music, of the world? We couldn't have so expressed it at that time but yes, I believe we did.

The Beatles played on Wednesday evening, when Paul travelled into town on the same bus as Sue, often paying her fare. They'd arrive together, chatting away, much to the envy of those of us who'd spent a couple of hours waiting in the doorway. Although not much more than five foot, she appeared nearly as tall as Paul. It must have been the cloud she was on. One day Gene Vincent performed at the Cavern, backed by The Beatles. Television cameras were there and hordes of non-regulars turned up, filling the archways, standing on each other's shoulders and heads to catch a glimpse of the stage, walls streaming, the heat and pulsating beat bouncing from the ceiling. What became of that film? The only one ever shown is a snatch of Paul singing 'Some Other Guy' with the backs of our heads in the foreground.

I remember the day Brian Epstein visited the Cavern for the first time. (I'd already met him when he interviewed me for a job at Nems, so I recognised him the moment I spotted him. Having decided halfway through a one-year commercial course that I knew enough to find myself work, I answered an advert in the *Liverpool Echo* for a junior secretary. Mum went mad and said I wasn't going to work for a tinpot record shop but must finish the college course and get a proper job.)

I think we sensed then that things were about to change. More outsiders began to appear and one day we arrived to find a different drummer. Where was Pete Best? Our world was falling apart. By now I had that 'proper job', in a shipping office at the Pierhead. My boss, Mr Burke, would tentatively lean towards me, sniff theatrically and wrinkle his nose with disdain: 'You've been pot-holing again in that dreadful dive.'

Perhaps by now he understands the attraction, and why I was sometimes a little late back from lunch.

Valerie Jukes

1962

I remember seeing The Beatles at the Cavern in the autumn of 1962. They stood out from the other Merseyside groups in a big way. They were the best. I thought they were so good that I even got their autographs on a piece of card. It was unheard of in those days to ask other blokes for their autographs; it was not the done thing, even if they were the best group on Merseyside! It laid you open to ridicule from your mates. After witnessing a great Beatles performance I caught the last bus home with a few mates. I can recall that another friend got on the same bus who had not been to the Cavern that night. After the fuss about Pete Best leaving the group he asked

me who was drummer with them now? None of us knew the new Beatle's name but I told him that I thought it was similar to a cowboy name, 'Lone Starr or something like that,' I replied. Remembering the autographed card that I had stuffed into my coat pocket earlier in the evening I pulled it out. After checking the signatures I informed the others that Ringo Starr was the new drummer. Some of them started ridiculing me for having acquired The Beatles' autographs. 'Only "Judys" collect autographs!' one of them said. After looking at it a few times I ripped it up and threw it out of the bus window. I wish I still had it…

Peter Thompson

The first time I saw The Beatles at the Cavern was on a Friday night. Although Brian Epstein had now signed them they were still in their leather outfits. I went with Tony Crane, who had seen them quite a lot. He said to me, 'You're gonna love this band.' I remember there was trad jazz on the bill as well and the jazz band were on stage as The Beatles entered the club, which caused quite a commotion at the stairway entrance. I was never a jazz fan and was on the verge of leaving when The Beatles arrived. When they came on stage and began to play I'd never seen anything like it in my life; they were incredible. Lennon sang the opening song, which was 'Memphis, Tennessee' and I was totally hooked.

Billy Kinsley, The Merseybeats

The girls would sleep out all night to make sure that they would get into the Cavern when The Beatles were on. I remember Easter Monday 1962 when there was a massive queue outside the club. We were the first group on at about four in the afternoon. As soon as we began to play there was a massive surge towards the stage to get the front seats. I thought, 'this lot are keen to hear us play'. They then all got their sandwiches and flasks out and began to eat their lunch. When they had finished eating they began to take their rollers out and get ready for The Beatles who were on later that night.

Dave Williams, Dale Roberts & The Jaywalkers

I was a trad jazz fan and was a Cavern and Iron Door regular from the day these clubs opened. I must have come across The Beatles on a number of occasions but did not really take much notice. One particular night I attended a 'Riverboat Shuffle' on board the Royal Iris. Acker Bilk was top of the bill and after he'd played his first set the leather-clad Beatles began to set their equipment up for their segment of the night's entertainment. From what I can remember I may have listened to a few bars of their first number but that was enough for me. I quickly departed the scene to get a pint and

some fresh air. It was jazz I'd come to hear, not this rock 'n' roll stuff. A lot of traditional jazz fans of this period felt the same. I must have had a lot of opportunities to catch The Beatles during this period with clubs such as the Cavern presenting a mixture of beat and jazz on the same night, but I chose not to take them, preferring to nip out for a pint instead.
Brian Thompson

I first saw The Beatles at the Aintree Institute and when they became Cavern regulars I became a Cavern Club member. I was probably a member of the club longer than anyone else on Merseyside and was still going to the club in the 1970s. My name is Brian but Paul McCartney nicknamed me 'Basil'. The Beatles would sometimes get me up on stage with them. I remember one night while I was dancing, the zip in my trousers broke and Cilla Black came to the rescue and put a safety pin in them. Gerry and the Pacemakers asked me to appear in their film, *Ferry Cross the Mersey*, but I worked for the council at the time and they wouldn't give me the time off work. It was like one big family at the Cavern and I remember when I was badly injured in an accident at work that the Cavern regulars had a collection for me and they turned up at the hospital with a paisley silk dressing gown and a pair of leather slippers. I never forgot their kindness. I used to go to all the Liverpool clubs: The Iron Door, Mardi Gras, Peppermint Lounge, Downbeat Club, Orrel Park Ballroom, but none of them meant as much to me as the Cavern.
Brian 'Basil' Clark

1962-63

Bob Wooler was a great help to all of us at the Cavern and I remember when he introduced us to the music press, who were arriving at the Cavern in droves after The Beatles became famous nationally. Norman Jopling of the *Record Mirror* interviewed us whilst we were sitting in the dressing room and he asked me for the names of the group. I told him mine and then introduced John McNally. But when it came to our drummer Chris Crummy I stuttered and it came out as Chris Curtis. It was the first name that came into my head. Finally, when it came to Mike Prendergast I stuttered again and it came out as Mike Pender. That's how two members of The Searchers were christened with new surnames in the bandroom of the Cavern.
Tony Jackson, The Searchers

Rock great Gene Vincent seen here with Eric London and Dave Williams of Wirral group Dale Roberts and The Jaywalkers. Gene Vincent appeared at the Cavern three times.

1962-64

When I was fifteen in 1963, my sister Alice, my friend Irene and I were frequent Cavern goers. I would borrow my elder sister's birth certificate, as she was eighteen, and Alice and Irene borrowed their two friends', in order that we could get in. I worked in London Road at the time, so every lunchtime I would meet my friends and go to the lunchtime sessions. We first went in November 1962, when Pete Best was still the drummer with The Beatles. I can still remember the smell of disinfectant, the stone floor, and perspiration running down the walls.

We continued to go to the Cavern for some time, then we moved to the Sink in Hardman Street.
Jean Tartt

1962-65

I was a member of the Cavern Club and witnessed the transition from a jazz-type club to a blues club and then to the better-known era.

Before we had our own transport we had to travel from the Northgate Station, Chester (now Northgate Arena) and if we were lucky we would catch the last bus through the tunnel and then hitch home.

Above left: The Searchers present copies of their first two albums to the mayors of Birkenhead and Wallasey before they performed at a Mayor's Charity Fund show at New Brighton Football Club ground in May 1964. Cavern DJ Bob Wooler compèred the show.

Above right: The Searchers performing in New Brighton in May 1964 at the Mayor's Charity Fund show. The Searchers appeared at the Cavern many times, but it was at the Iron Door club in nearby Temple Street that they really ruled the roost. The Beatles, on a 1964 edition of the *Juke Box Jury,* told the watching millions that The Searchers were their favourite Liverpool group.

Left: The Searchers' Tony Jackson, pictured here in 1964. The Searchers appeared at the Cavern fifty-five times, thirty with Johnny Sandon as lead vocalist. The classic Searchers' line-up of Tony Jackson, Mike Pender, Chris Curtis and John McNally was second to only The Beatles as the best and most inspirational group to come out of Liverpool in the 1960s. The Searchers had massive hits with 'Sweets for my Sweet', 'Sugar and Spice', 'Needles and Pins' and many more pop classics before Jackson and then Curtis left the group. Without them the magic was gone.

The Cavern Club was unique in many ways: the friendly atmosphere, the common interest in the blues and Merseybeat sound, the dress, etc.

On a typical night it would not be unusual to have groups like The Dennisons, the Big Three and a top name group of that time in one night. I was lucky to see The Beatles, The Hollies, Gerry Marsden, the fabulous Yardbirds, John Lee Hooker, Sonny Boy Williamson, etc., etc.
Barry Garrington

1963

Freda Kelly helped to run The Beatles' first fan club with its instigator Bobbie Brown. Freda would hear her workmates at Princes Food Company talking about how good The Beatles and the Cavern were. She decided to visit the club herself and quickly became a convert. She then decided to help Bobbie with The Beatles' Fan Club activities. Freda told *The Beatles Monthly* magazine in 1963 what attracted her to the group:

> It was their easy-going way on stage. They made the Cavern seem like their own front room and the crowd were all friends they'd invited round. Backstage The Beatles would relax in a tiny bandroom after their lunchtime session ended at 2.15. I was always after money so that I could buy stamps to reply to their fan mail. Paul used to have a whip-round amongst the lads and hand over as much as I asked for.
> *Freda Kelly, The Beatles Monthly 1963*

George Martin claims that the best version of 'Twist and Shout' that he saw The Beatles perform was actually on stage at the Cavern. George wanted the group's first LP to be recorded live at the Cavern but decided against it, reasoning that the conditions at the club were not conducive to a decent recording being made.

1964

Billed as 'Britain's most exciting R&B sound', The Cheynes (named after the fashionable Cheyne Walk in Chelsea) played the Cavern in 1964. Drummer in the group was fifteen-year-old Mick Fleetwood, who would find fame in the late 1960s with Fleetwood Mac. Recalling The Cheynes' Cavern debut in his autobiography, Mick said: 'The Cheynes played the Cavern Club in Liverpool at the height of Beatlemania. Our manager stuffed our equipment in a Daimler limousine and drove around Liverpool promoting the gig with our PA. We went on at the Cavern wearing fruity little suede jerkins and white shirts; the guitars weren't even tuned and the show was a disaster. But we had come from London and were identified with the Rolling Stones, so The Cheynes got some screamers in the provinces.'
Mick Fleetwood, Fleetwood Mac

It's amazing to think of all the talent from all the different strands of music that came together at the Cavern. I remember Luke Kelly, who was later to find fame with The Dubliners, appearing at the Cavern. The place was heaving and I was slightly apprehensive as to how Luke would go down with the kids at the club. I need not have worried. After we had finished our set we introduced Luke to the audience. He strode onto the stage, banjo slung over his shoulder, and launched into 'Plough the Rocks of Bawn', unaccompanied. He sang it as only Luke Kelly could and the whole club listened in silence, enraptured with this Irish ballad. He then went into a fast tempo song, plucking his banjo and they lapped it up. As long as the music was good, the kids at the Cavern appreciated it.
Mick Groves, The Spinners

1964-66

I was sixteen, just out of school and working in C&A in Church Street. I remember going to the Cavern with some friends, Pam, Monica, Colette and Pauline, all dolled up in our leather or suede coats dancing away the night to sounds from The Clayton Squares, The Hideaways (particular favourites) or The Masterminds, or just standing drinking bottles of Pepsi and listening as some really good music was played.

I'd first been introduced to the Cavern one lunchtime, it was just 1s to get in. Another bottle of Pepsi and a ham roll was usually my lunch there. I remember thinking 'what a dump' – it was dark and smelly and condensation ran down the walls, but oh! I was swept away by that music. Then an hour later there was the rush back to C&A to face a ferocious supervisor, Miss Kelly. 'You haven't been to that Cavern, have you?' 'No miss,' we'd pant breathless and red-faced from dancing. We'd then spend every other minute planning our next expedition to the Cavern, usually that very evening.

My parents couldn't understand the attraction, they thought we were rubbing shoulders with all sorts of unsavoury characters. Were we? They all seemed to be like we were, fresh-faced kids, enjoying the music. How harmless it all seems now or were we just naive? Yes we had great times, eyeing up the lads, terrible crushes on boys who never even noticed us.

The different fashions? We considered ourselves Mods at that time (1965). Most girls and boys had their coats and suits made by tailors such as John Colliers and Burtons. I remember the boys wearing Crombie coats and trilby

The great Wilson Pickett. Pickett wowed Cavern regulars with his soul classics: 'In the Midnight Hour' and 'Mustang Sally' during his November 1965 performance at the club.

hats – Robert De Niro eat your heart out. The Godfather? Goodfellas? I can't watch those movies without remembering.

Considering what a small venue it was I recall some great artists – at two all-day sessions. There was Stevie Wonder, dressed in a little tin soldiers jacket, all red with gold braiding, and Wilson Pickett screaming 'In the Midnight Hour'. We were all mad crazy Tamla Motown fans. A particular favourite of ours was the Spencer Davis Group; Steve Winwood was brilliant singing blues at the piano. I remember we even saw Dave Dee, Dozy, Beaky, Mick & Tich. We sneered at the dopey name, but the music was jolly and party-like.

In 1966 it closed its doors. I remember going into a zombie-like state, wondering where we would go, how we would see our favourite bands, but what we didn't realise was that we were growing up and sooner or later we'd have left the old Cavern anyway. It opened up a few doors down some time later, but it wasn't 'our Cavern' then, it wasn't special any more. By that time we'd found another club we loved, the Mardi Gras, but that's another story.
Yvonne Harris

1964-68

I was a regular at the Cavern from 1964 to 1968. As teenagers we used to queue up and the queue would extend sometimes past The Grapes pub. Many teenagers from Germany used to visit the Cavern and loved the atmosphere, with the strong smell of Jeye's pine disinfectant and the walls and arches streaming with condensation. There was a drinks machine at the bottom of the stairs and the chicken soup was delicious (6d a cup). The atmosphere was electric and the music was 'fab'.

I remember that the watch company Timex had a TV ad which was filmed at the Cavern. I think it was done off-spot as the cameras rolled without anyone really being aware of them. Of course in those days, cameras were no big deal, everyone was taking pictures and films. The big shock was when it was screened on TV. I was not allowed out after 10p.m., but when my dad was on the night shift, I would stay at the Cavern a bit later. I denied for months that it could have been me on the TV. It may not have been, but it sure looked like me, and my dad was convinced it was. Oh, those good days!
Molly Yates

I played in a skiffle group in 1961. Our one and only gig was on the Saturday morning matinee at the Regal Cinema, Broadway, Norris Green. Music was in my blood – I was the guitar player and lead vocalist. When I left school in 1964 at the age of sixteen, I was a member of a local group who were quite famous locally, called Solomon's Mines. We were all school mates. After playing as was usual in those days at most of the pub venues, we did all the top club venues: Mardi Gras, Victoriana, Iron Door, Blue Angel, and of course, the Cavern. Between 1965 and 1967 we played at the Cavern about thirty times. We won the 'Search for Sound' competition, held at the ice rink in Prescot Road – we beat a lot of local groups. In the final, which was held in London at Streatham Ice Rink, we were beaten by the group called Mud who went on to become famous. That was a brief history of my days playing and singing in the sixties. The Cavern was always something special, even though when I think back it was in its death throes in the mid-sixties, but what happy memories. We played with a lot of top names: The Searchers, The Escorts, the Bluegenes, Gerry and the Pacemakers, Rory Storm, as well as the international stars such as the Drifters, Zoot Money, Ben E. King, and many more. I remember our first time at the Cavern, it was an all-nighter. We had been playing somewhere else and when we arrived at the Cavern our manager told us our spot was 2.30. It was then roughly 1a.m. so we sat around. We had these red hipster trousers on, being naive, and we didn't half get the mickey taken out of us, especially from a group called The Hideaways who were one of my favourites.
Allan Devon, Solomon's Mines

1965

We made our Cavern debut at a Saturday afternoon Junior Cavern Club show. I remember Sonny Boy Williamson playing at the Cavern backed by The Yardbirds. After the show Sonny Boy sat in the Cavern bandroom with Judd Lander, our harmonica player, exchanging mouth organ licks. We backed a lot of the blues greats at the Cavern. On one occasion the doorman from the Cavern, Paddy Delaney, drove us to an out of town gig in a van that we had borrowed from the Merseybeats. On the return journey Paddy had to bring the van to a sudden halt at a set of lights and it went into a skid and overturned, causing considerable damage to the vehicle. Nobody was seriously hurt and after scrambling out of the van and dusting ourselves down we began to right the vehicle. We were surprised to find that the first people on the scene to give us a hand were Cavern regulars The Kubas, who had also been playing out of town. I remember Paddy having to drive the van back to Liverpool with no windscreen in it.

Ozzie Yue, The Hideaways

The legendary Eric Clapton, who was a member of The Yardbirds when they backed Sonny Boy Williamson at the Cavern on 26 February 1964. The Yardbirds played a blistering set during a lunchtime performance before backing the blues legend in the evening.

1966-69

I was a member of a pop group called The Tremas and we played at the Cavern no less than eighty times, from the time it reopened in 1966, to 1969 when we split up. I remember the day it reopened very well. Harold Wilson, the Prime Minister of the time, performed the opening ceremony and there were personal appearances of all the top pop groups including Billy J. Kramer, Gerry Marsden, Dave Dee, Dozy, Beaky, Mick and Tich, and DJ Jimmy Savile. Bob Wooler read to the audience a telegram from The Beatles themselves, who could not be there due to pressures of work. The ceremony started at 9a.m. and went on till 6a.m. next morning with celebrities popping in all the time. The exact date I cannot remember but it was around about March/April 1966. After that the club obtained a drinks licence and opened a bar and club on the ground floor above the original Cavern. I would say it was the happiest time of my musical career (still playing at forty-six!) and my ambition was fulfilled.

Roy Cooke, The Tremas

1970-73

I met my husband Tom in 1970 in a club in Liverpool. I was sixteen, he was eighteen. We started going to the Cavern Club on a Friday night, with our mates. We used to go then because they played all heavy music. The club was dirty but had a brilliant atmosphere.

We never saw any trouble there. We were married in 1971 and continued to go there until we had our daughter in 1973. We were totally devastated when we heard it was closing to put a rail line through – you can't replace a piece of history like that, can you?

We often tell our kids about the great times we had there and are sorry that they are unable to go to the Cavern. We are still into heavy metal and so are our kids. We will always have fond memories of this brilliant club.

Andrea & Tom Carey, two old metal heads

Chapter 17

THE CAVERN DIARY

The Cavern Diary is a first attempt to present in a logical order the thousands of groups and musicians who appeared at the club over its seventeen-year existence. Incomplete lists have been drawn up previously of groups who appeared during the Merseybeat era but without dates or number of appearances. Hopefully, this diary will give some indication of the quality (and quantity) of talent that graced the Cavern stage. Obviously all the great Liverpool groups made their appearances: The Beatles, Gerry and the Pacemakers, the Big Three, The Swinging Blue Genes, The Searchers, The Merseybeats, The Fourmost etc. So, too, did many of the great names in pop history including the Rolling Stones, The Hollies, The Yardbirds, The Kinks, The Animals and The Who. Blues legends were well represented with the likes of John Lee Hooker, Sonny Boy Williamson, Little Walter, Mose Allison and virtually all the great names in British post-war jazz appearing in the early years before rock and roll took over.

The information contained in this diary was compiled from the Entertainment advertisements section of the *Liverpool Echo*. With no other source of information available, the diary is based on the reliability of the advertisements. On occasions, however, bands advertised did not appear as a result of late cancellations or failure to turn up. On other nights bands not advertised would be brought in either to fill a cancellation or as a result of a last-minute booking which missed the *Echo's* deadline. As a result, artists who definitely appeared at the Cavern as booked performers including Queen, David Bowie (with the Lower Third) and Genesis are not in the diary because no dates for their appearances can be found. Additionally, many musicians gave impromptu performances at the club (particularly in the early jazz days). Tony Sheridan, Shirley Bassey and Alma Cogan are among the artists known to have taken the stage for (unpaid) sessions. Cilla Black regularly performed on stage but, because her appearances tended to be impromptu, she was never advertised as a booked artist.

The diary is, therefore, not foolproof and, hopefully, can be improved with more intensive research. The Cavern, for instance, was also advertised as the West Coast Jazz Club, the Riverside Jazz Club, the Muskrat Jazz Club and the Merseyside Jazz Union. On modern jazz nights it was known as the Club Perdido. Such confusions are perhaps incidental to the purpose of the listing, which is to give an accurate picture of the day-to-day activity of the Cavern. For the many members of the lesser-known groups who appeared, the diary will be a welcome confirmation of the part they played in the history of the world's best-known club.

Opposite, above left: The Animals, pictured here in 1966 after Dave Rowberry had replaced Alan Price in the group. The Animals made the first of their two Cavern performances at a lunchtime session on 10 December 1963. It was the group's first appearance outside Northumberland and at the time they were yet to have a chart hit. Early in 1964 The Animals' version of 'The House of the Rising Sun' propelled them to world fame. The group's Cavern show was just a brief stop on their way to London, where they became firm favourites in the capital's burgeoning R&B clubs.

Opposite, above right: Queen, who made an appearance at the Cavern Club as an unknown group in the early 1970s. Freddy Mercury was actually living in Liverpool at the time and was delighted to appear on the same stage that The Beatles had appeared on so many times.

1957

JANUARY
Wednesday 16th Evening
Merseysippi Jazz Band
Wall City Jazzmen
Ralph Watmough Jazz Band
Coney Island Skiffle Group
Friday 18th Evening
Muskrat Jazz Band
Gin Mill Skiffle Group
Liverpool University Jazz Band
Saturday 19th Evening
Ralph Watmough Jazz Band
Panama Jazz Band
Ron McKay Skiffle Group
Dolphin Jazz Band
Pete Galvin Jazz Band
Sunday 20th Evening
Merseysippi Jazz Band
Ralph Watmough Jazz Band
Liverpool University Jazz Band
Ron McKay Skiffle Group
Tuesday 22nd Evening
Merseysippi Jazz Band
Wednesday 23rd Evening
Blue Note Jazzmen
Ralph Watmough Jazz Band

Friday 25th Evening
Muskrat Jazz Band
Gin Mill Skiffle Group
Five Chevs Skiffle Group
Saturday 26th Evening
Zenith Six Jazz Band
Ron McKay Skiffle Group
Ralph Watmough Jazz Band
Sunday 27th Evening
Merseysippi Jazz Band
Panama Jazz Band
Wednesday 30th Lunchtime
Architects Jazz Band
Ron McKay Skiffle Group and guests
Evening
Merseysippi Jazz Band
Coney Island Skiffle Group
Tony Brown Quartet

FEBRUARY
Friday 1st Evening
Muskrat Jazz Band
Panama Jazz Band
Gin Mill Skiffle Group
Saturday 2nd Evening
Ralph Watmough Jazz Band
Panama Jazz Band
Ron McKay Skiffle Group
Sunday 3rd Evening
Merseysippi Jazz Band

Blue Note Jazzmen
Wednesday 6th Evening
Merseysippi Jazz Band
Ron McKay Skiffle Group
Friday 8th Evening
Muskrat Jazz Band
Gin Mill Skiffle Group
Saturday 9th Evening
White Eagles Jazz Band
Martin Roland Skiffle Group
Sunday 10th Evening
Merseysippi Jazz Band
Ralph Watmough Jazz Band
Wednesday 12th Evening
Merseysippi Jazz Band
Ron McKay Skiffle Group
Friday 15th Evening
Muskrat Jazz Band
Liverpool University Jazz Band
Gin Mill Skiffle Group
Saturday 16th Evening
Ralph Watmough Jazz Band
Muskrat Jazz Band
Panama Jazz Band
Sunday 17th Evening
The Saints Jazz Band
Gin Mill Skiffle Group
Wednesday 20th Evening
Merseysippi Jazz Band
Ron McKay Skiffle Group

Thursday 21st Evening
(Modern Jazz Session)
Dizzy Reece
Harry Klein
Trond Svennevig Quintet
Friday 22nd Evening
Muskrat Jazz Band
Ron McKay Skiffle Group
Saturday 23rd Evening
Eric Batty Jazz Aces
Sunday 24th Evening
Ralph Watmough Jazz Band
Merseysippi Jazz Band
Wednesday 27th Evening
Merseysippi Jazz Band
Ralph Watmough Jazz Band
Thursday 28th Evening
(Modern Jazz Session)
Don Rendell
Trond Svennevig Quintet

MARCH
Friday 1st Evening
Muskrat Jazz Band
Panama Jazz Band
Gin Mill Skiffle Group
Red Valley Skiffle Group
Saturday 2nd Evening
The Zenith Six Jazz Band

Sunday 3rd Evening
The Saints Jazz Band
Wednesday 6th Evening
Panama Jazz Band
Merseysippi Jazz Band
Thursday 7th Evening
(Modern Jazz Session)
Joe Harriot
Kiernan Forester Quintet
Trond Svennevig Quintet
Friday 8th Evening
Muskrat Jazz Band
Gin Mill Skiffle Group and three
    other groups
Saturday 9th Evening
South Side Stompers
Paul Beadle Skiffle Group
Sunday 10th Evening
Merseysippi Jazz Band
Ralph Watmough Jazz Band
Wednesday 13th Evening
Big Bill Broonzy
Merseysippi Jazz Band
Thursday 14th Evening
(Modern Jazz Session)
Tubby Hayes All Star Quintet
Trond Svennevig Quintet with US
    drum star Robbie Robinson
Friday 15th Evening
Muskrat Jazz Band

Gin Mill Skiffle Group and two
  surprise groups
Saturday 16th Evening
Ralph Watmough Jazz Band
Dick Bishop Skiffle Group
Martin Rowland Skiffle Group
Sunday 17th Evening
White Eagles Jazz Band
Wednesday 20th Evening
Merseysippi Jazz Band
Ralph Watmough Jazz Band
Thursday 21st Evening
(Modern Jazz Session)
Jimmy Deuchar
Derek Humble
Trond Svennevig Quintet
Friday 22nd Evening
Muskrat Jazz Band
Panama Jazz Band
Gin Mill Skiffle Group
Saturday 23rd Evening
Eric Batty Jazz Aces
Ron McKay Skiffle Group
Sunday 24th Evening
Merseysippi Jazz Band
Wednesday 27th Evening
Merseysippi Jazz Band
Ron McKay Skiffle Group
Thursday 28th Evening
(Modern Jazz Session)
Tommy Whittle
Harry Klein
Trond Svennevig Quintet
Friday 29th Evening
Muskrat Jazz Band
Gin Mill Skiffle Group and three
  surprise groups
Saturday 30th Evening
Blue Note Jazzmen
Panama Jazz Band
Sunday 31st Evening
Johnny Duncan and his skiffle group
Merseysippi Jazz Band

APRIL
Wednesday 3rd Evening
Alex Welsh Dixielanders
Thursday 4th Evening
(Modern Jazz Session)
Trend Svennevig Quintet
Jimmy Skidmore All Star Session
(Robbie Robinson Jazz Drummer)
Friday 5th Lunchtime
Don Lowe's Dixielanders
Evening
Muskrat Jazz Band
Ron McKay Skiffle Group
Gin Mill Skiffle Group
Pilgrims Skiffle Group

Saturday 6th Evening
Zenith Six Jazz Band
Ralph Watmough Jazz Band
Sunday 7th Evening
Eric Batty Jazz Aces
Ron McKay Skiffle Group
Monday 8th Lunchtime
Merseysippi Jazz Band
Wednesday 10th Lunchtime
Merseysippi Jazz Band
Don Lowe's Dixielanders
Evening
Merseysippi Jazz Band
Ron McKay Skiffle Group
Thursday 11th Evening
(Modern Jazz Session)
Kenny Graham
Trond Svennevig Quintet
Friday 12th Evening
Muskrat Jazz Band
Panama Jazz Band
Gin Mill Skiffle Group
Saturday 13th Evening
Yorkshire Jazz Band
Ron McKay Skiffle Group
Sunday 14th Evening
Merseysippi Jazz Band
Ralph Watmough Jazz Band
Monday 15th Lunchtime
Merseysippi Jazz Band
Wednesday 17th Lunchtime
Merseysippi Jazz Band
Evening
Ron McKay Skiffle Group
Ralph Watmough Jazz Band
Thursday 18th Evening
(Modern Jazz Session)
Tony Kinsey Quintet
Kiernan Forester Quintet
Saturday 20th Evening
The March Hares Jazz Band
The Liver Skiffle Group
Sunday 2lst Evening
The Saints Jazz Band
Wednesday 24th Lunchtime
Merseysippi Jazz Band
Don Lowe's Dixielanders
Evening
Merseysippi Jazz Band
Ron McKay Skiffle Group
Thursday 25th Evening
(Modern Jazz Session)
Dizzy Reece
Phil Seamen
Friday 26th Evening
Muskrat Jazz Band
Gin Mill Skiffle Group
Saturday 27th Evening
The Ceramics Jazz Band

Ron McKay Skiffle Group
Sunday 28th Evening
Merseysippi Jazz Band
Ralph Watmough Jazz Band
Monday 29th Lunchtime
Merseysippi Jazz Band
Tuesday 30th Lunchtime
Merseysippi Jazz Band

MAY
Wednesday 1st Lunchtime
Merseysippi Jazz Band
Evening
Merseysippi Jazz Band
Ralph Watmough Jazz Band
Thursday 2nd Evening
(Modern Jazz Session)
Don Rendell
Jimmy Skidmore
Trond Svennevig Quintet
Friday 3rd Evening
Muskrat Jazz Band
Gin Mill Skiffle Group
Saturday 4th Evening
Ceramic City Stompers
Ron McKay Skiffle Group
Sunday 5th Evening
Merseysippi Jazz Band
Ralph Watmough Jazz Band
Pilgrims Skiffle Group
Monday 6th Lunchtime
Merseysippi Jazz Band
Wednesday 8th Lunchtime
Merseysippi Jazz Band
Evening
Merseysippi Jazz Band
Ron McKay Skiffle Group
Thursday 9th Evening
(Modern Jazz Session)
Alan Branscombe
Bobby Ore
Stuart Hammer
Friday 10th Evening
Muskrat Jazz Band
Gin Mill Skiffle Group
Saturday 11th Evening
White Eagles Jazz Band
Martin Rowland Skiffle Group
Sunday 12th Evening
Merseysippi Jazz Band
Ralph Watmough Jazz Band
Ron McKay Skiffle Group
Wednesday 15th Lunchtime
Merseysippi Jazz Band Evening
Carl Barriteau Jazz Band
Ralph Watmough Jazz Band
Ron McKay Skiffle Group
Friday 17th Evening
Muskrat Jazz Band

Panama Jazz Band
Ron McKay Skiffle Group
Saturday 18th Evening
White Eagle Jazzmen
Ninety Five Skiffle Group
The Saints Jazz Band
Sunday 19th Evening
Hobo Skiffle Group
Wednesday 22nd Lunchtime
Merseysippi Jazz Band
Evening
Mike Peters Jazzmen
Ron McKay Skiffle Group
Friday 24th Evening
Muskrat Jazz Band
Gin Mill Skiffle Group
Texans Skiffle Group
Saturday 25th Evening
Merseysippi Jazz Band
Ron McKay Skiffle Group
Sunday 26th Evening
Merseysippi Jazz Band
Dickie Bishop Skiffle Group
Wednesday 29th Lunchtime
Merseysippi Jazz Band
Evening
Merseysippi Jazz Band
Ron McKay Skiffle Group
Thursday 30th Evening
(Modern Jazz Session)
Jackie Murray
Trond Svennevig Quintet
Alan Branscombe
Friday 31st Evening
Muskrat Jazz Band
Ron McKay Skiffle Group
Smokie River Skiffle Group

JUNE
Saturday 1st Evening
Ralph Watmough Jazz Band
Gin Mill Skiffle Group
Sunday 2nd Evening
Merseysippi Jazz Band
Bruce Turner
Ralph Watmough Jazz Band
Wednesday 5th Lunchtime
Merseysippi Jazz Band
Evening
(Skiffle Session)
Ron McKay Skiffle Group
Gin Mill Skiffle Group
Texans Skiffle Group
Demons Skiffle Group
Joe Shannon Skiffle Group and
  surprise feature
Thursday 6th Evening
(Modern Jazz Session)
Alan Alderson Quartet

Kiernan Forester Quintet
Riverboat Shuffle
Merseysippi Jazz Band
Ron McKay Skiffle Group
Ralph Watmough Jazz Band
Friday 7th Evening
Merseysippi Jazz Band
Gin Mill Skiffle Group
Saturday 8th Evening
Ron McKay Skiffle Group
Ralph Watmough Jazz Band
Sunday 9th Evening
Wall City Jazzmen
Ron McKay Skiffle Group
Wednesday 12th Lunchtime
Merseysippi Jazz Band
Evening
(Skiffle Session)
Gin Mill Skiffle Group
Texans Skiffle Group
Dark Town Skiffle Group
Smokey City Skiffle Group
Angelo Gamblers Skiffle Group
Thursday 13th Evening
(Modern Jazz Session)
Trond Svennevig Quintet
Alan Branscombe
US Quartet with Tim Bailey
Friday 14th Evening
Merseysippi Jazz Band
Ron McKay Skiffle Group
Gin Mill Skiffle Group
Saturday 15th Evening
Ralph Watmough Jazz Band
Mathew Street Skifflers
Sunday 16th Evening
Wall City Jazzmen
Ralph Watmough Jazz Band
Wednesday 19th Evening
(Skiffle Session)
Mathew Street Skifflers
Gin Mill Skiffle Group
Joe Shannon Skiffle Group
Thursday 20th Evening
(Modern Jazz Session)
Alan Branscombe
Jackie Murray
Tim Bailey
Friday 21st Evening
Merseysippi Jazz Band
Panama Jazz Band
Saturday 22nd Evening
Zenith Six Jazz Band
Mathew Street Skifflers
Sunday 23rd Evening
Merseysippi Jazz Band
Ralph Watmough Jazz Band
Wednesday 26th Evening
(Skiffle Festival)

Joe Shannon Skiffle Group
Smokie River Skiffle Group
The Deltones Skiffle Group
The Angela Skiffle Group
Calandonie Skiffle Group
Thursday 27th Evening
(Modern Jazz Session)
T. Bailey Quintet
Alan Alderson Quartet
Friday 28th Evening
Merseysippi Jazz Band
Gin Mill Skiffle Group
Saturday 29th Evening
Blue Note Jazz Band
Mathew Street Skifflers
Sunday 30th Evening
Merseysippi Jazz Band
Ralph Watmough Jazz Band

JULY
Wednesday 3rd Evening
Miss Cavern Contest
(Skiffle Session)
Gin Mill Skiffle Group
Mathew Street Skifflers
Black Cat Skiffle Group
Thursday 4th Evening
(Modern Jazz Session)
Stan Robinson Quintet with Jackie
  Murray
Alan Alderson Quartet
Friday 5th Evening
Merseysippi Jazz Band
Gin Mill Skiffle Group
Saturday 6th Evening
Ralph Watmough Jazz Band
Panama Jazz Band
Sunday 7th Evening
Merseysippi Jazz Band
Ralph Watmough Jazz Band

Wednesday 10th Evening
(Skiffle Session)
Gin Mill Skiffle Group
The Deltones Skiffle Group
Thursday 11th Evening
(Modern Jazz Session)
The New Alan Branscombe Quintet
Jackie Murray
Joe Palm
Robbie Robinson
Jack Stevenson
Tim Bailey Quartet
Friday 12th Evening
Wall City Jazzmen
Gin Mill Skiffle Group
Saturday 13th Evening
Panama Jazz Band
Joe Shannon Skiffle Group
Sunday 14th Evening
Merseysippi Jazz Band
Ralph Watmough Jazz Band
Wednesday 17th Evening
(Skiffle Session)
Gin Mill Skiffle Group
Dark Town Skiffle Group
Thursday 18th Evening
(Modern Jazz Session)
Alan Branscombe
Alan Alderson
Friday 19th Evening
White Eagles Jazz Band
Martin Rowland Skiffle Group
Saturday 20th Evening
Eric Batty Jazz Aces
Sunday 21st Evening
Merseysippi Jazz Band
Gin Mill Skiffle Group
Wednesday 24th Evening
(Skiffle Session)

Gin Mill Skiffle Group
Dusty Road Ramblers Skiffle Group
Calandonie Skiffle Group
Thursday 25th Evening
(Modern Jazz Session)
Alan Branscombe
Alan Alderson
Friday 26th Evening
Merseysippi Jazz Band
Gin Mill Skiffle Group
Saturday 27th Evening
Ralph Watmough Jazz Band
Joe Shannon Skiffle Group
Sunday 28th Evening
Merseysippi Jazz Band
Panama Jazz Band
Wednesday 31st
Miss Cavern Bathing Beauty Contest
Evening
(Skiffle Session)
Eddie Clayton Skiffle Group (Ringo
  Starr's Cavern debut. N.B. Ringo
  also sat in with the Dark Town
  Skiffle Group, so may have appeared
  at the club at an earlier date.)
Blue Genes Skiffle Group
Dusty Road Ramblers Skiffle Group

AUGUST
Thursday 1st Evening
(Modern Jazz Session)
Alan Branscombe Quintet featuring
  Jackie Murray
Friday 2nd Evening
Merseysippi Jazz Band
Joe Shannon Skiffle Group
Saturday 3rd Evening
Gin Mill Skiffle Group
Ralph Watmough Jazz Band
Sunday 4th Evening
The Saints Jazz Band
Wednesday 7th Evening
(Skiffle Session)
Ron McKay Skiffle Group
The Quarrymen Skiffle Group (John
  Lennon's Cavern debut)
Dark Town Skiffle Group
The Deltones Skiffle Group
Thursday 8th Evening
(Modern Jazz Session)
Alan Branscombe Quintet
The Darryl Dugdale Trio
Friday 9th Evening
Merseysippi Jazz Band
Joe Shannon Skiffle Group
Saturday 10th Evening
Merseysippi Jazz Band
Ralph Watmough Jazz Band
Ron McKay Skiffle Group

Sunday 11th Evening
Merseysippi Jazz Band
Panama Jazz Band
Wednesday 14th Evening
Ron McKay Skiffle Group
Thursday 15th Evening
(Modern Jazz Session)
Tommy Whittle Quartet
Jackie Murray
The Darryl Dugdale Trio
Friday 16th Riverboat Shuffle
(No Session at Cavern)
Merseysippi Jazz Band
Gin Mill Skiffle Group
Wall City Jazzmen
Saturday 17th Evening
Dickie Bishop Skiffle Group
Ralph Watmough Jazz Band
Sunday 18th Evening
Wall City Jazzmen
Dickie Bishop Skiffle Group
Wednesday 21st Evening
Ron McKay Skiffle Group
Thursday 22nd Evening
(Modern Jazz Session)
The Darryl Dugdale Trio
Alan Branscombe Quintet

Friday 23rd Evening
Merseysippi Jazz Band
Joe Shannon Skiffle Group
Ron McKay Skiffle Group
Saturday 24th Evening
Ralph Watmough Jazz Band
Ron McKay Skiffle Group
Sunday 25th Evening
Merseysippi Jazz Band
Panama Jazz Band
Wednesday 28th Evening
Ron McKay Skiffle Group
Thursday 29th Evening
(Modern Jazz Session)
Alan Branscombe Quintet
Tim Bailey Quartet
Friday 30th Evening
Wall City Jazzmen
Joe Shannon Skiffle Group
Saturday 31st Evening
Ron McKay Skiffle Group
Merseysippi Jazz Band

SEPTEMBER
Sunday 1st Evening
Cy Laurie Jazz Band
Gin Mill Skiffle Group

Wednesday 4th Evening
Ron McKay Skiffle Group
Thursday 5th Evening
(Modern Jazz Session)
Alan Branscombe Quintet
Friday 6th Evening
Merseysippi Jazz Band
Ron McKay Skiffle Group
Saturday 7th Evening
Ron McKay Skiffle Group
Ralph Watmough Jazz Band
Sunday 8th Evening
Blue Note Jazzmen
Paul Beattie Skiffle Group
Wednesday 11th Evening
Ron McKay Skiffle Group
Thursday 12th Evening
(Modern Jazz Session)
Alan Branscombe Quintet
Alan Alderson Quartet
Friday 13th Evening
Wall City Jazzmen with Pete Wright
Gin Mill Skiffle Group
Saturday 14th Evening
Ron Mc Skiffle Group
Ralph Watmough Jazz Band
Sunday 15th Lunchtime
Merseysippi Jazz Band
Royal Caribbean Calypso Steel Band
Evening
Gin Mill Skiffle Group
The Druids Jazz Band
Wednesday 18th Evening
Ron McKay Skiffle Group plus
  special guest
Thursday 19th Evening
(Modern Jazz Session)
Alan Branscombe Quintet
Tommy Whittle
Saturday 21st Evening
Ralph Watmough Jazz Band
Gin Mill Skiffle Group
Sunday 22nd Evening
Ron McKay Skiffle Group
Panama Jazzmen
Wednesday 25th Evening
Ron McKay Skiffle Group plus
  special guest
Thursday 26th Evening
(Modern Jazz Session)
Don Randall's All Stars
Friday 27th Evening
Wall City Jazzmen
Joe Shannon Skiffle Group
Saturday 28th Evening
Gin Mill Skiffle Group
Golden Era Jazz Band
Sunday 29th Lunchtime
Ron McKay Skiffle Group

Evening
Clinton Ford
Druids Jazz Band
Merseysippi Jazz Band

OCTOBER
Wednesday 2nd Lunchtime
Merseysippi Jazz Band
Thursday 3rd Evening
(Modern Jazz Session)
Alan Branscombe Quintet
Friday 4th Lunchtime
Merseysippi Jazz Band
Evening
Wall City Jazzmen
Pete Wright's Skiffle and Blues Group
Ron McKay Skiffle Group
Saturday 5th Evening
Joe Shannon Skiffle Group
Merseysippi Jazz Band
Clinton Ford
Sunday 6th Lunchtime
Druids Jazz Band
Gin Mill Skiffle Group
Evening
Ron McKay Skiffle Group
Blue Note Jazz Band
Clinton Ford
Ralph Watmough Jazz Band
Wednesday 9th Lunchtime
Merseysippi Jazz Band
Evening
Ron McKay Skiffle Group plus
  special guest
Thursday 10th Evening
(Modern Jazz Session)
Alan Branscombe Quintet
The Darryl Dugdale Trio
Friday 11th Lunchtime
Merseysippi Jazz Band
Evening
Johnny Parker
Joe Shannon Skiffle Group
Saturday 12th Evening
The Saints Jazz Band
Blue Genes Skiffle Group
Sunday 13th Lunchtime
Gin Mill Skiffle Group
The Druids Jazz Band
Royal Caribbean Calypso Steel Band
Evening
Royal Caribbean Calypso Steel Band
Ron McKay Skiffle Group
Johnny Parker
Wednesday 16th Lunchtime
Merseysippi Jazz Band
Evening
Ralph Watmough Jazz Band
Dark Town Skiffle Group

Thursday 17th Evening
(Modern Jazz Session)
Alan Branscombe Quintet
The Darryl Dugdale Trio
Friday 18th Lunchtime
Merseysippi Jazz Band
Evening
Wall City Jazzmen
Joe Shannon Skiffle Group
Saturday 19th Evening
Merseysippi Jazz Band
Sunday 20th Evening
Merseysippi Jazz Band
Wednesday 23rd Lunchtime
Merseysippi Jazz Band
Evening
Ralph Watmough Jazz Band with
  Bryan Newman
Red Valley Skiffle Group
Thursday 24th Evening
(Modern Jazz Session)
Alan Branscombe Quintet
The Vin Newton Trio
Friday 25th Lunchtime
Merseysippi Jazz Band
Evening
Merseysippi Jazz Band
The 95 Skiffle Group
Saturday 26th Evening
Alex Welsh Dixielanders
Joe Shannon Skiffle Group
Sunday 27th Evening
Dark Town Skiffle Group
Merseysippi Jazz Band
Wednesday 30th Lunchtime
Merseysippi Jazz Band
Evening
Ralph Watmough Jazz Band with
  Bryan Newman
Riversiders Skiffle Group
Thursday 31st Evening
(Modern Jazz Session)
Harry Klein
Alan Branscombe Quintet

NOVEMBER
Friday 1st Evening
Merseysippi Jazz Band
Cavendish Skiffle Group
Saturday 2nd Evening
The Saints Jazz Band
Joe Shannon Skiffle Group
Sunday 3rd Evening
Cavendish Skiffle Group
Merseysippi Jazz Band
Wednesday 6th Lunchtime
Merseysippi Jazz Band
Evening
Ralph Watmough Jazz Band with

Bryan Newman
Thursday 7th Evening
(Modern Jazz Session)
Alan Branscombe Quintet
Friday 8th Lunchtime
Merseysippi Jazz Band
Evening
Ralph Watmough Jazz Band
Dickie Bishop Skiffle Group
Panama Jazz Band
Saturday 9th Evening
Panama Jazz Band
Dickie Bishop Skiffle Group
Sunday 10th Evening
Merseysippi Jazz Band
Wednesday 13th Lunchtime
Merseysippi Jazz Band
Evening
Ralph Watmough Jazz Band with
  Bryan Newman
Dark Town Skiffle Group
Thursday 14th Evening
(Modern Jazz Session)
Kenny Graham
Alan Branscombe Quintet
Friday 15th Evening
Ralph Watmough Jazz Band with
  Bryan Newman
Los Torros Skiffle Group
Cavendish Skiffle Group
Saturday 16th Evening
Joe Shannon Skiffle Group
Eric Batty Jazz Aces
Sunday 17th Evening
Merseysippi Jazz Band
Panama Jazz Band
Wednesday 20th Lunchtime
Merseysippi Jazz Band
Evening
Ralph Watmough Jazz Band
Bryan Newman
Dark Town Skiffle Group
Thursday 21st Evening
(Modern Jazz Session)
Tubby Hayes
Ronnie Scott
The Jazz Couriers
Friday 22nd Lunchtime
Merseysippi Jazz Band
Evening
Merseysippi Jazz Band
Paul Beattie Skiffle Group
Saturday 23rd Evening
Cavendish Skiffle Group
Blue Genes Skiffle Group
The Saints Jazz Band
Sunday 24th Evening
Merseysippi Jazz Band
Joe Shannon Skiffle Group

Bryan Newman Skiffle Group
Monday 25th Evening
Vic Lewis Orchestra Big Band Jazz
Tuesday 26th Lunchtime
Merseysippi Jazz Band
Wednesday 27th Lunchtime
Merseysippi Jazz Band
Evening
Ralph Watmough Jazz Band
Dark Town Skiffle Group
Bryan Newman Skiffle Group
Thursday 28th Evening
(Modern Jazz Session)
Joe Harriot
Alan Branscombe Quintet
Friday 29th Lunchtime
Merseysippi Jazz Band
Evening
Merseysippi Jazz Band
Cavendish Skiffle Group
Saturday 30th Evening
Deltones Skiffle Group
Blue Note Jazz Band

DECEMBER
Sunday 1st Evening
Merseysippi Jazz Band
Dark Town Skiffle Group
Wednesday 4th Lunchtime
Merseysippi Jazz Band
Evening
Ralph Watmough Jazz Band
Bryan Newman Skiffle Group
Eddie Clayton Skiffle Group
Thursday 5th Evening
(Modern Jazz Session)
Tony Kinsey Quartet
Friday 6th Lunchtime
Merseysippi Jazz Band
Evening
Merseysippi Jazz Band
Deltones Skiffle Group
Saturday 7th Evening
Joe Shannon Skiffle Group
Eric Batty Jazz Aces
Sunday 8th Evening
Merseysippi Jazz Band
Red Sullivan Jazz Band
Tommy Smith
Clinton Ford
Blue Genes Skiffle Group
Bryan Newman Skiffle Group
Wednesday 11th Lunchtime
Merseysippi Jazz Band
Evening
Ralph Watmough Jazz Band
Bryan Newman Skiffle Group
Martinis Skiffle Group

Thursday 12th Evening
(Modern Jazz Session)
Alan Branscombe Quintet
Friday 27th Lunchtime
Merseysippi Jazz Band
Evening
Merseysippi Jazz Band
Martinis Skiffle Group
Saturday 28th Evening
Demons Skiffle Group
Terry Lightfoot's New Orleans
  Jazzmen
Sunday 29th Evening
Merseysippi Jazz Band
The Los Toros Skiffle Group
Tuesday 31st Evening
Merseysippi Jazz Band with Clinton
  Ford
Blue Genes Skiffle Group
Los Toros Skiffle Group

1958

JANUARY
Thursday 2nd Evening
(Modern Jazz Session)
Alan Branscombe Quintet
Friday 3rd Evening
Merseysippi Jazz Band with Clinton
  Ford
Texans Skiffle Group
Saturday 4th Evening
Deltones Skiffle Group
Blue Genes Jazz Band
Sunday 5th Evening
Merseysippi Jazz Band
Clinton Ford
Blue Genes Skiffle Group
Wednesday 8th Evening
Ralph Watmough Jazz Band
Bryan Newman Skiffle Group
Texans Skiffle Group
Thursday 9th Evening
(Modern Jazz Session)
Ronnie Scott
Tubby Hayes with The Jazz Couriers
Friday 10th Evening
Merseysippi Jazz Band
Red Valley Skiffle Group
Saturday 11th Evening
Blue Genes Skiffle Group
Eric Batty Jazz Aces
Sunday 12th Evening
(TV Contest Winners)
Second City Jazzmen
Deltones Skiffle Group

Wednesday 15th
Cavern Birthday Session: One Year
  Old
Evening
Merseysippi Jazz Band
Ralph Watmough Jazz Band
Bryan Newman Skiffle Group
Cooke's Dixielanders
Katz Skiffle Group
Thursday 16th Evening
(Modern Jazz Session – TV and
  Radio Stars)
Bill Jones Trio
Joe Harriot
Friday 17th Evening
Alex Welsh Dixielanders
Los Toros Skiffle Group
Saturday 18th Evening
Paul Beaton Skiffle Group
The Saints Jazz Band
Blue Note Jazzmen
Sunday 19th Evening
Terry Lightfoot Jazz Band
John Wilson Quartet
Bryan Newman Skiffle Group
Wednesday 22nd Evening
Wall City Jazzmen
Pete Wright Skiffle Group
Thursday 23rd Evening
(Modern Jazz Session)
Basil Kirchin Band
Friday 24th Evening
Merseysippi Jazz Band
The Quarrymen Skiffle Group (Paul
  McCartney's Cavern debut)
Saturday 25th Evening
Cavendish Skiffle Group
Zenith Six Jazz Band
Sunday 26th Evening
Merseysippi Jazz Band
The Druids Jazz Band
Blue Genes Skiffle Group
Wednesday 29th Evening
Ralph Watmough Jazz Band
Eddie Clayton Skiffle Group
Thursday 30th Evening
(Modern Jazz Session)
Tony Kinsey Quartet
Friday 31st Evening
Merseysippi Jazz Band
Clinton Ford
Bryan Newman Skiffle Group

FEBRUARY
Saturday 1st Evening
Blue Genes Skiffle Group
Wall City Jazzmen
Sunday 2nd Evening
Merseysippi Jazz Band

Bryan Newman Skiffle Group
Wednesday 5th Evening
Reg Guest Jazzmen
The Barmen Skiffle Group
Thursday 6th Evening
(Modern Jazz Session)
The Don Rendell All Stars
Friday 7th Evening
Merseysippi Jazz Band
Eddie Clayton Skiffle Group
Saturday 8th Evening
Eric Batty Jazz Aces
Sunday 9th Evening
Merseysippi Jazz Band
John Wilson Trio
Bryan Newman Skiffle Group
Wednesday 12th Evening
Ralph Watmough Jazz Band
Blue Genes Skiffle Group
Friday 14th Evening
Acker Bilk's Paramount Jazz Band
  with Ron McKay
Hy-Katz Skiffle Group
Saturday 15th Evening
Acker Bilk's Paramount Jazz Band
  with Ron McKay
Bryan Newman Skiffle Group
Sunday 16th Evening
Eddie Clayton Skiffle Group
Merseysippi Jazz Band
Wednesday 19th Evening
Ralph Watmough Jazz Band plus
  Guest Skiffle Groups
Friday 21st Evening
Merseysippi Jazz Band
Zenith Skiffle Group
Saturday 22nd Evening
Blue Genes Skiffle Group
Wall City Jazzmen
Sunday 23rd Evening
Merseysippi Jazz Band
Clinton Ford
Eddie Clayton Skiffle Group
Wednesday 26th Evening
Hy-Katz Skiffle Group
Friday 28th Evening
Merseysippi Jazz Band
Dark Town Skiffle Group

MARCH
Saturday 1st Evening
The Sandy Brown Jazz Band (from
  London)
Sunday 2nd Evening
The Sandy Brown Jazz Band
Merseysippi Jazz Band
Wednesday 5th Evening
Ralph Watmough Jazz Band
Red Valley Skiffle Group

Thursday 6th Evening
(Modern Jazz Session)
Tony Kinsey with Bill Le Sage
Friday 7th Evening
Merseysippi Jazz Band
Blue Genes Skiffle Group
Saturday 8th Evening
Eddie Clayton Skiffle Group
Wall City Jazzmen
Sunday 9th Evening
Merseysippi Jazz Band
Ralph Watmough Jazz Band
Clinton Ford
Bryan Newman Skiffle Group
Wednesday 12th Evening
Merseysippi Jazz Band
Zenith Skiffle Group
J.M.O. Skiffle Group
Thursday 13th Evening
(Modern Jazz Session)
Tommy Whittle Quintet with Harry
  Klein
The Eddie Thompson Trio
Friday 14th Evening
Merseysippi Jazz Band
The Demons Skiffle Group
Saturday 15th Evening
Alex Welsh Dixielanders
Eddie Clayton Skiffle Group
Sunday 16th Evening
Merseysippi Jazz Band
Wall City Jazzmen
Liverpool University Jazz Band
Beryl Bryden
Wednesday 19th Evening
(Skiffle Night)
Bryan Newman Skiffle Group
Dark Town Skiffle Group
Los Toros Skiffle Group
Thursday 20th Evening
(Modern Jazz Session)
Tubby Hayes and Ronnie Scott
The Jazz Couriers
Friday 21st Evening
Merseysippi Jazz Band
Bryan Newman Skiffle Group
Saturday 22nd Evening
Jackson Bradshaw Jazz Band
Zenith Six Jazz Band
Sunday 23rd Evening
Merseysippi Jazz Band
Dark Town Skiffle Group
Wednesday 26th Evening
(Skiffle Night)
Bryan Newman
Hy-Katz Skiffle Group
Blue Genes Skiffle Group

Thursday 27th Evening
(Modern Jazz Session)
Betty Smith Quintet
Friday 28th Evening
Merseysippi Jazz Band
Eddie Clayton Skiffle Group
Saturday 29th Evening
Los Toros Skiffle Group
Wall City Jazzmen
Sunday 30th Evening
Merseysippi Jazz Band
Bryan Newman Skiffle Group

APRIL
Wednesday 2nd Evening
(Skiffle Night)
Dark Town Skiffle Group
Red Valley Skiffle Group
Thursday 3rd Evening
(Modern Jazz Session)
Ronnie Ross Quintet
Joe Palin Quintet
Friday 4th Evening
Acker Bilk's Paramount Jazz Band
  with Ron McKay Skiffle Group
Blue Genes Skiffle Group
Saturday 5th Evening
Acker Bilk's Paramount Jazz Band
Ron McKay Skiffle Group
Sunday 6th Evening
Beryl Bryden
Merseysippi Jazz Band
Thursday 10th Evening
(Modern Jazz Session)
Joe Palin Quintet
Friday 11th Evening
Merseysippi Jazz Band
Los Toros Skiffle Group
Saturday 12th Evening
Sister Rosetta Tharpe (American star)
  backed by Wall City Jazzmen
Sunday 13th Evening
Merseysippi Jazz Band
Clinton Ford
Al Fairweather Jazz Band
Wednesday 16th Evening
(Skiffle Night)
Lonnie Donegan
Trophy Award Contest
Thursday 17th Evening
(Modern Jazz Session)
Ray Premru (American bass
  trombone and trumpet star)
Joe Palin Quintet
Friday 18th Evening
Merseysippi Jazz Band
Clinton Ford
Red Valley Skiffle Group

Saturday 19th Evening
Terry Lightfoot's Jazz Band
Blue Genes Skiffle Group
Dark Town Skiffle Group
Sunday 20th Evening
The Lime House Swing Quintet
Terry Lightfoot's Jazz Band
Blue Genes Skiffle Group
Dark Town Skiffle Group
Thursday 24th Evening
(Modern Jazz Session)
Bennie Green
Joe Palin Quintet
Friday 25th Evening
Acker Bilk
Ron McKay Skiffle Group
Texans Skiffle Group
Saturday 26th Evening
Bryan Newman Skiffle Group
Merseysippi Jazz Band
Harry Ormesher's Dixielanders
Sunday 27th Evening
Acker Bilk's Paramount Jazz Band
Merseysippi Jazz Band
Ron McKay Skiffle Group with
    Clinton Ford

MAY
Friday 2nd Evening
Merseysippi Jazz Band
Hy-Katz Skiffle Group
Saturday 3rd Riverboat Shuffle
Cy Laurie Jazz Band
Merseysippi Jazz Band
Sunday 4th Evening
Cy Laurie Jazz Band
Bryan Newman Skiffle Group
Thursday 8th Evening
(Modern Jazz Session)
Alan Branscombe Quintet
Joe Palin Quintet

Friday 9th Evening
Merseysippi Jazz Band
Saturday 10th Evening
Graham Stewart Seven Jazz Band
Alan Elsdon and John Parker
Dickie Bishop Skiffle Group with
    The Barrel House Three
Dusty Road Ramblers Skiffle Group
Sunday 11th Evening
Dusty Road Ramblers Skiffle Group
The Barrel House Three
Dickie Bishop Skiffle Group
Graham Stewart Seven Jazz Band
Alan Elsdon and John Parker
Friday 16th Evening
Marie Knight (Blues Star) and The
    Humphrey Lyttelton Jazz Band
Merseysippi Jazz Band
Saturday 17th Evening
Wall City Jazzmen
Dark Town Skiffle Group
Blue Genes Skiffle Group
Sunday 18th Evening
Bryan Newman Skiffle Group
Merseysippi Jazz Band
Clinton Ford
Thursday 22nd Evening
(Modern Jazz Session)
The Jazz Couriers
Tubby Hayes and Ronnie Scott
Friday 23rd Evening
Jackson Bradshaw Jazz Band Texans
    Skiffle Group
Saturday 24th Evening
Merseysippi Jazz Band
Sunday 25th Evening
Merseysippi Jazz Band
Monday 26th Evening
The Terry Lightfoot Jazz Band

Thursday 29th Evening
(Modern Jazz Session)
Don Rendell
Friday 30th Evening
Merseysippi Jazz Band
Black Cat Skiffle Group
Saturday 31st Evening
Dark Town Skiffle Group
Wall City Jazzmen

JUNE
Sunday 1st Evening
Merseysippi Jazz Band
Bryan Newman Skiffle Group
Thursday 5th Evening
(Modern Jazz Session)
Ronnie Ross
Red Price
Friday 6th Evening
Merseysippi Jazz Band
Blue Genes Skiffle Group
Saturday 7th Evening
Dark Town Skiffle Group
Wall City Jazzmen
Sunday 8th Evening
Merseysippi Jazz Band
Beryl Bryden
Thursday 12th Evening
(Modern Jazz Session)
Tony Kinsey
Friday 13th Evening
Ralph Watmough Jazz Band
Los Toros Skiffle Group
Saturday 14th Evening
Blue Genes Skiffle Group
Alex Welsh Dixielanders
Sunday 15th Evening
Wall City Jazzmen
Dark Town Skiffle Group
Friday 20th Evening
Wall City Jazzmen
Dark Town Skiffle Group
Saturday 21st Evening
Hy-Katz Skiffle Group
Merseysippi Jazz Band
Sunday 22nd Evening
Merseysippi Jazz Band
Friday 27th Evening
(Miss Liverpool Contest)
Merseysippi Jazz Band
Saturday 28th Evening
Merseysippi Jazz Band
Sunday 29th Evening
Acker Bilk's Paramount Jazz Band
Ron McKay Skiffle Group

JULY
Friday 4th Evening
Merseysippi Jazz Band

Saturday 5th Evening
Merseysippi Jazz Band
Sunday 6th Evening
Mick Mulligan Band with George
    Melly
Friday 11th Evening
(Miss Liverpool Contest)
Merseysippi Jazz Band with Jill
    Martin
Saturday 12th Evening
Druids Jazz Band
Wall City Jazzmen
Sunday 13th Evening
Merseysippi Jazz Band with Jill
    Martin
Thursday 17th Evening
(Modern Jazz Session)
Kenny Baker
Joe Palin Quintet
Friday 18th Evening
Ralph Watmough Jazz Band
Saturday 19th Evening
Wall City Jazzmen
Sunday 20th Evening
Terry Lightfoot Jazz Band
Thursday 24th Evening
(Modern Jazz Session)
Kenny Baker
Friday 25th Evening
Wall City Jazzmen
Saturday 26th Evening
The Yorkshire Jazz Band
Sunday 27th Evening
Acker Bilk's Paramount Jazz Band
Thursday 31st Evening
(Modern Jazz Session)
Kenny Baker

AUGUST
Friday 1st Riverboat Shuffle
Merseysippi Jazz Band
Wall City Jazzmen plus skiffle groups
Saturday 2nd Evening
The Yorkshire Jazz Bend
Sunday 3rd Evening
Merseysippi Jazz Band
Thursday 7th Evening
(Modern Jazz Session)
Kenny Baker
Friday 8th Evening
Merseysippi Jazz Band
Saturday 9th Evening
The Druids Jazz Band
Wall City Jazzmen
Sunday 10th Evening
Merseysippi Jazz Band
Thursday 14th Evening
(Modern Jazz Session)
Kenny Baker

Friday 15th Evening
Merseysippi Jazz Band
Saturday 16th Evening
Ralph Watmough Jazz Band
Sunday 17th Evening
Merseysippi Jazz Band
Thursday 21st Evening
Kenny Baker
Friday 22nd Evening
Merseysippi Jazz Band
Saturday 23rd Evening
Ralph Watmough Jazz Band
Sunday 24th Evening
Merseysippi Jazz Band
Thursday 28th Evening
(Modern Jazz Session)
Bert Courtney
Friday 29th Evening
The Sonny Morris Jazzmen
Saturday 30th Evening
The Sonny Morris Jazzmen
Sunday 31st Evening
Merseysippi Jazz Band
Sandy Brown and The Fairweather
    All Stars

SEPTEMBER
Thursday 4th Evening
(Modern Jazz Session)
Ronnie Ross
Friday 5th Evening
Merseysippi Jazz Band
Saturday 6th Evening
Druids Jazz Band
Ralph Watmough Jazz Band
Sunday 7th Evening
Merseysippi Jazz Band
Thursday 11th Evening
(Modern Jazz Session)
Ronnie Scott
Tubby Hayes
The Jazz Couriers
Friday 12th Evening
Merseysippi Jazz Band
Blue Genes Skiffle Group
Saturday 13th Evening
Wall City Jazzmen
Druids Jazz Band
Sunday 14th Evening
Merseysippi Jazz Band
Mick Mulligan
George Melly
Saturday 20th Riverboat Shuffle
No session at Cavern
Sunday 21st Evening
Merseysippi Jazz Band
Micky Ashman Jazz Band
Sonny Morris Jazz Band
Dickie Bishop Skiffle Group

Thursday 25th Evening
(Modern Jazz Session)
Tony Kinsey
Dizzy Reece
Joe Palin
Friday 26th Evening
Merseysippi Jazz Band
Ralph Watmough Jazz Band
Jimmy Rushing (American blues star)
Saturday 27th Evening
Wall City Jazzmen
The Druids Jazz Band
Sunday 28th Evening
Merseysippi Jazz Band
Ralph Watmough Jazz Band

OCTOBER
Thursday 2nd Evening
(Modern Jazz Session)
The Vic Ashe Sextet
Friday 3rd Evening
Merseysippi Jazz Band
Blue Genes Skiffle Group
Saturday 4th Evening
Cy Laurie Jazz Band
Druids Jazz Band
Sunday 5th Evening
Cy Laurie Jazz Band
Carl Barriteau Jazz Band
Merseysippi Jazz Band
Thursday 9th Evening
(Modern Jazz Session)
The Jazz Makers
Ronnie Ross and Alan Ganley
Art Ellefson
Friday 10th Evening
Merseysippi Jazz Band
Druids Jazz Band
Sandy Brown and The Fairweather
   All Stars
Saturday 11th Evening
Sandy Brown and The Fairweather
   All Stars
Druids Jazz Band
Sunday 12th Evening
Merseysippi Jazz Band
Sandy Brown and The Fairweather
   All Stars
Thursday 16th Evening
(Modern Jazz Session)
The Jazz Couriers
Ronnie Scott
Tubby Hayes
Friday 17th Evening
Graham Stewart Seven Jazz Band
Blue Genes Skiffle Group
Saturday 18th Evening
The Druids Jazz Band
Graham Stewart Seven Jazz Band

Sunday 19th Evening
Merseysippi Jazz Band
Graham Stewart Seven Jazz Band
Thursday 23rd Evening
(Modern Jazz Session)
Joe Palin Quintet
Friday 24th Evening
Merseysippi Jazz Band
Blue Genes Skiffle Group
Saturday 25th Evening
Wall City Jazzmen
The Druids Jazz Band
Sunday 26th Evening
Merseysippi Jazz Band
Thursday 30th Evening
(Modern Jazz Session)
Joe Palin Quintet
Friday 31st Evening
Merseysippi Jazz Band
Micky Ashman and his Ragtime Band

NOVEMBER
Saturday 1st Evening
Micky Ashman and his Ragtime Band
Dickie Bishop Skiffle Group
Blue Genes Skiffle Group
Sunday 2nd Evening
Dickie Bishop Skiffle Group
Merseysippi Jazz Band
Micky Ashman and his Ragtime Band
Thursday 6th Evening
(Modern Jazz Session)
Vic Ashe Sextet
Alan Branscombe
Friday 7th Evening
Alan Pendlebury's Jazzmen
Blue Genes Skiffle Group
Saturday 8th Evening
The Bobby Mickleburgh Jazz Band
The Druids Jazz Band
Sunday 9th Evening
Merseysippi Jazz Band
Blue Genes Skiffle Group
Thursday 13th Evening
(Modern Jazz Session)
Tony Kinsey Quartet
Friday 14th Evening
Merseysippi Jazz Band
Saturday 15th Evening
The Druids Jazz Band
Terry Lightfoot's Jazzmen
Sunday 16th Evening
Terry Lightfoot's Jazzmen
Merseysippi Jazz Band
Thursday 20th Evening
(Modern Jazz Session)
The Jazz Couriers
Tubby Hayes
Ronnie Scott

Friday 21st Evening
Merseysippi Jazz Band
Saturday 22nd Evening
Graham Stewart Seven Jazz Band
Druids Jazz Band
Sunday 23rd Evening
Graham Stewart Seven Jazz Band
Merseysippi Jazz Band
Thursday 27th Evening
(Modern Jazz Session)
Ronnie Ross and Alan Ganley
Friday 28th Evening
Merseysippi Jazz Band
Saturday 29th Evening
Druids Jazz Band
Graham Stewart Jazz Band
Sunday 30th Evening
Beryl Bryden
Alex Welsh Dixielanders
Merseysippi Jazz Band
Clinton Ford and Jill Martin

DECEMBER
Thursday 4th Evening
(Modern Jazz Session)
Joe Palin Quintet
Friday 5th Evening
Merseysippi Jazz Band
Blue Genes Skiffle Group
Saturday 6th Evening
Blue Genes Skiffle Group
Merseysippi Jazz Band
The Druids Jazz Band
Sunday 7th Evening
(Festival of Jazz)
Acker Bilk's Paramount Jazz Band
Cy Laurie Jazz Band
Bruce Turner Jump Band
Ron McKay Skiffle Group
Thursday 11th Evening
(Modern Jazz Session)
Harry Klein
Friday 12th Evening
Merseysippi Jazz Band
Blue Genes Skiffle Group
Saturday 13th Evening
Micky Ashman
Druids Jazz Band
Dickie Bishop Skiffle Group
Sunday 14th Evening
Graham Stewarts New Orleans Six
Merseysippi Jazz Band
Clinton Ford
Jill Martin
Thursday 18th Evening
(Modern Jazz Session)
Ronnie Scott and Tubby Hayes
The Jazz Couriers

Friday 19th Evening
Merseysippi Jazz Band
Blue Genes Skiffle Group
Eddie O'Donnel Band
Saturday 20th Evening
Wall City Jazzmen
The Druids Jazz Band
Sunday 21st Evening
Mick Mulligan Band with George
   Melley
Merseysippi Jazz Band
Wednesday 24th Evening
Wall City Jazzmen
Thursday 25th Evening
(Modern Jazz Session)
Alan Branscombe
Ian Rames
Joe Palin Quintet
Friday 26th Evening
Micky Ashman
Dickie Bishop Skiffle Group
Saturday 27th Evening
Terry Lightfoot's Jazzmen
Sunday 28th Evening
Acker Bilk's Paramount Jazz Band
Ron McKay Skiffle Group
Wednesday 31st Evening
Mick Mulligan Band with George
   Melly
Merseysippi Jazz Band

1959

JANUARY
Thursday 1st Evening
Vic Ashe
Friday 2nd Evening
Wall City Jazzmen
Blue Genes Skiffle Group
Saturday 3rd Evening
Merseysippi Jazz Band
Sunday 4th Evening
Merseysippi Jazz Band
Friday 9th Evening
Wall City Jazzmen
Blue Genes Skiffle Group
Saturday 10th Evening
Alex Welsh Dixielanders
Sunday 11th Evening
Mick Mulligan Jazz Band with
   George Melly and Beryl Bryden
Friday 16th Evening
Wall City Jazzmen
Blue Genes Skiffle Group
Saturday 17th Evening
Micky Ashman
New Orleans Jazz Band

Dickie Bishop Skiffle Group
Sunday 18th Evening
Micky Ashman
Dickie Bishop Skiffle Group
Friday 23rd Evening
Merseysippi Jazz Band
Clinton Ford
Saturday 24th Evening
Clinton Ford
Merseysippi Jazz Band
Sunday 25th Evening
Merseysippi Jazz Band
Clinton Ford
Acker Bilk's Paramount Jazz Band
Ron McKay Skiffle Group
Friday 30th Evening
Merseysippi Jazz Band
Clinton Ford
Saturday 31st Evening
Wall City Jazzmen

FEBRUARY
Sunday 1st Evening
Terry Lightfoot's New Orleans
   Jazzmen
Merseysippi Jazz Band
Clinton Ford and Beryl Bryden
Friday 6th Evening
Merseysippi Jazz Band
Clinton Ford
Jill Martin
Saturday 7th Evening
Graham Stewart Seven Jazz Band
Sunday 8th Evening
Merseysippi Jazz Band
Jill Martin and Beryl Bryden
Friday 13th Evening
Beryl Bryden
Alex Welsh Dixielanders
Merseysippi Jazz Band
Saturday 14th Evening
Terry Lightfoot's New Orleans
   Jazzmen
Friday 20th Evening
Merseysippi Jazz Band
Clinton Ford and Jill Martin
Saturday 21st Evening
Clinton Ford
Jill Martin
Merseysippi Jazz Band
Sunday 22nd Evening
The Saints Jazz Band
Friday 27th Evening
Merseysippi Jazz Band
Saturday 28th Evening
Merseysippi Jazz Band

MARCH

Sunday 1st Evening
Merseysippi Jazz Band
Micky Ashman
Dickie Bishop Skiffle Group
Saturday 7th Evening
Teddy Layton's New Orleans Jazz
  Band
Sonny Morris Jazz Band
Sunday 8th Evening
Sonny Morris Jazz Band
Teddy Leyton's New Orleans Jazz
  Band
Saturday 14th Evening
Wall City Jazzmen
Blue Genes Skiffle Group
Sunday 15th Evening
Humphrey Lyttelton Jazz Band
Merseysippi Jazz Band
Clinton Ford
Jill Martin
Saturday 21st Evening
Merseysippi Jazz Band
Clinton Ford
Jill Martin
Blue Genes Skiffle Group
Sunday 22nd Evening
Cy Laurie's Jazz Band
Blue Genes Skiffle Group
Friday 27th Evening
Bob Wallis and The Storeyville
  Jazzmen
Blue Genes Skiffle Group
Texans Skiffle Group
Saturday 28th Evening
Texans Skiffle Group
Blue Genes Skiffle Group
Bob Wallis Storeyville Jazzmen
Sunday 29th Evening
Mick Mulligan Jazz Band
George Molly
Texans Skiffle Group
Blue Genes Skiffle Group
Monday 30th Evening
Blue Genes Skiffle Group
Texans Skiffle Group
Dickie Bishop Trio
Micky Ashman

APRIL

Saturday 4th Evening
The Zenith Six Jazz Band
Blue Genes Skiffle Group
Sunday 5th Evening
Blue Genes Skiffle Group
Merseysippi Jazz Band
Alex Welsh Dixielanders
Beryl Bryden

Saturday 11th Evening
Wall City Jazzmen
Blue Genes Skiffle Group
Sunday 12th Evening
Blue Genes Skiffle Group
Merseysippi Jazz Band
Clinton Ford
Jill Martin
Beryl Bryden
Saturday 18th Evening
Syd Laurence Dixielanders with
  Peggy Karvelle
Sunday 19th Evening
Terry Lightfoot's New Orleans
  Jazzmen
Blue Genes Skiffle Group
Saturday 25th Evening
Syd Laurence Dixielanders with
  Peggy Karvelle
Blue Genes Skiffle Group
Sunday 26th Evening
Blue Genes Skiffle Group
Mick Mulligan Band
George Melly

MAY

Saturday 2nd Evening
Mike Daniels Jazz Band
'The Angel' (blues singer)
Swinging Blue Genes
Sunday 3rd Evening
Swinging Blue Genes
Alex Welsh Dixielanders
Beryl Bryden
Friday 8th Evening
Acker Bilk's Paramount Jazz Band
Climax Jazzmen
Ron McKay Skiffle Group
Saturday 9th Evening
Micky Ashman Jazz Band
Swinging Blue Genes
Sunday 10th Evening
Dr Jazz
Sonny Morris
Swinging Blue Genes
Friday 15th Evening
Climax Jazz Band
Swinging Blue Genes
Saturday 16th Evening
Swinging Blue Genes
Graham Stewart Jazz Band
Sunday 17th Evening
Mick Mulligan Band
George Melly
Swinging Blue Genes
Friday 22nd Evening
Climax Jazz Band
Swinging Blue Genes

Saturday 23rd Evening
Bob Wallis Storeyville Jazzmen
Garden City Jazz Band
Raving Texans Skiffle Group
Sunday 24th Evening
Bob Wallis Storeyville Jazzmen
Garden City Jazz Band
Raving Texans Skiffle Group
Friday 29th Evening
Squire Richard Colbreck's Jazz Band
Climax Jazz Band
Connaughts Skiffle Group
Metronomes Skiffle Group
Swinging Blue Genes
Saturday 30th Evening
Swinging Blue Genes
Syd Laurence Jazz Band
Sunday 31st Evening
Cy Laurie Jazz Band
Swinging Blue Genes Skiffle Group

JUNE

Friday 5th Evening
Climax Jazz Band
Blue Genes Skiffle Group
Saturday 6th All-Night Session
Blue Genes Skiffle Group
Graham Stewart Jazz Band
Climax Jazz Band
Sunday 7th Evening
(New cut-rate summer prices)
Micky Ashman Jazz Band
Blue Genes Skiffle Group
Friday 12th Evening
Climax Jazz Band
Swinging Blue Genes Skiffle Group
Texans Skiffle Group
Saturday 13th Evening
Swinging Blue Genes Skiffle Group
Syd Laurence Jazzmen
Sunday 14th Evening
Mick Mulligan Jazz Band
George Molly
Swinging Blue Genes Skiffle Group
Friday 19th Evening
Climax Jazz Band
Connaughts Jazz Band
Swinging Blue Genes Skiffle Group
Saturday 20th Evening
Texans Skiffle Group
Syd Laurence Jazz Band
Sunday 21st Evening
Dick Charlesworth
City Gents Jazz Band
Swinging Blue Genes Skiffle Group
Friday 6th Evening
Climax Jazz Band
Swinging Blue Genes Skiffle Group

Saturday 27th All-Night Session
Acker Bilk's Paramount Jazz Band
Sunday 28th Evening
Acker Bilk's Paramount Jazz Band

JULY

Friday 24th Evening
Humphrey Lyttelton Jazz Band
Mathew Street Six Skiffle Group
Saturday 25th Evening
Sonny Morris Jazz Band
Sunday 26th Evening
Sonny Morris Jazz Band
Friday 31st Evening
Climax Jazz Band
Mathew Street Six Skiffle Group

AUGUST

Saturday 1st Evening
Blue Genes Skiffle Group
Micky Ashman Jazz Band
The Blue Notes Jazz Band
Sunday 2nd Evening
Graham Stewart Seven Jazz Band
Blue Gene Skiffle Group
Friday 7th Evening
Mathew Street Six Skiffle Group
Dark Town Skiffle Group
Saturday 8th Evening
The Collegians Jazz Band
Sunday 9th Evening
Ken Colyer's Jazz Band
Blue Genes Skiffle Group
Friday 14th Evening
Mathew Street Six Skiffle
Group Texans Skiffle Group
Saturday 15th Evening
Texans Skiffle Group
Zenith Six Jazz Band
Sunday 16th Evening
Graham Stewart Seven Jazz Band
Blue Genes Skiffle Group
Friday 21st Evening
Mathew Street Six Skiffle Group
Johnny Goode and The Country
  Kinfolk
Saturday 22nd Evening
Blue Notes Jazz Band
Al Storm and The Hurricanes
Sunday 23rd Evening
Micky Ashman Jazz Band
Blue Genes Skiffle Group
Friday 28th Evening
Mathew Street Six Skiffle Group
Climax Jazz Band
Saturday 29th Evening
The Saints Jazz Band
Johnny Goode and The Country
  Kinfolk

Sunday 30th Evening
Alex Welsh Dixielanders
Blue Genes Skiffle Group

SEPTEMBER

Friday 4th Evening
The Southside Stompers
Hank Walters and The Dusty Road
  Ramblers
John Goode and The Country
  Kinfolk
Sunday 6th Evening
Sonny Morris Jazzmen
Friday 11th Evening
Ken Colyer Jazzmen
Red River Jazzmen
Saturday 12th Evening
Saints Jazz Band and Kenny Baker
Sunday 13th Evening
Bob Wallis Storeyville Jazzmen
Blue Genes Skiffle Group
Friday 18th Evening
The Jazz Hatters
Saturday 19th Evening
Collegians Jazz Band
The Climax Jazz Band
Sunday 20th Evening
Mick Mulligan Band
George Molly
Friday 25th Evening
The Jazz Hatters

Saturday 26th Evening
The Saints Jazz Band
Sunday 27th Evening
Dick Charlesworth Jazz Band
Blue Genes Skiffle Group

OCTOBER
Friday 2nd Evening
The Jazz Hatters
Dark Town Skiffle Group
Saturday 3rd Evening
Acker Bilk's Paramount Jazz Band
Sonny Terry (USA Guest Star)
Brownie McGhee (USA guest star)
Sunday 4th Evening
Micky Ashman Jazz Band
Blue Genes Skiffle Group
Friday 9th Evening
Red River Jazzmen
Dusty Road Ramblers
Saturday 10th Evening
Dark Town Skiffle Group
Kenny Baker
Zenith Six Jazz Band
Sunday 11th Evening
Cy Laurie Jazz Band
Swinging Blue Genes
Thursday 15th Evening
(Modern Jazz Session)
Tubby Hayes
Sid Levin
Friday 16th Evening
The Jazz Hatters
Dark Town Skiffle Group
Saturday 17th Evening
Yorkshire Jazz Band
Al Storm and The Hurricanes
Sunday 18th Evening
Mick Mulligan Band
George Melly
Swinging Blue Genes
Thursday 22nd Evening
(Modern Jazz Session)
Eric Ferguson
Syd Levin
Friday 23rd Evening
Red River Jazzmen
Al Storm and The Hurricanes
Saturday 24th Evening
Collegians Jazz Band
Johnny Goode and The County
  Kinfolk
Sunday 25th Evening
Dick Charlesworth and The City Gents
Swinging Blue Genes
Thursday 29th Evening
(Modern Jazz Session)
Joe Harriot
Eric Ferguson

Friday 30th Evening
Johnny Duncan and The Blue Grass
  Boys
Dusty Road Ramblers
Johnny Goode and The Country
  Kinfolk
Saturday 31st Evening
Tony Charlesworth Jazz Band

NOVEMBER
Sunday 1st Evening
Acker Bilk's Paramount Jazz Band
Swinging Blue Genes
Monday 2nd
Lonnie Donegan Club opening night
Thursday 5th Evening
(Modern Jazz Session)
Ronnie Ross
The Jazz Makers
Alan Ganley
Friday 6th Evening
The Jazz Hatters
Johnny Goode and The Country
  Kinfolk
Saturday 7th Evening
(All-Night Session)
A.J. Storm and The Hurricanes
Wall City Jazzmen
Bob Wallis Storeyville Jazzmen
Cy Laurie Jazz Band (after midnight)
Sunday 8th Evening
Bob Wallis Storeyville Jazzmen
Thursday 12th Evening
Humphrey Lyttelton Jazz Band
Friday 13th Evening
Sunset Seven Jazz Band
Connaughts Skiffle Group
Saturday 14th Evening
Yorkshire Jazz Band
Johnny Goode and The Country
  Kinfolk
Sunday 15th Evening
Micky Ashman Jazz Band
Swinging Blue Genes
Thursday 19th Evening
(Modern Jazz Session)
Dill Jones Trio
Eric Ferguson Quartet
Friday 20th Evening
Red River Jazzmen
Rory Storm and The Hurricanes
Saturday 21st Evening
Dizzy Burton's Aces
Johnny Goode and The Country
  Kinfolk
Sunday 22nd Evening
Mick Mulligan Jazz Band
George Melly
Swinging Blue Genes

Thursday 26th Evening
(Modern Jazz Session)
Coursley Rendell
Commitee Harvey
Friday 27th Evening
The Southern Stompers
Rory Storm and The Hurricanes
Saturday 28th Evening
The Collemans Jazz Band
Swinging Blue Genes
Sunday 29th Evening
Champion Jack Dupree
(American barrel house blues)
Cy Laurie Jazz Band

DECEMBER
Thursday 3rd Evening
(Modern Jazz Session)
Tony Kinsey Quartet plus Owen
  Thomas
Friday 4th Evening
Davenport Jazz Band
Johnny Goode and The Country
  Kinfolk
Saturday 5th Evening
The Saints Jazz Band
Eddie and The Cadillacs
Sunday 6th Evening
Mick Mulligan Jazz Band
George Melly
Swinging Blue Genes
Thursday 10th Evening
(Modern Jazz Session)
Tubby Hayes
The Ken O'Hara Trio
Friday 11th Evening
Dallas Jazz Band
Johnny Goode and The Country
  Kinfolk
Rory Storm and The Hurricanes
Saturday 12th All-Night Session
Terry Lightfoot's New Orleans Jazz
  Band
Yorkshire Jazz Band
Red River Jazzmen
Swinging Blue Genes
Sunday 13th Evening
Swinging Blue Genes
Terry Lightfoot's
New Orleans Jazz Band
Thursday 17th Evening
(Modern Jazz Session)
Kathy Stobart and The Glyn Evans
  Group
Friday 18th Evening
Sunset Seven Jazz Band
Hank Walters and The Dusty Road
  Ramblers

Saturday 19th Evening
Zenith Six Jazz Band
Rory Storm and The Hurricanes
Sunday 20th Evening
Alex Welsh Dixielanders
Swinging Blue Genes
Thursday 24th Evening
Wall City Jazzmen
Johnny Goode and The County
  Kinfolk
Saturday 26th Evening
Collegians Jazz Band
Hank Walters and The Dusty Road
  Ramblers
Sunday 27th Evening
Mick Mulligan Jazz Band
George Melly
Swinging Blue Genes
Thursday 31st All-Night Session
Micky Ashman Jazz Band
Yorkshire Jazz Band
Dallas Jazz Band
Swinging Blue Genes
Hank Walters and The Dusty Road
  Ramblers

1960

JANUARY
Friday 1st Evening
Cy Laurie Jazz Band
Swinging Blue Genes
Saturday 2nd Evening
Cy Laurie Jazz Band
Johnny Goode and The Country
  Kinfolk
Sunday 3rd Evening
Cy Laurie Jazz Band
Rory Storm and The Hurricanes
Thursday 7th Evening
(Modern Jazz Session)
Glynn Evans Quintet with The Ken
  O'Hara Trio
Friday 8th Evening
Red River Jazzmen
Southside Jazzmen
Little Bernie and The Drifting
  Cowboys
Saturday 9th Evening
Saints Jazz Band
Rory Storm and The Hurricanes
Terry Lightfoot's New Orleans Jazz
  Band
Sunday 10th Evening
(Liverpool Jazz Festival)
Acker Bilk's Paramount Jazz Band
Swinging Blue Genes

Monday 11th Evening
Hank Walters and The Dusty Road
  Ramblers
Tuesday 12th Evening
Alex Welsh Jazz Band
Wednesday 13th Evening
Saints Jazz Band
Collegians Jazz Band
Swinging Blue Genes
Thursday 14th Evening
(Modern Jazz Session)
All Star Modern Jazz Session
Johnny Duncan and The Blue Grass
  Boys
Friday 15th Evening
Merseysippi Jazz Band with Clinton
  Ford
Hank Walters and The Dusty road
  Ramblers
Johnny Goode and The Country
  Kinfolk
Saturday 16th Evening
Ken Colyer's Jazzmen
Johnny Goode and The Country
  Kinfolk
Sunday 17th Evening
Micky Ashman's Jazz Band
Swinging Blue Genes
Rory Storm and The Hurricanes
Thursday 21st Evening
(Modern Jazz Session)
Ronnie Ross
Eddie Thompson Trio
Friday 22nd Evening
Dallas Jazz Band
Little Bernie and The Drifting
  Cowboys
Saturday 23rd Evening
Sonny Morris Jazz Band
Johnny Goode and The Country
  Kinfolk
Sunday 24th Evening
Sonny Morris Jazz Band
Swinging Blue Genes
Thursday 28th Evening
(Modern Jazz Session)
Betty Smith Quintet
Friday 29th Evening
Johnny Tippett Jazzmen
Saturday 30th All-Night Session
Bob Wallis Jazz Band
Storeyville Jazz Band
Saints Jazz Band
Johnny Goode and The Country
  Kinfolk
Swinging Blue Genes
Hank Walters and The Dusty Road
  Ramblers

Sunday 31st Evening
Bob Wallis Jazz Band
Swinging Blue Genes

FEBRUARY
Thursday 4th Evening
(Modern Jazz Session)
Tubby Hayes Quintet
Friday 5th Evening
Sunset Seven Jazz Band
Johnny Goode and The Country
   Kinfolk
Saturday 6th Evening
Nat Gonella (The Great)
Red River Jazzmen
Sunday 7th Evening
Nat Gonella
Swinging Blue Genes
Thursday 11th Evening
(Modern Jazz Session)
Bert Courtley
Kathy Stobart
Eddie Thompson Trio
Friday 12th Evening
John Tippett Jazzmen
Eric Bell and his group
Saturday 13th Evening
Wall City Jazzmen
Johnny Goode and The Country
   Kinfolk
Sunday 14th Evening
Clyde Valley Stompers
Swinging Blue Genes
Thursday 18th Evening
(Modern Jazz Session)
The Jazzmakers
Ronnie Ross
Alan Ganley
Art Ellefson
Keith Christie
Friday 19th Evening
Wolverines Jazz Band
Swinging Blue Genes
Saturday 20th Evening
Zenith Six Jazz Band
Rory Storm and The Hurricanes
Sunday 21st Evening
Alex Welsh Jazz Band
Swinging Blue Genes
Thursday 25th Evening
(Modern Jazz Session)
Harry Klein
Pete King
Eddie Thompson Trio
Friday 26th Evening
Southside Jazzmen
Dale Roberts and The Jaywalkers
Saturday 27th Evening
Graham Stewart's New Orleans Six

Swinging Blue Genes
Sunday 28th Evening
Graham Stewart's New Orleans Six
Johnny Goode and The Country
   Kinfolk

MARCH
Thursday 3rd Evening
(Modern Jazz Session)
Vic Ashe
Jimmy Deuchar
Ken O'Hara Trio
Friday 4th Evening
Saints Jazz Band
Hank Walters and The Dusty Road
   Ramblers
Saturday 5th Evening
Yorkshire Jazz Band
Swinging Blue Genes
Sunday 6th Evening
Jessie Fuller
Terry Lightfoot's New Orleans
   Jazzmen
Thursday 10th Evening
(Modern Jazz Session)
Kenny Baker
Harry Klein
Alan Branscombe
Ken O'Hara Trio
Friday 11th Evening
Sonny Morris Jazzmen
Hank Walters and The Dusty Road
   Ramblers
Saturday 12th Evening
Sony Morris Jazzmen
Rory Storm and The Hurricanes
Sunday 13th Evening
Sonny Morris Jazzmen
Swinging Blue Genes
Thursday 17th Evening
(Modern Jazz Session)
The Jazzmakers
Ronnie Ross
Allan Ganley
Art Ellefson
Keith Christie
Friday 18th Evening
Wall City Jazzmen with Frank Knight
   and the Barons
Saturday 19th All-Night Session
Cisco Houston
Dick Charlesworth Big City Gents
Zenith Six Jazz Band
Johnny Goode and The Country
   Kinfolk
Hank Walters and The Dusty Road
   Ramblers
Sunday 20th Evening
Swinging Blue Genes

Clyde Valley Stompers
Thursday 24th All-Night Session
Tubby Hayes
Terry Shannon
Phil Seamen
Jeff Klein
Friday 25th Evening
Red River Jazzmen
Hank Walters and The Dusty Road
   Ramblers
Saturday 26th Evening
Nat Gonella and his Georgia Jazzmen
Johnny Goode and The Country
   Kinfolk
Sunday 27th Evening
Nat Gonella and his Georgia Jazzmen
Swinging Blue Genes
Thursday 31st Evening
Kenny Baker with Bill Le Sage

APRIL
Friday 1st Evening
Wolverines Jazz Band
Johnny Goode and The Country
   Kinfolk
Saturday 2nd Evening
Sunset Seven Jazz Band
Swinging Blue Genes
Sunday 3rd Evening
Humphrey Lyttelton Jazz Band
Hank Walters and The Dusty Road
   Ramblers
Thursday 7th Evening
(Modern Jazz Session)
Pete King Quartet
Friday 8th Evening
Red River Jazzmen
Saturday 9th All-Night Session
Sonny Morris Jazz Band
Yorkshire Jazz Band
Zenith Six Jazz Band
Sunday 10th Evening
Micky Ashman Ragtime Jazz Band
Swinging Blue Genes
Thursday 14th evening
(Modern Jazz Session)
Dill Jones Trio
Alan Branscombe
Friday 15th Evening
Collegians Jazz Band
Josh White
Saturday 16th Evening
Wall City Jazzmen
Hank Walters' Dusty Road Ramblers
Sunday 17th Evening
Johnny Goode and The Country
   Kinfolk
Mike Daniels
Delta Jazz Band

British trad jazz great Humphrey Lyttelton with *Merseyside Jazz* editor
Dave Eddie backstage at the Cavern in 1958. Lyttelton appeared at the
club on fourteen occasions.

Doreen Beatty
Monday 18th Evening
Cy Laurie Jazz Band
Swinging Blue Genes
Thursday 21st Evening
(Modern Jazz Session)
Tubby Hayes
Friday 22nd Evening
Chas McDevitt Four with Shirley
   Douglas
Southside Jazzmen
Saturday 23rd All-Night Session
Ken Colyer Jazz Band
Saints Jazz Band
Red River Jazzmen
Sunday 24th Evening
Ken Colyer Jazz Band
Swinging Blue Genes
Thursday 28th Evening
(Modern Jazz Session)
Vic Ashe
Harry Klein
Friday 29th Evening
Sunset Seven Jazz Band
Rory Storm and The Hurricanes
Saturday 30th Evening
Kenny Baker
Ken O'Hara Trio
Dizzy Burrows Jazz Aces

MAY
Sunday 1st Evening
Sister Rosetta Tharpe
Swinging Blue Genes
Micky Ashman's Ragtime Jazz Band
Thursday 5th Evening
(Modern Jazz Session)
Tony Kinsey Quintet
Friday 6th Evening
John Tippett Jazz Band
Hank Walters' Dusty Road Ramblers
Saturday 7th All-Night Session
Terry Lightfoot's Jazzmen
Sonny Morris Jazz Band
Collegians Jazz Band
Johnny Goode and The Country
   Kinfolk
Swinging Blue Genes
Sunday 8th Evening
Swinging Blue Genes
Terry Lightfoot's Jazzmen
Sonny Morris Jazz Band
Thursday 12th Evening
(Modern Jazz Session)
Tubby Hayes
Friday 13th Evening
Red River Jazzmen
Hank Walters
Dusty Road Ramblers
Saturday 14th All-Night Session
Bob Wallis Storeyville Jazz Band
Sunset Seven Jazz Band

Wall City Jazzmen
Johnny Goode and The Country
    Kinfolk
Black Cat Skiffle Group
Sunday 15th Evening
Bob Wallis Storeyville Jazz Band
Swinging Blue Genes
Thursday 19th Evening
(Modern Jazz Session)
Ross and Courtley Jazztet
Friday 20th Evening
Dallas Jazz Band
Dale Roberts and The Jaywalkers
Saturday 21st Evening
The Saints Jazz Band
Johnny Goode and The Country
    Kinfolk
Sims Wheeler Vintage Jazz Band
Swinging Blue Genes
Wednesday 25th Evening
(Rock Night)
Cass and The Cassanovas
Rory Storm and The Hurricanes
Thursday 26th Evening
(Modern Jazz Session)
Alan Branscombe
Ken O'Hara Trio
Friday 27th Evening
Sunset Seven Jazz Band
Johnny Goode and The Country
    Kinfolk
Saturday 28th Evening
Red River Jazzmen
Black Cat Rhythm Group
Sunday 29th Evening
Sonny Morris Jazz Band
Swinging Blue Genes

JUNE
Wednesday 1st Evening
(Direct from the Cliff Richard Show)
Billy Woods Five plus Rory Storm
    and The Hurricanes
Thursday 2nd Evening
(Modern Jazz Session)
Ken O'Hara Trio
Bobbie Wellins
Friday 3rd Evening
John Tippett Jazzmen
Vermont Quartet and Paul
Saturday 4th Evening
Yorkshire Jazz Band
Johnny Goode and The Country
    Kinfolk
Sunday 5th Evening
Pete Haslan's Collegians
Swinging Blue Genes
Thursday 9th Evening
(Modern Jazz Session)

Vic Ashe
Ken O'Hara Trio
Friday 10th Evening
Johnny Duncan and The Blue Grass
    Boys
Southside Jazzmen
Saturday 11th Evening
Red River Jazzmen
Johnny Goode and The Country
    Kinfolk
Sunday 12th Evening
Speckled Red (American blues singer
    and pianist)
Alex Welsh Jazz Band
Wednesday 15th Evening
(Rock Night)
Cass and The Cassanovas
Eddie Storm and The Clubmen
Thursday 16th Evening
(Modern Jazz Session)
Don Rendell
Keith Christie
Eddie Thompson Trio
Friday 17th Evening
Sunset Seven Jazz Band
The Hillbilly Bandits
Saturday 18th Evening
Zenith Six Jazz Band
Johnny Goode and The Country
    Kinfolk
Sunday 19th Evening
Swinging Blue Genes
The Saints Jazz Band
Wednesday 22nd Evening
Dale Roberts and The Jaywalkers
Danny Le Roy and The Tornados
Thursday 23rd Evening
(Modern Jazz Session)
Ken O'Hara Trio
Don Rendell
Friday 24th Evening
Red River Jazz Band
Hank Walters' Dusty Road Ramblers
Saturday 25th Evening
Sonny Morris
Johnny Goode and The Country
    Kinfolk
Sunday 26th Evening
Wall City Jazzmen
Swinging Blue Genes
Wednesday 29th Evening
Cass and The Cassanovas
Dale Roberts and The Jaywalkers
Thursday 30th Evening
(Modern Jazz Session)
Kenny Baker
Ken O'Hara Trio

JULY
Friday 1st Evening
Wolverines Jazz Band
Saturday 2nd Evening
Zenith Six Jazz Band
Johnny Goode and The Country
    Kinfolk
Sunday 3rd Evening
Red River Jazzmen
Swinging Blue Genes
Wednesday 6th Evening
(Rock Night)
Dale Roberts and The Jaywalkers
Wump and his Werbles
Thursday 7th Evening
(Modern Jazz Session)
Ross and Courtley Jazztet
Friday 8th Evening
Southside Jazzmen
Hank Walters and The Dusty Road
    Ramblers
Saturday 9th Evening
Wall City Jazzmen
Johnny Goode and The Country
    Kinfolk
Sunday 10th Evening
Humphrey Lyttelton Jazz Band
Swinging Blue Genes
Wednesday 13th Evening
Black Cat Rhythm group
The Delcados
Thursday 14th Evening
(Modern Jazz Session)
Ken O'Hara Trio
Friday 15th Evening
Sunset Seven Jazz Band
Saturday 16th Evening
Red River Jazzmen
Dusty Road Ramblers
Hank Walters
Sunday 17th Evening
Alex Welsh Jazz Band
Swinging Blue Genes
Wednesday 20th Evening
The Remo Quartet
Danny Leroy and The Tornados
Thursday 21st Evening
(Modern Jazz Session)
Kenny Baker
Ken O'Hara Trio
Saturday 23rd Evening
Zenith Six Jazz Band
Johnny Goode and The Country
    Kinfolk
Sunday 24th Evening
Micky Ashman's Ragtime Jazz Band
Swinging Blue Genes
Wednesday 27th Evening
Remo Quartet

Saturday 30th Evening
Yorkshire Jazz Band
Sunday 31st Evening
Clyde Valley Stompers
Fiona Duncan
Swinging Blue Genes

AUGUST
Wednesday 3rd Evening
Dale Roberts and The Jaywalkers
Thursday 4th Evening
(Modern Jazz Session)
Kathy Stobart
Ken O'Hara Trio
Friday 5th Evening
Sunset Seven Jazz Band
Saturday 6th Evening
Wall City Jazzmen
Hank Walters
Dusty Road Ramblers
Sunday 7th Evening
Swinging Blue Genes
Sims Wheeler Vintage Jazz Band
Wednesday 10th Evening
Dale Roberts and The Jaywalkers
The Remo Quartet
Thursday 11th Evening
(Modern Jazz Session)
Harry Klein
Tommy Smith
Ken O'Hara Trio
Friday 12th Evening
John Tippett Jazzmen
Saturday 13th Evening
Yorkshire Jazz Band
Sunday 14th Evening
Nat Gonella and his Georgia Jazz
    Band
Thursday 18th Evening
(Modern Jazz Session)
The Jazzmakers
Allan Ganley
Keith Christie
A. Wattis
Stan Robinson
Johnny Burcia
Friday 19th Evening
Wolverines Jazz Band
Saturday 20th Evening
Collegians Jazz Band
Sunday 21st Evening
Sonny Morris Jazz Band
Friday 26th Evening
Southern Jazzmen
Saturday 27th Evening
Sunset Seven Jazz Band
Johnny Goode and The Country
    Kinfolk

Sunday 28th Evening
Terry Lightfoot's Jazz Band
Swinging Blue Genes
Wednesday 31st Evening
(Rock Night)
Dave Samson and The Hunters
Remo Quartet
The Royal Bros
Dale Roberts and The Jaywalkers

SEPTEMBER
Thursday 1st Evening
(Modern Jazz Session)
Harold McNair
Ken O'Hara Trio
Friday 2nd Evening
John Tippett Jazz Band
The Vigilantes
Saturday 3rd Evening
Zenith Six Jazz Band
Johnny Goode and The Country
    Kinfolk
Sunday 4th Evening
Swinging Blue Genes
The Saints Jazz Band
Wednesday 7th Evening
Black Cat Rhythm Group
Nick Olsen and The Aces
Thursday 8th Evening
(Modern Jazz Session)
Ken O'Hara Trio
Tommy Smith
Ernie Tomasso
Friday 9th Evening
Red River Jazzmen
Saturday 10th Evening
Yorkshire Jazz Band
Sunday 11th Evening
Sonny Morris Jazz Band
Wednesday 14th Evening
Dale Roberts and The Jaywalkers
Remo Quartet
The Royal Bros
Thursday 15th Evening
(Modern Jazz Session)
Ken O'Hara Trio
Friday 16th Evening
Southside Jazzmen
Saturday 17th Evening
Riverboat Shuffle on board Royal Iris
(After Shuffle All-Night Session)
Acker Bilk Paramount Jazz Band
Red River Jazzmen
Terry Lightfoot
Swinging Blue Genes
Johnny Goode and The Country
    Kinfolk
Sunday 18th Evening
Swinging Blue Genes

Sims Wheelar Vintage Jazz Band
Thursday 22nd Evening
(Modern Jazz Session)
Ken O'Hara Trio
Friday 23rd Evening
Sunset Seven Jazz Band
Hank Walters' Dusty Road Ramblers
Saturday 24th Evening
Johnny Goode and The Country
   Kinfolk
Red River Jazzmen
Sunday 25th Evening
Ken Colyer Jazz Band
Swinging Blue Genes
Wednesday 28th Evening
Dale Roberts and The Jaywalkers
Remo Quartet
Thursday 29th Evening
(Modern Jazz Session)
Ken O'Hara Trio
Friday 30th Evening
Southside Jazzmen

OCTOBER
Saturday 1st Evening
Clayton Jones
Sunday 2nd Evening
Clyde Valley Stompers
Fiona Duncan
Wednesday 5th Evening
(Rock Night)
Duke Duval
Gerry and the Pacemakers
Ray Walker and The Del Renas
Thursday 6th Evening
(Modern Jazz Session)
Kathy Stobart
Ken O'Hara Trio
Friday 7th Evening
Sunset Seven Jazz Band
Saturday 8th Evening
Red River Jazzmen
Julie Kaye
Sunday 9th Evening
Nat Gonella and The New Georgians
   Jazz Band
Swinging Blue Genes
Wednesday 12th Evening
Remo Quartet
Dale Roberts and The Jaywalkers
Thursday 13th Evening
(Modern Jazz Session)
The Jazzmakers
Allan Ganley
Keith Christie
Stan Robinson
Friday 14th Evening
John Tippett Jazzmen
Julie Kaye

Connaughts Jazz Band
Saturday 15th Evening
Pete Haslam's Collegians Jazz Band
Julie Kaye
Johnny Goode and The Country
   Kinfolk
Sunday 16th Evening
Ken Colyer Jazz Band
Swinging Blue Genes
Wednesday 19th Evening
Cass and The Cassanovas
Ray Walker and The Delrenas
Thursday 20th Lunchtime
Tommy Lowe and The Metronomes
Evening
(Modern Jazz Session)
Jimmy Skidmore
Ken O'Hara Trio
Friday 21st Lunchtime
Tommy Lowe and The Metronomes
Evening
Wolverines Jazz Band
Noel Walker Stompers
Saturday 22nd Evening
The Saints Jazz Band
Sunday 23rd Evening
Micky Ashman's Ragtime Jazz Band
Swinging Blue Genes
Wednesday 26th Lunchtime
Cass and The Cassanovas
Evening
Dale Roberts and The Jaywalkers
Remo Quartet
Thursday 27th Lunchtime
Tommy Lowe and The Metronomes
Evening
(Modern Jazz Session)
Don Rendell
Ken O'Hara Trio
Friday 28th Evening
Sunset Seven Jazz Band
Connaughts Jazz Band
Saturday 29th All-Night Session
Yorkshire Jazz Band
Sonny Morris
Red River Jazzmen
Hank Walters and The Dusty Road
   Ramblers
Sunday 30th Evening
Swinging Blue Genes
Humphrey Lyttelton Jazz Band

NOVEMBER
Wednesday 2nd Evening
Lance Fortune (backed by The
   Jaywalkers)
Cass and The Cassanovas
Nick Olsen and The Aces

Thursday 3rd Evening
(Modern Jazz Session)
Don Rendell
Ken O'Hara Trio
Kenny Baker
Friday 4th Evening
Southside Jazzmen
Irene and Santa Fe's
Saturday 5th Evening
Clayton Jones Jazzmen
Johnny Goode and The Country
   Kinfolk
Sunday 6th Evening
Pete Ridge Jazz Band
Swinging Blue Genes
Wednesday 9th Evening
Remo Quartet
Dale Roberts and The Jaywalkers
Thursday 10th Evening
(Modern Jazz Session)
The Jazz Five
Vic Ashe
Harry Klein
Sunset Seven Jazzmen
Noel Walker's Stompers
Saturday 12th Evening
Wall City Jazzmen
Johnny Goode and The Country
   Kinfolk
Sunday 13th Evening
Cy Charlie Jazz Band
Swinging Blue Genes
Wednesday 16th Evening
Emile Ford and The Checkmates
Gerry and the Pacemakers
Cass and The Cassanovas
Thursday 17th Evening
(Modern Jazz Session)
Kenny Baker
Ken O'Hara Trio
Friday 18th Evening
Red River Jazzmen
Saturday 19th Evening
Saints Jazz Band
Sunday 20th Evening
Alex Welsh Jazz Band
Swinging Blue Genes
Wednesday 23rd Evening
Remo Quartet
Dale Roberts and The Jaywalkers
Thursday 24th Evening
(Modern Jazz Session)
Ross and Courtley
Friday 25th Evening
John Tippett Jazz Band
Saturday 26th All-Night Session
Yorkshire Jazz Band
Zenith Six Jazz Band
Collegians Jazz Band

Swinging Blue Genes
Hank Walters and The Dusty Road
   Ramblers
Johnny Goode and The Country
   Kinfolk
Sunday 27th Evening
Micky Ashman Jazz Band
Swinging Blue Genes
Wednesday 30th Evening
Gerry and the Pacemakers
Cass and The Cassanovas

DECEMBER
Thursday 1st Evening
(Modern Jazz Session)
Betty Smith Quintet
Friday 2nd Evening
Papa Blues Viking
(Denmark's Top Group)
Saturday 3rd Evening
Clayton Jones Jazz Band
Sunday 4th Evening
Humphrey Lyttelton Jazz Band
Swinging Blue Genes
Thursday 8th Evening
(Modern Jazz Session)
Ken O'Hara Trio
Friday 9th Evening
Sunset Seven Jazz Band
Connaughts Jazz Band
Saturday 10th Evening
Collegians Jazz Band
Sunday 11th Evening
Ray Ellington with Carol Simpson
Swinging Blue Genes
Tuesday 13th Lunchtime
J. Siler Sextet
Wednesday 14th Evening
John Barry Seven
Duke Duval
Cass and The Cassanovas
Thursday 15th Evening
(Modern Jazz Session)
Tubby Hayes
Friday 16th Evening
Wolverines Jazz Band
Saturday 17th All-Night Session
Zenith Six Jazz Band
Terry Lightfoot's Jazzmen
Swinging Blue Genes
Johnny Goode and The Country
   Kinfolk
Clyde Valley Stompers
Hank Walters and The Dusty Road
   Ramblers
Sunday 18th Evening
Swinging Blue Genes
Terry Lightfoot's Jazzmen

Wednesday 21st Evening
Remo Quartet
Dale Roberts and The Jaywalkers
Thursday 22nd Evening
(Modern Jazz Session)
Ken O'Hara Trio
Friday 23rd Evening
Sunset Seven Jazz Band
Blue Mountain Boys
Saturday 24th Evening
Yorkshire Jazz Band
Hill Billy Bandits
Monday 26th Evening
Charlie Gall Jazz Band
Johnny Goode and The Country
   Kinfolk
Tuesday 27th Evening
John Tippett Jazz Band
Swinging Blue Genes
Wednesday 28th Evening
Remo Quartet
Dale Roberts and The Jaywalkers
Friday 30th Evening
Sunset Seven Jazz Band
Blue Mountain Boys
Saturday 31st All Night Carnival
Yorkshire Jazz Band
Clayton Jones Jazz Band
Johnny Goode and The Country
   Kinfolk
After Midnight
Swinging Blue Genes
Hank Walters' Dusty Road Ramblers

1961

JANUARY
Sunday 1st Evening
Sims Wheelar Jazz Band
Swinging Blue Genes
Wednesday 4th Evening
Remo Quartet
Dale Roberts and The Jaywalkers
Thursday 5th Evening
The Bohemian Quintet
Friday 6th Evening
Sunset Seven Jazz Band
Saturday 7th Evening
Wall City Jazzmen
Johnny Goode and The Country
   Kinfolk
Sunday 8th Evening
Micky Ashman
Swinging Blue Jeans
Wednesday 11th Evening
Tommy Lowe and The Metronomes
Johnny Rocco and The Jets

This card is to be shown at all meetings attended, to the Door Staff and also to the Desk Staff, and any other Club Official on demand.

●

A member who does not produce his or her Membership Card must "sign in" as a visitor.

Cards and passes are not transferable. Anyone found using another person's Card or Pass will be liable to be barred from the Club.

●

This card does not guarantee admission if the management deems the premises full, or for any other reason.

THE MERSEYSIDE PRINTING CO.
21, DALE STREET - - LIVERPOOL, 2
TELEPHONE : CENTRAL 4895

THE Cavern CLUB

MEMBERSHIP CARD
1961 SEASON

Ending 31st December, 1961

A 1961 Cavern membership card.

Thursday 12th Evening
Tubby Hayes
Friday 13th Evening
Wolverines
Connaughts Jazz Band
Saturday 14th Evening
The Red River Jazzmen
Johnny Goode and The Country
   Kinfolk
Sunday 15th Evening
Terry Lightfoot's New Orleans
   Jazzmen
Swinging Blue Genes
Wednesday 18th Lunchtime
Liverpool's Fender Men
Remo Quartet
Evening
The Shadows
Dale Roberts and The Jaywalkers
Thursday 19th Evening
Art Reid's Sextet
Saturday 21st Evening
The Saints Jazz Band
Sunday 22nd Evening
Eric Allandale's New Orleans Knights
Wednesday 25th Evening
Kingsize Taylor and The Dominoes
The Pressmen
Saturday 28th Evening
The Zenith Six Jazz Sand
Johnny Goode and The Country
   Kinfolk

Sunday 29th Evening
Cy Laurie Jazz Band led by Terry Pitts
Swinging Blue Genes

FEBRUARY
Thursday 2nd Evening
The Jazz Five
Vic Ashe
Harry Klein
Brian Dee
Malcolm Cecil
Lennie Bresuau
Friday 3rd Evening
Sunset Seven Jazz Band
Saturday 4th Evening
The Collegians Jazz Band
Sunday 5th Evening
Alex Welsh and His Band
Swinging Blue Genes
Wednesday 8th Evening
The Skyliners
Gus and The Thunderclaps
Thursday 9th Evening
Art Reid's Sextet
Friday 10th Evening
Kenny Ball's Jazzmen
Clinton Ford
Blue Mountain Boys
Saturday 11th All-Night Session
Kenny Ball's Jazzmen
Clinton Ford
Swinging Blue Genes
Yorkshire Jazzband

Johnny Goode and The Country
   Kinfolk
Sunday 12th Evening
Bob Wallis
Storeyville Jazzmen
Swinging Blue Genes
Wednesday 15th Evening
Remo Quartet
Dale Roberts and The Jaywalkers
Thursday 16th Evening
Jimmy Skidmore
Art Reid's Sextet
Friday 17th Evening
Pete Haslam's Collegians Jazz Band
Hank Walters' Dusty Road Ramblers
Saturday 18th Evening
Red River Jazzmen
Johnny Goode and The Country
   Kinfolk
Sunday 19th Evening
Ken Colyer Jazzmen with Bobby
   Breen
Swinging Blue Genes
Tuesday 21st Lunchtime
The Beatles (George Harrison's
   Cavern debut, Stuart Sutcliffe's only
   Cavern appearance)
Evening
(Blue Genes Guest Night)
Remo Quartet
Wednesday 22nd Lunchtime
Derry and The Seniors
Evening
Kingsize Taylor and The Dominoes
Cliff Roberts and The Rockers
Thursday 23rd Lunchtime
Gerry and the Pacemakers
Evening
Tubby Hayes
Friday 24th Lunchtime
The Big Three
Evening
Pete Ridge Band
Saturday 25th Evening
White Eagles Jazz Band
Sunday 26th Evening
Cy Laurie Jazz Band led by Terry
   Pitts
Tuesday 28th Evening
(Blue Genes' Guest Night)
Derry and The Seniors

MARCH
Wednesday 1st Evening
Dale Roberts and The Jaywalkers
The Four Jays
Thursday 2nd Evening
Johnny Dankworth and his full band
Bobby Breen

Friday 3rd Evening
Wall City Jazzmen with Pat Field
Saturday 4th Evening
Clayton Jones Jazz Bend
Sunday 5th Evening
Alex Welsh Jazz Band
Monday 6th Lunchtime
The Beatles
Tuesday 7th Lunchtime
The Big Three
Evening
(Blue Genes' Guest Night)
Dale Roberts and The Jaywalkers
Wednesday 8th Lunchtime
The Beatles
Evening
Gerry and the Pacemakers
Faron's Tempest Tornados
Johnny Rocco and The Jets
Thursday 9th Lunchtime
Derry and The Seniors
Evening
Ronnie Ross
Art Reid
Friday 10th Lunchtime
The Beatles
Evening
Wall City Jazzmen
Hank Walters and The Dusty Road
   Ramblers
Saturday 11th Evening
The Saints Jazz Band
Johnny Goode and The Country
   Kinfolk
Sunday 12th Evening
Humphrey Lyttelton Jazz Band
Swinging Blue Genes
Monday 13th Lunchtime
(Sessions all week with compère Bob
   Wooler)
Derry and The Seniors
Tommy Lowes Metronomes
Tuesday 14th Lunchtime
The Beatles
Evening
(Blue Genes' Guest Night)
The Four Jays
Gerry and the Pacemakers
Wednesday 15th Lunchtime
The Beatles
Evening
Dale Roberts and The Jaywalkers
Gerry and the Pacemakers
Thursday 16th Lunchtime
The Beatles
Evening
Bert Courtley with Ken O'Hara's
   Half Dozen

Friday 17th Evening
Red River Jazzmen
Ray and The Delrenas
Gerry and the Pacemakers
Saturday 18th Evening
The Collegians Jazz Band
Johnny Goode and The Country
   Kinfolk
Sunday 19th Evening
Micky Ashman's Ragtime Jazz Band
Swinging Blue Genes
Monday 20th Lunchtime
The Beatles
Tuesday 21st Lunchtime
Cliff Robert and The Rockers
Derry and The Seniors
Evening
(Blue Genes' Guest Night)
Remo Quartet
Dale Roberts and The Jaywalkers
The Beatles (first evening
   performance)
Wednesday 22nd Lunchtime
The Beatles
Evening
(Rock Night)
Derry and The Seniors
The Four Jays
Cliff Roberts and The Rockers
Thursday 23rd Lunchtime
Derry and The Seniors
Evening
Tommy Whittle
Ken O'Hara's Half Dozen
Friday 24th Lunchtime
The Beatles
Evening
White Eagles Jazz Band
Blue Mountain Boys
Saturday 25th Evening
Yorkshire Jazz Band
Johnny Goode and The Country
   Kinfolk
Sunday 26th Evening
Ken Colyer's Jazzmen
Swinging Blue Genes
Tuesday 28th Evening
(Blue Genes' Guest Night)
The Pressmen
Kingsize Taylor and The Dominoes
Wednesday 29th Evening
Dale Roberts and The Jaywalkers
Remo Quartet
Kingsize Taylor and The Dominoes
Thursday 30th Evening
Jazzmakers
Allan Ganley
Keith Christie
Stan Robinson

Friday 31st Evening
Alex Welsh Jazz Band
Remo Four

APRIL
Saturday 1st Evening
Zenith Six Jazz Band
Johnny Goode and The Country
  Kinfolk
Sunday 2nd Evening
Cy Laurie Jazz Band led by Terry
  Pitts
Swinging Blue Genes
Tuesday 4th Evening
(Blue Genes' Guest Night)
Remo Four
Dale Roberts and The Jaywalkers
Wednesday 5th Evening
The Pressmen
The Searchers
Thursday 6th Evening
Johnny Scott
Ken O'Hara's Half Dozen
Friday 7th Evening
Bob Wallis and The Storeyville
  Jazzmen
Dale Roberts and The Jaywalkers
Saturday 8th Evening
Zenith Six Jazz Band
Sunday 9th Evening
Humphrey Lyttelton Jazz Band
Swinging Blue Genes
Tuesday 11th Evening
(Blue Genes' Guest Night)
The Four Jays
Kingsize Taylor and The Dominoes
Wednesday 12th Evening
Remo Quartet
Dale Roberts and The Jaywalkers
Thursday 13th Evening
Joe Harriot Quintet
Friday 14th Evening
Wall City Jazzmen
Saturday 15th Evening
The Saints Jazz Band
Sunday 16th Evening
Clyde Valley Stompers
Tuesday 18th Evening
(Blue Genes' Guest Night)
Johnny Sandon and The Searchers
Remo Quartet
Wednesday 19th Evening
The Pressmen
Faron's Tempest Tornados
Friday 21st Evening
Yorkshire Jazz Band
Kingsize Taylor and The Dominoes
Saturday 22nd Evening
Red River Jazzmen

Gerry and the Pacemakers
Sunday 23rd Evening
Nat Gonella's Georgians
Swinging Blue Genes
Tuesday 25th Evening
(Blue Genes' Guest Night)
Gerry and the Pacemakers
Robin and The Ravens
Wednesday 26th Evening
Remo Quartet
Dale Roberts and The Jaywalkers
Friday 28th Evening
Mike Cotton Jazz Band (formerly
  Pete Ridge Band)
Saturday 29th All-Night Session
Red River Jazzmen
Wall City Jazzmen
Collegians Jazz Band
Swinging Blue Genes
Gerry and the Pacemakers
Remo Four
Sunday 30th Evening
Terry Lightfoot's New Orleans
  Jazzmen
Swinging Blue Genes
Kenny Baker

MAY
Tuesday 2nd Evening
(Blue Genes' Guest Night)
Remo Quartet
The Pressmen
Wednesday 3rd Evening
The Four Jays
Kingsize Taylor and The Dominoes
Friday 5th Evening
Collegians Jazz Band
Gerry and the Pacemakers
Saturday 6th Evening
The White Eagles Jazz Band
Ian and The Zodiacs
Sunday 7th Evening
New Orleans Knights led by Eric
  Allen
Dale Roberts and The Jaywalkers
Swinging Blue Genes
Tuesday 9th Evening
(Blue Genes' Guest Night)
Gerry and the Pacemakers
Kingsize Taylor and The Dominoes
Wednesday 10th Evening
Dale Roberts and The Jaywalkers
Remo Quartet
Friday 12th Evening
Yorkshire Jazz Band
Saturday 13th Evening
Zenith Six Jazz Band
Remo Four

Sunday 14th Evening
Mac Duncan Jazz Band
Swinging Blue Genes
Monday 15th Lunchtime
Gerry and the Pacemakers
Tuesday 16th Lunchtime
Cliff Roberts and The Rockers
Evening
(Blue Genes' Guest Night)
Remo Four
Ian and The Zodiacs
Wednesday 17th Lunchtime
Remo Four
Evening
Gerry and the Pacemakers
Johnny Sandon and The Searchers
Frank Knight and The Barons
Thursday 18th Lunchtime
The Big Three
Friday 19th Lunchtime
Gerry and the Pacemakers
Evening
Kingsize Taylor and The Dominoes
River Red Jazzmen
Saturday 20th Evening
Casey's Hot Seven Jazz Band
Johnny Sandon and The Searchers
Sunday 21st Evening
Alex Welsh Jazz Band
Swinging Blue Genes
Monday 22nd Evening
Acker Bilk's Paramount Jazz Band
Tuesday 23rd Lunchtime
Gerry and the Pacemakers
Wednesday 24th Lunchtime
Johnny Sandon and The Searchers
Thursday 25th Lunchtime
The Big Three
Friday 26th Lunchtime
Cliff Roberts and The Rockers
Evening
Johnny Sandon and The Searchers
Wall City Jazzmen
Saturday 27th Evening
The Collegians Jazz Band
Kingsize Taylor and The Dominoes
Sunday 28th Evening
Clyde Valley Stompers
Swinging Blue Genes
Monday 29th Lunchtime
Gerry and the Pacemakers
Tuesday 30th Lunchtime
Cliff Roberts and The Rockers
Evening
(Blue Genes' Guest Night)
Remo Four
Johnny Sandon and The Searchers
Wednesday 31st Lunchtime
Robin and The Ravens

Evening
Gerry and the Pacemakers
The Pressmen
The Strangers

JUNE
Thursday 1st Lunchtime
The Big Three
Friday 2nd Lunchtime
Gerry and the Pacemakers
Evening
Yorkshire Jazz Band
Ian and The Zodiacs
Saturday 3rd Evening
Kenny Ball's Jazzmen
Gerry and the Pacemakers
Sunday 4th Evening
Charlie Galbraith Jazz Band
Swinging Blue Genes
Monday 5th Lunchtime
Cliff Roberts and The Rockers
Tuesday 6th Lunchtime
Gerry and the Pacemakers
Evening
(Blue Genes' Guest Night)
Four Jays
Kingsize Taylor and The Dominoes
Wednesday 7th Lunchtime
Cliff Roberts and The Rockers
Evening
Remo Four
Dale Roberts and The Jaywalkers

Thursday 8th Lunchtime
The Big Three
Friday 9th Lunchtime
Gerry and the Pacemakers
Evening
The Saints Jazz Band
Gerry and the Pacemakers
Saturday 10th Evening
Zenith Six Jazz Band
Sunday 11th Evening
Mike Clayton's Jazzmen
Swinging Blue Genes
Monday 12th Lunchtime
Gerry and the Pacemakers
Tuesday 13th Lunchtime
The Big Three
Evening
(Blue Genes' Guest Night)
Remo Four
Gerry and the Pacemakers
Wednesday 14th Lunchtime
Johnny Sandon and The Searchers
Evening
Kingsize Taylor and The Dominoes
Johnny Sandon and The Searchers
The Decker Rhythm Group
Thursday 15th Lunchtime
Gerry and the Pacemakers
Friday 16th Lunchtime
Gerry and the Pacemakers
Evening
The Collegians Jazz Band
Remo Four

AT THE CAVERN
10 Mathew St. off North John St.
TO-NIGHT: CLUB CLOSED
We'll all be on the
RIVERBOAT SHUFFLE
on M.V. ROYAL IRIS
7.45 from Landing Stage
Returning 11 p.m.
With MR. ACKER BILK'S
Paramount Jazz Band
And THE BEATLES
Tickets (8/6) on Sale at
CRANES. LEWIS'S. RUSHWORTHS AND
AT THE CAVERN
CENTRAL 1591

```
AT THE CAVERN
TO-NIGHT
THE GREAT
TUBBY HAYES QUARTET
FRIDAY AND SATURDAY:
BOB WALLIS'S
STORYVILLE JAZZ BAND
RIVERBOAT SHUFFLE
Aboard M.V. ROYAL IRIS
Friday, August 25.   7.45 p.m.
With MR. ACKER BILK'S
PARAMOUNT JAZZ BAND
AND THE BEATLES
Tickets (8 6) Now on Sale at
Lewis's, Cranes, Rushworth's and
AT THE CAVERN
CENTRAL 1591.
```

Saturday 17th Evening
The Saints Jazz Band
Gerry and the Pacemakers
Sunday 18th Evening
Cy Laurie Jazz Band led by Terry Pitts
Swinging Blue Genes
Monday 19th Lunchtime
Gerry and the Pacemakers
Tuesday 20th Lunchtime
The Big Three
Evening
(Blue Genes' Guest Night)
Dale Roberts and The Jaywalkers
Johnny Sandon and The Searchers
Wednesday 21st Lunchtime
Remo Four
Evening
Remo Four
The Four Jays
The Rockin' Blackcats
Thursday 22nd Lunchtime
Gerry and the Pacemakers
Friday 23rd Lunchtime
Gerry and the Pacemakers
Evening
The Saints Jazz Band
Remo Four
Saturday 24th Evening
Red River Jazzmen
Dale Roberts and The Jaywalkers
Sunday 25th Evening
Humphrey Lyttelton Jazz Band
Swinging Blue Genes

Monday 26th Lunchtime
Gerry and the Pacemakers
Tuesday 27th Lunchtime
The Big Three
Evening
(Blue Genes' Guest Night)
Gerry and the Pacemakers
Ian and The Zodiacs
Wednesday 28th Lunchtime
Gerry and the Pacemakers
Evening
Kingsize Taylor and The Dominoes
Robin and The Ravens
The Galvanizers
Thursday 29th Lunchtime
Mark Peters and The Cyclones
Friday 30th Lunchtime
Gerry and the Pacemakers
Evening
Yorkshire Jazz Band
The Strangers

JULY
Saturday 1st Evening
Ken Sims Vintage Jazz Band
Gerry and the Pacemakers
Sunday 2nd Evening
Ken Colyer's Jazzmen
Swinging Blue Genes
Tuesday 4th Evening
(Blue Genes' Guest Night)
Gerry and the Pacemakers
Johnny Sandon and The Searchers

Friday 7th Evening
Collegians Jazz Band
Kingsize Taylor and The Dominoes
Saturday 8th Evening
The Temperance Seven
The Saints Jazz Band
Sunday 9th Evening
Eric Allandale's New Orleans Knights
Swinging Blue Genes
Tuesday 11th Lunchtime
Gerry and the Pacemakers
Evening
(Blue Genes' Guest Night)
Remo Four
Gerry and the Pacemakers
Wednesday 12th Lunchtime
Gerry and the Pacemakers
Evening
Dale Roberts and The Jaywalkers
Mark Peters and The Cyclones
The Four Jays
Thursday 13th Lunchtime
Karl Terry and The Cruisers
Friday 14th Lunchtime
The Beatles
Evening
Ian and The Zodiacs
White Eagles Jazz Band
The Beatles
Monday 17th Lunchtime
The Beatles
Tuesday 18th Lunchtime
Gerry and the Pacemakers
Evening
(Blue Genes' Guest Night)
Gerry and the Pacemakers
Dale Roberts and The Jaywalkers
Wednesday 19th Lunchtime
The Beatles
Evening
The Beatles
Remo Four
Pressmen
Thursday 20th Lunchtime
Gerry and the Pacemakers
Friday 21st Lunchtime
The Beatles
Evening
Gerry and the Pacemakers
Yorkshire Jazz Band
Saturday 22nd Evening
The Saints Jazz Band
Ian and The Zodiacs
Sunday 23rd Evening
Terry Lightfoot's New Orleans Jazzmen
Swinging Blue Genes
Monday 24th Lunchtime
Gerry and the Pacemakers

Tuesday 25th Lunchtime
The Beatles
Evening
(Blue Genes' Guest Night)
The Beatles
Remo Four
Gerry and the Pacemakers
Wednesday 26th Lunchtime
Gerry and the Pacemakers
Evening
The Beatles
Johnny Sandon and The Searchers
The Four Jays
Thursday 27th Lunchtime
The Beatles
Friday 28th Lunchtime
Gerry and the Pacemakers
Evening
Collegians Jazz Band
Remo Four
Saturday 29th Evening
Mike Peters' Florida Jazz Band
Robin and The Ravens
Sunday 30th Evening
Micky Ashman's Ragtime Jazz Band
Swinging Blue Genes
Monday 31st Lunchtime
The Beatles

AUGUST
Tuesday 1st Lunchtime
The Strangers
Evening
(Blue Genes' Guest Night)
Remo Four
Ray and The Del Renas
Wednesday 2nd Lunchtime
The Beatles
Evening
Karl Terry and The Cruisers
The Beatles
Dale Roberts and The Jaywalkers
Thursday 3rd Lunchtime
The Hi Cats
Friday 4th Lunchtime
The Beatles
Evening
Red River Jazzmen
The Strangers
Saturday 5th All-Night Session
The Cimmarons
Panama Jazz Band
Mike Conan Jazz Band
Kenny Ball's Jazzmen
The Beatles
The Remo Four
Sunday 6th Evening
Mike Cotten Jazz Bend
The Remo Four

Tuesday 8th Lunchtime
The Beatles
Wednesday 9th Evening
The Beatles
Thursday 10th Lunchtime
The Beatles
Friday 11th Evening
The Beatles
Alan Elsdon's Jazz Band
Saturday 12th Evening
Zenith Six Jazz Band
Ian and The Zodiacs
Sunday 13th Evening
Mac Duncan's Jazz Band
Remo Four
Monday 14th Lunchtime
The Beatles
Tuesday 15th Lunchtime
Karl Terry and The Cruisers
Evening
Remo Four
The Four Jays
Kingsize Taylor and The Dominoes
Wednesday 16th Lunchtime
The Ravens
Evening
The Beatles
The Pressmen
Thursday 17th Lunchtime
The Hi Cats
Evening
Tubby Hayes
Friday 18th Lunchtime
The Beatles
Evening
Bob Wallis Storeyville Jazzmen
Saturday 19th Evening
Bob Wallis Storeyville Jazzmen
Sunday 20th Evening
Alex Revel's Jazz Band
The Four Jays
Monday 21st Lunchtime
The Beatles
Tuesday 22nd Evening
Johnny Sandon and The Searchers
The Four Jays
Carl Vincent and The Counts
Wednesday 23rd Lunchtime
The Beatles
Evening
The Beatles
The Rockin' Blackcats
Kingsize Taylor and The Dominoes
Friday 25th Lunchtime
The Beatles
River Boat Shuffle
The Beatles
Acker Bilk's Paramount Jazz Band

Saturday 26th Evening
Red River Jazzmen
Sunday 27th Evening
Micky Ashman's Ragtime Jazz Band
Monday 28th Lunchtime
The Beatles
Tuesday 29th Lunchtime
The Beatles
Evening
(Blue Genes' Guest Night)
Remo Four
Ian and The Zodiacs
Wednesday 30th Lunchtime
The Ravens
Evening
The Beatles
The Strangers
Thursday 31st Lunchtime
Karl Terry and The Cruisers

SEPTEMBER
Friday 1st Lunchtime
The Beatles
Evening
The Beatles
Dizzy Burton Jazz Band
Saturday 2nd Evening
Kenny Baker
Zenith Six Jazz Band
Sunday 3rd Evening
Clyde Valley Stompers
Monday 4th Lunchtime
Gerry and the Pacemakers
Tuesday 5th Lunchtime
The Beatles
Evening
Remo Four
Gerry and the Pacemakers
Wednesday 6th Lunchtime
Gerry and the Pacemakers
Evening
The Beatles
Johnny Sandon and The Searchers
Ian and The Zodiacs
Thursday 7th Lunchtime
The Beatles
Friday 8th Lunchtime
Gerry and the Pacemakers
Evening
Yorkshire Jazz Band
Karl Terry and The Cruisers
Saturday 9th Evening
Dick Williams and His Band
Gerry and the Pacemakers
Sunday 10th Evening
Len Baldwin's Dauphin St Six
Monday 11th Lunchtime
The Beatles

Tuesday 12th Lunchtime
Gerry and the Pacemakers
Evening
(Blue Genes' Guest Night)
Remo Four
Gerry and the Pacemakers
Johnny Sandon and The Searchers
Wednesday 13th Lunchtime
The Beatles
Evening
The Beatles
Remo Four
The Pressmen
Thursday 14th Lunchtime
Gerry and the Pacemakers
Friday 15th Lunchtime
The Beatles
Evening
The Collegians Jazz Band
The Remo Four
Saturday 16th Evening
White Eagles Jazz Bad
Gerry and the Pacemakers
Sunday 17th Evening
Doug Richford's Jazzmen
Swinging Blue Genes
Tuesday 19th Lunchtime
The Beatles
Evening
(Blue Genes' Guest Night)
Remo Four
Gerry and the Pacemakers
Wednesday 20th Evening
The Beatles
Karl Terry and The Cruisers
Ian and The Zodiacs
Thursday 21st Lunchtime
The Beatles
Evening
Eddie Harvey
Spike Heatley
Art Ellefson
Johnny Dankworth
Alan Ganley
Friday 22nd Evening
River Red Jazzmen
Johnny Sandon and The Searchers
Saturday 23rd Evening
The Saints Jazz Band
Gerry and the Pacemakers
Sunday 24th Evening
Ken Colyer's Jazzmen
Swinging Blue Genes
Monday 25th Lunchtime
The Beatles
Tuesday 26th Lunchtime
Gerry and the Pacemakers
Wednesday 27th Lunchtime
The Beatles

Evening
The Beatles
Gerry and the Pacemakers
Mark Peters and The Cyclones
Thursday 28th Lunchtime
Gerry and the Pacemakers
Friday 29th Lunchtime
The Beatles
Evening
Alan Elsdon Jazz Band
Remo Four
Gerry and the Pacemakers
The Collegians Jazz Band
Saturday 30th Evening
The Collegians Jazz Band
Gerry and the Pacemakers

OCTOBER
Sunday 1st Evening
Alex Welsh Jazz Band
Swinging Blue Genes
Tuesday 3rd Evening
(Blue Genes' Guest Night)
Gerry and the Pacemakers
Remo Four
Wednesday 4th Evening
Johnny Sandon and The Searchers
The Strangers
Kingsize Taylor and The Dominoes
Friday 6th Lunchtime
Ian and The Zodiacs
Yorkshire Jazz Band
Saturday 7th Evening
The Saints Jazz Band
The Four Jays
Sunday 8th Evening
Humphrey Lyttelton Jazz Band
Swinging Blue Genes
Tuesday 10th Evening
(Blue Genes' Guest Night)
Gerry and the Pacemakers
Kingsize Taylor and The Dominoes
Wednesday 11th Evening
Remo Four
Mark Peters and The Cyclones
Clay Ellis and The Raiders
Friday 13th Evening
Red River Jazzmen
Gerry and the Pacemakers
Saturday 14th Evening
Bob Wallis
Terry Lightfoot
Sonny Terry
Brownie McGhee
Sunday 15th Evening
The Melbourne New Orleans Jazz
   Band (from Australia)
Monday 16th Lunchtime
The Beatles

Tuesday 17th Lunchtime
Gerry and the Pacemakers
Evening
(Blue Genes' Guest Night)
Remo Four
Gerry and the Pacemakers
Wednesday 18th Lunchtime
The Beatles
Evening
The Beatles
Ian and The Zodiacs
The Four Jays
Thursday 19th Lunchtime
Gerry and the Pacemakers
Evening
Tubby Hayes
Friday 20th Lunchtime
The Beatles
Evening
The Saints Jazz Band
Gerry and the Pacemakers
Saturday 21st All-Night Session
The Beatles
Panama Jazz Band
Remo Four
Gerry and the Pacemakers
Yorkshire Jazz Band
The Collegians Jazz Band
Sunday 22nd Evening
Cyril Preston's Jazzmen
Swinging Blue Genes
Tuesday 24th Lunchtime
The Beatles
Evening
(Blue Genes' Guest Night)
Remo Four
Kingsize Taylor and The Dominoes
Wednesday 25th Evening
The Beatles
Gerry and the Pacemakers
The Strangers
Thursday 26th Lunchtime
The Beatles
Friday 27th Evening
Tony Smith Jazz Band
Gerry and the Pacemakers
Saturday 28th Evening
White Eagles Jazz Band
Johnny Sandon and The Searchers
Sunday 29th Evening
Terry Pitts Jazz Band
Swinging Blue Genes
Monday 30th Lunchtime
The Beatles
Tuesday 31st Evening
(Blue Genes' Guest Night)
Remo Four
Ian and The Zodiacs

NOVEMBER
Wednesday 1st Lunchtime
The Beatles
Evening
The Beatles
The Strangers
Gerry and the Pacemakers
Friday 3rd Lunchtime
The Beatles
Evening
The Saints Jazz Band
Gerry and the Pacemakers
Saturday 4th Evening
The Beatles
The Collegians Jazz Band
Sunday 5th Evening
Micky Ashman
Ragtime Jazz Band
Swinging Blue Genes
Tuesday 7th Lunchtime
The Beatles
Evening
(Blue Genes' Guest Night)
Gerry and the Pacemakers
The Strangers
Wednesday 8th Evening
The Beatles
Remo Four
Ian and The Zodiacs
Thursday 9th Lunchtime
The Beatles (allegedly the occasion
   when Brian Epstein saw The
   Beatles performing for the first
   time)
Evening
Zoot Sims
Ronnie Scott's Quintet
Jimmy Deuchar
Friday 10th Evening
Mike Cotten's Jazzmen
Remo Four
Saturday 11th Evening
Red River Jazzmen
The Four Jays
Sunday 12th Evening
Eric Allandale's New Orleans Knights
Swinging Blue Genes
Monday 13th Lunchtime
The Beatles
Tuesday 14th Evening
(Blue Genes' Guest Night)
Gerry and the Pacemakers
Remo Four
The Beatles
Wednesday 15th Lunchtime
The Beatles
Evening
The Beatles
The Four Jays

THE BEATLES FAN CLUB

PRESENTS

"THE BEATLES FOR THEIR FANS"

OR AN EVENING WITH GEORGE, JOHN, PAUL & PETE

GUEST ARTISTES WILL INCLUDE

THE FOUR JAYS

AND THE BEATLES' FAVOURITE COMPERE

BOB WOOLER

7-30 p.m., THURSDAY, APRIL 5th. 1962

AT THE CAVERN

TICKETS 6/6d.

Ticket holders will receive a FREE PHOTOGRAPH and may apply for
FREE Membership of the Fan Club   (See over).

Johnny Sandon and The Searchers
Thursday 16th Evening
Harold McNair
Friday 17th Lunchtime
The Beatles
Evening
Yorkshire Jazz Band
Mark Peters and The Cyclones
Saturday 18th Evening
White Eagles Jazz Band
The Beatles
Sunday 19th Evening
Doug Richford's Jazz Band
Swinging Blue Genes
Tuesday 21st Lunchtime
The Beatles
Evening
(Blue Genes' Guest Night)
Remo Four
Kingsize Taylor and The Dominoes
Wednesday 22nd Evening
The Beatles
Gerry and the Pacemakers
Earl Preston and The TTs
Thursday 23rd Lunchtime
The Beatles
Friday 24th Evening
Terry Lightfoot's New Orleans
 Jazzmen
Saturday 25th Evening
The Dallas Jazz Band
Gerry and the Pacemakers

Sunday 26th Evening
Swinging Blue Genes
Bob Wallis Storeyville Jazzmen
Monday 27th Lunchtime
The Beatles
Tuesday 28th Evening
(Blue Genes' Guest Night)
Gerry and the Pacemakers
Johnny Sandon and The Searchers
Wednesday 29th Lunchtime
The Beatles
Evening
The Beatles
Ian and The Zodiacs
The Remo Four
Thursday 30th Evening
Don Rendell Quintet

DECEMBER
Friday 1st Lunchtime
The Beatles
Evening
The Dallas Jazz Band
Gerry and the Pacemakers
Saturday 2nd Evening
The Beatles
Zenith Six Jazz Band
Sunday 3rd Evening
Swinging Blue Genes
Alan Elsdon Jazz Band
Tuesday 5th Lunchtime
The Beatles

Evening
(Blue Genes' Guest Night)
Johnny Sandon and The Searchers
Gerry and the Pacemakers
Wednesday 6th Evening
The Beatles
The Remo Four
The Strangers
Thursday 7th Evening
Tony Kinsey Quintet
Friday 8th Lunchtime
The Beatles
Evening
The Collegians Jazz Band
The Remo Four
Saturday 9th Evening
The Saints Jazz Band
Gerry and the Pacemakers
Sunday 10th Evening
Humphrey Lyttelton Jazz Band
Johnny Sandon and The Searchers
Monday 11th Lunchtime
The Beatles
Tuesday 12th Evening
(Blue Genes' Guest Night)
The Remo Four
Kingsize Taylor and The Dominoes
Wednesday 13th Lunchtime
The Beatles
Evening
The Beatles
Gerry and the Pacemakers
The Four Jays
Friday 15th Lunchtime
The Beatles
Evening
Yorkshire Jazz Band
Gerry and the Pacemakers
Saturday 16th Evening
The Beatles
White Eagles Jazz Band
Sunday 17th Evening
Terry Lightfoot's New Orleans
Jazzmen
Swinging Blue Genes
Tuesday 19th Lunchtime
The Beatles
Evening
(Blue Genes' Guest Night)
The Remo Four
Gerry and the Pacemakers
Wednesday 20th Evening
The Beatles
The Strangers
Mark Peters and The Cyclones
Thursday 21st Lunchtime
The Beatles
Evening
Tubby Hayes Quintet

Friday 22nd Evening
Red River Jazzmen
Gerry and the Pacemakers
Saturday 23rd All-Night Session
Micky Ashman Jazz Band
The Remo Four
Gerry and the Pacemakers
The Saints Jazz Band
The Beatles
The Searchers
Sunday 24th Evening
Eric Allandale's New Orleans Knights
The Searchers
Swinging Blue Genes
Tuesday 26th Evening
(Blue Genes' Christmas Party)
The Remo Four
The Four Jays
Wednesday 27th Evening
Compère Bob Wooler
(Beatles' Christmas Party)
Gerry and the Pacemakers
Kingsize Taylor and The Dominoes
Friday 29th Evening
The Beatles
Yorkshire Jazz Band
Saturday 30th Evening
The Beatles
White Eagles Jazz Band
Sunday 31st New Years Eve
Terry Pitt's Jazzmen
Swinging Blue Genes
Johnny Sandon and The Searchers

1962

JANUARY
Wednesday 3rd Lunchtime
The Beatles
Evening
The Beatles
Johnny Sandon and The Searchers
Kingsize Taylor and The Dominoes
Friday 5th Lunchtime
The Beatles
Evening
Tony Smith Jazzmen
Kingsize Taylor and The Dominoes
Saturday 6th Evening
The Collegians Jazz Band
The Beatles
Sunday 7th Evening
Alex Welsh Jazz Band
Swinging Blue Genes
Tuesday 9th Lunchtime
The Beatles

Evening
(Blue Genes' Guest Night)
The Remo Four
Johnny Sandon and The Searchers
Wednesday 10th Evening
Gerry and the Pacemakers
Thursday 11th Lunchtime
The Beatles
Friday 12th Evening
Mike Cotten Jazzmen
The Beatles
Saturday 13th Evening
The Saints Jazz Band
Gerry and the Pacemakers
Sunday 14th Evening
Micky Ashman's Ragtime Band
Swinging Blue Genes
Monday 15th Lunchtime
The Beatles
Tuesday 16th Evening
(Blue Genes' Guest Night)
Gerry and the Pacemakers
Kingsize Taylor and The Dominoes
Wednesday 17th Lunchtime
The Beatles
Evening
The Beatles
Ian and The Zodiacs
The Remo Four
Friday 19th Lunchtime
The Beatles
Evening
Red River Jazzmen
Gerry and the Pacemakers
Saturday 20th Evening
The Beatles
Yorkshire Jazz Band
Sunday 21st Evening
Melbourne New Orleans Jazz Band
(Australia's no.1 jazz band)
Swinging Blue Genes
Monday 22nd Lunchtime
The Beatles
Tuesday 23rd Lunchtime
Gerry and the Pacemakers
Evening
(Blue Genes' Guest Night)
The Remo Four
The Strangers
Wednesday 24th Lunchtime
The Beatles
Evening
The Four Jays
The Beatles
Gerry and the Pacemakers
Thursday 25th Lunchtime
Gerry and the Pacemakers
Friday 26th Lunchtime
The Beatles

Evening
The Yorkshire Jazz Band
The Beatles
Saturday 27th Evening
The Collegians Jazz Band
Johnny Sandon and The Searchers
Gerry and the Pacemakers
Sunday 28th Evening
Ken Colyer Jazz Band
Swinging Blue Genes
Monday 29th Lunchtime
Gerry and the Pacemakers
Tuesday 30th Lunchtime
The Beatles
Evening
(Blue Genes' Guest Night)
Johnny Sandon and The Searchers
Ian and The Zodiacs
Wednesday 31st Lunchtime
Gerry and the Pacemakers
Evening
The Beatles
The Remo Four
Kingsize Taylor and The Dominoes

FEBRUARY
Thursday 1st Lunchtime
The Beatles
Friday 2nd Lunchtime
Gerry and the Pacemakers
Evening
Red River Jazzmen
Pete McLaine and The Dakotas
Saturday 3rd Evening
The Beatles
The Saints Jazz Band
Gerry and the Pacemakers
Sunday 4th Evening
Ken Sims Vintage Jazz Band
Swinging Blue Genes
Monday 5th Lunchtime
The Beatles
Tuesday 6th Lunchtime
Gerry and the Pacemakers
Evening
(Blue Genes' Guest Night)
The Four Jays
The Strangers
Wednesday 7th Lunchtime
The Beatles
Evening
The Beatles
Dale Roberts and The Jaywalkers
Gerry and the Pacemakers
Thursday 8th Lunchtime
Gerry and the Pacemakers
Friday 9th Lunchtime
The Beatles

Evening
The Beatles
Gerry and the Pacemakers
The Collegians Jazz Band
Saturday 10th Evening
The Yorkshire Jazz Band
The Remo Four
Sunday 11th Evening
The Clyde Valley Stompers
Swinging Blue Genes
Tuesday 13th Lunchtime
The Beatles
Evening
(Blue Genes' Guest Night)
Gerry and the Pacemakers
Kingsize Taylor and The Dominoes
Wednesday 14th Evening
The Beatles
Johnny Sandon and The Searchers
The Strangers
Thursday 15th Lunchtime
The Beatles
Evening
Johnny Sandon and The Searchers
John Dean and The Tremors
Pete Hartigan's Jazzmen
Saturday 17th Evening
The Beatles
Cyril Preston's Exselsior Jazz Band
The Zenith Six Jazz Band
Sunday 18th Evening
Doug Richford's London Jazzmen
   featuring Nat Gonella
Swinging Blue Genes
Monday 19th Lunchtime
The Beatles
Evening
(Blue Genes' Guest Night)
The Four Jays
Johnny Sandon and The Searchers
Wednesday 21st Lunchtime
The Beatles
Evening
Ken Dallas and The Silhouettes
The Beatles
Steve Day and The Drifters
Friday 23rd Lunchtime
The Beatles
Evening
The Saints Jazz Band
Johnny Sandon and The Searchers
Saturday 24th All-Night Session
Red River Jazzmen
Tony Smith's Jazz Band
Ken Sims' Jazz Band
Gerry and the Pacemakers
The Beatles
Ken Dallas and The Silhouettes

Sunday 25th Evening
The Terry Lightfoot Jazz Band
Swinging Blue Genes
Monday 26th Lunchtime
Gerry and the Pacemakers
Tuesday 27th Lunchtime
The Beatles
Evening
(Blue Genes' Guest Night)
The Strangers
Ken Dallas and The Silhouettes
Wednesday 28th Lunchtime
Gerry and the Pacemakers
Evening
The Beatles
Gerry and the Pacemakers
The Searchers

MARCH
Thursday 1st Lunchtime
The Beatles
Friday 2nd Lunchtime
Gerry and the Pacemakers
Evening
Tony Smith's Jazzmen
Gerry and the Pacemakers
Saturday 3rd Evening
The Beatles
Jim McHarg's Storeyville Jazzmen
Sunday 4th Evening
Mike Cotten's Jazzmen
Swinging Blue Genes
Monday 5th Lunchtime
The Beatles
Tuesday 6th Lunchtime
Gerry and the Pacemakers
Evening
(Blue Genes' Guest Night)
The Beatles
Gerry and the Pacemakers
Wednesday 7th Lunchtime
The Remo Four
Johnny Sandon
Evening
The Remo Four
Kingsize Taylor and The Dominoes
The Morockans
Thursday 8th Lunchtime
Gerry and the Pacemakers
Friday 9th Lunchtime
The Beatles
Evening
The Beatles
The Saints Jazz Band
Saturday 10th Evening
Gerry and the Pacemakers
White Eagles Jazz Band
Remo Four featuring Johnny Sandon

Sunday 11th Evening
The Dauphin St Jazz Band
Swinging Blue Genes
Monday 12th Lunchtime
The Beatles
Tuesday 13th Lunchtime
The Beatles
Wednesday 14th Evening
The Beatles
Gerry and the Pacemakers
Clay Ellis and The Raiders
Thursday 15th Lunchtime
The Beatles
Friday 16th Evening
The Beatles
The Collegians Jazz Band
Saturday 17th Evening
The Saints Jazz Band
The Four Jays
Sunday 18th Evening
Papa Blue's Viking Jazz Band
Swinging Blue Genes
Monday 19th Lunchtime
Gerry and the Pacemakers
Tuesday 20th Lunchtime
Gerry and the Pacemakers
Evening
(Blue Genes' Guest Night)
The Beatles
The Remo Four
Johnny Sandon
The Zodiacs
Wednesday 21st Lunchtime
The Beatles
Evening
The Four Jays
The Strangers
Thursday 22nd Lunchtime
Peppy and The New York Twisters
Evening
The Beatles
Peppy and The New York Twisters
Friday 23rd Lunchtime
The Beatles
Evening
Pate Hartigan's Jazzmen
The Beatles
Gerry and the Pacemakers
Saturday 24th Evening
The Saints Jazz Band
Ian and The Zodiacs
Sunday 25th Evening
The Pitts Jazzmen
Swinging Blue Genes
Monday 26th Lunchtime
The Beatles
Tuesday 27th Lunchtime
Gerry and the Pacemakers

Evening
(Blue Genes' Guest Night)
Kingsize Taylor and The Dominoes
Ken Dallas and The Silhouettes
Wednesday 28th Lunchtime
The Beatles
Evening
Gerry and the Pacemakers
The Beatles
Remo Four with Johnny Sandon
Thursday 29th Lunchtime
Gerry and the Pacemakers
Friday 30th Lunchtime
The Beatles
Evening
The Beatles
The Dallas Jazz Band
Saturday 31st Evening
Alan Elson's Jazz Band
The Zenith Six Jazz Band
The Searchers

APRIL
Sunday 1st Evening
The Melbourne New Orleans Jazz
   Band
Swinging Blue Genes
Monday 2nd Lunchtime
The Beatles
Tuesday 3rd Lunchtime
Gerry and the Pacemakers
Wednesday 4th Lunchtime
The Beatles
Evening
The Beatles
The Searchers
Earl Preston and The TTs
Thursday 5th Lunchtime
Gerry and the Pacemakers
Evening
Compère Bob Wooler
The Beatles (last week in town before
   leaving for Hamburg)
The Four Jays
Friday 6th Lunchtime
The Beatles
Evening
Yorkshire Jazz Band
Mark Peters and The Cyclones
Saturday 7th Evening
The Saints Jazz Band
The Beatles Farewell Show
Sunday 8th Evening
Micky Ashman's Ragtime Jazz Band
Swinging Blue Genes
Tuesday 10th Evening
(Blue Genes' Guest Night)
The Searchers

Wednesday 11th Evening
Gerry and the Pacemakers
Ian and the Zodiacs
Johnny Peters and The Creates
Friday 13th Evening
The Collegians Jazz Band
Ian and The Zodiacs
Saturday 14th Evening
The Zenith Six Jazz Band
The Four Jays
Sunday 15th Evening
The Doug Richford Jazz Band (from London)
Swinging Blue Genes
Monday 16th Lunchtime
Gerry and the Pacemakers
Tuesday 17th Lunchtime
Gerry and the Pacemakers
Evening
(Blue Genes' Guest Night)
Gerry and the Pacemakers
The Four Jays
Wednesday 18th Lunchtime
The Dakotas
Evening
The Dakotas
The Searchers
Ken Dallas and The Silhouettes
Thursday 19th Lunchtime
The Dakotas
Friday 20th Evening
The Red River Jazzmen
The Zephyrs
Saturday 21st Evening
Tony Smith's Jazzmen
Clay Ellis and The Raiders
Sunday 22nd Evening
Humphrey Lyttelton Jazz Band
Swinging Blue Genes
Friday 27th Evening
Kingsize Taylor and The Dominoes
The Collegians Jazz Band
Saturday 28th Evening
The Four Jays
Red River Jazzmen
Sunday 29th Evening
Ken Sims Vintage Jazz Band
Swinging Blue Genes
Monday 30th Lunchtime
Gerry and the Pacemakers

MAY
Tuesday 1st Lunchtime
Pete McLaine and The Dakotas
Evening
(Blue Genes' Guest Night)
The Searchers
Group One

Wednesday 2nd Lunchtime
Gerry and the Pacemakers
Evening
Gerry and the Pacemakers
Ken Dallas and The Silhouettes
Sonny Webb and The Cascade
Thursday 3rd Lunchtime
Pete McLaine and The Dakotas
Friday 4th Lunchtime
Gerry and the Pacemakers
Evening
The Four Jays
Mike Cotten's Jazzmen
Saturday 5th Evening
Gerry and the Pacemakers
  (farewell appearance before leaving for Germany)
The Red River Jazzmen
Sunday 6th Evening
Mike Cotten's Jazzmen
Swinging Blue Genes
Tuesday 8th Evening
(Blue Genes' Guest Night)
Ken Dallas and The Silhouettes
Johnny Peters and The Crestas
Wednesday 9th Evening
The Dakotas
Clay Ellis and The Raiders
The Searchers
Friday 11th Evening
Evening
The Saints Jazz Band
The Dakotas
Saturday 12th Evening
The Collegians Jazz Band
The Olympics
Sunday 13th Evening
Mike Daniels' Delta Jazz Band
Swinging Blue Genes
Monday 14th Lunchtime
Johnny Kidd and The Pirates
Evening
Johnny Kidd and The Pirates
Tuesday 15th Lunchtime
Johnny Kidd and The Pirates
Evening
(Blue Genes' Guest Night)
Johnny Kidd and The Pirates
The Searchers
Wednesday 16th Lunchtime
Johnny Kidd and The Pirates
Evening
Ken Dallas and The Silhouettes
The Dakotas
Johnny Kidd and The Pirates
Thursday 17th Lunchtime
Johnny Kidd and The Pirates
Friday 18th Lunchtime
Johnny Kidd and The Pirates

Evening
Johnny Kidd and The Pirates
The Red River Jazzmen
Saturday 19th Evening
The Collegians Jazzmen
The Merseybeats
Sunday 20th Evening
The Clyde Valley Stompers
Swinging Blue Genes
Monday 21st Lunchtime
Mike Berry and The Outlaws
Evening
Mike Berry and The Outlaws
Tuesday 22nd Lunchtime
Mike Berry and The Outlaws
Evening
Mark Peters and The Cyclones
The Swinging Blue Genes
Mike Berry and The Outlaws
Wednesday 23rd Lunchtime
Mike Berry and The Outlaws
Evening
Johnny Peters and The Crestas
The Searchers
Mike Berry and The Outlaws
Thursday 24th Lunchtime
Mike Berry and The Outlaws
Evening
Mike Berry and The Outlaws
Friday 25th Lunchtime
Mike Berry and The Outlaws
Evening
The Dennisons
Mike Berry and The Outlaws
Saturday 26th Evening
The Zenith Six Jazz Band
The Spidermen
Sunday 27th Evening
The Swinging Blue Genes
The Dauphin St Six Jazz Band
Tuesday 29th Evening
The Swinging Blue Genes
Johnny Peters and The Crestas
The Dennisons
Wednesday 30th Lunchtime
The Dakotas
Evening
Mark Peters and The Cyclones
The Four Jays
The Dakotas

JUNE
Friday 1st Evening
Group One
The Red River Jazzmen
The Searchers
Saturday 2nd Evening
The Saints Jazz Band

Sunday 3rd Evening
Ken Sims Vintage Jazzmen
Swinging Blue Genes
Tuesday 5th Evening
The Swinging Blue Genes
The Merseybeats
The Sorrals
Wednesday 6th Evening
The Big Three
Clay Ellis and The Raiders
Mark Peters and The Cyclones
Friday 8th Evening
Johnny Templar's Hi Cats with Barbara
The Collegians Jazz Band
The Dennisons
Saturday 9th Evening
Beatles Welcome Home Show
The Red River Jazzmen
The Spidermen
The Four Jays
Ken Dallas and The Silhouettes
Sunday 10th Evening
Eric Allandale's New Orleans Knights
Swinging Blue Genes
Tuesday 12th Lunchtime
The Beatles
Evening
The Beatles
Wednesday 13th Lunchtime
The Beatles
Evening
The Beatles
The Dakotas
The Dennisons
Friday 15th Lunchtime
The Beatles
Evening
The Beatles
Group One
The Spidermen
Saturday 16th Evening
The Beatles
Tony Smith's Jazzmen
Sunday 17th Evening
Alan Elsdon's Jazzmen
Swinging Blue Genes
Tuesday 19th Lunchtime
The Beatles
Evening
The Beatles
The Merseybeats
The Swinging Blue Genes
Wednesday 20th Lunchtime
The Beatles
Evening
The Sorrals
The Beatles
Kingsize Taylor and The Dominoes

Thursday 21st Lunchtime
Bruce Channel ('Hey Baby')
Delbert McClinton and The Barons
Friday 22nd Lunchtime
The Beatles
Evening
The Beatles
Clay Ellis and The Raiders
The Olympics
Saturday 23rd Evening
Zenith Six Jazz Band
Swinging Blue Genes
The Spidermen
Sunday 24th Evening
Swinging Blue Genes
The Red River Jazzmen
Monday 25th Lunchtime
The Beatles
Tuesday 26th Evening
Swinging Blue Genes
The Four Jays
The Dakotas
Wednesday 27th Lunchtime
The Beatles
Evening
The Beatles
The Swinging Blue Genes
Friday 29th Lunchtime
The Beatles
Evening
Welcome Home to Gerry and the Pacemakers
Ian and The Zodiacs
Clay Ellis and The Raiders
Saturday 30th Evening
The Red River Jazzmen
The Searchers
Group One

JULY
Sunday 1st Evening
The Beatles
Gene Vincent with Sounds Incorporated
Tuesday 3rd Lunchtime
The Beatles
Evening
Freddie and The Dreamers
The Swinging Blue Genes
The Searchers
Wednesday 4th Evening
The Beatles
The Spidermen
Group One
Friday 6th River Boat Shuffle
The Beatles
Acker Bilk's Paramount Jazz Band
Saturday 7th Evening
Kingsize Taylor and The Dominoes

The Merseybeats
The Collegians Jazz Band
Sunday 8th Evening
The Beatles
The Swinging Blue Genes
Tony Smith's Jazzmen
Monday 9th Lunchtime
Jimmy Justice
Evening
Gus Travis and The Midnighters
Billy Kramer and The Coasters
Mark Peters and The Cyclones
Jimmy Justice
Tuesday 10th Lunchtime
The Beatles
Evening
The Swinging Blue Genes
Ian and the Zodiacs
Group One
Wednesday 11th Lunchtime
The Statesmen
Evening
The Statesmen
The Beatles
The Moreckans
Thursday 12th Lunchtime
The Beatles
Friday 13th Lunchtime
Pete McLaine and The Dakotas
Evening
Mark Peters and The Cyclones
The Midnighters
Ian and The Zodiacs
Pete McLain and The Dakotas
Saturday 14th Evening
Ken Dallas and The Silhouettes
Tony Smith's Jazzmen
Earl Preston and The TTs
Sunday 15th Evening
The Beatles
The Saints Jazz Band
The Swinging Blue Genes
The Four Jays
Monday 16th Lunchtime
The Beatles
Tuesday 17th Lunchtime
Gerry and the Pacemakers
Evening
Gerry and the Pacemakers
Swinging Blue Genes
Group One
Wednesday 18th Lunchtime
The Beatles
Evening
Ken Dallas and The Silhouettes
The Beatles
The Spidermen
Thursday 19th Lunchtime
Gerry and the Pacemakers

Friday 20th Lunchtime
The Beatles
Evening
Group One
The Merseybeats
Mark Peters and The Cyclones
The Moreckans
Saturday 21st Evening
The Searchers Tony Smith's Jazzmen
The Four Jays
Sunday 22nd Evening
The Beatles
The Swinging Blue Genes
The Red River Jazzmen
Ken Dallas and The Silhouettes
Monday 23rd Lunchtime
Gerry and the Pacemakers
Tuesday 24th Lunchtime
The Beatles
Evening
The Swinging Blue Genes
Gerry and the Pacemakers
Mark Peters and The Cyclones
Wednesday 25th Lunchtime
Gerry and the Pacemakers
The Beatles
Evening
The Dakotas
Ian and The Zodiacs
The Beatles
The Dennisons
Thursday 26th Lunchtime
Joe Brown and His Bruvvers
Friday 27th Lunchtime
Joe Brown and His Bruvvers
Evening
The Searchers
Billy Kramer and The Coasters
Saturday 28th Evening
The Beatles
The Red River Jazzmen
Dee Fenton and The Silhouettes
Sunday 29th Evening
The Saints Jazz Band
Lee Curtis and The All Stars
Mark Peters and The Cyclones
Monday 30th Lunchtime
The Beatles
Tuesday 31st Lunchtime
Gerry and the Pacemakers
Evening
Group One
The Swinging Blue Genes
The Dennisons

AUGUST
Wednesday 1st Lunchtime
The Beatles

Evening
Gerry and the Pacemakers
The Merseybeats
The Beatles
Thursday 2nd Lunchtime
Gerry and the Pacemakers
Friday 3rd Lunchtime
The Big Three
Evening
Clay Ellis and The Raiders
Ray Malcolm and The Sunsets
Alby and The Sorrals
Saturday 4th Evening
The Zenith Six Jazz Band
Mark Peters and The Cyclones
Dee Fenton and the Silhouettes
Sunday 5th Evening
The Beatles
The Saints Jazz Band
The Swinging Blue Genes
Tuesday 7th Lunchtime
The Beatles
Evening
Wayne Stevens and The Vikings
Ken Dallas and The Silhouettes
The Swinging Blue Genes
The Beatles
Wednesday 8th Lunchtime
Gerry and the Pacemakers
Evening
The Big Three
Gerry and the Pacemakers
Shane Fenton and The Fentones
Thursday 9th Lunchtime
The Beatles
Friday 10th Lunchtime
The Dakotas
River Boat Shuffle
The Beatles
The Dakotas
Johnny Kidd and The Pirates
Saturday 11th Evening
The Merseybeats
The Four Jays
The Collegians Jazz Band
Sunday 12th Evening
The Beatles
The Swinging Blue Genes
The Red River Jazzmen
Monday 13th Lunchtime
The Beatles
Tuesday 14th Lunchtime
Gerry and the Pacemakers
Evening
Swinging Blue Genes
Gerry and the Pacemakers
Dee Young and The Pontiacs
Wednesday 15th Lunchtime
The Beatles

Evening
The Beatles (Pete Best's last Beatles
  performance)
Thursday 16th Lunchtime
The Big Three
Friday 17th Lunchtime
Freddie and the Dreamers
Evening
Freddie and The Dreamers
Ray and The Del Renas
The Spidermen
Gus Travis and The Midnighters
Saturday 18th Evening
Bob Wallis Storeyville Jazzmen
Clay Ellis and The Raiders
Group One
Sunday 19th Evening
The Beatles
The Zenith Six Jazz Band
The Swinging Blue Genes
Peppy and The New York Twisters
  (return visit)
Monday 20th Lunchtime
The Big Three
Tuesday 21st Lunchtime
Gerry and the Pacemakers
Evening
The Swinging Blue Genes
Bill Kramer and The Coasters
Ken Dallas and The Silhouettes
Wednesday 22nd Lunchtime
The Beatles (with Granada TV
  cameras filming their live show)
Evening
Gerry and the Pacemakers
The Beatles
Dee Fenton and The Silhouettes
Thursday 23rd Lunchtime
Gerry and the Pacemakers
Friday 24th Lunchtime
The Beatles
Evening
The Big Three
Lee Curtis and The All Stars
Group One
Saturday 25th Evening
The Red River Jazzmen
The Searchers
Pete McLaine and The Dakotas
Sunday 26th Evening
Mike Berry and The Phantoms
The Red River Jazzmen
The Beatles
The Swinging Blue Genes
Monday 27th Lunchtime
Mike Berry and The Phantoms
Tuesday 28th Lunchtime
Gerry and the Pacemakers

Evening
The Swinging Blue Genes (last
  appearance before going to
  Germany)
The Beatles
Gerry Levine and The Avengers (from
  Birmingham)
Wednesday 29th Lunchtime
Nero and The Gladiators
Evening
Group One
Clay Ellis and The Raiders
Nero and The Gladiators
Thursday 30th Lunchtime
The Beatles
Friday 31st Lunchtime
The Big Three
Evening
Johnny Templar and The Hi Cats
Kirk Daniels and The Deltas
Ian and The Zodiacs
Mark Peters and The Cyclones

SEPTEMBER
Saturday 1st Evening
Gerry and the Pacemakers
The Four Jays
Pete Hartigan's Jazz Band
Sunday 2nd Evening
The Beatles
Kingsize Taylor and The Dominoes
The Zenith Six Jazz Band
Monday 3rd Lunchtime
The Beatles
Tuesday 4th Lunchtime
Gerry and the Pacemakers
Evening
Lee Curtis and The All Stars
Ken Dallas and The Silhouettes
Billy Kramer and The Coasters
Wednesday 5th Lunchtime
The Big Three
Evening
The Dennisons
Gus Travis and The Midnighters
Thursday 6th Lunchtime
The Beatles
Friday 7th Lunchtime
Gerry and the Pacemakers
Evening
Gerry and the Pacemakers
The Big Three
The Spidermen
The Merseybeats
Saturday 8th Evening
Kingsize Taylor and The Dominoes
Dee Young and The Pontiacs
Tony Smith's Jazzmen

Sunday 9th Evening
Cyril Preston's Jazz Band with
  Clinton Ford
Billy Kramer and The Coasters
The Beatles
Monday 10th Lunchtime
The Beatles
Tuesday 11th Lunchtime
Joe Brown and His Bruvvers
Evening
The Merseybeats
Gerry and the Pacemakers
Joe Brown and His Bruvvers
Wednesday 12th Lunchtime
Freddie and The Dreamers
Evening
The Beatles
Freddie and The Dreamers
Simone Jackson
The Spidermen
Group One
Thursday 13th Lunchtime
The Beatles
Friday 14th Evening
The Dakotas
Alby and The Sorrals
Clay Ellis and The Raiders
Dee Fenton and The Silhouettes
Saturday 15th Evening
The Saints Jazz Band
Kingsize Taylor and The Dominoes
Ian and the Zodiacs
Sunday 16th Evening
The Beatles
The Red River Jazzmen
Gerry and the Pacemakers
Monday 17th Lunchtime
The Beatles
Tuesday 18th Lunchtime
The Fleerekkers
Evening
Billy Kramer and The Coasters
Lee Curtis and The All Stars with
  Pete Best
The Fleerekkers
Wednesday 19th Lunchtime
The Dakotas
Evening
The Dakotas
The Beatles
The Big Three
Thursday 20th Lunchtime
The Beatles
Friday 21st Lunchtime
Gerry and the Pacemakers
Evening
Gerry and the Pacemakers
Group One
The Four Jays

The Dennisons
Saturday 22nd Evening
The Zenith Six Jazz Band
Lee Curtis and The All Stars
Mike and The Thunderbirds
Sunday 23rd Evening
The Beatles
The Saints Jazz Band
Kingsize Taylor and The Dominoes
Monday 24th Lunchtime
Gerry and the Pacemakers
Tuesday 25th Lunchtime
Lee Curtis and The All Stars
Evening
Lee Curtis and The All Stars
Ken Dallas and The Silhouettes
Mark Peters and The Cyclones
Wednesday 26th Lunchtime
The Beatles
Evening
The Beatles
The Spidermen
Kingsize Taylor and The Dominoes
Thursday 27th Lunchtime
The Big Three
Friday 28th Lunchtime
The Beatles
Evening
Billy Kramer and The Coasters
The Big Three
Ian and The Zodiacs
The Merseybeats
Saturday 29th Evening
Gerry and the Pacemakers
Grant Tracey and The Sunsets
Group One
The Four Jays
Sunday 30th Evening
The Red River Jazzmen
The Beatles
Clay Ellis and The Raiders

OCTOBER
Monday 1st Lunchtime
The Dakotas
Tuesday 2nd Lunchtime
The Beatles
Evening
Lee Curtis and The All Stars
The Merseybeats
The Nut Rockers
Wednesday 3rd Lunchtime
The Echoes
Evening
The Beatles
The Echoes
Billy Kramer and The Coasters

Thursday 4th Lunchtime
The Beatles
Friday 5th Evening
Ken Dallas and The Silhouettes
The Flintstones
Mark Peters and The Cyclones
Dee Young and The Pontiacs
Saturday 6th Evening
Lee Curtis and The All Stars
The Saints Jazz Band
Group One
Sunday 7th Evening
The Beatles (new record released
  today 'Love Me Do')
The Swinging Blue Genes (back from
  Germany)
The Red River Jazzmen
Ian and The Zodiacs
Monday 8th Lunchtime
The Dakotas
Tuesday 9th Lunchtime
The Big Three
Evening
The Strangers
Buddy Brittain and The Regents
The Big Three
The Undertakers
Wednesday 10th Lunchtime
The Beatles
Ken Dallas and The Silhouettes
The Four Jays
The Beatles
Thursday 11th Lunchtime
Freddie and The Dreamers
Friday 12th Lunchtime
The Beatles
Evening
The Flintstones
The Del Renas
The Spidermen
Karl Terry and The Cruisers
Saturday 13th Evening
The Beatles
The Zenith Six Jazz Band
Group One
The Dennisons
Sunday 14th Evening
The Saints Jazz Band
The Swinging Blue Genes
Mark Peters and The Cyclones
Dee Young and The Pontiacs
Monday 15th Lunchtime
The Merseybeats
Tuesday 16th Lunchtime
The Big Three
Evening
The Strangers
The Swinging Blue Genes
The Undertakers

Wednesday 17th Lunchtime
The Beatles
Johnny Sandon and The Remo Four
  (first show since returning from
  France)
Evening
Group One
Johnny Sandon and The Remo Four
The Swinging Blue Genes
The Beatles (with Granada TV)
Friday 19th Lunchtime
The Beatles
Evening
Dee Fenton and The Silhouettes
The Pressmen
Billy Kramer and The Coasters
The Fourmost
B Bumble and The Stingers
  (American group)
Saturday 20th Evening
Tommy Quickley and The
  Challengers
The Memphis Three
The Merseybeats
B Bumble and The Stingers
Ian and the Zodiacs
Sunday 21st Evening
The Beatles
The Fourmost
The Red River Jazzmen
Monday 22nd Lunchtime
The Merseybeats
Tuesday 23rd Lunchtime
Freddie and The Dreamers
Evening
Freddie and The Dreamers
The Merseybeats
The Undertakers
Wednesday 24th Lunchtime
The Dakotas
Evening
Mark Peters and The Cyclones
The Big Three
The Dakotas
The Strangers
Thursday 25th Lunchtime
The Big Three
Friday 26th Lunchtime
The Beatles (off to Hamburg)
Evening
Group One
The Del Renas
Dee Young and The Pontiacs
The Spidermen
Saturday 27th Evening
The Saints Jazz Band
The Dennisons
The Fourmost

Sunday 28th Evening
The Zenith Six Jazz Band
The Swinging Blue Genes
The Merseybeats
Tuesday 30th Evening
The Swinging Blue Genes
The Undertakers
Ken Dallas and The Silhouettes
Wednesday 31st Evening
Johnny Sandon and The Remo Four
The Big Three
The Dakotas

NOVEMBER
Friday 2nd Evening
The Fourmost
The Spidermen
The Dennisons
Johnny Martin and The Tremors
Saturday 3rd Evening
The Tony Dallas Jazz Band
Group One
The Merseybeats
Pete Hartigan's Jazz Band
Sunday 4th Evening
The Big Three
The Swinging Blue Genes
Johnny Sandon and The Remo Four
Joe Silmons Dixielanders
Monday 5th Lunchtime
Lee Curtis and The All Stars
Tuesday 6th Evening
Freddie and The Dreamers
The Undertakers
Alby and The Sorrals
Wednesday 7th Evening
The Dakotas
The Big Three
Lee Curtis and The All Stars
Friday 9th Evening
Ian and The Zodiacs
The Statesmen
The Flintstones
The Fourmost
Saturday 10th Evening
The Merseybeats
The Dennisons
Joe Silmon's Dixielanders
Sunday 11th Evening
The Zenith Six Jazz Band
The Swinging Blue Genes
Johnny Sandon and The Remo Four
Monday 12th Lunchtime
Freddie and The Dreamers
Tuesday 13th Lunchtime
Johnny Sandon and The Remo Four
Wednesday 14th Lunchtime
The Dakotas

Evening
The Merseybeats
The Dakotas
The Fourmost
Thursday 15th Lunchtime
The Merseybeats
Friday 16th Lunchtime
The Fourmost
Evening
Ken Dallas and The Silhouettes
Alan Elsdon's Jazz Band
The Flintstones
Dee Fenton and The Pontiacs
Saturday 17th Evening
The Red River Jazzmen
Dee Fenton and The Pontiacs
The Renegades
Sunday 18th Evening
The Beatles (return from Hamburg)
The Merseybeats
The Pete Hartigan Jazz Band
Monday 19th Lunchtime
The Beatles
Tuesday 20th Lunchtime
The Statesmen
Evening
The Statesmen
The Del Renas
The Spidermen
Wednesday 21st Lunchtime
The Beatles
Evening
Johnny Templar and The Hi Cats
The Beatles
Ian and The Zodiacs
Thursday 22nd Lunchtime
The Beatles
Friday 23rd Lunchtime
Johnny Sandon and The Remo Four
Evening
Johnny Martin and The Tremors
The Del Renas
The Merseybeats
Johnny Sandon and The Remo Four
Saturday 24th Evening
The Saints Jazz Band
Group One
The Spidermen
Alby and The Sorrals
Sunday 25th Evening
The Zenith Six Jazz Band
The Beatles
The Fourmost
The Swinging Blue Genes
The Dennisons
Monday 26th Lunchtime
The Merseybeats
Tuesday 27th Lunchtime
Lee Curtis and The All Stars

Evening
The Merseybeats
Lee Curtis and The All Stars
Gerry Levine and The Avengers
Wednesday 28th Lunchtime
Johnny Sandon and The Remo Four
Evening
The Beatles
Johnny Sandon and The Remo Four
Dee Young and The Pontiacs
Thursday 29th Lunchtime
Freddie and The Dreamers
Friday 30th Lunchtime
The Beatles
The Dakotas
Evening
The Fourmost
The Dakotas
Group One
The Spidermen

DECEMBER
Saturday 1st Evening
Johnny Sandon and The Remo Four
Dee Young and The Pontiacs
Joe Silmon's Dixielanders
Sunday 2nd Evening
Lee Curtis and The All Stars
The Spidermen
The Swinging Blue Genes
The Red River Jazzmen
Monday 3rd Lunchtime
Lee Curtis and The All Stars
Tuesday 4th Lunchtime
The Dakotas
Evening
The Del Renas
The Swinging Blue Genes
The Dakotas
Wednesday 5th Lunchtime
The Beatles
Evening
The Beatles
Gerry and the Pacemakers (back from
   Germany)
Johnny Sandon and The Remo Four
The Statesmen
Friday 7th Lunchtime
The Beatles
Evening
Gerry and the Pacemakers
The Fourmost
The Merseybeat
Ian and The Zodiacs
Saturday 8th Evening
The Saints
The Spidermen
Tommy Quickley and The
   Challengers

Sunday 9th Evening
The Beatles
The Fourmost
The Swinging Blue Genes
The Zenith Six Jazz Band
Monday 10th Lunchtime
The Beatles
Tuesday 11th Evening
The Swinging Blue Genes
Freddie and The Dreamers
The Lee Eddy Five
Wednesday 12th Lunchtime
The Beatles
Evening
The Beatles
The Fourmost
The Merseybeats
Robin Hall and Jimmy MacGregor
   (guest stars)
Friday 14th Evening
The Dakotas
Ken Dallas and The Silhouettes
The Dennisons
The Delrenas
Saturday 15th Evening
The Merseybeats
Vic and The Spidermen
Pete Hartigan's Jazz Band
Sunday 16th Evening
The Beatles
The Fourmost
The Swinging Blue Genes
Gerry and the Pacemakers
The Red River Jazzmen
Tuesday 18th Lunchtime
The Tornados
Evening
Ken Dallas and The Silhouettes
The Panthers
Earl Preston and The TTs
The Tornados
Wednesday 19th Lunchtime
The Tornados
Evening
Vic and The Spidermen
Ian and The Zodiacs
Gerry and the Pacemakers
The Tornados
Thursday 20th Lunchtime
Gerry and the Pacemakers
Friday 21st Lunchtime
The Big Three
Evening
Johnny Sandon and The Remo Four
The Delrenas
Mike Foster's Jazzmen
Vic and The Spidermen
Saturday 22nd Evening
The Fourmost

Group One
The Merseybeats
The Zenith Six Jazz Band
Sunday 23rd Evening
The Big Three
Gerry and the Pacemakers
The Red River Jazzmen
Vic and The Spidermen
Monday 24th Lunchtime
The Big Three
Gerry and the Pacemakers
Evening
Johnny Sandon and The Remo Four
The Flintstones
Tommy Quickley and The
   Challengers
The Merseybeats
Wednesday 26th Evening
Gerry and the Pacemakers
Vic and The Spidermen
The Fourmost
Dee Young and The Pontiacs
Saturday 29th Evening
Group One
The Spidermen
The Dakotas
Joe Silmon's Dixielanders
Sunday 30th Evening
Gerry and the Pacemakers
The Swinging Blue Genes
Ian and The Zodiacs
The Zenith Six Jazz Band
Monday 31st Lunchtime
Gerry and the Pacemakers
All-Night Session
The Delrenas
The Big Three
Johnny Sandon and The Remo Four
The Fourmost
The Spidermen
The Escorts
The Flintstones

1963

JANUARY
Wednesday 2nd Evening
The Merseybeats
Group One
The Dakotas
Alby and The Sorrals
Thursday 3rd Lunchtime
Lee Curtis and The All Stars
Friday 4th Evening
The Merseybeats
Group One
The Dakotas

Alby and The Sorrals
Saturday 5th Evening
The Fourmost
The Delrenas
Dallas Jazz Band
Sunday 6th Evening
Pete Hartigan's Jazzmen
Ken Dallas and The Silhouettes
The Swinging Blue Genes
Lee Shondell and The Boys
Monday 7th Lunchtime
The Remo Four
Evening
Susan Maughan (Bobby's Girl)
Vic and The Spidermen
The Fourmost
Gerry and the Pacemakers
Tuesday 8th Lunchtime
Gerry and the Pacemakers
Evening
Lee Curtis and The All Stars
The Swinging Blue Genes
A.N. Other and The Rest
Wednesday 9th Lunchtime
The Swinging Blue Genes
Evening
Johnny Sandon and The Remo Four
Vic and The Spidermen
Tommy Quickly and The Challengers
Thursday 10th Lunchtime
The Big Three
Friday 11th Lunchtime
The Beatles ('Please Please Me'
   released today)
Kingsize Taylor and The Dominoes
Evening
The Fourmost
Gerry and the Pacemakers
Sonny Webb and The Cascades
The Delrenas
Saturday 12th Evening
Johnny Sandon and The Remo Four
Group One
Zenith Six Jazz Band
Sunday 13th Evening
Johnny and Mike with the Shades
Dallas Jazz Band
The Swinging Blue Genes
The Blue Mountain Boys
Vic and The Spidermen
Monday 14th Lunchtime
Gerry Levine and The Avengers
Tuesday 15th Lunchtime
The Big Three
Wednesday 16th Lunchtime
Johnny Sandon and The Remo Four
Evening
Gerry and the Pacemakers
Johnny Martin and The Tremors

The Merseybeats
Thursday 17th Lunchtime
The Beatles (first record in charts for
    fourteen weeks and has reached
    no.17)
Friday 18th Lunchtime
Billy Kramer and The Coasters
Evening
Vic and The Spidermen
The Big Three
Mark Peters and The Cyclones
Dee Fenton and The Silhouettes
Saturday 19th Evening
The Red River Jazzmen
The Fourmost
Pete McLaine and The Dakotas
Sunday 20th Evening
The Beatles
Pete Hartigan's Jazzmen
The Dennisons
The Merseybeats
The Swinging Blue Genes
Tuesday 22nd Evening
Lee Curtis and The All Stars
The Big Three
The Four Clefs
Wednesday 23rd Lunchtime
The Big Three
Evening
The Beatles
The Fourmost
Ken Dallas and The Silhouettes
Freddie Starr and The Midnighters
Thursday 24th Lunchtime
Johnny Sandon and The Remo Four
Friday 25th Evening
Johnny Sandon and The Remo Four
Gerry and the Pacemakers
The Merseybeats
Saturday 26th Evening
The Big Three
The Delrenas
Pete Hartigan's Jazzmen
Sunday 27th Evening
The Marauders
The Swinging Blue Genes
The Zenith Six Jazz Band
The Merseybeats
Tuesday 29th Evening
Lee Curtis and The All Stars
Gerry and the Pacemakers
The Young Ones
Wednesday 30th Evening
The Beatles
Johnny Sandon and The Remo Four
The Dakotas
Thursday 31st Lunchtime
The Beatles

FEBRUARY
Friday 1st Lunchtime
Gerry and the Pacemakers
Evening
The Fourmost
Vic and The Spidermen
Ken Dallas and The Silhouettes
Saturday 2nd Evening
The Merseybeats
Billy Kramer and The Coasters
Pete Hartigan's Jazzmen
Sunday 3rd Eight-hour marathon
The Beatles
The Fourmost
The Dominoes
The Hollies
Earl Preston and The TTs
The Merseybeats
The Swinging Blue Genes
The Roadrunners
Monday 4th Lunchtime
The Beatles
Tuesday 5th Lunchtime
The Big Three
Evening
Lee Curtis and The All Stars
The Dennisons
The Easybeats
Wednesday 6th Lunchtime
Gerry and the Pacemakers
Evening
Gerry and the Pacemakers
The Big Three
Alby and The Sorrals
Thursday 7th Lunchtime
Lee Curtis and The All Stars
Friday 8th Lunchtime
The Blue Mountain Boys
Evening
Beat Session
Saturday 9th Evening
The Big Three
The Merseybeats
The Red River Jazzmen
Sunday 10th Evening
The Zenith Six Jazz Band
Johnny Sandon and The Remo Four
Earl Preston and The TTs
The Renegades
The Escorts
Tuesday 12th Evening
Lee Curtis and The All Stars
The Top Spots
Ken Dallas and The Silhouettes
Wednesday 13th Lunchtime
The Swinging Blue Genes
Evening
Gerry and the Pacemakers
The Big Three

The Coasters
Thursday 14th Lunchtime
Gerry and the Pacemakers
Friday 15th Lunchtime
The Big Three
Evening
The Fourmost
The Merseybeats
The Memphis Three
The Dennisons
Saturday 16th Evening
The Saints Jazz Band
Johnny Sandon and The Remo Four
The Roadrunners
Vic and The Spidermen
Sunday 17th Evening
John Tippet's Jazzmen
The Dennisons
Tommy Quickley and The
    Challengers
The Nomads
Freddie Starr and The Midnighters
Monday 18th Lunchtime
Johnny Sandon and The Remo Four
Tuesday 19th Lunchtime
The Merseybeats
Evening
The Beatles
Lee Curtis and The All Stars
The Pathfinders
Freddie Starr and The Midnighters
Wednesday 20th Lunchtime
Gerry and the Pacemakers
Evening
Gerry and the Pacemakers
The Delrenas
Johnny Ringo and The Colts
Earl Preston and The TTs
Thursday 21st Lunchtime
The Big Three
Friday 22nd Lunchtime
The Swinging Blue Genes
Evening
The Big Three
Johnny Sandon and The Remo Four
The Panthers
Vic and The Spidermen
Saturday 23rd Evening
The Zenith Six Jazz Band
Group One
The Easybeats
Ken Dallas and The Silhouettes
Sunday 24th Evening
The Red River Jazzmen
Vic and The Spidermen
The Swinging Blue Genes
The Coasters
Dean Stacy and The Detonators

Birkenhead group The Pathfinders. The group appeared at the Cavern
four times, once on the same bill as The Beatles in February 1963.

Monday 25th Evening
Mike Berry and The Marauders
Johnny Sandon and The Remo Four
The Delrenas
Earl Preston and The TTs
Tuesday 26th Lunchtime
Gerry and the Pacemakers
Evening
The Merseybeats
Clay Campbell and The Classics
Wednesday 27th Lunchtime
Kingsize Taylor and The Dominoes
Evening
The Big Three
Lee Curtis and The All Stars
Freddie Starr and The Midnighters
Thursday 28th Lunchtime
Johnny Sandon and The Remo Four

MARCH
Friday 1st Lunchtime
The Merseybeats
Evening
Johnny Sandon and The Remo Four
The Merseybeats
The Delrenas
Ken Dallas and The Silhouettes

Saturday 2nd Evening
The Red River Jazzmen
The Fourmost
The Flintstones
The Four Just Men
Sunday 3rd Evening
Gerry and the Pacemakers (first
    record released today 'How Do You
    Do It?')
The Swinging Blue Genes
Earl Preston and The TTs
Joe Silmon's Dixielanders
The Beathovens
Monday 4th Lunchtime
Gerry and the Pacemakers
Tuesday 5th Lunchtime
Faron and The Flamingos
Evening
The Big Three
The Spidermen
The Dennisons
Wednesday 6th Evening
The Merseybeats
Vic and The Spidermen
The Aarons
Freddie Starr and The Midnighters

Thursday 7th Lunchtime
Kingsize Taylor and The Dominoes
Friday 8th Lunchtime
Johnny Sandon and The Remo Four
Evening
Johnny Sandon and The Remo Four
Lee Curtis and The All Stars
The Fourmost
The Dennisons
The Photons
Saturday 9th Evening
Joe Silmon's Dixielanders
The Delrenas
The Escorts
Ken Dallas and The Silhouettes
Sunday 10th Evening
(Twist and Trad Night)
The Swinging Blue Genes
Johnny Sandon and The Remo Four
The Merseybeats
Zenith Six Jazz Band
City Kings Jazz Band
Monday 11th Lunchtime
The Merseybeats
Tuesday 12th Lunchtime
Johnny Sandon and The Remo Four
Evening
Gerry and the Pacemakers
The Fourmost
The Southerners
Faron's Flamingos
Wednesday 13th Lunchtime
Billy Kramer and The Dakotas
Thursday 14th Lunchtime
Gerry and the Pacemakers
Friday 15th Lunchtime
The Big Three
Evening
Group One
The Merseybeats
The Coasters
The Flintstones
The Hispanos
Saturday 16th Evening
(Twist and Trad Night)
Pete Hartigan's Jazzmen
Vic and The Spidermen
Johnny Templar and The Hi Cats
The Memphis Three
Sunday 17th Evening
The Red River Jazzmen
The Dennisons
The Swinging Blue Genes
Ken Dallas and The Silhouettes
Monday 18th Lunchtime
Kingsize Taylor and The Dominoes
Tuesday 19th Lunchtime
The Big Three

Evening
Gerry and the Pacemakers
Freddie Starr and The Midnighters
The Easybeats
The Harlequins
Wednesday 20th Lunchtime
The Swinging Blue Genes
Thursday 21st Lunchtime
Johnny Sandon and The Remo Four
Friday 22nd Lunchtime
Gerry and the Pacemakers
Evening
The Fourmost
The Searchers
The Merseybeats
The Delrenas
The Executioners
The Big Three
The Dennisons
The Spidermen
The Easybeats
Saturday 23rd Evening
The Zenith Six Jazz Band
Johnny Sandon and The Remo Four
Group One
Four Just Men
Sunday 24th Evening
Billy Kramer and The Dakotas
The Merseybeats
The Swinging Blue Genes
The Rainy City Jazz Band
Earl Royce and The Olympics
Monday 25th Lunchtime
Billy Kramer and The Dakotas
Tuesday 26th Lunchtime
The Merseybeats
Evening
Faron's Flamingos
The Panthers
The Chessmen
Ken Dallas and The Silhouettes
Wednesday 27th Lunchtime
The Hollies
Evening
Karl Denver Trio
The Big Three
The Hollies
Earl Preston and The TTs
Friday 29th Lunchtime
Gerry and the Pacemakers
Evening
The Falcons
The Nomads
Gerry and the Pacemakers
The Spidermen
The Escorts
Saturday 30th Evening
The Saints Jazz Band
The Silhouettes

Liverpool group Faron's Flamingos pictured here in 1963. Faron (Billy Russley, centre) also appeared at the Cavern with Faron's Tempest Tornadoes and Faron and the TTs. He later joined The Big Three. Bob Wooler dubbed Faron 'the panda-footed prince of prance'. Faron's reputation as a dynamic stage performer made him one of the most popular acts on Merseyside in the 1960s and there was always the nagging feeling that if he had found the right management he could have been a national star.

Freddie Starr and The Midnighters
Tommy Quickly and The Challengers
Sunday 31st Evening
The Swinging Blue Genes
Johnny Sandon and The Remo Four
The Merseybeats
Pete Fenton and The Landsliders
The Red River Jazzmen

APRIL
Monday 1st Lunchtime
The Searchers
Evening
Ian and The Zodiacs
The Bachelors
Steve Perry
The Escorts
The Nomads
The Aarons
Tuesday 2nd Lunchtime
Faron's Flamingos
Evening
The Dennisons
Lee Shondel and The Boys
The Citrons

The Black Knights
Wednesday 3rd Lunchtime
Rory Storm and The Hurricanes
Evening
Vic and The Spidermen
Sonny Webb and The Cascades
The Citadels
The Crusaders
Thursday 4th Lunchtime
Johnny Sandon and The Remo Four
Friday 5th Lunchtime
The Merseybeats
Evening
The Merseybeats
Tommy Quickly and The Challengers
The Silhouettes
The Coasters
Saturday 6th Evening
Johnny Sandon and The Remo Four
Joe Silmon's Dixielanders
The Chessmen
Dean Stacy and The Detonators
Sunday 7th Evening
Alan Elsdon's Jazz Band
The Zenith Six Jazz Band

The Fourmost
The Swinging Blue Genes
The Flintstones
Monday 8th Lunchtime
Faron's Flamingos
Tuesday 9th Lunchtime
Johnny Sandon and The Remo Four
Evening
Sonny Webb and The Cascades
Freddie Starr and The Midnighters
The Senators
The Riot Squad
Wednesday 10th Lunchtime
The Merseybeats
Evening
The Merseybeats
Group One
The Classics
Al Stone's Earthquakes
Thursday 11th Lunchtime
Rory Storm and The Hurricanes
Friday 12th Evening
(R&B Marathon)
The Beatles
The Fourmost

Faron is almost dragged off the stage by his adoring admirers during a 1960s show. By all accounts this is the earliest known picture of Faron in action.

Ireland's original boy band The Bachelors at a record signing session in Liverpool before they appeared on the bill at the reopening of the Cavern in July 1966. The Bachelors had many chart hits in the 1960s, with their version of 'I Believe' perhaps the most famous. They appeared at the Cavern twice.

The Dennisons
The Nomads
The Panthers
Faron's Flamingos
The Flintstones
The Roadrunners
Group One
Saturday 27th Evening
The Red River Jazzmen
The Dennisons
Vic and The Spidermen
Tommy Quickly and The Challengers
Sunday 28th Evening
Billy J. Kramer and The Dakotas (first record now on sale 'Do You Want to Know a Secret?')
Bruce Bakewell's Rainy City Jazz Band
The Swinging Blue Genes
The Coasters
Monday 29th Lunchtime
Gerry and the Pacemakers
Tuesday 30th Evening
Earl Preston and The TTs
Count Linsey and The Skeletons
Dean Stacy and The Detonators

MAY
Wednesday 1st Lunchtime
Billy J. Kramer and The Dakotas
Evening
Billy J. Kramer and The Dakotas
Faron's Flamingos
The Vegas Four
The Scorpions
Friday 3rd Evening
The Big Three
The Merseybeats
Vic and The Spidermen
The Executioners
Saturday 4th Evening
(TV cameras present for recording of *Rave Wave*)
Johnny Sandon and The Remo Four
The Silhouettes
Joe Silmon's Dixielanders
The Delrenas
Sunday 5th Evening
(The third R&B marathon televised live for ABC TV for *Sunday Break* programme)
The Zenith Six Jazz Band
The Dennisons
The Escorts
Earl Preston and The TTs
The Merseybeats
Faron's Flamingos
The Nomads
Deny Wilkie and The Pressmen

Tommy Quickly and The Challengers
Tuesday 7th Evening
Group One
The Huntsmen
Vince Reno and The Sabres
Alby and The Sorrals
Wednesday 8th Lunchtime
The Merseybeats
Evening
The Fourmost
The Flintstones
The Cheetahs
Freddie Starr and The Midnighters
Thursday 9th Lunchtime
The Swinging Blue Genes
Friday 10th Evening
The Dennisons
The Coasters
Johnny Sandon and The Remo Four
Lee Curtis and The All Stars
Saturday 11th Evening
Group One
The Easybeats
The Roadrunners
The Rainy City Jazz Band
Sunday 12th Evening
The Red River Jazzmen
The Silhouettes
Tommy Quickley and The Challengers
Monday 13th Lunchtime
Freddie Starr and The Midnighters
Tuesday 14th Lunchtime
Faron's Flamingos
Evening
Faron's Flamingos
The Delrenas
The Panthers
The Mustangs
Wednesday 15th Lunchtime
Johnny Sandon and The Remo Four
Evening
The Dennisons
The Merseybeats
The Fourmost
Robby and The Halers
Thursday 16th Lunchtime
The Delrenas
Johnny Sandon and The Remo Four
Friday 17th Lunchtime
The Merseybeats
Evening
Group One
Vic and The Spidermen
Alby and The Sorrals
The Silhouettes
(Royal Iris 'Big Five Jive')
Freddie and The Dreamers
Johnny Sandon and The Remo Four

Kansas City Five
JJ and The Hi-Lites
Saturday 18th Evening
The Zenith Six Jazz Band
Johnny Sandon and The Remo Four
The Flintstones
Earl Preston and The TTs
Sunday 19th Evening
Gene Vincent
The Hollies
Tommy Quickley and The
  Challengers
Deny Wilkie and The Pressmen
JJ and The Hi-Lites
The Incas
Monday 20th Lunchtime
The Merseybeats
Tuesday 21st Lunchtime
The Escorts
Wednesday 22nd Lunchtime
Faron's Flamingos
Thursday 23rd Lunchtime
Rory Storm and The Hurricanes
Friday 24th Lunchtime
Freddie Starr and The Midnighters
Evening
Johnny Sandon and The Remo Four
Mark Peters and The Silhouettes
Lee Shondel and The Boys
Rick and The Delmonts
Saturday 25th Evening
The Merseybeats
Vic and The Spidermen
Joe Silmon's Dixielanders
Sunday 26th Evening
Johnny Kidd and The Pirates
The Dennisons
Lee Curtis and The All Stars
Earl Preston and The TTs
Monday 27th Lunchtime
Lee Curtis and The All Stars
The Escorts
Tuesday 28th Evening
The Hollies
Faron's Flamingos
Sonny Webb and The Cascades
The Decibels
Wednesday 29th Lunchtime
The Escorts
Evening
Group One
Rory Storm and The Hurricanes
The Coasters
The Four Quarters
Friday 31st Evening
Johnny Sandon and The Remo Four
The Merseybeats
The Flintstones
Johnny Templar and The Hi-Cats

JUNE
Saturday 1st Evening
The Fourmost
The Silhouettes
Dean Stacy and The Detonators
The Rainy City Jazz Band
Sunday 2nd Evening
The Zenith Six Jazz Band
The Panthers
Johnny Sandon and The Remo Four
Friday 7th Lunchtime
Billy J. Kramer and The Dakotas
Evening
The Fourmost
Mark Peters and The Cyclones
The Challengers
Earl Preston and The TTs
Saturday 8th Evening
The Golly Golly Boys
The Top Spots
Johnny Sandon and The Remo Four
The Delrenas
Sunday 9th Evening
Sonny Webb and The Cascades
Riverside Jazzmen with Julie
Mark Peters and The Silhouettes
Tuesday 11th Evening
The Dennisons
Johnny Sandon and The Remo Four
The Easybeats
The Allekats
Wednesday 12th Lunchtime
The Hollies
Evening
The Hollies
The Ravons
Faron's Flamingos
Vince Earl and The Talismen
Friday 14th Lunchtime
The Merseybeats
Evening
Gerry Deville and The City Kings
Gay and The Guys
Tommy Quickley and The
  Challengers
Saturday 15th Evening
The Fourmost
The Delrenas
Joe Silmon's Dixielanders
Mark Peters and The Silhouettes
Sunday 16th Evening
Johnny Sandon and The Remo Four
The Sapphires
The Big Three
The Red River Jazzmen
Alexis Korner's R&B
Tuesday 18th Evening
Faron's Flamingos
Mark Peters and The Silhouettes

Rory Storm and The Hurricanes
Rhythm and Blues Inc.
Wednesday 19th Evening
The Fourmost
Denny Seyton and The Sabres
The Panthers
Earl Preston and The TTs
Friday 21st Evening
The Merseybeats
The Nomads
Vic and The Spidermen
The Coasters
Saturday 22nd Evening
The Searchers
The Escorts
Roy and The Falcons
The Zenith Six Jazz Band
Sunday 23rd Evening
The Fourmost
The Roadrunners
The Delrenas
Wednesday 26th Evening
The Hollies
Vic and The Spidermen
Chick Graham and The Coasters (Ted
  Knibbs' latest discovery)
Thursday 27th Lunchtime
The Searchers
Friday 28th Lunchtime
Faron's Flamingos
Evening
Sonny Webb and The Cascades
The Escorts
The Panthers
Some People
Saturday 29th Evening
The Merseybeats (back from Fontana
  recording session)
Earl Preston and The TTs
Johnny Templar and The Hi-Cats
Sunday 30th Evening
Ketty Lester
The Hollies
The Red River Jazzmen
Vince Earl and The Talismen

JULY
Tuesday 2nd Evening
The Merseybeats
Group One
The Huntsmen
The Dateliners
Wednesday 3rd Lunchtime
The Country Gentlemen
Evening
Gerry and the Pacemakers
Vic and The Spidermen
The Country Gentlemen

Thursday 4th Lunchtime
Faron's Flamingos
Friday 5th Lunchtime
Pete McLaine and The Clan
Evening
The Delrenas
Pete McLaine and The Clan
The Nomads
The Pathfinders
Saturday 6th Evening
Deny Wilkie and The Pressmen
Lee Shondell and The Boys
The Panthers
Steve Aldo and The Challengers
Sunday 7th Evening
Johnny Sandon and The Remo Four
Faron's Flamingos
The Zenith Six Jazz Band
Monday 8th Lunchtime
The Nomads
Tuesday 9th Lunchtime
Rory Storm and The Hurricanes
Evening
Stomp night competition judged by
  Bill Harry. Winners receive copies
  of LP 'This is Merseybeat' Vols. 1
  and 2.
The Merseybeats
Roy and The Dions
The Kinsmen
Wednesday 10th Lunchtime
Freddie Starr and The Midnighters
Evening
The Dennisons
Wayne Fontana and The Mindbenders
Group One
Lee Shondell and The Boys
Thursday 11th Lunchtime
Sonny Webb and The Cascades
Friday 12th Lunchtime
The Hollies
Evening
The Hollies
Vic and The Spidermen
Mark Peters and The Cyclones
Faron's Flamingos
Saturday 13th Evening
The Paladins
The Escorts
The Nomads
The Delrenas
The Chris Nava Combo
Sunday 14th Evening
The Merseybeats
The Memphis Three
The Tributes
The Red River Jazzmen
Monday 15th Lunchtime
Earl Preston and The TTs

Tuesday 16th Lunchtime
The Young Ones
Wednesday 17th Lunchtime
Faron's Flamingos
Evening
The Big Three
The Chants
The Roadrunners
Johnny Sandon and The Remo Four
Thursday 18th Lunchtime
The Escorts
Friday 19th Lunchtime
Johnny Sandon and The Remo Four
Evening
Derry Wilkie and The Pressmen
Lee Shondell and The Boys
The Delmonts
Saturday 20th Evening
Sonny Webb and The Cascades
The Four Just Men
The Panthers
Steve Aldo and The Challengers
Sunday 21st Evening
The Chants
Chick Graham and The Coasters
The Delrenas
Joe Silmon's Dixielanders
Monday 22nd Lunchtime
Steve Aldo and The Challengers
Tuesday 23rd Lunchtime
The Hollies
Evening
Alexis Korner's Blues Band
The Hollies
Denny Seyton and The Sabres
The Motifs
The Bob Ross Group
Wednesday 24th Lunchtime
The Merseybeats
Evening
The Dennisons
The Roadrunners
The Georgians
Thursday 25th Lunchtime
Freddie Starr and The Midnighters
Friday 26th Lunchtime
The Searchers
Evening
Rory Storm and The Hurricanes
Wayne Fontana and The Mindbenders
The Nomads
The Panthers
Saturday 27th Evening
Mark Peters and The Cyclones
The Chris Nava Combo
Rhythm and Blues Inc.
Dean Stacey and The Detonators
Sunday 28th Evening
The Dennisons

The Merseybeats
The Valkyries
The Red River Jazzmen
Monday 29th Lunchtime
Faron's Flamingos
Tuesday 30th Evening
The Merseybeats
Evening
Ian and The Zodiacs
The Moonrakers
The Nomads
Wednesday 31st Lunchtime
Earl Preston and The TTs
Evening
The Dennisons
The Escorts
Mark Peters and The Silhouettes
The Black Knights

AUGUST
Saturday 3rd Evening
The Beatles (last Cavern performance
– first two members to buy tickets
[at 9s 6d] get autographed copies of
EP 'Twist and Shout')
The Merseybeats
Johnny Ringo and The Colts
The Escorts
The Roadrunners
The Sapphires
Sunday 4th Evening
Dave Curtis and The Tremors
Chick Graham and The Coasters
Lee Shondell and The Boys
The Victors
Tuesday 6th Evening
The Hollies
Derry Wilkie and The Pressmen
The Cordelles
Group 5
Wednesday 7th Evening
Rockin' Henry and The Hayseeds
The Four Sounds
The Nomads
Earl Preston and The TTs
Friday 9th Evening
Vince Earl and The Talismen
The Chants
Dave Berry and The Cruisers
The Defenders
Johnny Sandon and The Remo Four
Saturday 10th Evening
Joe Silmon's Dixielanders
The Easybeats
Vince Earl and The Talismen
Gerry de Vile and The City Kings
Sunday 11th Evening
Wayne Fontana and The Mindbenders
The Zenith Six Jazz Band

The Triffids
Chick Graham and The Coasters
Monday 12th Lunchtime
Wayne Fontana and The Mindbenders
Tuesday 13th Lunchtime
The Dennisons
Evening
Earl Preston and The TTs
The Dennisons
The Renegades
The Stereos
Wednesday 14th Lunchtime
Johnny Sandon and The Remo Four
Evening
The Marauders
Lee Shondell and The Boys
The Escorts
Ian and The Zodiacs
Thursday 15th Lunchtime
The Fourmost
Friday 16th Lunchtime
The Jetblacks (Jet Harris's former
backing group, with John Paul Jones
on bass)
Evening
The Jetblacks
The Dennisons
Vic and The Spidermen
Karl Terry and The Cruisers
Saturday 17th Evening
The Mojos
Group One
Chick Graham and The Coasters
Derry Wilkie and The Pressmen
Sunday 18th Evening
Johnny Sandon and The Remo Four
Ian and The Zodiacs
The Hytones
The Rainy City Jazzmen
Monday 19th Lunchtime
The Paladins
**Tuesday 20th
Lunchtime**
The Escorts
Evening
The Four Quarters
The Mojos
The Escorts
Vic and The Spidermen
Wednesday 21st Lunchtime
Wayne Fontana and The Mindbenders
Evening
The Defenders
The Bachelor Boys
Wayne Fontana and The Mindbenders
The Escorts
The Merseybeats (first record out
Friday 23 August 1963)

Thursday 22nd Lunchtime
The Merseybeats
Friday 23rd Lunchtime
The Fourmost
Evening
The Fourmost
Chick Graham and The Coasters
Gerry De Villa and The City Kings
The Sapphires
Saturday 24th Evening
The Chants
The Easybeats
Johnny Sandon and The Remo Four
The Dennisons
Dean Stacy and The Detonators
Sunday 25th Evening
Red River Jazzmen
The Escorts
Steve Aldo and The Challengers
Monday 26th Lunchtime
The Dennisons
Tuesday 27th Lunchtime
The Merseybeats
Evening
Faron's Flamingos
The Leemen
Ian and The Zodiacs
The Delmont Four
Wednesday 28th Lunchtime
The Hollies
Evening
Chick Graham and The Coasters
The Hollies
The Citadels
Sonny Webb and The Cascades
Thursday 29th Lunchtime
The Escorts
Evening
The Big Three (free admission to live
recording session [Decca])
Friday 30th Lunchtime
The Mojos (free show, new record
'They Say' twenty-five copies to
give away)
The Panthers
Vince Earl and The Talisman
The Mobs
Ian and The Zodiacs
Saturday 31st Evening
The Marauders
The Nocturns
Chick Graham and The Coasters
The Young Ones

SEPTEMBER
Sunday 1st Evening
The Clyde Valley Stompers Jazz Band
Johnny Sandon and The Remo Four
The Escorts

Bobby Lame and The Confederates
(from Manchester)
Monday 2nd Lunchtime
Faron's Flamingos
Tuesday 3rd Lunchtime
Earl Preston and The TTs
Evening
The Merseybeats
The Beatcombers
Bobby and The Bachelors
Dean Stacy and The Detonators
Wednesday 4th Lunchtime
The Merseybeats
Evening
The Roadrunners
(direct from the Beatles' touring
show)
Tommy Quickley and The
Challengers
Sons of the Piltdownmen
Garry and Lee
The Escorts
Thursday 5th Lunchtime
The Mojos
Friday 6th Lunchtime
Ricky Valance
Jimmy Powell and The Jumping Jacks
Evening
The Mojos
The Easybeats
The Merseybeats
Ricky Valance and The Questions
Jimmy Powell and The Jumping Jacks
Saturday 7th Evening
Earl Preston and The TTs
The Dee Jays
The Jokers
The Excheckers
Sunday 8th Evening
The Dennisons
Sonny Webb and The Cascades
The Master Sounds
The Rainy City Jazz Band
Monday 9th Lunchtime
Rory Storm and The Hurricanes
Tuesday 10th Lunchtime
Johnny Sandon and The Remo Four
Evening
Bishop and The Curates
The Panthers
The Merseybeats
Four Hits and A Miss
Wednesday 11th Lunchtime
Chris Nays Combo
Evening
Chris Nava Combo
Vic and The Spidermen
Paul and The Diamonds
The Beatcombers

Thursday 12th Lunchtime
Faron's Flamingos
Friday 13th Lunchtime
The Escorts
Evening
Ian and The Zodiacs
Group One
Sonny Kaye and The Reds
Steve Aldo and The Challengers
Saturday 14th Evening
The Escorts
Rory Storm and The Hurricanes
Roy and The Dions
The Black Knights
Sunday 15th Evening
The Merseybeats
The Beatcombers
Dave Roman and The Chariots
The Red River Jazzmen
Tuesday 17th Evening
Vic and The Spidermen
Rory Storm and The Hurricanes
The Asteroids
The Exiles
Wednesday 18th Lunchtime
The Escorts
Evening
The Merseybeats
The Four Just Men
The Defenders
The Crusaders
Thursday 19th Lunchtime
The Swinging Blue Genes
(free pictures)
Friday 20th Evening
Wayne Gibson and The Dynamic
Sounds
Evening
The Roadrunners
Mike and The Thunderbirds
The Mark Four
Saturday 21st Evening
Group One
The Mojos
The Tomboys
The Panthers
Vince Earl and The Talismen
Sunday 22nd Evening
The Merseybeats
The Zenith Six Jazz Band
The Psychos
The Dateliners
Monday 23rd Lunchtime
Sonny Webb and The Cascades
Tuesday 24th Lunchtime
The Escorts
Evening
Earl Preston and The TTs
The Mojos

The Four Clefs
The Counts
Wednesday 25th Lunchtime
The Mojos
Evening
The Chants
The Escorts
Rory Storm and The Hurricanes
The Harlems
The Quintones
Thursday 26th Lunchtime
The Merseybeats
Friday 27th Lunchtime
The Swinging Blue Genes
Evening
The Stormers
The Shondells
The Beatcombers
The Bachelor Boys
Saturday 28th Evening
Alexis Korner's Blues Inc.
Derry Wilkie and The Pressmen
Dean Stacy and The Detonators
Sunday 29th Evening
The Mojos
Vic and The Spidermen
The Countdowns
Riverside Jazzmen with Julie
Monday 30th Lunchtime
Earl Preston and The TTs

OCTOBER
Tuesday 1st Lunchtime
The Merseybeats
Evening
The Cyclones
The Kinsmen
The Merseybeats
The Fortunes
Wednesday 2nd Lunchtime
Faron's Flamingos
Thursday 3rd Lunchtime
Rory Storm and The Hurricanes
Friday 4th Lunchtime
The Escorts
Evening
Freddie Starr and The Midnighters
The Panthers
The Memphis 3
The Four Tralelars
Saturday 5th Evening
The Beatcombers
The Washington DCs
Group One
The Easybeats
Sunday 6th Evening
Wayne Fontana and The Mindbenders
The Defenders
The Nightwalkers

The Rainy City Jazzmen
Monday 7th Lunchtime
Wayne Fontana and The Mindbenders
Tuesday 8th Lunchtime
The Mojos
Evening
The Escorts
The Roadrunners
The Paladins
The Cracksmen
Wednesday 9th Lunchtime
Wayne Fontana and The Mindbenders
Evening
Wayne Fontana and The Mindbenders
Sonny Webb and The Cascades
The Sterios
The Beathovens
Thursday 10th Lunchtime
The Escorts
Friday 11th Lunchtime
Faron's Flamingos
Evening
Freddie Starr and The Midnighters
Vic and The Spidermen
The Nashpool Four
The Easybeats
Saturday 12th Evening
Mel Turner and The Souvenirs
The Mission Men
The Delrenas
The Mark Four
Bobby and The Bachelors
Sunday 13th Evening
The Merseybeats
The Dennisons
The Kubas
The Zenith Six Jazz Band
Monday 14th Lunchtime
The Merseybeats
Tuesday 15th Lunchtime
Sonny Webb and The Cascades
Evening
The Dennisons
The Moonrakers
The Black Knights
The Beatcombers
Wednesday 16th Lunchtime
Earl Preston and The TTs
Evening
The Escorts
The Shondells
Johnny Marlowe and The Whipcords
The Country Gentlemen
Thursday 17th Lunchtime
The Escorts
Friday 18th Lunchtime
Faron's Flamingos
Evening
Faron's Flamingos

The Mojos
The Roadrunners
The Victors
Saturday 19th Evening
The Kubas
The Panthers
Vince Earl and The Talisman
The Mission Men
Sunday 20th Evening
The Escorts
The Mark Four
The Paladins
The Emperors of Rhythm
Tuesday 22nd Evening
Danny Havoc and The Secrets
The Mojos
Clay Ellis and The Landsliders
The Karacters
Wednesday 23rd Lunchtime
The Escorts
Evening
The Dennisons
The Incas
Earl Royce and The Olympics
The Valkyries
Thursday 24th Lunchtime
The Merseybeats
Friday 25th Lunchtime
Faron's Flamingos
Evening
Vic and The Spidermen
The Beatcombers
Bobby and The Bachelors
JJ and The Hi-Lites
Saturday 26th Evening
The Escorts
The Roadrunners
The Mark Four
The Black Knights
Sunday 27th Evening
Jimmy Powell and The 5th
    Dimension (with Rod Stewart on
    harmonica)
The Delrenas
The Zenith Six Jazz Band
The Notions
Monday 28th Lunchtime
The Mojos
Tuesday 29th Lunchtime
The Merseybeats
Evening
The Cordelles
The Dennisons
Vic and The Spidermen
Wednesday 30th Lunchtime
The Hollies
Evening
Bobby and The Bachelors
The Hollies

The Hustlers
The Beatcombers
Thursday 31st Lunchtime
The Chants

NOVEMBER
Friday 1st Lunchtime
Wayne Fontana and The Mindbenders
Evening
Dean Stacey and The Detonators
The Fourmost ('Hello Little Girl')
Wayne Fontana and The Mindbenders
The Panthers
The Boys
Saturday 2nd Evening
The Mojos
The Beatcombers
Johnny Ringo and The Colts
Dino and The Wildfires
Sunday 3rd Evening
The Dennisons
The Five Shillings
Sonny Webb and The Cascades
Zenith Six Jazz Band
Monday 4th Lunchtime
Derry Wilkie and The Pressmen
Tuesday 5th Lunchtime
The Mojos
Evening
The Master Sounds
The Rolling Stones (4s 6d admission)
The Escorts
The Roadrunners
Wednesday 6th Lunchtime
Wayne Fontana and The Mindbenders
Evening
Wayne Fontana and The Mindbenders
The Shondells
Gerry De Ville and The City Kings
Thursday 7th
Closed all day for television recording
    – The Big Three
Friday 8th Lunchtime
The Merseybeats
Evening
The Roadrunners
The Master Sounds
JJ and The Hi-Lites
Gerry and The Pontiacs
Saturday 9th Evening
The Escorts
The Mark Four
Derry and The Pressmen
Dean Stacy and The Detonators
Sunday 10th Lunchtime
The Big Three (filmed on stage)
Freddie and The Dreamers
Wayne Fontana and The Mindbenders
Dave Berry and The Cruisers

Pete McLaine and The Clan
Evening
Alexis Korner Blues Inc. (Graham
    Bond on keyboards, Ginger Baker
    on drums, Jack Bruce on bass)
Vic and The Spidermen
The Four Musketeers
Monday 11th Lunchtime
Earl Preston and The TTs
Evening
Television filming taking place
Tuesday 12th Lunchtime
The Shouts
Evening
The Tempos
The Beatcombers
The Shouts
The Panthers
The Shondells
Wednesday 13th Lunchtime
Cadillac and The Playboys
Evening
The Escorts
Cadillac and The Playboys
The Cruisaders
The Five Aces
Thursday 14th Lunchtime
The Mojos
Friday 15th Lunchtime
Vic and The Spidermen
Jimmy Tarbuck
Saturday 16th Evening
The Roadrunners
The Classics
Bobby and The Bachelors
Bobby Laine and The Confederates
Sunday 17th Evening
The Dennisons
The Escorts
Pete Hartigan's Jazz Band
The In Beateens
Tuesday 19th Evening
Wayne Fontana and The Mindbenders
The Escorts
The Rainchecks
The Cossacks
Wednesday 20th Evening
Johnny Sandon and The Remo Four
Friday 22nd Evening
The Escorts
The Beatcombers
Derry Wilkie and The Pressmen
The Asteroids
Saturday 23rd Evening
Vic and The Spidermen
The Roadrunners
The Kinsmen
The Paladins

Sunday 24th Evening
(R&B marathon)
The Big Three
The Merseybeats
The Escorts
The Roadrunners
The Astrals
The Panthers
The Notions
Derry and The Pressmen
Monday 25th Lunchtime
The Dennisons
Tuesday 26th Lunchtime
Earl Preston and The TTs
Evening
Derry and The Pressmen
Alby and The Sorrals
Karl Terry and The Cruisers
The Four Gents
Wednesday 27th Lunchtime
The Escorts
Evening
The Escorts
Earl Preston and The TTs
The Roadrunners
The Chandels
Thursday 28th Lunchtime
The Merseybeats
Friday 29th Lunchtime
Earl Preston and The TTs
Saturday 30th Evening
Jimmy Powell and The 5th
   Dimension
The Mark Four

DECEMBER
Sunday 1st Evening
The Cresters (from Manchester)
Earl Preston and The TTs
Derry and The Pressmen
The Paladins
Monday 2nd Lunchtime
Chick Graham and The Coasters
Tuesday 3rd Evening
Chick Graham and The Coasters
The Roadrunners
The Mighty Avengers
Roy and The Dions
Wednesday 4th Lunchtime
The Roadrunners
Evening
Dean Stacy and The Detonators
The Dennisons
The City Beats
The Notions
Thursday 5th Lunchtime
The Classics
Evening
The Rattles (from Germany)

The Classics
The Mark Four
Friday 6th Lunchtime
Earl Preston and The TTs
Evening
The Rattles
Earl Preston and The TTs
The Escorts
The Mark Four
Denny Seyton and The Sabres
Saturday 7th Evening
The Rattles
The Master Sounds
Vic and The Spidermen
The Black Knights
The Connoisseurs
Sunday 8th Evening
The Rattles
The Notions
The Escorts
The Panthers
The Red River Jazzmen
Monday 9th Lunchtime
The Rattles
Tuesday 10th Lunchtime
The Animals (from Newcastle)
Evening
Cliff Bennet and The Rebel Rousers
The Mojos
Chris and The Classics
The Shondells
Wednesday 11th Lunchtime
The Rattles
Evening
The Big Three
The Notions
The Roadrunners
The Mafia
Thursday 12th Lunchtime
The Rattles
Evening
The Rattles
The Master Sounds
The Escorts
The Panthers
Friday 13th Lunchtime
The Escorts
Evening
The Fourmost
Derry and The Pressmen
The Mark Four
The Easybeats
Saturday 14th Evening
The Rattles
The Beatcombers
Dean Stacy and The Detonators
Bobby and The Bachelors
Johnny Ringo and The Colts

Sunday 15th Evening
Vic and The Spidermen
The Zenith Six Jazz Band
Denny Seyton and The Sabres
The Beatcombers
Monday 16th Lunchtime
The Merseybeats
Tuesday 17th Lunchtime
The Roadrunners
Evening
The Merseybeats
The Rattles
The Notions
The Mark Four
Wednesday 18th Lunchtime
The Rattles
Evening
The Big Three
Earl Preston and The TTs
The Escorts
The Animals
Cy Tucker and The Friars
Friday 20th Lunchtime
The Rattles
Evening
The Rattles (Farewell show before
   returning to Germany. Record out
   now: 'The Stomp')
Vic and The Spidermen
The Valkyries
The Young Ones
Saturday 21st Evening
Derry and The Pressmen
The Mastersounds
The Shondells
The Beatcombers
Sunday 22nd Evening
The Escorts
The Zenith Six Jazz Band
Derry and The Pressmen
The Naspool Four
Tuesday 24th Evening
The Merseybeats
The Mastersounds
Derry and The Pressmen
The Secrets
The Beatcombers
Thursday 26th Evening
The Escorts
Vic and The Spidermen
The Notions
The Riot Squad
The Beatcombers
Friday 27th Lunchtime
Johnny Mike and The Shades
Evening
The Mastersounds
The Shondells
The Cordelles

Johnny Mike and The Shades
Saturday 28th Evening
The Mark Four
The Panthers
The Beathovens
Derry and The Pressmen
Tuesday 31st Lunchtime
The Mobs
All-Night Session
The Shondells
The Detonators
The Easybeats
Chick Graham and The Coasters
The Remo Four
The Big Three
The Escorts
The Mark Four
Vic and The Spidermen
Deny and The Pressmen
The Riot Squad (John Lord on
   keyboards, Mitch Mitchell on drums)

1964

JANUARY
Wednesday 1st Evening
The Escorts
The Notions
The Casuals
Gerry De Ville and The City Kings
Thursday 2nd Lunchtime
The Escorts
Friday 3rd Lunchtime
The Undertakers
Evening
The Escorts
The Notions
The Casuals
Herman and The Hermits
Saturday 4th Evening
Chick Graham and The Coasters
The Liver Birds
The Master Sounds
The Mark Four
Sunday 5th Evening
The Mojos
The Panthers
The Notions
The Shondells
Ian and The Zodiacs
Monday 6th Lunchtime
Ian and The Zodiacs
The Merseybeats
Tuesday 7th Lunchtime
The Escorts
Evening
The Remo Four

The Premiers
The Georgians
Wednesday 8th Lunchtime
The Cresters
Evening
The Cresters
The Hungry 1's
Adam and The Sinners
Lorraine Gray and The Chaperones
Thursday 9th Lunchtime
The Remo Four
Friday 10th Lunchtime
The Liver Birds
Evening
The Mark Four
The Pawns
The Notions
The Rainmakers
Saturday 11th Evening
The Escorts
Johnny Anger and The Wild Ones
Herman and The Hermits
Savva and The Democrats
Sunday 12th Evening
Denny Seyton and The Sabres
The Nocturns
The Spidermen
The Dixielanders

Monday 13th Lunchtime
Ricky Gleason and The Top Spots
Tuesday 14th Lunchtime
Mark Peters and The Silhouettes
Evening
Cadillac and The Play Boys
Take Four
The Diamonds
The Georgians
Wednesday 15th Lunchtime
The Chants
The Harlems
Evening
The Country Gentlemen
Denny Seyton and The Sabres
The Boys
The Caverners
Thursday 16th Lunchtime
The Dennisons
Friday 17th Lunchtime
The Fortunes
Evening
The Fortunes
The Mastersounds
Bobby and The Bachelors
The Connoisseurs
Saturday 18th Evening
The Four Pennies
The Panthers
The Stereos
The Valkyries
Sunday 19th Evening
The Crestas
The Notions
The Mafia
Denny Seyton and The Sabres
Tuesday 21st Evening
The Kubas
The Liver Birds
The Rats
The Panthers
Wednesday 22nd Lunchtime
The Remo Four
Evening
Sonny Boy Williamson (blues star)
The Yardbirds – direct from London
The Master Sounds (featuring Adrian
   Lord)
The Pawns
The Champions
Friday 24th Lunchtime
The Roadrunners
Saturday 25th Evening
The Escorts
The Mastersounds
The Kinsmen
The Huntsmen
The Notions

Sunday 26th Evening
Alexis Korner Blues Inc.
Vic and The TTs
The Liver Birds
The Georgians
Tuesday 28th Evening
The Roadrunners
Lee Castle and The Barons
The Inmates
The Panthers
Wednesday 29th Lunchtime
The Chants
The Harlems
Evening
The Escorts
The Kubas
The Mastersounds
Friday 31st Evening
The Notions
The Riot Squad
The Spidermen
The Cordelles

FEBRUARY
Saturday 1st Lunchtime
(Opening of the Junior Cavern Club)
The Mark Four
The Notions
Personal appearance by Billy J.
   Kramer (new record 'Little
   Children')
Evening
Deke Rivers and The Big Sound
The Mark Four
The Valkyries
Bobby and The Bachelors
Sunday 2nd Evening
The Chants
The Harlems
The Panthers
Evening
The Mersey Blue Beats
Monday 3rd Lunchtime
(Decca recording the day's sessions)
The Big Three
Dave Berry and The Cruisers
Evening
Lee Curtis and The All Stars
The Dennisons
The Fortunes
Tuesday 4th Evening
The Kubas
The Crestas
The Nashpool Four
Sundown Valley
The Boys
Wednesday 5th Lunchtime
(Film cameras to record *Look at Life*
   programme for Rank Organisation)

The Escorts
Evening
Free Disco
The Undertakers
The Roadrunners
The Panthers
The Page Boys
Thursday 6th Lunchtime
(Decca recording the day's sessions)
The Marauders
The Four Just Men
Beryl Marsden
Evening
(Admission free)
Bern Elliot and The Fenmen
The Marauders
Heinz
Vic and The TTs
Friday 7th Lunchtime
The Merseybeats (new record 'I
   Think of You')
Saturday 8th Lunchtime
Junior Cavern Club
The Escorts
Chick Graham and The Coasters
Tuesday 11th Evening
Denny Seyton and The Sabres
Cadillac and The Playboys
The Pilgrims
The Ghost Riders
The Mark Four
Wednesday 12th Lunchtime
The Undertakers
Evening
The Merseybeats
The Escorts
The Valkyries
The Georgians
Thursday 13th Lunchtime
The Vernons Girls
Johnny Mike and The Shades
Friday 14th Evening
The Remo Four
The Liver Birds
The Riot Squad
Alby and The Sorrals
Saturday 15th Lunchtime
Junior Cavern club
The Escorts
The Panthers
The Deans
Evening
The Escorts
The Mark Four
The Panthers
The Executioners
Sunday 16th Evening
The Escorts
The Notions

Billy Butler and The Tuxedos
Bobby and The Bachelors
Monday 17th Evening
(Oriole recording session taking
   place)
Wayne Fontana and The Mindbenders
Tuesday 18th Evening
The Roadrunners
The Spidermen
The Ivan D Juniors
The Vibrators
Wednesday 19th Evening
The Kubas
The Panthers
The Concords
The Corvettes
Friday 21st Lunchtime
The Kinks (new record 'Long Tall
   Sally')
Saturday 22nd Evening
The Roadrunners
The Astrals
The Georgians
The Spidermen
Sunday 23rd Evening
Alexis Korner Blues Inc.
The Remo Four
The Dominant Four
The Georgians
Monday 24th Evening
(Rael Brook Contest Night)
The Escorts
The Hawks
The Defenders
The Interns
The Cavels
The Fortunes
Tuesday 25th Evening
Billy Butler and The Tuxedos
The Cresters
The Silverstones
The Georgians
Wednesday 26th Lunchtime
The Undertakers
The Yardbirds (Eric Clapton on
   guitar)
Evening
Sonny Boy Williamson
The Yardbirds
The Mersey Blue Beats
The Roadrunners
The Valkyries
The St Louis Checks
Thursday 27th Lunchtime
Phil Ryan and The Crescents
Friday 28th Lunchtime
The Escorts
Saturday 29th Evening
Sonny Webb and The Cascades

The Notions
The Riot Squad
The Nocturnes

MARCH
Sunday 1st Evening
Herman's Hermits
The Sheffields
The Bumbles
The Detonators
Monday 2nd Evening
Rael Brook Competition
Six bands including Deek's
   Bohemians
Tuesday 3rd Evening
(First recording session for Radio 208
   show *Sunday Night at the Cavern*)
Bobby Sampson and The Giants
The Dions
The Roadrunners
The Rockin' Rivals
Thursday 5th Evening
The Merseybeats
Saturday 7th Evening
The Notions
The Huntsmen
The Spidermen
The Georgians
Sunday 8th Evening
The Mastersounds
The Notions
Gerry De Ville and The City Kings
Monday 9th Evening
The Fortunes
Tuesday 10th Evening
The Chants
The Harlems
The Notions
The Black Knights
The Caverners
Wednesday 11th Evening
Lorraine Gray and The Chaperones
The Secrets
The Kirbys
The Vampires
Thursday 12th Evening
Rael Brook Competition
The Cresters – plus five bands
Friday 13th Lunchtime
The Roadrunners
Evening
The Roadrunners
The Notions
The Mersey Blue Beats
The Concords
The Georgians
Saturday 14th Lunchtime
(Junior Cavern Club)
Herman's Hermits

Cavern favourites Earl Preston's Realms, 1963. Earl Preston's Realms appeared at the Cavern 144 times in the 1960s. Earl Preston (real name Georgie Spruce) also made other appearances at the Cavern as Earl Preston and the TTs and Earl Preston and The Reflections. His tally of 182 appearances at the club is bettered by just a handful of Cavern performers.

The Mark Four
The Fallons
Evening
Herman's Hermits
The Mark Four
The Pilgrims
L'Ringos
Sunday 15th Evening
The Saints Jazz Band
The Mersey Blue Beats
The Feelgoods
The Hideaways
The Georgians
The Chequers
Monday 16th Evening
The Rattles
Tuesday 17th Evening
Ian Crawford and The Boomerangs
Sonny Kaye and The Reds
Le Paul and The Boys
The Jokers
Wednesday 18th Evening
The Kubas
The Country Gentlemen
The Liverbirds
The Shimmy Shakers
Friday 20th Lunchtime
The Merseybeats
Evening
The Roadrunners

The Mersey Blue Beats
The Motifs
The Vigilantes
Saturday 21st Lunchtime
(Junior Cavern Club)
Denny Seyton and The Sabres
Earl Preston's Realms
The Four Aces
Evening
The Kirbys
The Secrets
The Georgians
The Skeletons
Group One
Sunday 22nd Evening
Lorraine Gray and The Chaperones
The Roadrunners
The Cordes
The Megatones
Monday 23rd Lunchtime
The Delameres
Tuesday 24th Evening
Earl Preston's Realms
The Secrets
The Photons
The Riot Squad
The Country Gentlemen
Wednesday 25th Evening
The Roadrunners
Ricky Gleason and The Top Spots

The Triffids
The Feelgoods
Thursday 26th Evening
The Escorts
Saturday 28th Evening
The Nashpool Four
The Acoustics
JJ and The Executives
Mike Cotten's R&B Band
The Mark Four
Sunday 29th Evening
Earl Preston's Realms
Billy Butler and The Tuxedos
The Secrets
The Hideaways
The Pilgrims
Chick Graham and The Coasters
Tuesday 31st Lunchtime
The Green Beats (from Ireland)

APRIL
Wednesday 1st lunchtime
The Green Beats
Evening
The Clayton Squares
The Kubas
The Riot Squad
Vince Earl and The Talismen
Thursday 2nd Lunchtime
The Green Beats
Evening
The Roadrunners
Friday 3rd Lunchtime
The Escorts
The Valkyries
The Green Beats
The Chants
The Harlems
Evening
The Four Pennies
The Clayton Squares
The Notions
The Kubas
Group One
Saturday 4th Lunchtime
(Junior Cavern Club)
The Green Beats
Evening
The Roadrunners
The Feelgoods
The Hideaways
The Black Velvets
Deek's Weirdos
Sunday 5th Evening
Millie ('My Boy Lollipop')
The Five Embers
The Kubas
The Mark Four
The Rockefellers

The Pretenders
The Executioners
Monday 6th Evening
The Raffles
Thursday 9th Evening
Millie
The Four Pennies
The Five Embers
Ricky Gleason and The Top Spots
Friday 10th Lunchtime
The Kubas
Evening
The Escorts
The Executioners
The Kubas
The Mark Four
The Riot Squad
The Legends
Saturday 11th Lunchtime
(Junior Cavern Club)
Millie
The Escorts
The Five Embers
Carol and The Corvettes
Arrow and The Archers
Evening
Millie
The Five Embers
The Notions
The Clayton Squares
Billy Butler and The Tuxedos
Bobby and The Bachelors
Sunday 12th Evening
Compère Bob Wooler
The Roadrunners
The Kirbys
The Hideaways
The Clayton Squares
The Escorts
Monday 13th Evening
The Rattles
Tuesday 14th Evening
The Raffles
Earl Preston's Realms
Denny Seyton and The Sabres
The Blackwells
Wednesday 15th Lunchtime
The Rattles
Evening
The Rattles
The Notions
The Clayton Squares
St Louis Checks
Thursday 16th Evening
The Rattles
The Clayton Squares
The Pretenders
The Billy Kinsley Group

Friday 17th Evening
The Kubas
The Illusions
The Notions
The Hideaways
The Riot Squad
The Feelgoods
Saturday 18th Lunchtime
(Junior Cavern Club)
Cole Young and The Graduates (from Bristol)
The Flyaways
The Scorchers
The Nocturns
The Mosquitos
Evening
The Mark Four
Billy Butler and The Tuxedos
Cole Young and The Graduates
The Georgians
The New Pressmen
The Varasounds
Wednesday 22nd Evening
The Kirbys
The Pawns
The Hideaways
The Valkyries
Thursday 23rd Lunchtime
The Valkyries
The Billy Kinsley Group
Friday 24th Lunchtime
The Four Pennies
Evening
The Clayton Squares
The Notions
The Gruff Parry Five
The Feelgoods
The Chessmen
Saturday 25th Lunchtime
(Junior Cavern Club)
The Hideaways
The Soundsmen
Bobby Sampson and The Giants
Evening
The Valkyries
Bobby Sampson and The Giants
The Soundsmen
Sunday 26th Evening
Bobby and The Bachelors
Mike Cotten Sound
The Mark Four
The Kirbys
The Black Cats
Monday 27th Lunchtime
Freddy Starr and The Flamingos

MAY
Friday 1st Evening
The Clayton Squares

J.B. Bishop and The Curates
The Feelgoods
The Dions
The Climaks
Saturday 2nd Lunchtime
(Junior Cavern Club)
Chick Graham and The Coasters
Billy Butler and The Tuxedos
Earl Preston's Realms
The Hideaways
Evening
Russ Saunders and The V Tones
The Colts with Johnny Ringo
The Executioners
Sunday 3rd Evening
Alexis Korner's Blues Inc.
The Cordes
The Tempests
The Clayton Squares
Monday 4th Lunchtime
The Valkyries
Tuesday 5th Lunchtime
Herman's Hermits
Evening
(Sounds of '64 Big Beat Competition Night. Judged by Norrie Paramor)
The Dolly Mixtures
The Merseybeats
Wednesday 6th Evening
Ian Crawford and The Boomerangs
The Notions
The Pilgrims
The Mysteries
Friday 8th Evening
The Valkyries
The Cordes
The Incas
The Huntsmen
Saturday 9th Lunchtime
(Junior Cavern Club)
Vic and The TTs
The Dions
The Jaguars
Evening
The Mike Cotten Sound
The Feelgoods
The Lectrons
The Mersey Blue Beats
Bobby and The Bachelors
Sunday 10th Evening
The Cordes
Lee Paul and The Boys
The Four Pennies
The Dolly Mixtures
Monday 11th Lunchtime
The Escorts
Tuesday 12th Lunchtime
Bobby Sampson and The Giants
The Redcaps

TO-NIGHT, TO-NIGHT, TO-NIGHT
At The Cavern
THE ROADRUNNERS
THE ASTRALS
THE SPIDERMEN
THE GEORGIANS

Don't Miss This Great Sunday
Night At The Cavern
Once Again We Feature That
Terrific Act
ALEXIS KORNER'S BLUES INC
PLUS
THE REMO FOUR
PLUS
THE DOMINANT FOUR
PLUS
THE GEORGIANS

WEDNESDAY LUNCHTIME IS A MUST
TWO FAB. ACTS FOR YOU
THE UNDERTAKERS
PLUS
THE YARDBIRDS
Thursday Lunchtime:
PHIL RYAN & THE CRESCENTS
Friday Lunchtime:
THE ESCORTS

Evening
Bobby Sampson and The Giants
The Diamonds
The Clayton Squares
Carol and The Corvettes
Wednesday 13th Lunchtime
The Trends
Tony Rivers and The Castaways
Evening
The Notions
The Redcaps
The Kirbys
The Renicks
Vic and The TTs
Thursday 14th Lunchtime
Billy Kinsley Group
Friday 15th Lunchtime
The Escorts
Evening
Lorraine Gray and The Chaperones
The Riot Squad

The Detonators
The Connoisseurs
Saturday 16th Lunchtime
(Junior Cavern Club)
Ricky Gleason and The Top Spots
The Mark Four
Evening
The Mark Four
The Cordes
The Feelgoods
The Pretenders
Sunday 17th Evening
Ricky Gleason and The Top Spots
The Notions
The Dions
Dene and The Citizens
Monday 18th All Day Session
3.30-11.30p.m.
(Beatrama no.2)
The Clayton Squares
The Roadrunners

Billy Kinsley's New Group
The Centremen
The Mastersounds
The Hideaways
The Nashpool Four
Freddy Starr and The Flamingos
The Spidermen
St Louis Checks
The Georgians
The Blackwells
The Coins
The Schatz

Tuesday 19th Lunchtime
The Schatz
The Escorts
The Rats
The Notions
Vic and The TTs
The Four Travellers

Wednesday 20th Lunchtime
The Roadrunners

Evening
The Georgians
St Louis Checks
Johnny Ringo and The Colts
Phil's Feelgoods

Thursday 21st Lunchtime
Denny Seyton and The Sabres

Friday 22nd Lunchtime
The Mojos
The Griff Parry Five

Evening
The Escorts
The Roadrunners
The Easybeats
The Notions
The Cordes

Saturday 23rd Lunchtime
(Junior Cavern Club)
Herman's Hermits
The Motifs
The Fractions

Evening
The Kirbys
Herman's Hermits
The Mark Four
The Pilgrims
The Motifs

Sunday 24th Evening
The Kinsleys
Ian Crawford and The Boomerangs
The Connoisseurs
The Premiers
Them Grimbles

Tuesday 26th Evening
The Notions
The Kinsleys
The Tabs
The Georgians

**Wednesday 27th Lunchtime and
  Afternoon Session**
Wayne Fontana and The Mindbenders
Earl Preston's Realms
The Big Three

Evening
Long John Baldry
The Hoochie Coochie Men (with
  Rod Stewart on vocals)
The Clayton Squares
The Griff Parry Five

Friday 29th Evening
The Kinsleys
The Pilgrims
Billy Butler and The Tuxedos
The 12345

Saturday 30th Lunchtime
(Junior Cavern Club)
The Escorts
The Calderstones
Chick Graham and The Coasters

Evening
The Georgians
The Cordes
The Dions
Bobby and The Bachelors
The Rockin' Rivals

Sunday 31st Evening
Shorty and Them
Vic and The TTs
Earl Preston's Realms
The Riot Squad
The Inmates

JUNE
Monday 1st Lunchtime
The Escorts

Tuesday 2nd Evening
The Roadrunners
The Notions
Herman's Hermits

Wednesday 3rd Evening
Dave Lee and The Staggerlees
The Hideaways
The Ivan D Juniors
The Elements

Thursday 4th Evening
The Escorts
Denny Seyton and The Sabres
The Kinsleys

Friday 5th Evening
Vic and The TTs
The Georgians
Mickey Most and The Gear
The Triumphs
Kris Ryan and The Questions

Saturday 6th Lunchtime
(Junior Cavern Club)
The Kirbys

The Kinsleys
The J Beats
The Fractions

Evening
The Nightwalkers
The Cordes
The Kinsleys
The Mark Four

Sunday 7th Evening
The Kirbys
The Griff Parry Five
Bobby and The Bachelors
The Pilgrims
The Cyclones

Monday 8th Lunchtime
The Escorts

Tuesday 9th Evening
Freddy Starr and The Flamingos
The Dions
The Mysteries
The Elektons

Wednesday 10th Evening
The Escorts
Vic and The TTs
The Notions
J and The Juniors

Friday 12th Lunchtime
The Clayton Squares

Evening
The St Louis Checks
The Clayton Squares
The Cordes
The Hideaways
The John Lee Hooker Show
John Mayall's Bluesbreakers

Saturday 13th Lunchtime
(Junior Cavern Club)
The Escorts

Evening
The Notions
The Hideaways
The Spidermen
The St Louis Checks

Sunday 14th Evening
The Countdowns
Mike Cotton Sound
The Kubas (Back from Spanish tour)
The Jensons

Tuesday 16th Evening
The Roadrunners
The Kirbys
The Mersey Blue Beats
The Interludes

Wednesday 17th Evening
The Country Gentlemen
The Georgians
The Kruzads
The Jacobeats

Thursday 18th Evening
The Yardbirds
Freddy Starr and The Flamingos
Jimmy Powell and The Five
  Dimensions

Friday 19th Lunchtime
The Chants

Evening
Billy Butler and The Tuxedos
The TTs
The Dell Stars
The Pilgrims

Saturday 20th Lunchtime
(Junior Cavern Club)
Arrow and The Archers
Chick Graham and The Coasters
The Kinsleys

Evening
The Kinsleys
The Cordes
The Paladins
The Riot Squad
The Connoisseurs

Sunday 21st Evening
The Roadrunners
The Plebs
The Notions
The St Louis Checks

Monday 22nd Lunchtime
The Escorts

Tuesday 23rd Evening
Chick Graham and The Coasters
Cy Tucker and The Friars
The Kirbys

Wednesday 24th Evening
The Notions
Herman's Hermits
The Escorts
The Memphis Three

Thursday 25th Evening
Gerry and the Pacemakers
Kris Ryan and The Questions
The Pretenders

Friday 26th Evening
The Spidermen
The Riot Squad
The Pretenders
The Nocturnes

Saturday 27th Evening
Billy Butler and The Tuxedos
The Doodle Bugs
The TTs
The Kinsleys

Sunday 28th Evening
Earl Preston's Realms
Tiffany and The Four Dimensions
The Moonrakers
The Georgians

Tuesday 30th Evening
The Redcaps
The Vikings
The Roadrunners
The Pilgrims
The Mark Four

JULY
Wednesday 1st Evening
The Escorts
The Mark Four
The Mersey Four
The Notions
Bobby and The Bachelors

Thursday 2nd Evening
The Georgians
The Spencer Davis Group (Steve
  Winwood on vocals and organ)
Inez and Charlie Foxx (soul singers)

Friday 3rd Evening
Cy Tucker and The Friars
Vic and The TTs
The Poets
The Notions

Saturday 4th Lunchtime
(Junior Cavern Club)
The Dions
The Cresters

Evening
The Lectrons
Earl Preston's Realms
The Mark Four
The Riot Squad
The Dee-Jays

Sunday 5th Evening
The Roadrunners
The Spidermen
The Cheetahs
Them Grimbles

Tuesday 7th Evening
Herman's Hermits
The Dions
The Tributes
Gerry De Ville and The City Kings

Wednesday 8th Evening
The Kirbys
The Notions
The Riot Squad
The Alphas

Thursday 9th Evening
Kingsize Taylor and The Dominoes
The Griff Parry Five
The Hideaways
The St Louis Checks

Friday 10th Lunchtime
The Undertakers

Evening
The Notions
Billy Butler and The Tuxedos

The Feelgoods
Savva and The Democrats
Saturday 11th Evening
Earl Preston's Realms
The Georgians
Them Grimbles
Sunday 12th Evening
The Mastersounds
The Hideaways
The Silverstones
The Dolly Mixtures
Monday 13th Lunchtime
The Clayton Squares
Tuesday 14th Evening
The Four Pennies
The Escorts
The Undertakers
Thursday 16th Evening
Earl Preston's Realms
The Four Pennies
The Escorts
The Undertakers
The Kinsleys
Saturday 18th Lunchtime
(Junior Cavern Club)
The Merseybeats
The Hideaways
The Flyaways
The Calderstones
Tuesday 21st Evening
Mark Peters and The Silhouettes
Savva and The Democrats
The Coins
The Casuals
Wednesday 22nd Evening
The Cresters
The Chequers
Gerry De Ville and The City Kings
Friday 24th Evening
The Mighty Avengers
The Dions
Them Grimbles
The Travellers
Saturday 25th Lunchtime
(Junior Cavern Club)
The Kinsleys
Jackie Martin with The Dominators
Evening
The TTs
The Pathfinders
Bobby and The Bachelors
The Chessmen
Sunday 26th Evening
Ian and The Zodiacs
The Pilgrims
The Boot Hillbillies
Monday 27th Lunchtime
The Escorts

Tuesday 28th Evening
The Kirbys
Mr Smith and Sum People
The Pilgrims
Wednesday 29th Evening
The Chants
Friday 31st Evening
Mark Peters and The Silhouettes
The Connoisseurs
Johnny Darren and The Corvettes

AUGUST
Saturday 1st Lunchtime
(Junior Cavern Club)
The Escorts
The Hideaways
The Song Peddlars
Evening
The Song Peddlars
The Hideaways
The Mark Four
The Delmont Four
Monday 3rd R&B Marathon
(Bank Holiday Show)
Prince Khan and The Babes
Savva and The Democrats
The Valkyries
The Dions
Earl Preston's Realms
The Kubas
Them Grimbles
The Strangers
The Smoke Stacks
Tuesday 4th Lunchtime
The Apple Jacks
Evening
The Merseybeats
The Kinsleys
The Cresters
Friday 7th Evening
The Kirbys
The Spidermen
Ian and The Zodiacs
Saturday 8th Lunchtime
(Junior Cavern Club)
Billy Butler and The Tuxedos
Jimmy Nicol and The Shub Dubs
   (Jimmy stood in for Ringo Starr on
   a recent Beatles tour)
Evening
Jimmy Nicol and The Shub Dubs
The Coins
The Mysteries
Sunday 9th Evening
Lorraine Gray and The Chaperones
Vic Takes Four
The Interns
Monday 10th Lunchtime
The Kingsleys

(Cavern finals for the Rael Brook
   Contest taking place at the New
   Brighton Tower Ballroom)
Dale Young and The Semiholes
The Downbeats
Bobby and The Bachelors
Rik E. Dame and The Defenders
The Hustlers
The Jay Els
The Mark Four
The Tokens
J Taylor and The Top Spots
The Trekkers
The Wyverns
Evening
(Presented by the Cavern at the New
   Brighton Tower Ballroom)
The Rolling Stones
Tuesday 11th Evening
The Escorts
The Vampires
Tiffany and The Four Dimensions
Wednesday 12th Evening
The Hideaways
The Notions
The Mighty Avengers
Thursday 13th Evening
The Alex Harvey Big Soul Band
   (from Scotland)
The Hideaways
The Clayton Squares
Friday 14th Evening
Earl Preston's Realms
The Top Spots
The Pretenders
Savva and The Democrats
Saturday 15th Lunchtime
(Junior Cavern Club)
The Escorts
The Feelgoods
The Defiants
Evening
The Clayton Squares
The Spidermen
The Dions
The Feelgoods
Sunday 16th Evening
The Escorts
The Cordes
The Impacts
Monday 17th Lunchtime
Rory Storm and The Hurricanes
Tuesday 18th Evening
The Kinsleys
The Spidermen
The Pretenders
Wednesday 19th Lunchtime
The Escorts

Evening
Earl Preston's Realms
Phil's Feelgoods
The Notions
Thursday 20th Evening
(R&B Show)
The Blues System
Derry and The Others
The Clayton Squares
Mose Allison (blues singer from
   America)
The T Bones
Friday 21st Evening
Denny Seyton and The Sabres
The Notions
The Mighty Avengers
The Blackwells
Saturday 22nd Lunchtime
(Junior Cavern Club)
The Notions
The Zephyrs
The Calderstones
Evening
Earl Preston's Realms
The Cordes
The Pilgrims
Sunday 23rd Evening
The Mark Four
The Spidermen
The Feelgoods
The Spectors
Monday 24th Lunchtime
The Escorts
Tuesday 25th Evening
The Escorts
The Notions
The Dions
Wednesday 26th Evening
Lorraine Gray and The Chaperones
The Pilgrims
Savva and The Democrats
Thursday 27th Lunchtime
The Clayton Squares
Friday 28th Evening
Earl Preston's Realms
Mr Smith and Sum People
The Tokens
Saturday 29th Lunchtime
(Junior Cavern Club)
The Clayton Squares
The Kinsleys
Evening
The Clayton Squares
The Kinsleys
The Detonators
The Nightwalkers
Sunday 30th Evening
The Calderstones
Earl Preston's Realms

The Pilgrims
Monday 31st Lunchtime
The Clayton Squares

SEPTEMBER
Tuesday 1st Lunchtime
Earl Preston's Realms
Evening
The Roadrunners
The Hideaways
The Kinsleys
Wednesday 2nd Lunchtime
The Mighty Avengers
Evening
The Mighty Avengers
The Notions
The Beat Boys
Thursday 3rd Lunchtime
The Kirbys
Friday 4th Lunchtime
The Cresters
Evening
The Feelgoods
The TTs
The Cresters
Saturday 5th Lunchtime
(Junior Cavern Club)
Chick Graham and The Coasters
The Notions
The Traders
Evening
The Hideaways
The Calderstones
The Spidermen
Earl Preston's Realms
Sunday 6th Evening
The Chants
The Harlems
Billy Butler and The Tuxedos
The Dions
The Outcasts
**Monday 7th Beat Week for Oxfam
Lunchtime**
The Bluesville Bats
Evening
The Escorts
Tuesday 8th Evening
Herman's Hermits
The Notions
Denny Seyton and The Sabres
Thursday 10th Evening
The Clayton Squares
Friday 11th Evening
Earl Preston's Realms
Saturday 12th Evening
Kris Ryan and The Questions plus
   eight other top groups
Sunday 13th Evening
Earl Preston's Realms

The TTs
The Detonators
The Merseybeats
The Torreadors
Tuesday 15th Evening
Kris Ryan and The Questions
The Dions
The Vampires
The Riot Squad
Wednesday 16th Evening
The Hideaways
Thursday 17th Evening
(Blues Night)
Jimmy Powell and The Five
    Dimensions
The Hideaways
The Clayton Squares
The Music Students
Friday 18th Evening
The Kirbys
The Toggery Five
The Pilgrims
Saturday 19th Lunchtime
(Junior Cavern Club)
Chick Graham and The Coasters
The Chancellors
Evening
The Chessmen
The Notions
The Riot Squad
The Chancellors
Sunday 20th Eight-Hour Show
(starts 3.30p.m.)
Jimmy Witherspoon (Blues Star)
The Cordes
The Mark Four
The Excerts
Mark Anthony and The Avengers
The Bluesounds
The Abstracts
The Faces
Monday 21st Lunchtime
The Escorts
Tuesday 22nd Evening
The Kirbys
The Saints Jazz Band
The Notions
The TTs
Wednesday 23rd Evening
The Escorts
The Hideaways
The Ivan D Juniors
Saturday 26th Evening
Kris Ryan and The Questions
Group One
Billy Butler and The Tuxedos
The Lectrons
The Factotums

Sunday 27th Evening
The Clayton Squares
The Kubas
The Coins
Tony Lindell and The Sabres
Monday 28th Lunchtime
Denny Seyton and The Sabres
Tuesday 29th Evening
The Hideaways
The Saints Jazz Band
The VIPs
Wednesday 30th Lunchtime
The Escorts
Evening
The Rustiks (Brian Epstein's latest
    recording discovery)
The Notions
The Kirbys

OCTOBER
Thursday 1st Evening
Little Eva ('The Locomotion')
The Kirbys
Earl Preston's Realms
The Hideaways
Danny Storm and The Strollers
Saturday 3rd Evening
The Hideaways
The Kubas
The Chessmen
The Mark Four
Sunday 4th Evening
Mark Peters and The Silhouettes
The Hideaways
The Notions
Billy Butler and The Tuxedos
Monday 5th Lunchtime
The Escorts
Tuesday 6th Lunchtime
The Kinsleys
Evening
Earl Preston's Realms
The Notions
The Toplins
The Spinning Tops (from Manchester)
Wednesday 7th Lunchtime
The Clayton Squares
Evening
The Escorts
The Riot Squad
The Georgians
Thursday 8th Evening
Kris Ryan and The Questions
Alexis Korner's Blues Inc.
The Dennisons
The Hideaways
Friday 9th All-Night Session
The Abstracts
TL's Bluesicians

The TTs
Savva and The Democrats
John Lee Hooker
The Power House Six
The Clayton Squares
John Lee' Groundhogs
Saturday 10th Lunchtime
(Junior Cavern Club)
The Escorts
The Hideaways
Evening
The Kingsleys
The Riot Squad
The Kruzads
The Outcasts
Sunday 11th Evening
The Alex Harvey Big Soul Band
The Clayton Squares
The Abstracts
The St Louis Checks
Wednesday 14th Evening
The Clayton Squares
The Kubas
The Cordes
Thursday 15th Evening
The Abstracts
The Hideaways
The Sheffields
The St Louis Checks
The Tabs
Friday 16th Evening
The Mike Cotton Sound
The Notions
The Coins
The Cordes
Saturday 17th Evening
The Notions
The Dions
The Feelgoods
The Georgians
Uzz Strangers
Sunday 18th Evening
The Clayton Squares
The Spidermen
The Tributes
The Sapphires
Monday 19th Evening
(All Folk Night)
The Spinners
The Green Ginger Four
The Silkie
Luke Kelly (Irish singer)
Tuesday 20th Evening
Denny Seyton and The Sabres
The Notions
The Excerts
Wednesday 21st Evening
Vic Takes Four
The Defiants

The Connoisseurs
Thursday 22nd Evening
The Yardbirds
The Aintree Four
The Clayton Squares
The Abstracts
Friday 23rd Lunchtime
The Escorts
Saturday 24th Evening
The Kubas
The Premiers
Billy Butler and The Tuxedos
The Tributes
Sunday 25th Evening
The Hipster Image
The Cordes
The Riot Squad
Little Boys Blue
Tuesday 27th Lunchtime
The Escorts
Evening
The Faces
The Liberators
The Escorts
Wednesday 28th Lunchtime
The Dennisons
Evening
The Clayton Squares
The Notions
The Chessmen
Thursday 29th Lunchtime
The Kubas
Evening
TL's Bluesicians
The Hideaways
Little Walter (US blues star)
The Sheffields
The Abstracts
Friday 30th Lunchtime
The Clayton Squares
Evening
Ian and The Zodiacs
The Georgians
Uzz Strangers
The Countdowns
Saturday 31st Lunchtime
(Junior Cavern Club)
The Hideaways
The T Beats
The Principals
Evening
Bobby and The Bachelors
The Jacobeats
The Feelgoods
The Outer Limits

NOVEMBER
Sunday 1st Evening
The Clayton Squares

The Notions
The Dions
The Playboys
Monday 2nd Lunchtime
The Clayton Squares
Tuesday 3rd Evening
The Cresters
Amos Bonnie with The TTs
The Sett
Wednesday 4th Evening
Denny Seyton and The Sabres
The Masterminds
The Pretenders
Thursday 5th Evening
The Excelles
The Sheffields
The Blues System
The Hideaways
The St Louis Checks
Friday 6th Lunchtime
(Cavern opening Pop Record Inn for
    all your hit records – free Cavern
    haircut by Romanoffs Hair Stylists)
Kris Ryan and The Questions
The Roadrunners
Evening
The Clayton Squares
The Roadrunners
The Notions
Saturday 7th Lunchtime
(Junior Cavern Club)
The Seftons
The Dennisons
The Principals
All-Night Session
The St Louis Checks
The Excelles
The Hoochie Coochie Men
Long John Baldry
The Clayton Squares
Earl Preston's Realms
The Abstract Minds
The Hideaways
The Riot Squad
TL's Bluesicians
Sunday 8th Evening
The Clayton Squares
The Blues Giants
Billy Butler and The Tuxedos
Monday 9th Lunchtime
The Clayton Squares
Tuesday 10th Evening
The Moody Blues (from
    Birmingham)
Sonny Boy Williamson (blues star)
The Hideaways
The Easybeats
Wednesday 11th Lunchtime
The Takers

Liverpool group The Klaxons.

Friday 13th Evening
The Clayton Squares
The Motifs
Chris and The Autocrats
Saturday 14th Lunchtime
(Junior Cavern Club)
The Clayton Squares
The Hideaways
Evening
The Cordes
The Riot Squad
The Viceroys
The Executioners
Sunday 15th Evening
Earl Preston's Realms
The Notions
The Senators
The St Louis Checks
The Excelles
Monday 16th Lunchtime
Earl Preston's Realms
Tuesday 17th Lunchtime
The Kubas

Evening
Billy Butler and The Tuxedos
The Notions
The Strolling Bones
The Hideaways
Wednesday 18th Lunchtime
The Kinsleys
Evening
Freddy Starr and The Flamingos
The Music Students
The Trend-Setts
Thursday 19th Lunchtime
The St Louis Checks
Evening
(Folk at the Cavern)
The Spinners
The Silkie
The Leesides
The Billy Boys
Tina and Mardi
Friday 20th Lunchtime
The Clayton Squares

Evening
Earl Preston's Realms
The Thundermen
The Pretenders
Savva and The Democrats
Saturday 21st Lunchtime
(Junior Cavern Club)
The Soul Agents (Rod Stewart on
   vocals)
The Kubas
Evening
The Soul Agents
The Easybeats
The Spidermen
The Merseybeats
The Kreeps
Sunday 22nd Evening
(*Sunday Night at the Cavern* on Radio
   Luxembourg)
The Cordes
The Secrets
The Bluesicians
The Hideaways
The New Chariots
Tuesday 24th Evening
The Hollies
The Kirbys
Earl Preston's Realms
Wednesday 25th Lunchtime
The Addicts
Evening
The Notions
The Drumbeats
The Klaxons
The Spidermen
Friday 27th Evening
The Kinsleys
The Tagg
The Easybeats
The Kruzads
Saturday 28th Lunchtime
(Junior Cavern Club)
The Escorts
The Hideaways
Evening
Earl Preston's Realms
The Dions
The Defiants
Sunday 29th Evening
(*Sunday Night at the Cavern* on Radio
   Luxembourg)
The Merseybeats
The Excelles
The Notions
The TTs with Amos Bonny

DECEMBER
Tuesday 1st Evening
The Cresters

The Sad Saks
Steve Brett and The Mavericks
Wednesday 2nd Lunchtime
The Escorts
Evening
Earl Preston's Realms
The St Louis Checks
US Ltd
The Saracens
Thursday 3rd Lunchtime
Rory Storm and The Hurricanes
Friday 4th Lunchtime
The Clayton Squares
Evening
The Escorts
Earl Preston's Realms
The Smokestacks
Mark Peters and The Silhouettes
Saturday 5th Lunchtime
(Junior Cavern Club)
The Hideaways
Formula 1
Evening
Formula 1
The Sabres
The Kirbys
The Cordes
Gerry De Ville And The City Kings
Sunday 6th Evening
(*Sunday Night at the Cavern* on Radio
   Luxembourg)
The Kubas
The Georgians
The Litter
The Harpos
Monday 7th Lunchtime
The Mojos
Tuesday 8th Lunchtime
The Kubas
Evening
Kris Ryan and The Questions
Earl Preston's Realms
The Montanas
The Aztecs
Wednesday 9th Evening
Howlin Wolf (blues star)
The T Bones
Hubert Sumline (USA blues)
The Hideaways
The Michael Allen Group
The St Louis Checks
Thursday 10th Evening
Long John Baldry
Friday 11th Evening
The Escorts
The Notions
The Spidermen
The Dennisons
The Cordes

Sunday 12th Lunchtime
(Junior Cavern Club)
Earl Preston's Realms
The Hoboes
The Strettons
Evening
The Clayton Squares
The Detonators
Earl Preston's Realms
Sunday 13th Evening
(*Sunday Night at the Cavern* on Radio
   Luxembourg)
Steve Aldo
The Jokers
The Griff Parry Five
The Fontanas
The Kubas
The St Louis Checks
Monday 14th Lunchtime
The Escorts
Tuesday 15th Evening
(Twin Beat Nights – All twins get
   in free)
Earl Royce and The Olympics
The Cresters
The Pretenders
The Stormers
Wednesday 16th Evening
The Chants
Rory Storm and The Hurricanes
The Clayton Squares
The Harlems
Earl Royce and The Olympics
The Cordes
Friday 18th Evening
The Dennisons
The Notions
The Kruzads
The Abstracts
Saturday 19th All-Night Session
The Takers
The Pawns
The Kirbys
The Hideaways
The Tabs
The Riot Squad
The Georgians
The Nightwalkers
The Michael Allen Group
Sunday 20th Evening
(*Sunday Night at the Cavern* on Radio
   Luxembourg)
The Hideaways
The St Louis Checks
The Hipster Image
Tuesday 22nd Evening
Earl Preston's Realms
The Cordes

Wednesday 23rd Evening
Kris Ryan and The Questions
The Hideaways
The Kubas
Thursday 24th Lunchtime
Earl Preston's Realms
The Hoboes
Evening
(Christmas Eve Show)
The Escorts
The Clayton Squares
The Notions
The Kinsleys
Saturday 26th Evening
(Boxing Day Big Show)
The Chants
The Hideaways
The Roadrunners
The Kirbys
The Cordes
The Pretenders
Thursday 31st All-Night Session
The Escorts
The Notions
Earl Preston's Realms
The Kirbys
The Clayton Squares
The Pretenders
The Hideaways
The Kinsleys

1965

JANUARY
Tuesday 5th Evening
The Roadrunners
Earl Preston's Realms
Wednesday 6th Evening
The Clayton Squares
The St Louis Checks
Friday 8th Evening
The Hideaways
Fitz and Startz
Saturday 9th Evening
Earl Preston's Realms
The Michael Allen Group
The Factotums
Sunday 10th Evening
The Clayton Squares
The Almost Blues
The Brian Auger Trinity
Tuesday 12th Evening
The Roadrunners
The Notions
Wednesday 13th Evening
The Clayton Squares
The Hideaways

Friday 15th Evening
Earl Preston's Realms
Kris Ryan and The Questions
Saturday 16th All-Night Session
The St Louis Checks
The Clayton Squares
The Roadrunners
The Victor Brox Blues Train
The TTs with Amos Bonny
The TL's Bluesicians
The Jensons
The Gibsons
Sunday 17th Evening
(*Sunday Night at the Cavern* on
    Radio Luxembourg)
Earl Preston's Realms
The Notions
The Hillsiders
The Feelgoods
The Hoboes
Tuesday 19th Evening
The Roadrunners
The Michael Allen Group
Wednesday 20th Evening
Earl Preston's Realms
The Clayton Squares
Thursday 21st Lunchtime
The Hideaways
Friday 22nd Lunchtime
The Undertakers
Evening
The Undertakers
The St Louis Checks
Saturday 23rd Evening
The Spidermen
TL's Bluesicians
Johnny Ringo and The Colts
Sunday 24th Evening
(*Sunday Night at the Cavern* on
    Radio Luxembourg)
Kris Ryan and The Questions
The Victor Brox Blues Train
Rory Storm and The Hurricanes
Tuesday 26th Evening
Earl Preston's Realms
The Roadrunners
Wednesday 27th Evening
The Clayton Squares
TL's Bluesicians
Friday 29th Evening
Fitz and Startz
Lorraine Gray and The Playboys
Saturday 30th Evening
Earl Preston's Realms
The Excerts
The TTs (with Amos and Karl)
Sunday 31st Evening
(*Sunday Night at the Cavern* on Radio
    Luxembourg)

The Johnny Gus Set
The Undertakers
The Blues Syndicate
The Clayton Squares

FEBRUARY
Monday 1st Lunchtime
The Undertakers
Tuesday 2nd Evening
The Roadrunners
The Notions
Wednesday 3rd Evening
The Clayton Squares
Earl Preston's Realms
Friday 5th Lunchtime
Kris Ryan and The Questions
The St Louis Checks
Kris Ryan and The Questions
The Hideaways
Saturday 6th Evening
The Sheffields
The Juliens
The Bluesicians
Sunday 7th Evening
The Undertakers
The Roadrunners
The Maracas
Monday 8th Lunchtime
The Undertakers
Tuesday 9th Evening
The Roadrunners
The Clayton Squares
Wednesday 10th Evening
Earl Preston's Realms
Kris Ryan and The Questions
Friday 12th Evening
The Roadrunners
The Notions
Johnny Ringo and The Colts
Saturday 13th Evening
The Clayton Squares
Earl Preston's Realms
The Dions
Sunday 14th Evening
The Hideaways
The Hipster Image
The Expressions
Monday 15th Evening
(The Black and White Show Against
    Apartheid, produced by Adrian
    Henri)
The Clayton Squares
Wednesday 17th Evening
The Prowlers
The Spidermen
The Clayton Squares
Friday 19th Lunchtime
The Undertakers
The Defiants

The Hideaways
The Black Knights
Saturday 20th All-Night Session
Alexis Korner's Blues Inc.
The Hideaways
The Notions
The Roadrunners
The Excerts
The Spidermen
The St Louis Checks
Sunday 21st Evening
The Undertakers
The Music Students
The Earthlings
Monday 22nd Lunchtime
The Undertakers
Tuesday 23rd Evening
The Roadrunners
The Victor Brox Blues Train
Wednesday 24th Evening
The Clayton Squares
Earl Preston's Realms
Thursday 25th Lunchtime
The St Louis Checks
Friday 26th Evening
The Mersey Monsters
The Kinsleys
The TTs with Amos Bonny
Saturday 27th Evening
The Hideaways
The Spidermen
The Michael Allen Group
Sunday 28th Evening
The Roadrunners
The St Louis Checks

MARCH
Tuesday 2nd Evening
The Hideaways
Earl Royce and The Olympics
Wednesday 3rd Lunchtime
The Clayton Squares
Evening
The Clayton Squares
The Cordes
The Defiants
Thursday 4th Lunchtime
Earl Preston's Realms
Friday 5th Evening
Earl Preston's Realms
The Victor Brox Blues Train
The Michael Allen Group
Saturday 6th Evening
The Pete Best Combo
The Easybeats
The Poets
The Feelgoods
Sunday 7th Evening
The Lawbreakers

The Denny Mitchell Soundsations
The TTs with Amos and Karl
Monday 8th Lunchtime
The Denny Mitchell Soundsations
Tuesday 9th Evening
Earl Preston's Realms
The Prowlers
Wednesday 10th Lunchtime
The Clayton Squares
Evening
The Clayton Squares
The St Louis Checks
Thursday 11th Lunchtime
Earl Preston's Realms
Friday 12th Evening
The Coins
The Hideaways
The Ranchers
Tiffany and The Four Dimensions
Saturday 13th All-Night Session
Kris Ryan and The Questions
The Clayton Squares
Earl Preston's Realms
The Roadrunners
The Black Knights
The Factotums
The Hideaways
The Notions
The St Louis Checks
Sunday 14th Evening
Annette and The Riverdales
The Sheffields
The Masterminds
The Blue Angels
The Shakespears
Monday 15th Lunchtime
Earl Preston's Realms
Tuesday 16th Evening
The Clayton Squares
The Warriors
US Limited
Wednesday 17th Lunchtime
Earl Preston's Realms
Evening
Earl Preston's Realms
The Roadrunners
The Poets
Saturday 20th Evening
The Clayton Squares
The Feelgoods
The Prowlers
The Interns
Sunday 21st Evening
Earl Preston's Realms
Earl Royce and The Olympics
The Black Knights
The St Louis Checks
Tuesday 23rd Evening
Earl Preston's Realms

The Notions
The Dischords
Wednesday 24th Lunchtime
The Clayton Squares
Evening
The Measles
The Masterminds
The Blue Angela
Thursday 25th Lunchtime
Earl Preston's Realms
Friday 26th Evening
Them Grimbles
The St Louis Checks
The Smokestacks
The Aztec
Saturday 27th Evening
The Clayton Squares
The Roadrunners
The Michael Allen Group
Sunday 28th Evening
The Feelgoods
The Hideaways
The Masterminds
The Excelles
Tuesday 30th Lunchtime
The Clayton Squares
Evening
Earl Preston's Realms
The Hideaways
Wednesday 31st Evening
(Broadcast live on French TV)
Manfred Mann
The Kinks
Sandie Shaw
Petula Clark
Gene Vincent
The Clayton Squares

APRIL
Thursday 1st Lunchtime
Earl Preston's Realms
Friday 2nd Evening
Earl Preston's Realms
Lorraine Gray and The Playboys
Saturday 3rd All-Night Session
Terry Hines Sextet
The Cordes
The St Louis Checks
The Johnny Gus Set
The Big Three
The Spencer Lewis Soul Band
The Richmond Group
The Blue Angels
Sunday 4th Evening
The Sheffields
Earl Preston's Realms
Tuesday 6th Evening
The Hideaways
The Clayton Squares

Wednesday 7th Lunchtime
Earl Preston's Realms
Evening
Earl Preston's Realms
The Richmond Group
Thursday 8th Lunchtime
The Clayton Squares
Friday 9th Lunchtime
DJ Billy Butler
The Cresters
Evening
The Hideaways
The Cresters
The Warriors
Saturday 10th Evening
The Notions
Terry Hines Sextet
The St Louis Checks
The Escorts
Sunday 11th Evening
The Roadrunners
The Pretenders
Tuesday 13th Evening
Earl Preston's Realms
The Hideaways
Wednesday 14th Lunchtime
The Clayton Squares
Evening
The Clayton Squares
The St Louis Checks
Thursday 15th Lunchtime
Earl Preston's Realms
Friday 16th Eight-Hour Session
Kris Ryan and The Questions
The Notions
The St Louis Checks
The Runaways
The Richmond Group
The Roadrunners
Earl Preston's Realms
The Seftons
Saturday 17th Evening
The Clayton Squares
The TTs with Amos Bonny
The Renicks
Sunday 18th Evening
The Masterminds
The Measles
The Cordes
The Georgians
Tuesday 20th Lunchtime
The Clayton Squares
Evening
The Richmond Group
The Roadrunners
The Michael Allen Group
Wednesday 21st Lunchtime
Dave Dee, Dozy, Beaky, Mick and
    Tich

Evening
Earl Preston's Realms
Dave Dee, Dozy, Beaky, Mick and
    Tich
Thursday 22nd Lunchtime
Earl Preston's Realms
Friday 23rd Lunchtime
The Boomerangs
Evening
The St Louis Checks
The Boomerangs
The Clayton Squares
Saturday 24th Evening
Amos Bonny and The TTs
The Hideaways
The Notions
The Peasants
Sunday 25th Evening
The Blue Lotus Jazzmen
The Hideaways
The Pretenders
The Masterminds
Tuesday 27th Lunchtime
The Clayton Squares
Evening
The Clayton Squares
The Hideaways
Wednesday 28th Lunchtime
The Downliners Sect
Evening
The Downliners Sect
Amos Bonny and The TTs
Thursday 29th Lunchtime
The St Louis Checks
Friday 30th Lunchtime
Kris Ryan and The Questions
Evening
Kris Ryan and The Questions
The Clayton Squares
The Richmond Group

MAY
Saturday 1st Evening
The Blues Angels
Them Grimbles
The Masterminds
The Mersey Gonks
Sunday 2nd Evening
Earl Preston's Realms
The Hideaways
The Kirbys
Monday 3rd Evening
Them Grimbles
Wednesday 5th Evening
Earl Preston's Realms
The St Louis Checks
Thursday 6th Lunchtime
The St Louis Checks

Friday 7th Evening
The Roadrunners
The Warriors (Jon Anderson on
    vocals)
The Richmond Group
Saturday 8th All-Night Session
The Merseybeats
Terry Hines Sextet
The Clayton Squares
Earl Preston's Realms
The Blue Lotus Jazzmen
The Easybeats
The Defenders
The Blues Angels
The Flower Pot Men
Sunday 9th Evening
The Richmond Group
The Exit
The Hideaways
The Big Three
Monday 10th Lunchtime
The Big Three
Tuesday 11th Evening
Kris Ryan and The Questions
The Hideaways
The Stereos
Wednesday 12th Evening
The Clayton Squares
Earl Preston's Realms
Thursday 13th Lunchtime
The Easybeats
Friday 14th Evening
The St Louis Checks
Earl Royce and The Olympics
Saturday 15th Evening
The Hideaways
The Delmont Four
The Masterminds
The Exit
Sunday 16th Evening
The Feelgoods
The Clayton Squares
The Richmond Group
Tuesday 18th Evening
The Exit
The Hideaways
The Dawnbreakers
Wednesday 19th Lunchtime
Earl Preston's Realms
Evening
Earl Preston's Realms
The Thundermen
The Richmond Group
Friday 21st Evening
Earl Preston's Realms
The Kirbys
Terry Hines Sextet
Saturday 22nd All-Night Session
The Johnny Gus Set

The Hideaways
The Roadrunners
Amos Bonny and The TTs
The St Louis Checks
The Richmond Group
The Experts
The Blues Pentagon
Billy Butler and The Tuxedos
Sunday 23rd Evening
The Seftons
The Clayton Squares
Lorraine Gray and The Playboys
Tuesday 25th Evening
The Hideaways
The Boomerangs
Wednesday 26th Lunchtime
Kris Ryan and The Questions
Evening
Earl Preston's Realms
Kris Ryan and The Questions
Thursday 27th Lunchtime
Earl Preston's Realms
Friday 28th Evening
The Feelgoods
The Warriors
The Measles
Saturday 29th Evening
Earl Preston's Realms
The Exit
The Hideaways
The Georgians
Sunday 30th Evening
The St Louis Checks
Terry Hines Sextet
The Richmond Group
The Apaches

JUNE
Tuesday 1st Evening
The Clayton Squares
The Hideaways
Wednesday 2nd Lunchtime
The VIPs (became Spooky Tooth)
Evening
The VIPs
Earl Preston's Realms
Thursday 3rd Lunchtime
The Kirbys
Friday 4th Evening
The St Louis Checks
Terry Hines Sextet
Saturday 5th Evening
Earl Preston's Realms
The Roadrunners
The Feelgoods
Sunday 6th Evening
Kris Ryan and The Questions
The Hideaways

Monday 7th Eight-Hour Session
3.30-11.30p.m.
The Maracas
Earl Preston's Realms
The Clayton Squares
The Notions
The Michael Allen Group
The Richmond Group
The Johnny Gus Set
Tuesday 8th Evening
The Hideaways
The Soul Sisters (blues)
The Brian Auger Trinity (Rod
    Stewart, Julie Driscoll, Long John
    Baldry on vocals)
Wednesday 9th Evening
The Exit
The Clayton Squares
Thursday 10th Lunchtime
Earl Preston's Realms
Friday 11th Lunchtime
Kris Ryan and The Questions
Evening
Kris Ryan and The Questions
The Hideaways
The Georgians
Saturday 12th Evening
Earl Preston's Realms
The Dions
The Michael Allen Group
Sunday 13th Evening
The Spidermen
The Richmonds
The Feelgoods
Monday 14th Lunchtime
Record Session with Billy Butler
Tuesday 15th Evening
The Clayton Squares
Wednesday 16th Lunchtime
Earl Preston's Realms
Evening
Earl Preston's Realms
The Richmond Group
Friday 18th Evening
Dave Dee, Dozy, Beaky, Mick and
    Tich
The Richmond Group
The Dekkas
Saturday 19th All-Night Session
The Aztecs
The Clayton Squares
The Hideaways
The Kirbys
The Richmond Group
Earl Royce and The Olympics
The Michael Allen Group
The Smoke Stack
The Music Students

Sunday 20th Evening
The Escorts
The Defiants
Monday 21st Lunchtime
Dave Dee, Dozy, Beaky, Mick and
    Tich
Tuesday 22nd Evening
The Clayton Squares
The Hideaways
Wednesday 23rd Lunchtime
Fitz and Startz
Evening
Earl Preston's Realms
Fitz and Startz
Thursday 24th Lunchtime
Earl Preston's Realms
Friday 25th Evening
The Hideaways
The Notions
The Richmond Group
The Calderstones
Saturday 26th Evening
The Johnny Gus Set
The Blues Angels
The Dimensions
Earl Preston's Realms
Sunday 27th Evening
Tiffany's Thoughts
The St Louis Checks
Monday 28th Lunchtime
The Kirbys
Tuesday 29th Evening
Earl Preston's Realms
The Hideaways
Wednesday 30th Evening
The Clayton Squares
The Richmond Group

JULY
Friday 2nd Evening
The Clayton Squares
The Spidermen
The Motifs
Saturday 3rd All-Night Session
The Clayton Squares
The Dimensions
Earl Preston's Realms
Davy Morgan (folk)
The Music Students
The Michael Allen Group
The Warriors
The Richmond Group
Tuesday 6th Evening
The Hideaways
The Dimensions
Wednesday 7th Evening
The Clayton Squares
Earl Preston's Realms

Saturday 10th Evening
The Clayton Squares
The Big Three
The Michael Allen Group
Sunday 11th Evening
The Hideaways
The Roadrunners
The Richmond Group
Monday 12th Evening
The Ram Jam Band (from London
    featuring Geno Washington)
The Richmond Group
The Exit
Thursday 13th Evening
The Clayton Squares
The Hideaways
Wednesday 14th Lunchtime
The Warriors (from Accrington
    with Jon Anderson on vocals)
Thursday 15th Lunchtime
Earl Preston's Realms
Friday 16th Evening
The Four Just Men
The Pretenders
Tiffany's Thoughts
Saturday 17th Evening
Earl Preston's Realms
The Hideaways
The Richmond Group
Solomon's Mines
Sunday 18th Evening
The Kirbys
The Tabs
The Spidermen
Tuesday 20th Evening
The Hideaways
The Thee (from London)
Wednesday 21st Evening
The Clayton Squares
Earl Preston's Realms
Thursday 22nd Lunchtime
Earl Preston's Realms
Friday 23rd Evening
Earl Preston's Realms
The Sheffields
Frankenstein and The Monsters
The Georgians
Saturday 24th All-Night Session
The Seftons
The Richmond Group
The Exit
The Clayton Squares
The Brian Auger Trinity
Long John Baldry
The Hideaways
The Tarantulas
Rod Stewart
Julie Driscoll

Sunday 25th Evening
The Richmond Group
The Masterminds
The Calderstones
Monday 26th Twelve Hour
Session
12 noon-12 midnight
(Cavern Benefit Show)
Kris Ryan and The Questions
The Undertakers
The Scaffold
The Measles
The Five Aces
The Power House Six
The Hobos
The Boomerangs
The Masterminds
Hank Walters and The Dusty Road
    Ramblers
The Cresters
The Blue Secrets
The Clayton Squares
The Spinners
The Escorts
The Steve Aldo Quintet
The Richmond Group
The Dimensions
The Connoisseurs
Earl Preston's Realms
The Lancastrians
The Merseybeats
Lorraine Gray
The Manchester Playboys
Tuesday 27th Evening
The Denny Seyton Show Band
The Richmond Group
Wednesday 28th Lunchtime
The Escorts
Evening
Earl Preston's Realms
The Escorts (leaving for Germany)
Friday 30th Evening
The Spencer Davis Group
The Clayton Squares
The Richmond Group
Saturday 31st Evening
The Clayton Squares
Earl Preston's Realms
The Harpos

AUGUST
Sunday 1st Evening
The Richmond Group
The Terry Hines Sextet
The Masterminds
Tuesday 3rd Evening
The Hideaways
The Warriors

Wednesday 4th Evening
The Easybeats
Earl Preston's Realms
Thursday 5th Lunchtime
The Hideaways
Friday 6th Evening
The Richmond Group
The Black Knights
The Clayton Squares
Saturday 7th Evening
The Hideaways
The Masterminds
The Bobby Gray Soul Band
Sunday 8th Evening
Dave Dee, Dozy, Beaky, Mick and
    Tich
Alexis Korner's R&B Band
Tuesday 10th Evening
The Hideaways
The Problems
The Richmond Group
Wednesday 11th Evening
The Clayton Squares
Earl Preston's Realms
Friday 13th Evening
Earl Preston's Realms
The Masterminds
The Aztecs
Saturday 14th All-Night Session
Earl Preston's Realms
The Steve Aldo Quintet
The Hideaways
The Bumblies
The Dimensions
The Richmond Group
The Mike Hart Group
The Masterminds
Sunday 15th Evening
The Hideaways
The Outer Limits
Tuesday 17th Evening
Earl Preston's Realms
The Hideaways
Wednesday 18th Lunchtime
The Warriors
Evening
The Warriors
The Clayton Squares
Friday 20th Evening
The Clayton Squares
The Easybeats
The Hillsiders
Saturday 21st Evening
Earl Preston's Realms
The Richmond Group
The Connoisseurs
Sunday 22nd Evening
The Black Knights
The Nashville Teens (from London)

The Hideaways
Tuesday 24th Evening
The Clayton Squares
The Stylos
Wednesday 25th Evening
The Hideaways
Earl Preston's Realms
Friday 27th Evening
The Richmond Group
Earl Preston's Realms
The Dimensions
Saturday 28th Evening
The Clayton Squares
The Terry Hines Seventet
The Lee Eddy Show Group
The Mike Hart Group
Sunday 29th Evening
Earl Preston's Realms
The Hideaways
The Pretenders
The Four Shades
Monday 30th Eight-Hour Session
The Fourmost
The Silkie
The Hideaways
The Clayton Squares
The Masterminds
The Richmond Group
The Aztecs
The Aarons
Tuesday 31st Lunchtime
The Warriors

SEPTEMBER
Wednesday 1st Evening
The Kirbys
Earl Preston's Realms
Friday 3rd Evening
The Action
The Masterminds
Fritz, Mike and Mo
Saturday 4th Evening
Earl Preston's Realms
The Resistance
The Easybeats
Sunday 5th Evening
The Escorts
The Warriors
The Initials
Tuesday 7th Evening
Earl Preston's Realms
Earl Royce and The Olympics
Wednesday 8th Lunchtime
The Warriors
Evening
The Warriors
The Masterminds
Thursday 9th Lunchtime
The Hideaways

Friday 10th Evening
The Clayton Squares
The Cresters
The Aztecs
Saturday 11th All-Night Session
The Richmond Group
The Tabs
The Dark Ages
The Hideaways
The Clayton Squares
Gary Farr and The T Bones
The Masterminds
The Resistance (From Scotland)
Sunday 12th Evening
The Four Blues
The Masterminds
The Richmond Group
The Dresdens
Tuesday 14th Evening
The Clayton Squares
The Hideaways
Wednesday 15th Lunchtime
The Masterminds
Evening
The Richmond Group
The Masterminds
Thursday 16th Lunchtime
The Warriors
Friday 17th Evening
The Manchester Playboys
The Verbs
The Richmond Group
Saturday 18th Evening
The Roadrunners
The Easybeats
The Aztecs
Sunday 19th Evening
Sir Franklyn Show Band
The Masterminds
The Basic Five
The Connoisseurs
Tuesday 21st Evening
The Hideaways
The Dawnbreakers
Wednesday 22nd Evening
The Clayton Squares
The Masterminds
Friday 24th Evening
The Hideaways
Stu James and The Mojos
The Power House Six
The Big Three
Saturday 25th Evening
The Denny Seyton Show Band
The Harpos
The Excerts
Sunday 26th Evening
The Four Blues
The Richmond Group

The Crescendos
Tuesday 28th Evening
The Clayton Squares
The Warriors
Wednesday 29th Evening
The Richmond Group
Tiffany's Thoughts

OCTOBER
Friday 1st Evening
The Richmond Group
The Silkie
The Hideaways
Saturday 2nd Evening
162
Earl Preston's Realms
The Aztecs
The Calderstones
Sunday 3rd Evening
Mark Peters Method
The Big Three
The Richmond Group
Tuesday 5th Evening
The Dawnbreakers
Wynder K. Frog
Wednesday 6th Evening
Kris Ryan and The Questions
The Motown Sect
The Hideaways
Friday 8th Evening
The Prowlers
The Pretenders
The Dresdens
The Dimensions
Saturday 9th All-Night Session
Cliff Bennet and The Rebel Rousers
The Clayton Squares
David John and The Mood
The Roadrunners
The Hideaways
The Klubs
The Blue Angels
The Richmond Group
Sunday 10th Evening
Earl Preston's Realms
The Richmond Group
The Defiants
Tuesday 12th Evening
The Hideaways
The Warriors
Wednesday 13th Evening
The Hideaways
The Masterminds
Friday 15th Evening
Kris Ryan and The Questions
Earl Preston's Realms
Tiffany's Thoughts

Saturday 16th All-Night Session
4a.m.-4p.m.
(Will be attempting a world record
for playing non-stop)
The Merseybeats
Gideon's Few (from Yorkshire)
Earl Royce and The Olympics
The Hideaways
The Masterminds
The Du Fay
The Notions
Sunday 17th Evening
The Easybeats
The Dresdens
Wynder K. Frog
Tuesday 19th Evening
The Stylos
The Richmond Group
Wednesday 20th Evening
The Jimmy Brown Squad (from
London)
The Clayton Squares
The Hideaways
The Almost Blues
Ben E. King (from America)
Friday 22nd Evening
The Cresters
The Dimensions
Saturday 23rd Evening
The Escorts
The Four Blues
The Gremlins
Sunday 24th Twelve-Hour Session
Earl Preston's Realms
The Crying Shames
The Aztecs
The Verbs
Benny and The Others
The Clayton Squares
Johnny B Great and The Quotations
The Warriors
The Hideaways
The Masterminds
Tuesday 26th Evening
The Manchester Playboys
Earl Preston's Realms
Wednesday 27th Evening
The Warriors
The Masterminds
Friday 29th Evening
The Big Three
The Notions
The Tributes
Sunday 31st Evening
The Who (from London, new
single out soon 'My Generation')

NOVEMBER
Tuesday 2nd Evening
Earl Preston's Realms
The Hideaways
Wednesday 3rd Evening
The Cresters
The Masterminds
Friday 5th Evening
The Action
Earl Preston's Realms
Saturday 6th All-Night Session
The Baskerville Hounds (blues)
The Verbs
The Drifting Sands
The Richmond Group
The Dresdens
The Almost Blues
The Fourmost
Hedge Hoppers Anonymous
  ('It's Good News Next Week')
The Harpos
The Masterminds
Sunday 7th Evening
Denny Seyton's Show Band
The Cordes
The Four Blues
Tuesday 9th Evening
The Hideaways
The Victors
The Richmond Group
Wednesday 10th Evening
The Fairies
The Masterminds
The Pikkins
Friday 12th Evening
The Victor Brox Blues Train
The Coins
The Aztecs
Saturday 13th All-Night Session
Rory Storm and The Hurricanes
The Crescendos
The Dimensions
The Sect
Earl Royce and The Olympics
The Escorts
John Lee Hooker (blues star)
Earl Preston's Realms
The Hideaways
The Big Three
Sunday 14th Evening
The Bootleggers
Earl Royce and The Olympics
Tuesday 16th Evening
The Masterminds
Earl Preston's Realms
Wednesday 17th Evening
The Hideaways
The Untamed

Friday 19th Evening
The Cymerons
The Spencer Davis Group
The Fix
Saturday 20th Evening
The Almost Blues
The Aztecs
The Detonators
Sunday 21st Nine Hour Session
The Richmond Group
Tiffany's Thoughts
The Monos
The Tony Colton Big Boss Band
Wilson Pickett (soul star from
   America)
Earl Preston's Realms
The Hideaways
The Verbs
Tuesday 23rd Evening
Fitz and Startz
The Richmond Group
Wednesday 24th Evening
The Hideaways
The Big Three
Friday 26th Evening
Earl Preston's Realms
The Fix
The Cordes
Saturday 27th Evening
Steve Day's Kinsmen
The Secrets
The Principals
Sunday 28th Evening
The Easybeats
The Almost Blues
The Richmond Group
Tuesday 30th Evening
The Warriors
The Richmond Group

DECEMBER

Wednesday 1st Evening
Earl Preston's Realms
The Hideaways
Friday 3rd Evening
The Fix
The Excerts
The Dimensions
Saturday 4th All-Night Session
The Richmond Group
The Crying Shames
The Hideaways
The Big Three
The Masterminds
Georgie Fame and The Blue Flames
The Cordes
The Crescendos
Earl Preston's Realms

Sunday 5th Evening
The Runaways
The Richmond Group
Tiffany's Thoughts
Tuesday 7th Evening
The Big Three
The Richmond Group
Wednesday 8th Evening
Earl Preston's Realms
The Hickory Stix
Friday 10th Evening
The Hideaways
The Richmond Group
The Five Tributes
Saturday 11th Evening
Earl Royce and The Olympics
The Aztecs
The Detonators
Sunday 12th Nine hour session
The Well Respected Men
The Crying Shames
Rory Storm and The Hurricanes
The Easybeats
The Fix
The Verbs
The Escorts
Earl Preston's Realms
The Hideaways
Tuesday 14th Evening
Deny Wilkie and The Pressmen
The Richmond Group
Wednesday 15th Evening
The Hideaways
The Masterminds
Friday 17th All-Night Session
The Hickory Stix
The Richmond Group
The Hideaways
The Kirbys
Earl Preston's Realms
Earl Royce and The Olympics
Zoot Money's Big Roll Band
   (Andy Summers on guitar)
Paul Williams
The Fix
The Sect
Saturday 18th Evening
The Masterminds
The Invaders
The Harpos
Sunday 19th Evening
The Big Three
The Dimensions
The Richmond Group
Wednesday 22nd Evening
The Masterminds
The Hideaways
Friday 24th Evening
Christmas Eve Show

The Richmond Group
The Crying Shames
The Sect
The Aztecs
Sunday 26th Nine hour session
DJ Billy 'Kelly' Butler
The Richmond Group
The Masterminds
The Fix
The Hideaways
Earl Preston's Realms
The Escorts
The Big Three
Wednesday 29th Evening
The Hideaways
The Masterminds
Friday 31st Twelve hour session
DJ Billy Butler
Earl Preston's Realms
The Masterminds
The Richmond Group
The Fix
The Crying Shames
The Aztecs
The Sect
The Monos
The Script
The Five Tributes

1966

JANUARY

Saturday 1st Evening
Earl Preston's Realms
The Runaways
The Buffaloes
Sunday 2nd Evening
The Masterminds
The Richmond Group
The Fix
Tuesday 4th Evening
The Alan Price Set
The Fix
The Power House Six
Wednesday 5th Evening
The Masterminds
The Richmond Group
Thursday 6th Lunchtime
The Cresters
Friday 7th Evening
Earl Preston's Realms
The Handfull
The St Franklyn
Saturday 8th Evening
The Masterminds
Steve Day's Kinsmen
The Runaways

Sunday 9th Nine hour session
Lawrence James Federation
The Escorts
The Hideaways
The Masterminds
Earl Preston's Realms
The Almost Blues
The Crying Shames
Tuesday 11th Evening
The Masterminds
The Hideaways
Wednesday 12th Evening
Earl Preston's Realms
The Richmond Group
Friday 14th Evening
Earl Preston's Realms
The Hideaways
The Richmond Group
Saturday 15th All-Night Session
Freddie Starr and The Delmonts
The Almost Blues
The Crying Shames
The Dresdens
The Exciters (from USA)
The Fix
The Masterminds
The Calderstones
The League of Gentlemen
   (Robert Fripp on guitar)
Sunday 16th Evening
The Pathfinders
The Richmond Group
The Connoisseurs
Tuesday 18th Evening
The Big Three
The Hideaways

Wednesday 19th Evening
The Masterminds
The Richmond Group
Thursday 20th Evening
The Crew
Lee Dorsey (from USA)
The Fix
Earl Preston's Realms
Friday 21st Evening
The Hideaways
The Calderstones
The Crying Shames
Saturday 22nd Evening
The Roadrunners
The Almost Blues
Karl Terry and The TTs
Sunday 23rd Nine-Hour Session
The Aztecs
The Sidewinders
The Almost Blues
The Crying Shames
Little Stevie Wonder (from USA)
The Hideaways
Earl Preston's Realms
The Fix
The Richmond Group
Tuesday 25th Evening
The Copy Cats
The Hideaways
Friday 28th Evening
The Ying Tongs (from China)
The Fix
The Hideaways
Saturday 29th All-Night Session
The Sect
The Fix
The Trendsetters

Edge Hill College Students Union
with
Kirby Fields College Students Union
presents

CAVERN

ZOOT MONEY | THE ORIGINAL DRIFTERS
HAYDOCKS ROCKHOUSE | THE FIX
THE KONDA GROUP | THE ALMOST BLUES

Friday June 30th 8·00pm until Saturday July 1st 8·00am

Bar open until later than late

Admission by Ticket only   **12/6**

The Hideaways
Earl Preston's Realms
The Drifters (from USA)
The Plain and Fancy
The Richmond Group
The Aztecs
Sunday 30th Evening
Earl Preston's Realms
The Hideaways
The Fix
Monday 31st Lunchtime
(Beat and Eat Session)

FEBRUARY
Tuesday 1st Lunchtime
(Beat and Eat Session)
Evening
(Disco Night)
DJs Bob Wooler, Billy Butler, Barry
  Mac, Bob McGrae
The Private Eyes
Wednesday 2nd Lunchtime
The Plain and Fancy
Mike Donohue (comedian)
Evening
The Plain and Fancy
The Hideaways
Friday 4th Evening
The Warriors
The Richmond Group
Baskerville Hound (blues)
Saturday 5th All-Nighter
Earl Preston's Realms
The Aztecs
The Lawrence James Federation
The Hideaways
Inez and Charlie Foxx (from USA)
The League of Gentlemen
The Fix
The Richmond Group
Sunday 6th Evening
The Hideaways
The Richmond Group
The Maracas
Monday 7th Evening
Bluesology (with Elton John on
  piano)
Doris Troy (from USA)
The Fix
Earl Preston's Realms
Tuesday 8th Evening
(Disco Night)
DJs Bob Wooler, Bob McGrae, Pat
  Delaney
Wednesday 9th Evening
The Power House Six
The Hideaways
Friday 11th Evening
The Richmond Group

The Dark Ages
The Principals
Saturday 12th All-Nighter
The Fortunes
The Fix
The Newtowns
The Dresdens
The Hideaways
The Richmond Group
Solomon's Mines
Sunday 13th Evening
The Hideaways
The Richmond Group
Tuesday 15th Evening
(Disco Night)
DJs Bob Wooler, Billy Butler
The Private Eyes
Wednesday 16th Evening
Earl Preston's Realms
The Hideaways
Thursday 17th Lunchtime
The Crying Shames
Friday 18th Evening
Earl Preston's Realms
The Runaways
The Hideaways
Saturday 19th All-Nighter
The Crescendos
The Dark Ages
The Kwans
The Realm
The Hideaways
The Precinct
Tiffany's Thoughts
The Richmond Group
The Kirbys
Sunday 20th Evening
The Sect
The Hideaways
The Realm
The Rigg
Tuesday 22nd Evening
Disco
Wednesday 23rd Evening
The Hideaways
The Richmond Group
Friday 25th Evening
The Dark Ages
The Hideaways
The Sect
The Richmond Group
Saturday 26th Evening
The Mersey Boys
The Dresdens
The Crescendos
Sunday 27th All-Nighter
The Kwans
The Rekords
The Richmond Group

The Dark Ages
Rory Storm and The Hurricanes
The Sect
The Hideaways
The Big Three
The Rigg
The Runaways
The Crying Shames
The Realm
The Pro-tems

MARCH
Wednesday 4th
Ad in the *Liverpool Echo* reads 'Thank
  you for all you did to help the
  Cavern.'
Monday 7th
Liverpool Echo: 'Jimmy Savile Sends
  £100. Cavern appeals for money
  from all over the world. Public
  invited to buy shares in Cavern Ltd
  for £1. Donations to buy shares
  should be sent. District Bank Ltd,
  61 Dale Street, Liverpool.'

APRIL
Tuesday 5th
Liverpool Echo: 'Cavern Owner's
  Bankruptcy Hearing. Andrew Ray
  McFall, proprietor of Cavern said
  he had been throwing money
  about like confetti at his public
  examination in Bankruptcy in
  Liverpool today.'

JULY
Saturday 23rd
Reopening of Cavern, three fab
  sessions in one day.
Cavern reopened by Prime Minister,
  Harold Wilson
Daytime
Ken Dodd
Georgie Fame
Dave Dee, Dozy, Beaky, Mick and
  Tich
The Bachelors
The Searchers
Billy J. Kramer
The Fourmost
Jonathan King
Tony Jackson
The Merseys
Solomon Burke
Rufus Thomas
Jimmy Savile
Simon Dee
Marty Wilde
Johnny Hackett
Bessie Bradock, MP

HERE'S WISHING A FRESH ERA OF SUCCESS TO
THE CAVERN

THE BEATLES: GERRY AND THE PACEMAKERS: CILLA BLACK:
BILLY J. KRAMER WITH THE DAKOTAS: THE FOURMOST:
THE REMO FOUR: AND BRIAN EPSTEIN

Brian Epstein and his stable of stars sent this telegram to the Cavern
Club when it reopened in 1966.

The Champs
Liverpool and Everton Football Teams
Brian London (boxer)
Lunchtime
12.30 start – DJ Billy Butler
The Hideaways
The Signs
The Escorts
The Dark Ages
Georgia's Germs
The Excelles
The Strandmen
The Seftons
The Prowlers
The Dollies
The Tremas
The Carrols
The Pete Best Combo
Evening
The Hideaways
The Signs
The Dark Ages
The Prowlers
The Excelles
The Dions
The Tremas
Georgia's Germs
All-Night Session
Solomon Burke
Rufus Thomas
The Senates
The Escorts
The Hideaways
The Dark Ages

The Rockhouse Band
Sunday 24th Evening
DJ Billy Butler
The Signs
The Seftons
Georgia's Germs
Monday 25th Evening
The Monday Show with Billy Butler
The Platter Parade
Tuesday 26th Evening
The 5a.m. Event (Combo, first record
  'Hungry')
The Sinisters
The Hideaways
Wednesday 27th Evening
Disco, Billy Butler
The New Sygnets
Thursday 28th Evening
Georgia's Germs
The Magic Lanterns
The Signs
Friday 29th Evening
The Outrage
Saturday 30th All-Nighter
The Escorts
The Hideaways
The Signs
The Kop
The Dark Ages
The Pete Best Combo
Becket's Kin
Georgia's Germs

Sunday 31st Evening
The Dions
The Pro-tems
Carol and The Memories

AUGUST
Monday 1st Evening
Billy Butler's Platter Parade
The Senators
Tuesday 2nd Evening
The Creation (from London)
Wednesday 3rd Evening
Midweek Spin Around Show with
   Billy Butler
The Hideaways
Thursday 4th Evening
The Countdowns
Paul Cram and The Crying Shames
Friday 5th Evening
The Pro-tems
The Hideaways
American Fred
Saturday 6th All-Nighter
The Excelles
The Fix
The Dions
The Boz
The lkettes (from USA)
The Hideaways
The Kop
The Signs
Sunday 7th Evening
The Worrying Kynde
The Dark Ages
Monday 8th Evening
The Monday Show with Billy
   Butler – 100 special free tickets
   given out for free film to be
   shown Wednesday 10th. Northern
   Premiere
The Twigg
Tuesday 9th Evening
Tony River and The Castaways
Wednesday 10th 2.30p.m.
Film Show – 'Gather No Moss'
Evening
Billy Butler's Mid-week Spin Around
The Heatwave
Thursday 11th Evening
The Hideaways
The Prowlers
The Chuckles
Friday 12th Evening
The Warriors
The Dark Ages
The Times
Saturday 13th All-Night Rave
She Trinity (All-girl group from USA
   – hit record 'Yellow Submarine')

The Almost Blues
The Outrage (from Manchester)
The Signs
The Prowlers
Sunday 14th Evening
The Kop
The Rigg
Georgia's Germs
Monday 15th Evening
The Billy Butler Show
The Dark Ages
Tuesday 16th Evening
Paul and Richie and The Crying
   Shames
Wednesday 17th Evening
The Billy Butler Show
The Doug Barry Sound
Thursday 18th Evening
The Ivan Meads
The Seftons
Friday 19th Evening
The Hideaways
The Chuckles
Saturday 20th All-Night Rave
The Dark Ages
The Kop
The Connoisseurs
The St Louis Union
The Hideaways
Becket's Kin
Sunday 21st Evening
The Signs and The Times
The Rekorde
Monday 22nd Evening
The Billy Butler Show
The Hideaways
Tuesday 23rd Evening
The Signs and The Times
John's Children (from London)
Wednesday 24th Evening
The Prowlers
Thursday 25th Evening
Eddie Cave and The Fix
The Dark Ages
Friday 26th Evening
The Hideaways
Ivan's Mead
Saturday 27th All-Night Rave
Becket's Kin
The Signs
The Koobas
Crispian St Peters
(Jimmy Page, Albert Lee and Vic Slick
   in backing group)
The Puppets
John Evans Smash
Mad Monks

Sunday 28th Evening
The Hideaways
The Dawnbreakers
Monday 29th
(Bank Holiday Marathon)
The Times
Mommie's Darlings
Paul and Richie and The Crying
   Shames
The Prowlers
The Iveys (became Badfinger)
The Doug Barry Sound
Tuesday 30th Evening
The Hideaways
The Chuckles
Wednesday 31st Evening
DJ Billy Butler
The Seftons

SEPTEMBER
Thursday 1st Evening
The Signs and The Times
The Dark Ages
Friday 2nd Evening
John Evan's Smash (Ian Anderson on
   vocals)
Becket's Kin
Saturday 3rd All-Night Rave
The Times
The Hideaways
The Manchester Playboys
The Mixture
The Dollies
The Dark Ages
The Prowlers
Sunday 4th Evening
The Signs
The Times
The Kop
Tuesday 6th Evening
The Warriors
The Times
Wednesday 7th Evening
DJ Billy Butler
The Seftons
Thursday 8th Evening
The Hideaways
The Outrage
Friday 9th Evening
The Dark Ages
Paul and Richie and The Crying
   Shames
The Doug Barry Sound
Saturday 10th All-Night Rave
The Mack Sound
Eddie Cave and The Fix
The Kop
The Hideaways
The Seftons

The Rocking Vicars
Sunday 11th Evening
The Signs
The Times
The Prowlers
The Sextion Four
Monday 12th Evening
DJ Billy Butler
The Kop
Tuesday 13th Evening
The Cymerons
The Chuckles
Wednesday 14th Evening
DJ Billy Butler
The Dark Ages
Thursday 15th Evening
The Outrage
The Hideaways
Friday 16th Evening
The Shakedowns
The Signs
The Prowlers
Mommie's Darlings
Saturday 17th All-Night Rave
The Noblemen
Sooner or Later
Intent and Purpose
The Klubs
The Signs
The Times
The Vibrations
The Tremas
Jimmy James and The Vagabonds
The Dark Ages
Sunday 18th Evening
Eddie Cave and The Fix

The Calderstones
Monday 19th Evening
Billy Butler Show
Wednesday 21st Evening
DJ Billy Butler
The Doug Barry Sound
Thursday 22nd Evening
The Dawnbreakers (from Leeds)
Sooner or Later
Friday 23rd Evening
The Prowlers
The Times
Saturday 24th All-Night Rave
7.30-11.15p.m.
The Dark Ages
The Kop
The Klubs
Bo-Lynx
12.00-6.30a.m.
The Dark Ages
Neil Christian
Look Twice
The Crusaders
The Heatwave
Sunday 25th Evening
The Escorts
The Twiggs
Monday 26th Evening
DJ Billy Butler
Disco
Tuesday 27th Evening
The Chuckles
The Dark Ages
The Signs
The Times

Birkenhead's finest, the Klubs. The Klubs appeared at the Cavern an estimated 173 times in the late 1960s and early '70s. They changed the spelling of their name to the Klubbs at one stage and had a huge local following. Big things were expected of them but a national breakthrough failed to materialise. The Klubs appeared on the same bill at the Cavern with legendary acts such as John's Children (Marc Bolan), Chuck Berry and Edwin Starr.

Wednesday 28th Evening
The Hideaways
Thursday 29th Evening
The Manchester Playboys
Georgia's Germs
Friday 30th Evening
The Pro-tems
The Chuckles
The Klubs

OCTOBER
Saturday 1st Evening
The Bojacs
The Gates of Eden
The Knack (from London)
Chapter Five
The Prowlers
The Ivey League
The Mad Lads (from USA)
Sunday 2nd Evening
The Tiffany Show
The Dark Ages
The Pro-tems

Monday 3rd Evening
DJ Billy Butler
The Times
Tuesday 4th Evening
The Escorts
The Hideaways
Wednesday 5th Evening
The Calderstones
Thursday 6th Evening
The Signs and The Times
The Pitiful
Friday 7th Evening
The Doug Barry Sound
The Dark Ages
The Kop
Saturday 8th All-Night Rave
The Times
The Wheels (from Belfast)
The Prowlers
The Tremas
The Bo Lynx
The Fix

Sunday 9th Evening
Paul and Richie and The Crying
  Shames
The Signs and The Times
Monday 10th Evening
DJ Billy Butler
Disco
Tuesday 11th Evening
The Hideaways
The Prowlers
The Dark Ages
Wednesday 12th Evening
Juke Box Disco
Thursday 13th Evening
The Warriors
Look Twice
Friday 14th Evening
The Doug Barry Sound
The Cymerons (from Manchester)
Saturday 15th All-Night Rave
Rhythm and Blues Inc.
Eddie Cave and The Fix
The All Night Workers
The Wild Wild Klubs
The Seftons
Sunday 16th 3-11 Marathon
Lee Dorsey (from USA)
The Hideaways
The Dark Ages
The Gates of Eden
Tuesday 18th Evening
The Creation
The Hideaways
Wednesday 19th Evening
Big Disco Session
Thursday 20th Evening
The Escorts
The Seftons
Friday 21st Evening
Victor Brox and The Brox Band
The Doug Barry Sound
Saturday 22nd All-Night Rave
7.30-11.15p.m.
The Dark Ages
The Excelles
The Calderstones
The States
12.00-6.00a.m.
The Hideaways
The Family
The Calderstones
The Excelles
The Dark Ages
Sunday 23rd Evening
The Prowlers
The Chuckles
The Pro-ferns
Monday 24th Evening
Disco

Tuesday 25th Evening
The Searchers
The Excelles
The Hideaways
Solomon's Mines
Wednesday 26th Evening
The Avengers
The Klubs
Tamla Disco
Thursday 27th Evening
The Hideaways
The Klubs
Saturday 29th All-Night Rave
7.30-11.15p.m.
The Fix with Steve Aldo
The Prowlers
The Impact
12.00-6.00a.m.
The Senate
The Signs and The Times
The B Jays
The Talismen
Edwin Starr (from USA)
The Prowlers
The Fix
Sunday 30th Evening
The Times
The Seftons
The Katoz
Monday 31st Evening
Tamla Disco

NOVEMBER
Tuesday 1st Evening
The Signs and The Times
The Mistake
Wednesday 2nd Evening
Tamla Disco
The Action
Friday 4th Evening
John's Children – From London
The Klubs
Saturday 5th All-Night Rave
7.30-11.15p.m.
The Hideaways
The Prowlers
The Sect
Quiz and Query and Co.
12.00-6.30a.m.
Alvin Robinson
Herbie Goins
The Sect
The Nightimers
Johnny Breeze and The Atlantics
The Herb Set
The Interns
The First Lites
Sunday 6th Evening
The Signs and The Times

The Kids
Monday 7th Evening
Disco
Tuesday 8th Evening
The Dark Ages
The Seftons
Wednesday 9th Evening
Tamla Disco
The Impact
Thursday 10th Evening
The Klubs
The Mistake
Friday 11th Evening
The Dark Ages
The Home Grown
Solomon's Mines
Saturday 12th All-Night Rave
7.30-11.15p.m.
The Dollies
The Klubs
The Mixture
The Kruzads
12.00-6.30a.m.
The Hideaways
The Dollies
The Cock-a-Hoops
The Executives
The Kruzads
The Beechwoods
The Mixtures
Sunday 13th Evening
The Times
The Dark Ages
The Prowlers
Monday 14th Evening
Disco
Wednesday 16th Evening
DJs Bob Wooler and Billy Butler
The Klubs
The Mistake
Samantha Juste (from *Top of the Pops*)
The LSD
The Signs
Friday 18th Evening
The Fix (with Steve Aldo)
The Kids
The Runaways
Saturday 19th All-Night Rave
7.30-11.15p.m.
The Klubs
The Shades
The Love Trade
12.00-6.30a.m.
The Original Coasters (from USA)
The Hideaways
The Kids
The Love Trade
The Escorts
The Noblemen

The Houston Brothers
Sunday 20th Evening
(Marathon Show)
Barbara Lynn (from USA)
The Signs and The Times
The Hideaways
The Kids
Paul Richie and The Crying Shames
The Cordes
The Escorts
The Tremas
Monday 21st Evening
Disco
Wednesday 23rd Evening
The Hideaways
The Klubs
Friday 25th Evening
The Klubs
The Prowlers
The Cock-a-Hoops
Saturday 26th Evening
7.30–11.15p.m.
The Signs and The Times
Mommie's Darlings (from
   Manchester)
The Beechwoods
The Reaction
Ben E. King Show
The Reaction
12.00–6.30a.m.
The Signs and The Times
The Senate
The Joystrings
Mommie's Darlings
Sunday 27th Evening
The Dark Ages
The Mistake
The Kruzads
Monday 28th Evening
Disco
Wednesday 30th Evening
The Times
The Prowlers
Time and Motion

DECEMBER
Thursday 1st Evening
Free Tamla Sounds Disco
Friday 2nd Evening
Liverpool University Night Dance
   – Cavern Let
Saturday 3rd All-Nighter
Tony Rivers and The Castaways
The Kids
The Defenders
The Twilites
The Tatters
T.D. Backus and The Powerhouse

Sunday 4th Evening
(Marathon Show)
Bobby Hebb ('Sunny' from USA)
Lynn Randell
The Beechwoods
The States
The Hideaways
The Avengers
The Prowlers
Chapter Five
The Kids
Tuesday 6th Evening
Tamla Sounds Free Disco
Wednesday 7th Evening
The Prowlers
The Signs and The Times
Paul Richie and The Crying Shames
Thursday 8th Evening
Free Tamla Show
Friday 9th Evening
The Klubs
The Cordes
The Doug Barry Sound
Saturday 10th All-Nighter
The Prowlers
The Beechwoods
The Lemon Line
The Mistake
The Factotums
Sunday 11th Evening
The Calderstones
The Cordes
The Top
Tuesday 13th Evening
Tamla Disco
Wednesday 14th Evening
DJ Billy Butler
The Signs and The Times
Jason Hertz Quintet
The State
Thursday 15th Evening
Tamla Disco
Friday 16th Evening
Steve Aldo and The Fix
The Kids
The Cordes
Sunday 17th All-Nighter
The Cosmonauts
The Bo-Lynx
The Orlons (from USA)
The Kids
The Hideaways
The Gates of Eden
The Beechwoods
The Reaction
Normie Rowe (Australian singer)
Sunday 18th Evening
The Canadians (from USA)
The Prowlers

The Mead
The Defenders
Times Five
Monday 19th Evening
Disco
Tuesday 20th Evening
Disco
Wednesday 21st Evening
The Beechwoods
The Mistake
Cleo's Mood
The Reason Why
Thursday 22nd Evening
Disco
Friday 23rd Evening
The Cordes
The Hideaways
The Klubs
Saturday 24th Evening
Free Turkeys for Christmas
Peter Jay and The Jaywalkers
The Klubs
Sunday 25th Evening
Nine-hour spectacular meet all the
   stars!
Monday 26th Evening
Bumper Pop Marathon
Wednesday 28th Evening
The Dark Ages
Friday 30th Evening
The Calderstones
The Hideaways
The Mistake
Saturday 31st All-Nighter
7p.m.–7a.m.
The Prowlers
The Beechwoods
The Tatters
The States
The Klubs
The Kids
The Signs and The Times
The Soul Sisters
The Canadians
The Hideaways
The Shades

1967

JANUARY
Sunday 1st Evening
The Kids
The Defenders
The Pro-tems
Wednesday 4th Evening
The Hideaways
The Klubs

The Majority Plus
Thursday 5th Evening
The Dodoes
Friday 6th Evening
Sign and The Times
The Kop
Saturday 7th All-Nighter
The Peeps
The Principals
The Prowlers
Solomon's Mines
The All Night Workers
Sunday 8th Evening
The Richard Kent Style
The Tremas
The Phoenix Sound
Tuesday 10th Evening
The Bentics
Thursday 12th Evening
Compère D. Terry
The Dodoes
Friday 13th Evening
The Beechwoods
The Principles
The Sinisters and Kenny B.
Saturday 14th All-Nighter
7.30–11.15p.m.
The Klubs
The Tremas
The Pro-tems
12.00–6.30a.m.
Compère Bob Wooler
Alvin Cash and The Crawlers
Victor Brox and The Brox Band
Solomon's Mines
The Tremas
Majority Plus
Sunday 15th Evening
Compère Bob Wooler
The Magic Lanterns
Tyme and Motion
The Friendly Persuasion

Tuesday 17th Evening
The Dodoes
Wednesday 18th Evening
The Hideaways
Georgia's Germs
Majority Plus
Thursday 19th Evening
The Fix
Solomon's Mines
Friday 20th Evening
The Calderstones
The Seftons
The Kop
Kenny B.
Saturday 21st All-Nighter
7.30–11.15p.m.
The Beechwoods
The King Bs
The Avengers
12.00–6.30a.m.
The Kids
The Beechwoods
Johnny Breeze and The Atlantics
The King Bs
The Avengers
Sunday 22nd Evening
3.00–11p.m.
Majority Plus
Alvin Crash and The Crawlers
The Klubs
The Kids
The Principles
Solomon's Mines
The Signs
Tuesday 24th Evening
Tyme and Motion
Wednesday 25th Evening
The Klubs
The Prowlers
The All-Night Workers
Thursday 26th Evening
Georgia's Germs

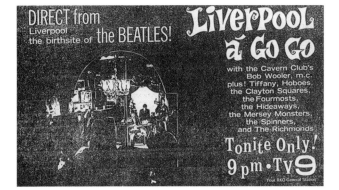

Friday 27th Evening
The Dwellers
The Signs
The Prowlers
Saturday 28th All-Nighter
7.30–11.15p.m.
The Admins
Majority Plus
The Friendly Persuasions
Mommie's Darlings
12.00–6.30a.m.
The Tatters
Solomon's Mines
The Admins
Mommie's Darlings
Majority Plus
Sunday 29th Cavern Marathon
3.00–11p.m.
The Cool Combination
The Beechwoods
The Klubs
The Hideaways
Edwin Starr (from America)
The Crazy Chains
Tyme and Motion
Tuesday 31st Evening
The Dodoes

FEBRUARY
Wednesday 1st Evening
The Hideaways
The Blue Diamonds
The WJs
Thursday 2nd Evening
The Admins
Friday 3rd Evening
Majority Plus
The Prowlers
The Pro-tems
Saturday 4th All-Nighter
7.30–11.15p.m.
The Signs
The Mead
The Kop
12.00–6.30a.m.
Solomon's Mines
The Kop
The Signs
The Mead
Sunday 5th Evening
Hari Karl
The Notions
The Prowlers
Tuesday 7th Evening
The Prowlers
Wednesday 8th Evening
The Signs
Winston Fumbs
The Multivation

Thursday 9th Evening
(Country and Western Night)
The Millars
Friday 10th Evening
The Hideaways
The Prowlers
The Kop
Saturday 11th Evening
Georgia's Germs
The Untouchables
Sunday 12th Evening
(Light Show. Films projected while
   they play. Carl-King Projection.)
The Hideaways
Tyme and Motion
Monday 13th Evening
Special Vox Amp demonstration night
   free to all groups
Tuesday 14th Evening
The Admins
Wednesday 15th Evening
The Signs
Tyme and Motion
The Fables
Thursday 16th Evening
The Multivation
Friday 17th Evening
The States
The Prowlers
Pride and Joy
Saturday 18th Evening
The Kop
The Reason Why
The Flowers
Sunday 19th Evening
The Signs
The Beechwoods
The Hardwear
Tuesday 21st Evening
The Multivation
Wednesday 22nd Evening
The Hideaways
The Klubs
The Original Sinisters
Thursday 23rd Evening
The Mistake
Friday 24th Evening
The Signs
Majority Plus
The Kop
Saturday 25th Evening
Tyme and Motion
The Multivation
The Kop
Sunday 26th Evening
The Klubs
The Beechwoods
The Kegmen

Monday 27th Evening
Compère Bob Wooler
The Multivation
The Canadians
The Klubs
The Tremas
Chuck Berry (from USA)
Tuesday 28th Evening
The Troubles

MARCH
Wednesday 1st Evening
The Hideaways
The Klubs
The Chances Are
Thursday 2nd Evening
Private Party – club let
Friday 3rd Evening
The Klubs
The Heatwave
The Reason Why
Saturday 4th Evening
Paul Young's Toggery
Two Top Tamla Groups
Sunday 5th Evening
The Signs
The Mistake
Tuesday 7th Evening
The Shades
Wednesday 8th Evening
The Hideaways
The Jigsaws
Thursday 9th Evening
Solomon's Mines
Friday 10th Evening
The Exception
The Hip Hooray Band
Saturday 11th Evening
Quiz, Query and Co.
The Shades
The Dimensions
Sunday 12th 3–11p.m.
The Friendly Persuasion
Gale Blues
Scots of St James
The Hideaways
The Signs
Lee Dorsey (from USA)
The Ox
The Rogues
The Michael Henry Group
Tuesday 14th Evening
The Friendly Persuasion
Wednesday 15th Evening
Georgia's Germs
Thursday 16th Evening
The Michael Henry Group
Friday 17th Evening
The Untouchables

Chuck Berry appeared at the Cavern just once, 27 February 1967. It should have been a great night but Chuck came across as a very cold fish. 'He did his famous duck walk though,' said Bob Wooler.

Saturday 18th Evening
Three Top Groups
Sunday 19th Evening
All-star line-up – including The
   Drifters from USA
Wednesday 22nd Evening
Jigsaw
Thursday 23rd Evening
The Fix
The Klubs
Cris Farlowe and The Thunderbirds
Friday 24th Evening
The Night Train
The Exception
The Beacons
The Crossbeats
Georgia's Germs
Saturday 25th Evening
The Purple Affair
The Tremas
The Big Sleep
Sunday 26th Evening
The Klubs
Tyme and Motion
The Ox

Monday 27th Evening
Paul and Richie and The Crying
   Shames
The Tremas
The Mistake
The Urge
The Denims
The Track
Wednesday 29th Evening
The Shades
Friday 31st Evening
The Impact

APRIL
Saturday 1st Evening
The Friendly Persuasion
Georgia's Germs
The Life 'n' Soul
Sunday 2nd Evening
The Tremas
The Waterboard
Changing Times
Friday 7th Evening
The Ox

Saturday 8th Evening
Three groups, no names
Sunday 9th Evening
The Tremas
The Candy Choir
The Senate
Ben E. King Show (from USA)
Friday 14th
Club shut for alterations during week
except for Sat, Sun and lunchtimes
Saturday 15th Evening
The Friendly Persuasion
Tyme and Motion
The Bentics
The Invasion
Sunday 16th Evening
42nd Light Infantry
The Unluv'd
Tuesday 18th Evening
The Unluv'd
Friday 21st Evening
Solomon's Mines
Saturday 22nd Evening
Security Nyshe Trende
The Klubs
The Tremas
Sunday 23rd Evening
The Calderstones
The Untouchables
Friday 28th Evening
The Track
Saturday 29th Evening
The Original Sinisters
Solomon's Mines
The Mad Monks
The States
Sunday 30th Evening
Pride and Joy
The Bo-Lynx
Big Lox Blues Band

MAY
Friday 5th Evening
The Marvellous Marbles
Saturday 6th Evening
The Klubs
The Efekt
The Lomax Alliance
Sunday 7th Evening
The Wild Things
The Bunkum Band
Wednesday 24th Evening
Liverpool Colleges of Buildings
Students' Union Presents…
DJ Tony Prince
The Crying Shames
The Signs
The Escorts
The Mad Monks

The Jets
The Wild Cat Strike
Richie's Persuasion

JUNE
**Saturday 10th All Night
Happening**
7p.m.–7a.m.
(The Bonzo Dog Doo Dah Band
turned up but did not perform)
The Escorts
The Scaffold
The Klubs
Brian Patten (poet)
Merseysippi Jazz Band
Tamla Disco
Thursday 15th Evening
In aid of the Simon Community Club
The Klubs
The Tremas
The Multivation
The Marbles

AUGUST
Wednesday 9th
To Cavern Members – your club is
now licensed, new members by
personal application only
Friday 11th Evening
The Klubs
Tuesday 15th Evening
Earl Preston and The Reflections
Wednesday 16th Evening
Earl Preston and The Reflections
Thursday 17th Evening
Earl Preston and The Reflections
Friday 18th Evening
The Troubles
Tuesday 22nd Evening
The Tremas
Saturday 26th Evening
The Bobby Gray Soul Band
The Washington Soul Band
Sunday 27th Evening
The Klubs
The Tremas
Monday 28th 3–7p.m.
Music by the resident organist, Barry
Edwards
Evening
7.30p.m.–1.00a.m.
The Bobby Gray Soul Band
The Times
The Munchkins
Wednesday 30th Evening
All girls admitted free until end of
September. Each Thursday Search
for Talent and Songwriters night
– successful artists will be recorded

on disc by Chart Records
Thursday 31st Evening
(Free to all members on Thursdays)
The Klubs

SEPTEMBER
Saturday 2nd Evening
Top groups, no names
(also Sunday)
Thursday 14th Evening
(Country and Western Night)
DJ Billy Butler
The String Dusters
The Carl Fenton Trio
The Hillsiders
The Ranch Hands
Saturday 16th Evening
The Tremas
The Klubs
The Detours
Sunday 17th Evening
The Washington Soul Band
Chapter 1
Thursday 21st Evening
(Country and Western Night)
The Blue Mountain Boys – featuring
John E. Paul
Friday 22nd Evening
(Beat Night)
The Fairy Tale
Saturday 23rd Evening
The Klubs
Thursday 28th Evening
(Beat Night)
The Bee-Jays
Friday 29th Evening
(Jazz Night)
The Savoy Jazzmen
Saturday 30th Evening
The King Bees
The George King Group

OCTOBER
Sunday 1st Evening
The Admins
The Tremas
Thursday 5th Evening
The Tremas
Friday 6th Evening
(Jazz Night)
Max Collie's Rhythm Aces
Saturday 7th Evening
The Excelles
Sunday 8th Evening
The In Times
The Illusion
Wednesday 11th Evening
The B Jays
The Cee Trio

Thursday 12th Evening
The Tremas
The Cee Trio
Friday 13th Evening
The Klubs
The Cee Trio
Saturday 14th Evening
DJ Tony Wolfe
The Dream Weavers
The Tremas
The Cee Trio
Friday 27th Evening
The Tremas
Saturday 28th Evening
Dei Meisenhop and The 2nd Edition
The Tremas
The Cee Trio
Sunday 29th Evening
The Washington Soul Band

NOVEMBER
Saturday 4th Evening
Cherished Memories
The States
The Cee Trio
Mechanical Camel
Sunday 5th Evening
The Tremas
The Admins
The Cee Trio
Friday 10th Evening
The Excelles
The Cobalt Complex
The Tremas
The Bicycle
Jerry Shaw's Background
Saturday 11th Evening
The Cobalt Complex
The Metric System
The Tremas
The Bicycle
Jerry Shaw's Background
Sunday 12th Evening
The Detours
The Dream Weavers
The Bicycle
Tuesday 14th Evening
The Tremas
The Bicycle
Friday 17th Evening
Billy Butler's Midnight Phonographic
Soul Explosion
The Detours
The Go-Go Girls
Earl Preston's Reflections
The Spare Tyres
The Bicycle
Wednesday 22nd
(BBC Radio Merseyside joins the

Cavern on board the Royal Daffodil)
DJs Tony Wolfe, Keith Macklin
The Detours
The Tremas
The Excelles
The King Bees
Jerry Shaw's Background
Friday 24th Evening
DJ Billy Butler
The Go-Go Girls
The Bicycle
The Washington Soul Band
Saturday 25th Evening
The Detours
The Bee-Jays
The Bicycle
Sunday 26th Evening
The Tremas

DECEMBER
Friday 1st Evening
Billy Butler's Tamla and Soul Party
with The Bare Essentials
Fred Lloyd's Bicycle (resident group)
The Tee Time Shock (from
Blackpool)
The Metric System
Saturday 2nd Evening
Billy Butler's Tamla and Soul Party
with The Bare Essentials
Fred Lloyd's Bicycle
The Mojos
The Tee Time Shock
Friday 8th Evening
The Bicycle
The Temptations (from USA)
The Chants
The Clockwork Orange (from
London)
Granny's Attic (soul band)
Sunday 10th Evening
The Metric System
Fred Lloyd's Herculese
Friday 15th Evening
(Cavern Lounge)
DJs Billy Butler, Fred 'Organ Grinder'
Lloyd
Gerry Shaw and The Bare Essentials
The Detours
The Beechwoods
Ronnie Pimlett
Saturday 16th Evening
Cavern Lounge
DJs Billy Butler, Fred 'Organ Grinder'
Lloyd
Gerry Shaw and The Bare Essentials
The Locomotive Soul Band
The Good Times
The Equadors

Ronnie Pimlett
Sunday 17th Evening
The Tremors
Gerry Shaw
Fred Lloyd's Bicycle
Wednesday 20th Evening
Fred Lloyd's Bicycle
Thursday 21st Evening
Fred Lloyd's Bicycle
Friday 22nd Evening
DJ Billy Butler
The Bare Essentials
Fred Lloyd
The Pattern People
Gerry Shaw
Steve Day's Kinsmen
Ron Pimlett
Saturday 23rd Evening
DJ Billy Butler
Gerry Shaw
Fred Lloyd
The King Bees
The Mechanical Camel
The Tremors
Sunday 24th Evening
The Perfumed Garden
The Beechwoods
The Mojos
Fred Lloyd
Gerry Shaw
Tuesday 26th Evening
DJ Billy Butler
The Rubber Soul Band
The Spoken Word
Friday 29th Evening
DJ Ron Pimlett
The Bare Essentials
The Perfumed Garden
The Times
Fred Lloyd
Gerry Shaw
Saturday 30th Evening
(Cavern Lounge)
DJs Billy Butler, Gerry Shaw, Ron
 Pimlett, Fred Lloyd
The Bare Essentials
Fred Lloyd
The Mechanical Camel
Steve Day's Kinsmen
Sunday 31st Evening
DJs Billy Butler, Fred Lloyd, Gerry
 Shaw
Dancer: Pearl
The Beechwoods
The Purple Haze

1968

JANUARY
Friday 5th Evening
DJs Billy Butler, Fred Lloyd, Gerry
 Shaw
The Bare Essentials
Rock and Roll Session
The King Bees
The Scene
The Pattern People
Saturday 6th Evening
DJs Billy Butler, Fred Lloyd, Gerry
 Shaw, Ron Pimlett
The Bare Essentials
Rock and Roll Session
Steve Day's Kinsmen
Sunday 7th Evening
DJs Fred Lloyd, Ron Pimlett
The Incident
Friday 12th Evening
DJs Billy Butler, Fred Lloyd
The Bare Essentials
The Section Four
Rock and Roll Session with Billy
 Butler
Saturday 13th Evening
Chapter Six
Friday 19th Evening
Billy Butler Disco Show
(Cavern Lounge)
Country and Western Show
The Westerners
Saturday 20th Evening
DJ Ron Pimlett
The Pattern People
(Cavern Lounge)
Country and Western Show,
DJ Fred Lloyd
The Carl Fenton Four
Sunday 21st Evening
Ron Pimlett's Disco
The Mad Monks
Friday 26th Evening
Billy Butler's Tamla and Soul Party
 with the Bare Essentials
Herald's Angels (from Bolton)
1.15-2.30a.m.
Rock and Roll Session with Billy
 Butler
Saturday 27th Evening
Kaspar's Engine
(Cavern Lounge)
Country and Western Show
The Driftwoods
The Texans

Evening
Disco with Fred Lloyd and The Bare
 Essentials

FEBRUARY
Friday 2nd Evening
(Cavern Lounge)
Tamla Disco with Gerry Shaw
The Vampires
Rock and Roll with Billy Butler and
 The Bare Essentials
DJ Ronnie Pimlett
Tamla Sound with The Dee Jays
Saturday 3rd Evening
DJs Billy Butler, Gerry Shaw
Idle Hours (country and western)
Sinton's Dream (show band)
Saturday 10th Evening
The Mighty Joe Young Show Band
Billy Butler Show with The Bare
 Essentials plus C&W
The Rock Springs
Friday 16th Evening
Billy Butler with The Bare Essentials
 plus Disco
The Pattern People
Saturday 17th Evening
(Cavern Lounge)
The Millars Country and Western
Kasper's Engine
Friday 23rd Evening
DJ Billy Butler plus Ron's Disco
Hell's Angels
Jamie's Jigsaw
Saturday 24th Evening
Children of the Ashes
Kasper's Engine
Rock and Roll with Billy Butler and
 The Bare Essentials
The Pattern People
Thursday 29th Evening
The Chants
Granny's Attic
The Hideaways
The Curiosity Shop

MARCH
Friday 1st Evening
Rock and Roll with Billy Butler and
 The Bare Essentials
The Times
Saturday 2nd Evening
Rock and Roll with Billy Butler and
 The Bare Essentials
Kasper's Engines
The Beechwoods
The Times
Monday 4th Evening
(C&W Night)

Gerry Shaw and The Blue Mountain
 Boys
The Idle Hours
The Carl Fenton Four
Thursday 7th Evening
Rock and Roll Night
DJ Billy Butler
Farron and The TTs
Mike Hart and The Moon Dogs
Friday 8th Evening
Mighty J Young
Familiar Compound
Spirit
Billy Butler's Beat Bonanza Rock
Revival
Saturday 9th Evening
DJ Billy Butler
The Watson Brown Show Band
Kasper's Engine
Monday 11th Evening
The Blue Mountain Boys with Gerry
 Shaw
Thursday 14th Evening
(Rock and Roll Night)
DJ Billy Butler
Farron and The TTs
The Flintstones
Friday 15th Evening
Billy Butler's Rock and Roll Show
The Fables
The Mojo Band
Saturday 16th Evening
Billy Butler's Rock and Roll Show
Farron and The TTs
The Big Sleep (show band)
The Fables
Monday 18th Evening
The Blue Mountain Boys with Gerry
 Shaw
Thursday 21st Evening
DJ Billy Butler
The Escorts
The Tremas
Saturday 23rd Evening
DJ Billy Butler
The Bare Essentials
Marvin Young and The Sound
 Package
Monday 25th Evening
The Blue Mountain Boys with Gerry
 Shaw
Thursday 28th Evening
Upstairs:
Gerry Shaw and The Blue Mountain
 Boys
In the Cellar:
Kasper's Engines
Tire Perfumed Garden
The Tremas

Saturday 30th Evening
DJ Billy Butler
The Bare Essentials
Marvin Young and The Sound Package
PP's Attraction

APRIL
Monday 1st Evening
The Blue Mountain Boys with Gerry
 Shaw
Thursday 4th Evening
Upstairs:
Billy Butler with the Rock A-Go-Go
 Show
Mighty Joe Young
Kasper's Engines
Farron and The TTs
Friday 5th Evening
Marvin Young and The Sound
 Package
Rock and Roll Special with Bob
 Wooler
Ron's Disco
Kenny Bee
Saturday 6th Evening
DJ Billy Butler
The Bare Essentials
Ron's Disco
Watson Brown Show Band
The Baltimore Switch Show Band
Wednesday 10th Evening
The Liverpool Scene:
Adrian Henri
Andy Roberts
Mike Hart
Mike Evans
Percy Jones
Brian Dodson
Thursday 11th Evening
Kasper's Engine
The Tremas
Ron's Disco
Billy Butler
Saturday 13th Evening
DJ Billy Butler
The Bare Essentials
Ron's Disco
Marvin Young's Sound Package
Tyme and Motion
Monday 15th Evening
Billy Butler Rock Show
The Watson Brown Show Band
The Baltimore Switch Show Band
Wednesday 17th Evening
The Liverpool Scene:
Adrian Henri
Andy Roberts
Mike Evans
Percy Jones

Mike Hart
Brian Dodson
Thursday 18th Evening
Billy Butler's Rock and Roll Show
  plus Ron's Disco
The Tremas
Saturday 20th Evening
The Locomotives Show Band
The Tremas
Wednesday 24th Evening
The Liverpool Scene:
Adrian Henri
Mike Evans
Mike Hart
Andy Roberts
Percy Jones
Brian Dodson
Thursday 25th Evening
The Perfumed Garden
Friday 26th Evening
The Motivation (show band)
Billy Butler's Rock A-Go-Go Show
  with The Bare Essentials
Billy Butler's Rock Show
The Locomotive Show Band
The Shady Lane (Tamla soul group
  from Wales)
The White News Generator
Monday 29th
New Merseyside paper *The Scene* on
  sale at Cavern with news by Billy
  Butler and Alf Geoghegan

MAY
Wednesday 1st Evening
The Liverpool Scene:
Adrian Henri
Mike Evans
Mike Hart
Andy Roberts
Percy Jones
Brian Dodson
Thursday 2nd Evening
Mike Gregg
Carl Terry
Mike Hart
Pete Clark
Billy Kinsley
The Tremas
Billy Butler and Disco
Friday 3rd Evening
DJ Tony Royce
Kasper's Engine
Billy Butler's Rock Show
Saturday 4th Evening
Marvin Young Sound Package (from
  Manchester)
The Tuxedos featuring Billy Butler
Disco and The Bare Essentials

Sunday 5th
Football Match: Cavern Kickers *v.*
  Merseybeat Eleven at Longview
  Playing Fields
Wednesday 8th Evening
The Liverpool Scene:
Adrian Henri
Mike Evans
Mike Hart
Andy Roberts
Percy Jones
Brian Dodson
Thursday 9th Evening
DJ Billy Butler plus Disco
The Tremas
Friday 10th Evening
DJ Billy Butler plus Disco
The Tremas
Saturday 11th Evening
The Baltimore Switch Show Band
Kasper's Engines
Friday 17th Evening
The Alan Henry Blend Show Band
Saturday 18th Evening
The Watson Brown Show Band
The Perfumed Garden
Billy Butler and The Go-Go Girls
Monday 27th Evening
The Tremas
Tuesday 28th Evening
The Night Life
Wednesday 29th Evening
Billy Butler's Tuxedos
Friday 31st Evening
The Tremas

JUNE
DJ Billy Butler
The Iveys
The Marvin Young Sound
Sunday 2nd Evening
DJ Billy Butler
The Baltimore Switch
The Tremas
Monday 3rd Evening
Billy Butler's Disco
The Soul Supply
The Baltimore Switch
The Edward John Concern

JULY
Wednesday 10th Evening
The Hideaways
Thursday 18th Evening
The Hideaways
Saturday 20th Evening
The Iveys
Hinge
Tuesday 23rd Evening
The Hideaways

Friday 26th Evening
Bernie's Buzz Band
Saturday 27th Evening
The Curiosity Shoppe
The Baltimore Switch
Billy Butler and Ron's Disco
Tuesday 30th Evening
The Curiosity Shoppe
Wednesday 31st Evening
The Perfumed Garden

AUGUST
Thursday 1st Evening
The Hideaways (back from Scottish
  tour)
Friday 2nd Evening
DJ Billy Butler
Bernie's Buzz Band
Saturday 3rd Evening
Shady Lane
Circulation
Billy Butler and Ron's Disco
Wednesday 7th Evening
The Hideaways
Thursday 8th Evening
The Hermit Sound
Friday 9th Evening
Circles
Wednesday 14th Evening
The Perfumed Garden
Thursday 15th Evening
The Mayo Band
Friday 16th Evening
In the Cavern cellar:
DJ Billy Butler
The Merseys
The Hideaways
The Curiosity Shoppe
Saturday 17th Evening
The Magic Lanterns (from London)
The Libra (from Manchester)
Billy Butler and Ron's Disco
Friday 23rd Evening
The Baltimore Switch
Thursday 29th Evening
The Perfumed Garden
Friday 30th Evening
In the Cavern cellar:
The Curiosity Shoppe
Purple Wedding
Saturday 31st Evening
The Hideaways
Mighty Joe Young
Billy Butler and Ron's Disco

SEPTEMBER
Thursday 5th Evening
The Condemned Valley
Friday 6th Evening
Two floors of non-stop entertainment

The Tremas
The Spoken Word
Saturday 7th Evening
DJ Billy Butler
The Curiosity Shoppe
NSU
Tuesday 10th Evening
Living Soul
Wednesday 11th Evening
The Michael Henry Group
Thursday 12th Evening
The Curiosity Shoppe
Friday 13th Evening
The Rubber Soul Band
The Jump
Saturday 14th Evening
DJ Billy Butler
Liquid Umbrella
The Tremas
Tuesday 17th Evening
The Kinsmen
Wednesday 18th Evening
The Dominoes
Thursday 19th Evening
DJ Billy Butler
The Tremas
The Curiosity Shoppe
Friday 20th Evening
The Curiosity Shoppe
The Kinsmen
Saturday 21st Evening
The Baltimore Switch
Focal Point
Tuesday 24th Evening
The Tremas
Wednesday 25th Evening
DJ Billy Butler
Bruce Channel (from USA)
The Curiosity Shoppe
The Baltimore Switch
Thursday 26th Evening
The Mojo Band
Friday 27th Evening
The Pattern People
NSU

OCTOBER
Friday 4th Evening
Mr Tim Rose (from USA)
(John Bonham on drums)
Wednesday 9th Evening
The Curiosity Shoppe
Thursday 10th Evening
Colonel Bagshot's Incredible Bucket
  Band
Thursday 17th Evening
DJ Billy Butler
The Rubber Soul Band

Friday 18th Evening
Gary Walker and The Rain (first time
  in Liverpool)
The Tremas
The Curiosity Shoppe
New Mojo Band
Wednesday 23rd Evening
The Curiosity Shoppe
Thursday 24th Evening
The Curiosity Shoppe
Tuesday 29th Evening
The Michael Henry Group
Thursday 31st Evening
DJ Billy Butler
The Curiosity Shoppe

NOVEMBER
Friday 1st Evening
The Curiosity Shoppe
The Memories
Saturday 2nd Evening
Sweet Marriage
Adam
Wednesday 6th Evening
The Mumbles
Thursday 7th Evening
DJ Billy Butler
The Rubber Soul Band
Friday 8th Evening
The Passion Wagon
Jug
Saturday 9th Evening
DJ Billy Butler
Sponge
The Baltimore Switch
Wednesday 13th Evening
The Mumbles
Thursday 14th Evening
DJ Billy Butler
The Tremas
Wednesday 27th Evening
The Mojo Band
Thursday 28th Evening
DJ Billy Butler
The Mumbles
Saturday 30th Evening
House of Lords (from London)
The Original Soul Bro Boogaloo
  Band

DECEMBER
Thursday 5th Evening
DJ Billy Butler
The Polka Dot Train
Friday 6th Evening
NSU
Third Stone From The Sun
Saturday 7th Evening
The Curiosity Shoppe
The Magic Lanterns

Wednesday 11th Evening
The Mojo Band
Thursday 12th Evening
DJ Billy Butler
The Curiosity Shoppe
Friday 13th Evening
The Klubs
The Baltimore Switch
Saturday 14th Evening
NSU
Tangerine
Thursday 19th Evening
DJ Billy Butler
The Mojo Band
Friday 20th Evening
Kasper's Engine
The Windy City Agreement
Saturday 21st Evening
DJ Billy Butler
Art Nouveaux
The Mojo Band
Tuesday 24th Evening
DJ Billy Butler
The Curiosity Shoppe
The Mojo Band
The Techniques
Thursday 26th Evening
DJ Billy Butler
The Curiosity Shoppe
Granny's Attic
Friday 27th Evening
The Verge
Saturday 28th Evening
The Curiosity Shoppe
Sin-Bad
Tuesday 31st Evening
The Curiosity Shoppe
The Mojo Band
Kasper's Engines

1969

JANUARY
Thursday 2nd Evening
The Curiosity Shoppe
Friday 3rd Evening
The Curiosity Shoppe
The Baltimore Switch
Saturday 4th Evening
DJ Billy Butler
Rare Amber
Harlem John's Reshuffle
Thursday 9th Evening
The Curiosity Shoppe
Northern Drift
Saturday 11th Evening
The Curiosity Shoppe

The New Generation
Wednesday 15th Evening
The Curiosity Shoppe
Thursday 16th Evening
DJ Billy Butler
Buzzer
Friday 17th Evening
The Curiosity Shoppe
The Baltimore Switch
Saturday 18th Evening
DJ Billy Butler
The Magoos
Jason Cord
Wednesday 22nd Evening
(Free membership given tonight and
    Thursday)
The Mumbles
Thursday 23rd Evening
Hurles Jinks
Friday 24th Evening
Reception Almost
Saturday 25th Evening
DJ Billy Butler
Sin-Bad
The Microbes
Wednesday 29th Evening
The Mumbles
Thursday 30th Evening
DJ Billy Butler
The Perfumed Garden
Friday 31st Evening
The Baltimore Switch
Lemon Cartoon

FEBRUARY
Saturday 1st Evening
DJ Billy Butler
The Iveys
Wednesday 5th Evening
The Incident
Thursday 6th Evening
The Mumbles
Friday 7th Evening
East of Eden
Smokestack
Saturday 8th Evening
DJ Billy Butler
Watson T. Brown
The Explosive
The Answers
Wednesday 12th Evening
The Mumbles
Friday 14th Evening
Jack Truth
Saturday 15th Evening
DJ Billy Butler
The Variation
The Wonder Band

Friday 21st Evening
NSU
Mighty Joe Young
Saturday 22nd Evening
DJ Billy Butler
Dream
Smokestack
Thursday 27th Evening
DJ Billy Butler
Shuffle's Sound

MARCH
Friday 7th Evening
Sweet Wine
Another
Saturday 8th Evening
DJ Billy Butler
State Express
Chapter Six
Thursday 13th Evening
DJ Billy Butler
Buzzell
Friday 14th Evening
Sunshine
Chapter Six
Saturday 15th Evening
DJ Billy Butler
The Perishers
Colour Supplement
Friday 21st Evening
Tribute
Chapter Six
Saturday 22nd Evening
Sellophane
Smokestack
Saturday 29th Evening
DJ Billy Butler
East of Eden
Petrus Booncamp

APRIL
Wednesday 2nd Evening
DJ Clem Dalton
Saturday 5th Evening
Billy Munder and The Liquid
    Umbrellas
The Variations
Sunday 6th Evening
Chapter Six
Tribute
Friday 11th Evening
DJ Clem Dalton
The Zombies
Hemlock
Saturday 12th Evening
DJ Billy Butler
Sellophane
Sweet Marriage

Thursday 17th Evening
DJ Billy Butler
Billy Kinsley
Peter Clark and Chris
Jackie Lomax (Beatles recording
    artist)
Petrus Booncamp
Friday 18th Evening
DJ Clem Dalton
The Business
White Summer
The New Scene
Wednesday 23rd Evening
September
Thursday 24th Evening
DJ Billy Butler
Sweet Marriage
The Cymbaline
Friday 25th Evening
The Royal Seed
Shuffle's Sound
Saturday 26th Evening
The Explosive
Tuesday's Mood
Wednesday 30th Evening
Smokestack

MAY
Thursday 1st Evening
The Iveys
Friday 2nd Evening
NSU
Jasmin T.
Saturday 3rd Evening
The Bitter Suite
Silence
Thursday 8th Evening
DJs Billy Butler, Robbie Rave
Bunker's Brain
Bubble Gum
Friday 9th Evening
Beryl Marsden
Sin-Bad
Lemon Cartoon
Saturday 10th Evening
Colonel Bagshot
Peter and The Alphabet
Wednesday 14th Evening
White Summer
Thursday 15th Evening
DJ Billy Butler
The Demon Fizz
The Business
Friday 16th Evening
DJ Robbie Rave The Pop Slave
The System
Lemon Cartoon
Saturday 17th Evening
DJ Billy Butler

House of Lords
Apple
Thursday 22nd Evening
The Explosive
The Stroll Band
Friday 23rd Evening
DJs Billy Butler, Robbie the Rave
East of Eden
White Summer
Saturday 24th Evening
DJs Billy Butler, Robbie Rave
Colour Supplement
Petrus Booncamp
Thursday 29th Evening
DJ Billy Butler
The Chris Carma Road Show
Friday 30th Evening
DJ Robbie Rave
The Kensington Mews
Gerrards Own
Saturday 31st Evening
Wellington Kitch
Frankie and The Countdowns

JUNE
Wednesday 4th Evening
Sin-Bad
Thursday 5th Evening
DJ Billy Butler
Family Circle
Friday 6th Evening
Small Piece of Paradise
The Midnight Hour
Saturday 7th Evening
DJs Billy Butler, Robbie the Rave
Only The Best
Justin Marts
The Baltimore Switch
The Kissing Game
Wednesday 11th Evening
The Mumbles
Thursday 12th Evening
DJ Billy Butler
The Baltimore Switch
Friday 13th Evening
Eastern Crowd
Marma
Saturday 14th Evening
DJs Billy Butler, Robbie Rave
Technique
Arishema
Wednesday 18th Evening
Chapter Six
Thursday 19th Evening
DJ Billy Butler
The Clayton Squares
Wednesday 25th Evening
DJ Robbie Rave
The Highfield

Thursday 26th Evening
DJ Billy Butler
The Exemption
Friday 27th Evening
DJ Robbie Rave
The Pepper Tree
The Shy Lambs
Saturday 28th Evening
DJs Billy Butler, Robbie Rave
Art Nouveaux
The Carleton

JULY
Wednesday 2nd Evening
The Exemption
Thursday 3rd Evening
DJ Billy Butler
The Highfield
Friday 4th Evening
DJ Robbie Rave
Golliwog
The Method Saturday
5th Evening
DJs Billy Butler, Robbie Rave
Cherry Blossom Clinic
The Hi-Coes
Wednesday 9th Evening
DJ Robbie Rave
The Highfield
Thursday 10th Evening
DJ Billy Butler
The Exemption
Friday 11th Evening
DJ Robbie Rave
Sunshine
The Midnight Hour
Saturday 12th Evening
DJs Billy Butler, Robbie Rave
The State Express
The Population
Wednesday 9th Evening
DJ Robbie Rave
The Exemption
Friday 18th Evening
DJ Robbie Rave
Harvey Brooks
Purple Haze
Saturday 19th Evening
DJs Billy Butler, Robbie Rave
The Perishers
The Stroll Band
In-Transit
Wednesday 23rd Evening
The Exemption
Thursday 24th Evening
The Highfields
Friday 25th Evening
The Story Book
The Variations

Saturday 26th Evening
Frank and The Countdowns
The Dimensions
Monday 28th Evening
The Scaffold (backed by The
  Business)
Wednesday 30th Evening
The Highfields
Thursday 31st Evening
The Curiosity Shoppe

AUGUST
Friday 1st Evening
The Magic Lanterns
Mighty Joe Young
Saturday 2nd Evening
Soul Staxx
Mighty Joe Young
Wednesday 6th Evening
The Exemption
Thursday 7th Evening
The Juice
Friday 8th Evening
The Klubs
Pandora's Box
Saturday 9th Evening
Explosive
The Population
Black Velvet
Wednesday 13th Evening
Chapter Six
Thursday 14th Evening
Guthile's Klokke
Friday 15th Evening
Jasmin T.
The Exception
Saturday 16th Evening
The Stroll Band
The Pavement
Thursday 21st Evening
DJ Robbie Rave
Chapter Six
Friday 22nd Evening
Petrus Booncamp
Frisby Dyke
Saturday 23rd Evening
The Bitter Suite
Monday 25th Evening
Underground Night
Blind Eye
The Klubs

SEPTEMBER
Thursday 4th Evening
The Clayton Squares
Friday 5th Evening
Guthrie's Klokke
Pandora's Box

Saturday 6th Evening
Ebony Blush
The Clayton Squares
Monday 8th Evening
The Scaffold
Thursday 11th Evening
The Village Band
Friday 12th Evening
The Klubs
The Gift Band
Saturday 13th Evening
The Almanac
The Friends
Monday 15th Evening
The Klubs
Thursday 18th Evening
St James Infirmary (from London)
Friday 19th Evening
St James Infirmary
Peter and The Alphabet
Saturday 20th Evening
The troll Band
The Balloons
Monday 22nd Evening
St James Infirmary
Thursday 25th Evening
Puritan
Friday 26th Evening
Greasy Bear
St James Infirmary
Saturday 27th Evening
Petrus Booncamp
Little Free Rock
Monday 29th Evening
(Underground Night)
The Klubs

OCTOBER
Thursday 3rd Evening
Colonel Bagshot
Friday 3rd Evening
The Pepper Tree
The Perfumed Garden
Saturday 4th Evening
Greasy Bear
The Klubs
Thursday 9th Evening
DJ Robby Rave
The Klubs
The Iveys
Friday 10th Evening
Fascination and Candy
Saturday 11th Evening
Frisby Dyke
Candy
Monday 13th Evening
The Iveys
Guthrie's Klokke

Thursday 16th Evening
Chapter Six
Friday 17th Evening
Anton Farmer
Creeping Vine
Saturday 18th Evening
The Mafia
Colonel Bagshot
Monday 20th Evening
(Underground Night)
The Sleep
Thursday 23rd Evening
The Klubs
Friday 24th Evening
Coconut Mushroom
Anton Farmer
Saturday 25th Evening
Coconut Mushroom
Puritan
Monday 27th Evening
(Underground Night)

The Klubs
Thursday 30th Evening
The Hunchy Band
Friday 31st Evening
Petrus Booncamp
Spring

NOVEMBER
Saturday 1st Evening
Life
Sleep
Thursday 6th Evening
The Klubs
Friday 7th Evening
Gravy Train
Pepper Tree
Saturday 8th Evening
Revolver
The Perfumed Garden
Monday 10th Evening
(Underground Night)
Turn Pike

Thursday 13th Evening
The Klubs
Friday 14th Evening
DJs Robbie Rave, Gray Donna
Peaceful Soul
Turnpike
Saturday 15th Evening
The Atlantics
The Klubs
Monday 17th Evening
(Underground Night)
Arnold Greenyard
Thursday 20th Evening
The Klubs
Friday 21st Evening
Golliwog
The Perfumed Garden
Saturday 22nd Evening
DJs Robbie Rave, Gray Donna
Grit
Frisby Dyke
Monday 24th Evening
Progressive Night Out
Progressive
Thursday 27th Evening
DJ Robbie Rave
The Hunchy Band
Friday 28th Evening
Golliwog
Strawberry Blues
Saturday 29th Evening
DJs Robbie Rave, Gray Donna
Little Free Rock
Greasy Bear

DECEMBER
Monday 1st Evening
The Klubs
Friday 5th Evening
Max Cannon
The Klubs
Saturday 6th Evening
Purple Gang
Life
Monday 8th Evening
Greasy Bear
Thursday 11th Evening
Afterglow
Friday 12th Evening
Colour Supplement
Daniel Boon
Saturday 13th Evening
DJs Robbie Rave, Gray Donna
The Staircase
Matthew
Monday 15th Evening
DJ Robbie Rave
The Klubs

Thursday 18th Evening
DJ Robbie Rave
The Klubs
Friday 19th Evening
DJs Robbie Rave, Gray Donna
Almanac
Mighty Joe Young
Saturday 20th Evening
Baby (from London)
Worn Dust
Monday 22nd Evening
The Original Sin
Wednesday 24th Evening
The Perishers
The Perfumed Garden
Friday 26th Evening
Golliwog
The Klubs
Saturday 27th Evening
The Perishers
St James Infirmary
Sunday 28th Evening
Mighty Joe Young
Wednesday 31st Evening
DJs Robbie Rave, Gray Donna
Frisby Dyke
The Klubs

1970

JANUARY
Friday 2nd Evening
DJs Robbie Rave, Gray Donna
Life
Variation
Saturday 3rd Evening
Max Cannon
Almanac
Monday 5th Evening
Isambard Kingdom
Thursday 8th Evening
DJ Robbie Rave
Chapter Six
Friday 9th Evening
Disco, Robbie Rave, Gray Donna
Staircase
Time Machine
Saturday 10th Evening
Disco, Daniel Boon, Robbie Rave,
  Gray Donna
Little Free Rock
Monday 12th Evening
Barbed Wire Soup
Thursday 15th Evening
DJ Robbie Rave
Dusty

Friday 16th Evening
DJs Robbie Rave, Gray Donna
Golliwog
Review
Saturday 17th Evening
DJs Robbie Rave, Gray Donna
The Purple Gang
Sleep
Monday 19th Evening
DJ Robbie Rave
Simon Dupree and The Big Sound
The Klubs
Thursday 22nd Evening
DJ Robbie Rave
The Toy Town Express
Friday 23rd Evening
Gravy Train
Cleveland Fox Band
Saturday 24th Evening
DJs Robbie Rave, Gray Donna
Daniel Boon
Bitter Suite
Monday 26th Evening
Wild Mouth (from London)
The Klubs
Thursday 29th Evening
DJ Robbie Rave
Tynefoil
Friday 30th Evening
Weather
Afterglow
Saturday 31st Evening
DJs Robbie Rave, Gray Donna
Applejacks
Almanac

FEBRUARY
Monday 2nd Evening
Wishbone Ash
Thursday 5th Evening
Disco with Robbie Rave, Gray
  Donna
The Klubs
Badfinger (New Record – 'Come
  and Get It')
Friday 6th Evening
DJs Robbie Rave, Gray Donna
Harlem John's Reshuffle
Justin Tyme
Saturday 7th Evening
Disco with Robbie Rave, Gray
  Donna
Barbed Wire Soup
Isambard Kingdom
Monday 9th Evening
DJ Robbie Rave
Status Quo
The Klubs

The Purple Gang, who made only a handful of Cavern appearances in the late 1960s but certainly managed to create a stir. They set off smoke bombs in the club (the type used as rodent repellent) and the club had to be evacuated.

Thursday 12th Evening
DJ Robbie Rave
Optimist Incorporated
Friday 13th Evening
DJs Robbie Rave, Gray Donna
Money
Max Cannon
Saturday 14th Evening
Disco with Robbie Rave, Gray Donna
Ned Ludd
Galliard
Monday 16th Evening
DJ Robbie Rave
Shmoels
Thursday 19th Evening
DJ Robbie Rave
The Klubs
Friday 20th Evening
DJs Robbie Rave, Gray Donna
Sunshine (from London)

Honda
Saturday 21st Evening
DJs Robbie Rave, Gray Donna
Hammer
Mighty Joe Young
Monday 23rd Evening
DJ Robbie Rave
The Klubs
Thursday 26th Evening
DJ Robbie Rave
Isambard Kingdom
Time Machine
Friday 27th Evening
DJs Robbie Rave, Gray Donna
Black Velvet
Dear John
Saturday 28th Evening
Little Free Rock
Revolver

MARCH
Monday 2nd Evening
South California Purple
Thursday 5th Evening
DJ Robbie Rave
Winters Tale
Friday 6th Evening
DJs Robbie Rave, Gray Donna
Locomotive
The Balloons
Saturday 7th Evening
DJs Robbie Rave, Gray Donna
Frisby Dyke
Hard Rock
Monday 9th Evening
DJ Robbie Rave
The Klubs
Thursday 12th Evening
DJ Robbie Rave
Stevie's Fix
Friday 13th Evening
Crossroads
Santa-Fe-Reunion
Saturday 14th Evening
Pepper Tree
Big Idea
Monday 16th Evening
The Klubs
Thursday 19th Evening
Isambard Kingdom
Friday 20th Evening
DJs Robbie Rave, Gray Donna
Almanac
Max Cannon
Saturday 21st Evening
DJs Robbie Rave, Gray Donna
Barbed Wire Soup
Kansas Hook
Monday 23rd Evening
DJ Robbie Rave
Arcadium (from London)
Saturday 28th Evening
DJs Robbie Rave, Gray Donna
Love Machine (from London)

APRIL
Thursday 2nd Evening
DJ Robbie Rave
Lemon Wood
Friday 3rd Evening
DJ Robbie Rave
Cartridge
Apricot Brandy
Saturday 4th Evening
DJs Robbie Rave, Gray Donna
The Klubs
Shelley
Monday 6th Evening
The Klubs

Thursday 9th Evening
DJ Robbie Rave
The Klubs
Friday 10th Evening
DJs Robbie Rave, Gray Donna
Toy Shop
Britain
Saturday 11th Evening
Galliard
Daniel Boon
Thursday 16th Evening
DJ Robbie Rave
Zelda Plum
Friday 17th Evening
DJs Robbie Rave, Gray Donna
Revolver
Magic Box
Saturday 18th Evening
DJs Robbie Rave, Gray Donna
Wishbone Ash
Magic Box
Monday 20th Evening
DJ Robbie Rave
The Klubs
Thursday 23rd Evening
DJ Robbie Rave
Match Box
Friday 24th Evening
Beatwave
The Jug
Saturday 25th Evening
DJs Robbie Rave, Gray Donna
Rupert's People
Angelique
Monday 27th Evening
The Klubs
Thursday 30th Evening
DJ Robbie Rave
Dusty

MAY
Friday 1st Evening
DJs Robbie Rave, Gray Donna
Magic Factory
Cathedral
Saturday 2nd Evening
DJs Robbie Rave, Gray Donna
Herbert Warninks
Magic Elixier
Cathedral
Monday 4th Evening
DJ Robbie Rave
The Klubs
Thursday 7th Evening
DJ Robbie Rave
The Perfumed Garden
Friday 8th Evening
DJs Robbie Rave, Gray Donna
Orange Tea Cup

Blind Eye
Saturday 9th Evening
DJs Robbie Rave, Gray Donna
Galliard
Orange Tea Cup
Monday 11th Evening
DJ Robbie Rave
The Klubs
Thursday 14th Evening
DJ Robbie Rave
Barbed Wire Soup
Friday 15th Evening
Samantha Krisp (From London)
Goliath
Nazareth
Saturday 16th Evening
DJs Robbie Rave, Gray Donna
Samantha Krisp
Goliath
Monday 18th Evening
DJ Robbie Rave
The Klubs
Thursday 21st Evening
DJ Robbie Rave
South California Purple
Friday 22nd Evening
DJs Robbie Rave, Gray Donna
Marble Arch
Merlin
Saturday 23rd Evening
DJs Robbie Rave, Gray Donna
Marble Arch
Kets Rebellion
Thursday 28th Evening
DJ Robbie Rave
Population
Friday 29th Evening
DJs Robbie Rave, Gray Donna
Balloons
Revolver
Saturday 30th Evening
DJs Robbie Rave, Gray Donna
Honda
The Klubs
Revolver

JUNE
Monday 1st Evening
DJ Robbie Rave
Slaughterhouse
Thursday 4th Evening
DJ Robbie Rave
Zelda Plum
Friday 5th Evening
DJs Robbie Rave, Gray Donna
The Jump
Aaron's Rod
Saturday 6th Evening
DJs Robbie Rave, Gray Donna

The Perfumed Garden
Kansas Hook
Monday 8th Evening
DJ Robbie Rave
Ned Pringe
Thursday 11th Evening
DJ Robbie Rave
Dusty
Friday 12th Evening
DJs Robbie Rave, Gray Donna
Tipp
Nazareth
Saturday 13th Evening
Gravy Train
Almanac
Monday 15th Evening
DJ Robbie Rave
Golliwog
Thursday 18th Evening
Spandrel
Friday 19th Evening
Whisky Martin
Penelope White
Thursday 25th Evening
DJ Robbie Rave
Zelda Plum
Friday 26th Evening
Titus Oates
Colour Supplement
Saturday 27th Evening
Technique
Isambard Kingdom
Monday 29th Evening
Slaughterhouse

JULY
Thursday 2nd Evening
Purple Gang
Friday 3rd Evening
State Express
Purple Gang
Saturday 4th
Evening State Express
Slaughterhouse
Monday 6th Evening
Isambard Kingdom
Thursday 9th Evening
The Scot James Band
Friday 10th Evening
DJs Robbie Rave, Gray Donna
The Acorns
Marble Orchard
Saturday 11th Evening
DJs Robbie Rave, Gray Donna
Kansas Hook
Ned Bludd
Monday 13th Evening
Slaughterhouse

Thursday 16th Evening
Ned Pringe
Friday 17th Evening
Rupert's People
Impact
Saturday 18th Evening
DJs Robbie Rave, Gray Donna
Dusty
Rupert's People
Monday 20th Evening
Euphoria
Tuesday 21st Evening
Colonel Bagshot
Acropolis
Thursday 23rd Evening
The Klubs
Friday 24th Evening
DJs Robbie Rave, Gray Donna
Kansas Hook
Slaughterhouse
Saturday 25th Evening
DJs Robbie Rave, Gray Donna
Barbed Wire Soup
Galliard
Monday 27th Evening
The Bells
Thursday 30th Evening
Impact
Friday 31st Evening
DJs Robbie Rave, Gray Donna
Zelda Plum
Salamanda

AUGUST
Saturday 1st Evening
DJs Robbie Rave, Gray Donna
Salamanda
South California Purple
Monday 3rd Evening
The Klubs
Thursday 6th Evening
Axis
Friday 7th Evening
DJs Robbie Rave, Gray Donna
The Klubs
Uncle Sam
Saturday 8th Evening
DJs Robbie Rave, Gray Donna
The Perfumed Garden
The Pink Engine
Monday 10th Evening
Zelda Plum
Thursday 13th Evening
The Klubs
Friday 14th Evening
DJs Robbie Rave, Gray Donna
Justin Tyme
Ned Pringe

Saturday 15th Evening
DJs Robbie Rave, Gray Donna
Almanak
Justin Tyme
Monday 17th Evening
Boadicea
Thursday 20th Evening
The Klubs
Friday 21st Evening
DJs Robbie Rave, Gray Donna
Greasy Bear
Zelda Plum
Saturday 22nd Evening
DJs Robbie Rave, Gray Donna
The Klubs
Greasy Bear
Thursday 27th Evening
Zelda Plum
Friday 28th Evening
DJs Robbie Rave, Gray Donna
Barabus
Barbed Wire Soup
Saturday 29th Evening
DJs Robbie Rave, Gray Donna
Galliard
Barabus

SEPTEMBER
Thursday 3rd Evening
The Klubs
Friday 4th Evening
DJs Robbie Rave, Gray Donna
The Perfumed Garden
Barbed Wire Soup
Saturday 5th Evening
DJs Robbie Rave, Gray Donna
Elton Chess
Penny Arcade
Monday 7th Evening
Isambard Kingdom
Tuesday 8th Evening
Schmoes
Thursday 10th Evening
Schmoes
Saturday 12th Evening
DJs Robbie Rave, Gray Donna
The Klubs
Arcadium
Monday 14th Evening
Zelda Plum
Thursday 17th Evening
The Klubs
Friday 18th Evening
DJs Robbie Rave, Gray Donna
Kansas Hook
South California Purple
Saturday 19th Evening
DJs Robbie Rave, Gray Donna
Kansas Hook

Jeff's-Chu-Chu
Monday 21st Evening
Currency
Thursday 24th Evening
Ned Prince
Friday 25th Evening
DJs Robbie Rave, Gray Donna
Innocent Child
The Norman Haines Band
Saturday 26th Evening
DJs Robbie Rave, Gray Donna
The Norman Haines Band
Isambard Kingdom
Monday 28th Evening
The Klubs

OCTOBER
Thursday 1st Evening
Barbed Wire Soup
Friday 2nd Evening
DJs Robbie Rave, Gray Donna
Possessed
Zelda Plum
Saturday 3rd Evening
DJs Robbie Rave, Gray Donna
Possessed
Santa Maria
Monday 5th Evening
Isambard Kingdom
Thursday 8th Evening
Zelda Plum
Friday 9th Evening
DJs Robbie Rave, Gray Donna
Trapeze
Bram Stoker
Saturday 10th Evening
DJs Robbie Rave, Gray Donna
Ghost
Super Group
Monday 12th Evening
Ned Prince
Thursday 15th Evening
The Klubs
Friday 16th Evening
DJs Robbie Rave, Gray Donna
Ginger
Bram Stoker
Saturday 17th Evening
DJs Robbie Rave, Gray Donna
Ginger
Axis
Thursday 22nd Evening
Currency
Friday 23rd Evening
DJs Robbie Rave, Gray Donna
Balloons
The Klubs
Saturday 24th Evening
DJs Robbie Rave, Gray Donna

Heavy Boots
Tear Gas
Monday 26th Evening
Just Us
Thursday 29th Evening
Zelda Plum
Friday 30th Evening
DJs Robbie Rave, Gray Donna
Quick Sand
Money

NOVEMBER
Monday 2nd Evening
Isambard Kingdom
Thursday 5th Evening
Currency
Friday 6th Evening
DJs Robbie Rave, Gray Donna
Kansas Hook
Salamanda
Saturday 7th Evening
DJs Robbie Rave, Gray Donna
Salamanda
The Klubs
Monday 9th Evening
Axis
Thursday 12th Evening
Uncle Sam
Friday 13th Evening
DJs Robbie Rave, Gray Donna
Isambard Kingdom
Impact
Saturday 14th Evening
DJs Robbie Rave, Gray Donna
Zelda Plum
Galliard
Monday 16th Evening
Geoff's-Chu-Chu
Thursday 19th Evening
Birth
Friday 20th Evening
DJs Robbie Rave, Gray Donna
Peace
Fisher
Saturday 21st Evening
DJs Robbie Rave, Gray Donna
Fisher
The Perfumed Garden
Monday 23rd Evening
Brandy
Thursday 26th Evening
The Klubs
Friday 27th Evening
DJs Robbie Rave, Gray Donna
Charges
Able Fletcher
Saturday 28th Evening
DJs Robbie Rave, Gray Donna
Charge

Able Fletcher
Monday 30th Evening
Zelda Plum

DECEMBER
Thursday 3rd Evening
The Circular State Band
Friday 4th Evening
DJs Robbie Rave, Gray Donna
Spring
Axis
Saturday 5th Evening
The Klubs
Spring
Monday 7th Evening
Bluto
Thursday 10th Evening
Uncle Sam
Friday 11th Evening
DJs Robbie Rave, Gray Donna
Balloons
Zelda Plum
Saturday 12th Evening
The Perfumed Garden
Heavy Boots
Monday 14th Evening
The Klubs
Thursday 17th Evening
Peaceful Nature
Friday 18th Evening
Racking Chair
The Circular State Band
Saturday 19th Evening
Rocking Chair
Salamanda
Monday 20th Evening
Curtesey
Thursday 24th Evening
The Klubs
Zelda Plum
Saturday 26th Evening
The Klubs
Sunday 27th Evening
DJ Robbie Rave
The Klubs
Thursday 31st Evening
DJs Robbie Rave, Gray Donna
The Klubs
Bram Stoker

1971

JANUARY
Friday 1st Evening
DJs Robbie Rave, Gray Donna
Explosion

Birth
Saturday 2nd Evening
Felix
Crazy Mabel
Sunday 3rd Evening
The Klubbs
Monday 4th Evening
DJ Robbie Rave
Apricot Brandy
Thursday 7th Evening
DJ Robbie Rave
Uncle Sam
Friday 8th Evening
DJs Robbie Rave, Gray Donna
The Seige Band
Impact
Saturday 9th Evening
The Seige Band
The Klubbs
Hannable
Sunday 10th Evening
Kansas Hook
Monday 11th Evening
DJ Robbie Rave
Peaceful Nature
Thursday 14th Evening
DJ Robbie Rave
Ned Prince
Friday 15th Evening
DJs Robbie Rave, Gray Donna
Strange Fox
Just Us
Saturday 16th Evening
DJs Robbie Rave, Gray Donna
Strange Fox
Romany Rye
Sunday 17th Evening
DJ Robbie Rave
The Klubbs
Thursday 21st Evening
DJ Robbie Rave
Average Cabbage
Friday 22nd Evening
DJs Robbie Rave, Gray Donna
Mead
Stackwaddy
Saturday 23rd Evening
Mead
Schmoes
Sunday 24th Evening
Currency
Monday 25th Evening
DJ Robbie Rave
Sheba
Thursday 28th Evening
DJ Robbie Rave
Axis

Friday 29th Evening
DJs Robbie Rave, Gray Donna
The Dog
Birth
Saturday 30th Evening
The Dog
Currency
Sunday 31st Evening
DJ Robbie Rave
The Klubbs

FEBRUARY
Monday 1st Evening
DJ Robbie Rave
Confucius
Thursday 4th Evening
DJ Robbie Rave
Uncle Sam
Friday 5th Evening
DJs Robbie Rave, Gray Donna
The Klubbs
Graphite
Saturday 6th Evening
Graphite
Impact
Sunday 7th Evening
DJ Robbie Rave
Ginger
Monday 8th Evening
DJ Robbie Rave
Time
Thursday 11th Evening
DJ Robbie Rave
Heated Blood
Friday 12th evening
DJs Robbie Rave, Gray Donna
The Klubbs
Woodfall
Saturday 13th Evening
DJs Robbie Rave, Gray Donna
Average Cabbage
Woodfall
Sunday 14th Evening
DJ Robbie Rave
The Klubbs
Monday 15th Evening
DJ Robbie Rave
Rupert
Thursday 18th Evening
DJ Robbie Rave
Confucius
Friday 19th Evening
DJ Robbie Rave
Kansas Hook
Bilbo Baggins Band
Saturday 20th Evening
DJs Robbie Rave, Gray Donna
Axis
Bilbo Baggins Band

Sunday 21st Evening
DJ Robbie Rave
The Klubbs
Monday 22nd Evening
DJ Robbie Rave
Confucius
Thursday 25th Evening
DJ Robbie Rave
Dhyana
Friday 26th Evening
DJs Robbie Rave, Gray Donna
Killing Floor
Explosion
Saturday 27th Evening
DJs Robbie Rave, Gray Donna
The Klubbs
Birth
Sunday 28th Evening
DJ Robbie Rave
The Klubbs

MARCH
Thursday 4th Evening
DJ Robbie Rave
Confucius
Friday 5th Evening
DJs Robbie Rave, Gray Donna
Galliard
Paladin
Saturday 6th Evening
DJs Robbie Rave, Gray Donna
Gentle Giant
Gass
Sunday 7th Evening
DJ Robbie Rave
The Klubbs
Monday 8th Evening
DJ Robbie Rave
Time
Thursday 11th Evening
DJ Robbie Rave
The Klubbs
Friday 12th Evening
DJs Robbie Rave, Gray Donna
Ronno
Paladin
Currency
Saturday 13th Evening
Ronno
Salamander
Sunday 14th Evening
DJ Robbie Rave
Salamander
Monday 15th Evening
DJ Robbie Rave
The Klubbs
Thursday 18th Evening
Confucius

Friday 19th Evening
DJs Robbie Rave, Gray Donna
Gringo
Perfumed Garden
Saturday 20th Evening
DJs Robbie Rave, Gray Donna
Northwind
Nothin' Ever 'Appens
Sunday 21st Evening
DJ Robbie Rave
Northwind
Monday 22nd Evening
DJ Robbie Rave
The Klubbs
Thursday 25th Evening
DJ Robbie Rave
Strife
Friday 26th Evening
DJs Robbie Rave, Gray Donna
Argent
Orphens
Saturday 27th Evening
DJs Robbie Rave, Gray Donna
Aubrey Small
Strife
Sunday 28th Evening
DJ Robbie Rave
The Klubbs
Monday 29th Evening
DJ Robbie Rave
Money
DJ Robbie Rave

APRIL
Thursday 1st Evening
DJ Robbie Rave
The Klubbs
Friday 2nd Evening
DJs Robbie Rave, Gray Donna
Bronco
Rhino
Saturday 3rd Evening
DJs Robbie Rave, Gray Donna
The Klubbs
Orgin
Sunday 4th Evening
DJ Robbie Rave
Confucius
Monday 5th Evening
DJ Robbie Rave
The Klubbs
Thursday 8th Evening
DJ Robbie Rave
Strife
Friday 9th Evening
DJs Robbie Rave, Gray Donna
Possessed
Mushroom

Saturday 10th Evening
DJ Robbie Rave
Mushroom
Confucius
Sunday 11th Evening
DJ Robbie Rave
Confucius
Larry Adlis and His Group
Monday 12th Evening
DJ Robbie Rave
The Klubbs
Thursday 15th Evening
DJ Robbie Rave
Confucius
Friday 16th Evening
DJs Robbie Rave, Gray Donna
Warhorse
Kansas Hook
Saturday 17th Evening
DJs Robbie Rave, Gray Donna
Kansas Hook
Perfumed Garden
Sunday 18th Evening
DJ Robbie Rave
The Klubbs
Monday 19th Evening
DJ Robbie Rave
Strife
Thursday 20th Evening
DJ Robbie Rave
Brewer's Droop
Friday 21st Evening
DJs Robbie Rave, Gray Donna
Upstairs:
Soul Disco
Downstairs:
Bethany
Satisfaction
Tea and Sympathy
Saturday 22nd Evening
DJs Robbie Rave, Gray Donna
Upstairs:
Soul Disco
Downstairs:
Bethany
The Klubbs
Sunday 25th Evening
DJ Robbie Rave
Graphite
Monday 26th Evening
DJ Robbie Rave
Confucius
Thursday 29th Evening
DJ Robbie Rave
The Purple Gang
Friday 30th Evening
DJs Robbie Rave, Gray Donna
Blitz (From USA)
Axis

MAY
Saturday 1st Evening
DJs Robbie Rave, Gray Donna
Ginger
Sebastian Cork
Sunday 2nd Evening
DJ Robbie Rave
Ginger
Spring Fever
Monday 3rd Evening
DJ Robbie Rave
The Klubbs
Thursday 6th Evening
DJ Uncle Joey Wall
Strife
Friday 7th Evening
DJs Joey Wall, Gray Donna
Dada (twelve-piece band with Robert
  Palmer and Elkie Brooks on vocals)
Gravy Train
Saturday 8th Evening
DJs Joey Wall, Gray Donna
Gravy Train
Ferry
Sunday 9th Evening
DJ Joey Wall
Possessed
Monday 10th Evening
DJ Joey Wall
The Klubbs
Thursday 13th Evening
DJ Robbie Rave
RA
Friday 14th Evening
DJs Robbie Rave, Gray Donna
Tear Gas
Ronno
Saturday 15th Evening
DJs Robbie Rave, Gray Donna
Tear Gas
Ronno
Sunday 16th evening
DJ Robbie Rave
The Klubbs
Monday 17th Evening
The Klubbs
Thursday 20th Evening
DJ Robbie Rave
Confucius
Friday 21st Evening
DJs Robbie Rave, Gray Donna
Renaissance
Galliard
Saturday 22nd Evening
DJs Robbie Rave, Gray Donna
Galliard
Strife
Sunday 23rd Evening
DJ Robbie Rave

Strife

Monday 24th Evening
DJ Robbie Rave
The Alan Bown Set

Thursday 27th Evening
DJ Robbie Rave
Kansas Hook

Friday 28th Evening
DJs Robbie Rave, Gray Donna
Fairfield Parlour
Cottage

Saturday 29th Evening
DJs Robbie Rave, Gray Donna
Karakorum
The Klubbs

Sunday 30th Evening
DJ Robbie Rave
Karakorum

Monday 31st Evening
The Klubbs

JUNE
Thursday 3rd Evening
DJ Robbie Rave
Ned Pringe

Friday 4th Evening
May Blitz (from USA)
Northwind (From Scotland)

Saturday 5th Evening
DJs Robbie Rave, Gray Donna
Northwind
The Klubbs

Sunday 6th Evening
DJ Robbie Rave
The Flying Hat Band

Monday 7th Evening
DJ Robbie Rave
Strife

Thursday 10th Evening
DJ Robbie Rave
Kansas Hook

Friday 11th Evening
Possessed
Confucius

Saturday 12th Evening
DJs Robbie Rave, Gray Donna
Possessed
Confucius

Sunday 13th Evening
DJ Robbie Rave
Confucius

Monday 14th Evening
DJ Robbie Rave
The Klubbs

Thursday 17th Evening
DJ Robbie Rave
Jerico Jones

Friday 18th Evening
DJs Robbie Rave, Gray Donna

Conchise
Killing Floor

Saturday 19th Evening
DJs Robbie Rave, Gray Donna
Killing Floor
The Klubbs

Sunday 20th Evening
DJ Robbie Rave
The Klubbs

Monday 21st Evening
DJ Robbie Rave
Confucius

Thursday 24th Evening
DJ Robbie Rave
The Klubbs

Friday 25th Evening
DJs Robbie Rave, Gray Donna
Kansas Hook
Egg

Saturday 26th Evening
DJs Robbie Rave, Gray Donna
Graphite
Rhino

Sunday 27th Evening
Ned Pringe

Monday 28th Evening
DJ Robbie Rave
The Klubbs

JULY
Thursday 1st Evening
DJ Robbie Rave
Confucius

Friday 2nd Evening
DJs Robbie Rave, Gray Donna
Tear Gas (from Scotland)
Time

Saturday 3rd Evening
DJs Robbie Rave, Gray Donna
Tear Gas
Strife

Sunday 4th Evening
DJ Robbie Rave
Hamster

Monday 5th Evening
DJ Robbie Rave
Fatgut

Thursday 8th Evening
DJ Robbie Rave
The Klubbs

Friday 9th Evening
DJs Robbie Rave, Gray Donna
Salamander
Fernhill

Saturday 10th Evening
DJs Robbie Rave, Gray Donna
Beggars' Opera (from Scotland)
Spring Fever

Sunday 11th Evening
Confucius

Monday 12th Evening
DJ Robbie Rave
The Klubbs

Thursday 15th Evening
DJ Robbie Rave
Strife

Friday 16th Evening
DJs Robbie Rave, Gray Donna
Trapeze
RA

Saturday 17th Evening
DJs Robbie Rave, Gray Donna
Kansas Hook
Wave

Sunday 18th Evening
DJ Robbie Rave
The Klubbs

Monday 19th Evening
DJ Robbie Rave
The Klubbs

Thursday 22nd Evening
DJ Robbie Rave
Confucius

Friday 23rd Evening
DJs Robbie Rave, Gray Donna
Galliard
Strife

Saturday 24th Evening
DJs Robbie Rave, Gray Donna
Galliard
9.30 Fly

Sunday 25th Evening
DJ Robbie Rave
Strife

Monday 26th Evening
DJ Robbie Rave
The Klubbs

Thursday 29th Evening
DJ Robbie Rave
Rhino

Friday 30th Evening
DJs Robbie Rave, Gray Donna
The Klubbs
Wave

Saturday 31st Evening
DJs Robbie Rave, Gray Donna
Ginger
Possessed

AUGUST
Sunday 1St Evening
DJ Robbie Rave
Ginger

Monday 2nd Evening
DJ Robbie Rave
Hamster

Thursday 5th Evening
DJ Robbie Rave
Hamster

Friday 6th Evening
DJs Robbie Rave, Gray Donna
Ned Pringe
Nothin' Ever 'Appens

Saturday 7th Evening
DJs Robbie Rave, Gray Donna
White Heat
Nothin' Ever 'Appens

Sunday 8th Evening
DJ Robbie Rave
The Klubbs

Monday 9th Evening
DJ Robbie Rave
Strife

Thursday 12th Evening
DJ Robbie Rave
White Heat

Friday 13th Evening
DJs Robbie Rave, Gray Donna
Northwind
Confucius

Saturday 14th Evening
DJs Robbie Rave, Gray Donna
Quicksand
Rebecca

Sunday 15th Evening
DJ Robbie Rave
Confucius

Monday 16th Evening
DJ Robbie Rave
Strife

Thursday 19th Evening
DJ Robbie Rave
The Klubbs

Friday 20th Evening
DJs Robbie Rave, Gray Donna
Possessed
Hamster

Saturday 21st Evening
DJs Robbie Rave, Gray Donna
Possessed
Hamster

Sunday 22nd Evening
DJ Robbie Rave
Confucius

Monday 23rd Evening
DJ Robbie Rave
Strife

Thursday 26th Evening
DJ Robbie Rave
Ned Pringe

Friday 27th Evening
DJs Robbie Rave, Gray Donna
Strife
Spontaneous Combustion

Saturday 28th Evening
DJs Robbie Rave, Gray Donna
Gypsy
Brewers' Droop

Sunday 29th Evening
DJ Robbie Rave
Brewers' Droop

Monday 30th Evening
DJ Robbie Rave
Strife

SEPTEMBER
Thursday 2nd Evening
DJ Robbie Rave
Confucius

Friday 3rd Evening
DJs Robbie Rave, Gray Donna
Northwind
Orpheus

Saturday 4th Evening
DJs Robbie Rave, Gray Donna
Northwind
Ned Pringe

Sunday 5th Evening
DJ Robbie Rave
Strife

Monday 6th Evening
DJ Robbie Rave
Strife

Thursday 9th Evening
DJ Robbie Rave
Ned Pringe

Friday 10th Evening
DJ Robbie Rave
Good Habits
Woodfall

Saturday 11th Evening
DJs Robbie Rave, Gray Donna
Strife
Good Habits

Sunday 12th Evening
DJ Robbie Rave
Hamster

Monday 13th Evening
DJ Robbie Rave
Strife

Thursday 16th Evening
DJ Robbie Rave
Confucius

Friday 17th Evening
DJs Robbie Rave, Gray Donna
Blonde on Blonde
Wave

Saturday 18th Evening
DJs Robbie Rave, Gray Donna
Hackensack Myth

Sunday 19th Evening
DJ Robbie Rave
Strife

Monday 20th Evening
DJ Robbie Rave
Confucius
Thursday 23rd Evening
DJ Robbie Rave
Volcano
Saturday 25th Evening
DJs Robbie Rave, Gray Donna
Smokestack
Crumble
The Klubbs
Sunday 26th Evening
DJ Robbie Rave
Hamster
Monday 27th Evening
DJ Robbie Rave
Strife
Thursday 30th Evening
DJ Robbie Rave
Stackwaddy

OCTOBER
Friday 1st Evening
DJs Robbie Rave, Gray Donna
Renaissance
Hamster
Saturday 2nd Evening
DJs Robbie Rave, Gray Donna
Cotton Wood (from USA)
Headstone
Monday 4th Evening
DJ Robbie Rave
Confucius
Thursday 7th Evening
DJ Robbie Rave
Strife
Friday 8th Evening
DJs Robbie Rave, Gray Donna
Anion Din (ex-Hawkwind)
The Sutherland Bros
Saturday 9th Evening
DJs Robbie Rave, Gray Donna
Gravy Train
The Sutherland Bros
Sunday 10th Evening
DJ Robbie Rave
The Klubbs
Monday 11th Evening
DJ Robbie Rave
Strife
Thursday 14th Evening
DJ Robbie Rave
Filibuster
Friday 15th Evening
DJs Robbie Rave, Gray Donna
Tear Gas
Jumbo
Saturday 16th Evening
DJs Robbie Rave, Gray Donna

Tear Gas
Graphite
Sunday 17th Evening
DJ Robbie-Rave
Confucius
Monday 18th Evening
DJ Robbie Rave
Strife
Thursday 21st Evening
DJ Robbie Rave
Stackwaddy
Friday 22nd Evening
Stackridge
Saturday 23rd Evening
DJs Robbie Rave, Gray Donna
Home
Ginger
Sunday 24th Evening
DJ Robbie Rave
The Klubbs
Monday 25th Evening
DJ Robbie Rave
Confucius
Thursday 28th Evening
DJ Robbie Rave
Ned Pringe
Friday 29th Evening
DJs Robbie Rave, Gray Donna
Glencoe
Sattva
Saturday 30th Evening
DJs Robbie Rave, Gray Donna
Glencoe
Sattva
Sunday 31st Evening
DJ Robbie Rave
Strife

NOVEMBER
Monday 1st Evening
DJ Robbie Rave
Strife
Thursday 4th Evening
DJ Robbie Rave
Wave
Friday 5th Evening
DJs Robbie Rave, Gray Donna
Galliard
Graphite
Saturday 6th Evening
DJs Robbie Rave, Gray Donna
Galliard
RA
Sunday 7th Evening
DJ Robbie Rave
Strife
Monday 8th Evening
DJ Robbie Rave
Easy Street

Thursday 11th Evening
DJ Robbie Rave
Confucius
Friday 12th Evening
DJs Robbie Rave, Gray Donna
Northwind
Strife
Saturday 13th Evening
DJs Robbie Rave, Gray Donna
Northwind
Wave
Sunday 14th Evening
DJ Robbie Rave
Confucius
Monday 15th Evening
DJ Robbie Rave
Strife
Thursday 18th Evening
DJ Robbie Rave
Scorpion
Friday 19th Evening
DJs Robbie Rave, Gray Donna
Vinegar Joe (Robert Palmer and
   Elkie Brooks on vocals – ex-Dada)
Tobias Wolfe
Saturday 20th Evening
DJs Robbie Rave, Gray Donna
Fatgut
Volcano
Sunday 21st Evening
DJ Robbie Rave
Ned Pringe
Monday 22nd Evening
DJ Robbie Rave
Wave
Thursday 25th Evening
DJ Robbie Rave
Confucius
Friday 26th Evening
DJs Robbie Rave, Gray Donna
Tear Gas
Pluto
Saturday 27th Evening
DJs Robbie Rave, Gray Donna
Possessed
Sunday 28th Evening
DJ Robbie Rave
Axis
Monday 29th Evening
DJ Robbie Rave
Strife

DECEMBER
Thursday 2nd Evening
DJ Robbie Rave
Wave
Saturday 4th Evening
DJs Robbie Rave, Gray Donna
Hackensack

Greasy Bear
Sunday 5th Evening
The Klubbs
Monday 6th Evening
DJs Robbie Rave, Gray Donna
The Klubbs
Thursday 9th Evening
Confucius
Friday 10th Evening
DJs Robbie Rave, Gray Donna
9.30 Fly
Paradise
Saturday 11th Evening
DJs Robbie Rave, Gray Donna
Sassafras
Paradise
Sunday 12th Evening
Confucius
Monday 13th Evening
Strife
Thursday 16th Evening
Hamster
Friday 17th Evening
Tapestry
Wave
Saturday 18th Evening
Tear Gas
The Klubbs
Sunday 19th Evening
The Klubbs
Monday 20th Evening
Timothy
Friday 24th Evening
DJs Robbie Rave, Gray Donna
Gravy Train
Hamster
Sunday 26th Evening
DJs Robbie Rave, Gray Donna
The Klubbs
Confucius
Monday 27th Evening
DJ Robbie Rave
The Klubbs
Strife
Thursday 30th Evening
DJ Robbie Rave
Strife
Friday 31st Evening
DJs Robbie Rave, Gray Donna
Strife
Confucius

1972

JANUARY
Saturday 1st Evening
DJs Robbie Rave, Gray Donna

The Klubbs
Jug
Sunday 2nd Evening
DJ Robbie Rave
Dogfeet
Monday 3rd Evening
DJ Robbie Rave
Top Group
Thursday 6th Evening
DJ Robbie Rave
Wave
Friday 7th Evening
DJ Robbie Rave
Woodfall
Chips
Saturday 8th Evening
DJ Robbie Rave
Ginger
Chips
Sunday 9th Evening
DJ Robbie Rave
Tobias Wolfe
Monday 10th Evening
DJ Robbie Rave
Tobias Wolfe
Thursday 13th Evening
DJ Robbie Rave
The Klubbs
Friday 14th Evening
DJs Joey Wall, Robbie Rave
The Klubbs
Amoeba
Saturday 15th Evening
DJ Joey Wall, Robbie Rave
Silverwood
Amoeba
Sunday 16th Evening
DJ Robbie Rave
Wave
Monday 17th Evening
DJ Robbie Rave
Strife
Thursday 20th Evening
DJ Robbie Rave
Timothy
Friday 21st Evening
DJs Joey Wall, Robbie Rave
The Klubbs
Spring Feeling
Saturday 22nd Evening
DJs Robbie Rave, Joey Wall
Anvil
Spring Feeling
Sunday 23rd Evening
DJ Robbie Rave
Anvil
Monday 24th Evening
DJ Robbie Rave
Potomac

Thursday 27th Evening
DJs Robbie Rave, Joey Wall
The Klubbs
Friday 28th Evening
DJs Robbie Rave, Joey
Galliard
Wave
Saturday 29th Evening
DJs Robbie Rave, Joey Wall
Galliard
Spontaneous Combustion
Sunday 30th Evening
DJ Robbie Rave
Confucius
Monday 31st Evening
DJ Robbie Rave
The Klubbs

FEBRUARY
Thursday 3rd Evening
No disco, power cut
Strife
Friday 4th Evening
DJs Robbie Rave, Joey Wall
Scapa Flow
Timothy
Saturday 5th Evening
DJs Robbie Rave, Joey Wall
Jug
Timothy
Sunday 6th Evening
DJ Robbie Rave
Wave
Monday 7th Evening
DJ Robbie Rave
Fatgut
Thursday 10th Evening
DJs Robbie Rave, Joey Wall
Confucius
Saturday 12th Evening
DJs Robbie Rave, Joey Wall
Hackensack
Pugmaho
Sunday 13th Evening
DJ Robbie Rave
Hackensack
Thursday 17th Evening
DJs Robbie Rave, Joey Wall
Soul Disco
Red Dirt
Friday 18th Evening
DJs Robbie Rave, Joey Wall
Red Dirt
Wave
Saturday 19th Evening
DJs Robbie Rave, Joey Wall
The Klubbs
Wave

Sunday 20th Evening
DJ Robbie Rave
Confucius
Monday 21st Evening
DJ Robbie Rave
Graphite
Thursday 24th Evening
DJs Robbie Rave, Joey Wall
Nu-Frame
Friday 25th Evening
DJs Robbie Rave, Joey Wall
The Klubbs
Nu-Frame
Saturday 26th Evening
DJs Robbie Rave, Joey Wall
The Klubbs
Dusk
Sunday 27th Evening
DJ Robbie Rave
Dusk
Monday 28th Evening
DJ Robbie Rave
Wave

MARCH
Thursday 2nd Evening
DJs Robbie Rave, Joey Wall
Plum Cottage
Friday 3rd Evening
DJs Robbie Rave, Joey Wall
Plum Cottage
Saturday 4th Evening
DJs Robbie Rave, Joey Wall
Dusk
Confucius
Sunday 5th Evening
DJ Robbie Rave
Dusk
Monday 6th Evening
DJ Robbie Rave
Confucius
Thursday 9th Evening
DJs Robbie Rave, Joey Wall
Squidd
Friday 10th Evening
DJs Robbie Rave, Joey Wall
Squidd
Sassafras
Saturday 11th Evening
DJs Robbie Rave, Joey Wall
The Klubbs
Sassafras
Sunday 12th Evening
DJ Robbie Rave
The Klubbs
Monday 13th Evening
DJ Robbie Rave
Wave

Thursday 16th Evening
DJs Robbie Rave, Joey Wall
Quicksand
Friday 17th Evening
DJs Robbie Rave, Joey Wall
Quicksand
Wave
Saturday 18th Evening
DJs Robbie Rave, Joey Wall
Wolf
Fatgut
Sunday 19th Evening
DJ Robbie Rave
Wolf
Monday 20th Evening
DJ Robbie Rave
Wolf
Thursday 23rd Evening
Upstairs: Disco – DJs Robbie Rave,
   Joey Wall
Quicksand
Downstairs:
Strife
Friday 24th Evening
DJ in disco Joey Wall
Ginger
Hamster
Saturday 25th Evening
DJs Robbie Rave, Joey Wall
Ginger
Hamster
Sunday 26th Evening
DJ Robbie Rave
Strife
Monday 27th Evening
DJ Robbie Rave
Strife
Thursday 30th Evening
DJs Robbie Rave, Joey Wall
Graphite
Friday 31st Evening
DJs Robbie Rave, Joey Wall
Graphite
The Klubbs

APRIL
Thursday 6th Evening
DJs Joey Wall, Robbie Rave
Acid
Havoc
Friday 7th Evening
DJs Joey Wall, Robbie Rave
Strife
Havoc
Saturday 8th Evening
DJs Joey Wall, Robbie Rave
Strife
The Klubbs

Sunday 9th Evening
DJ Robbie Rave
Argon
Monday 10th Evening
DJ Robbie Rave
Tobias Wolfe
Thursday 13th Evening
DJs Robbie Rave, Joey Wall
Wave
Friday 14th Evening
DJs Joey Wall, Robbie Rave
The Klubbs
Waterloo
Saturday 15th Evening
DJs Robbie Rave, Joey Wall
Smith Perkins and Smith (from USA)
The Klubbs
Sunday 16th Evening
DJ Robbie Rave
Smith Perkins and Smith
Monday 17th Evening
DJ Robbie Rave
Smith Perkins and Smith
Thursday 20th Evening
DJs Robbie Rave, Joey Wall
Wave
Friday 21st Evening
DJs Robbie Rave, Joey Wall
Pahana
The Living Dead
Saturday 22nd Evening
DJs Joey Wall, Robbie Rave
The Klubbs
Jon Damboro
Sunday 23rd Evening
DJ Robbie Rave
The Klubbs
Monday 24th Evening
DJ Robbie Rave
White Heat
Thursday 27th Evening
DJ Robbie Rave
The Klubbs
Friday 28th Evening
DJs Robbie Rave, Joey Wall
9.30 Fly
Waterloo
Saturday 29th Evening
DJs Joey Wall, Robbie Rave
Strife
9.30 Fly
Saturday 30th Evening
DJ Robbie Rave
Strife

MAY
Monday 1st Evening
DJ Robbie Rave
Acid

Thursday 4th Evening
DJ Robbie Rave
The Klubbs
Friday 5th Evening
DJs Robbie Rave, Joey Wall
Gravy Train
Pugma-ho
Saturday 6th Evening
DJs Robbie Rave, Joey Wall
Pugma-ho
The Living Dead
Sunday 7th Evening
DJ Robbie Rave
Wave Rave
Monday 8th Evening
DJ Bobbie Rave
The Klubbs
Thursday 11th Evening
DJ Robbie Rave
Confucius
Friday 12th Evening
DJs Robbie Rave, Joey Wall
Acid
Tobias Wolfe
Saturday 13th Evening
DJs Robbie Rave, Joey Wall
Pete Tidy
Tea and Symphony
The Klubbs
Sunday 14th Evening
DJ Robbie Rave
Strife
Monday 15th Evening
DJ Robbie Rave
Wave
Thursday 18th Evening
DJ Robbie Rave
Wave
Friday 19th Evening
DJs Robbie Rave, Joey Wall
Unicorn
The Klubbs
Saturday 20th Evening
DJs Robbie Rave, Joey Wall
Unicorn
Judas Priest (from Birmingham)
Sunday 21st Evening
DJ Robbie Rave
Acid
Monday 22nd Evening
DJ Robbie Rave
Confucius
Thursday 25th Evening
DJ Robbie Rave
Gravy Train
Friday 26th Evening
DJs Robbie Rave, Joey Wall
Possessed
Graphite

Saturday 27th Evening
DJs Robbie Rave, Joey Wall
Possessed
Graphite
Sunday 28th Evening
DJ Robbie Rave
Strife

JUNE
Thursday 1st Evening
DJ Robbie Rave
The Klubbs
Friday 2nd Evening
DJs Robbie Rave, Joey Wall
Gravy Train
Confucius
Saturday 3rd Evening
DJs Robbie Rave, Joey Wall
Gravy Train
Jerusalem Smith
Sunday 4th Evening
DJ Robbie Rave
Strife
Monday 5th Evening
DJ Robbie Rave
The Living Dead
Thursday 8th Evening
DJ Robbie Rave
Gary Wright and The Wonder Wheel
  (ex-Spooky Tooth)
Jerusalem Smith
Friday 9th Evening
DJs Robbie Rave, Joey Wall
Abednego
Grit Band
Saturday 10th Evening
DJs Robbie Rave, Joey Wall
The Klubbs
Abednego
Sunday 11th Evening
DJ Robbie Rave
The Klubbs
Monday 12th Evening
DJ Robbie Rave
Strife
Thursday 15th Evening
DJ Robbie Rave
The Klubbs
The Pretty Things
Friday 16th Evening
DJs Robbie Rave, Joey Wall
The Loon Street Gas Band
Victor Brox
Saturday 17th Evening
DJs Robbie Rave, Joey Wall
Tobias Wolfe
The Klubbs
Sunday 18th Evening
DJ Robbie Rave

Tea and Symphony
Monday 19th Evening
DJ Robbie Rave
Tea and Symphony
Thursday 22nd Evening
DJ Robbie Rave
Dante (afro rock)
Waterloo
Friday 23rd Evening
DJ Joey Wall, Robbie Rave
Hackensack
Waterloo
Saturday 24th Evening
DJ Joey Wall, Robbie Rave
Acid
Jerusalem Smith
Sunday 25th Evening
DJ Robbie Rave
Jerusalem Smith
Monday 26th Evening
DJ Robbie Rave
Gravy Train
Thursday 29th Evening
DJ Robbie Rave
Budgie (from Wales)
Bilf Slat
Friday 30th Evening
DJs Robbie Rave, Joey Wall
War Dog
Sergeant Jack

JULY
Saturday 1st Evening
DJs Robbie Rave, Joey Wall
War Dog
The Living Dead (from Stoke)
Sunday 2nd Evening
DJ Robbie Rave
The Living Dead
Monday 3rd Evening
DJ Robbie Rave
Confucius
Thursday 6th Evening
DJ Robbie Rave
Vinegar Joe (Elide Brooks and
  Robert Palmer on vocals)
Gravy Train
Friday 7th Evening
DJs Robbie Rave, Joey Wall
Gravy Train
Necromandus
Saturday 8th Evening
DJs Robbie Rave, Joey Wall
Stallion
Argon
Sunday 9th Evening
DJ Robbie Rave
Stallion

Monday 10th Evening
DJ Robbie Rave
Glass Fields
Thursday 13th Evening
DJ Robbie Rave
War Dog
East of Eden
Friday 14th Evening
DJs Robbie Rave, Joey Wall
Fusion Orchestra
War Dog
Saturday 15th Evening
DJs Robbie Rave, Joey Wall
Fusion Orchestra
Marble Orchard
Sunday 16th Evening
DJ Robbie Rave
Confucius
Monday 17th Evening
DJ Robbie Rave
Strife
Thursday 20th Evening
DJ Robbie Rave
Strife
Saturday 22nd Evening
DJs Robbie Rave, Joey Wall
Tea and Symphony
Evolution
Sunday 23rd Evening
DJ Robbie Rave
War Dog
Thursday 27th Evening
DJ Robbie Rave
Brinsley Schwartz (Nick Lowe)
Confucius
Friday 28th Evening
DJs Robbie Rave, Joey Wall
Bono
Hawthorn
Saturday 29th Evening
DJs Robbie Rave, Joey Wall
Bono
War Dog
Sunday 30th Evening
DJ Robbie Rave
Flying Hat Band
Monday 31st Evening
DJ Robbie Rave
Flying Hat Band

AUGUST
Thursday 3rd Evening
DJ Robbie Rave
Juicy Lucy
Jerusalem Smith
Friday 4th Evening
DJs Robbie Rave, Joey Wall
Butch
Pugmaho

Saturday 5th Evening
DJs Robbie Rave, Joey Wall
Butch
Pugmaho
Sunday 6th Evening
DJ Robbie Rave
Strife
Monday 7th Evening
DJ Robbie Rave
Confucius
Thursday 10th Evening
DJ Robbie Rave
Sergeant Jack
Gypsy
Friday 11th Evening
DJs Robbie Rave, Joey Wall
Gravy Train
Shaw Green Lane
Saturday 12th Evening
DJs Robbie Rave, Joey Wall
Gravy Train
9.30 Fly
Sunday 13th Evening
DJ Robbie Rave
Strife
Monday 14th Evening
DJ Robbie Rave
Hello Sailor
Thursday 17th Evening
DJ Robbie Rave
Patto
Grit Band
Friday 18th Evening
DJs Robbie Rave, Joey Wall
Frump (from Belfast)
Grit Band
Saturday 19th Evening
DJs Robbie Rave, Joey Wall
Frump
Sergeant Jack
Sunday 20th Evening
DJ Robbie Rave
The Shot
Monday 21st Evening
DJ Robbie Rave
Wardog
Thursday 24th Evening
DJ Robbie Rave
Thin Lizzy
Mahatma Kane Jeeves
Friday 25th Evening
DJs Robbie Rave, Joey Wall
Confucius
Mahatma Kane Jeeves
Saturday 26th Evening
DJs Robbie Rave, Joey Wall
Strife
Jerusalem Smith

Sunday 27th Evening
DJ Robbie Rave
Strife
Monday 28th Evening
DJ Robbie Rave
Wardog
Thursday 31st Evening
DJ Robbie Rave
Wardog
Strife

SEPTEMBER
Friday 1st Evening
DJs Robbie Rave, Joey Wall
Victor Brox
Necromandus
Saturday 2nd Evening
DJs Robbie Rave, Joey Wall
Victor Brox
Wardog
Sunday 3rd Evening
DJ Robbie Rave
Confucius
Monday 4th Evening
DJ Robbie Rave
Argon
Thursday 7th Evening
DJ Robbie Rave
Parachute
Gary Glitter
Saturday 9th Evening
DJ Robbie Rave
Strife
Flesh
Sunday 10th Evening
DJ Robbie Rave
Strife
Monday 11th Evening
DJ Robbie Rave
Fatgut
Thursday 14th Evening
DJ Robbie Rave
Gravy Train
The Roy Young Band
Friday 15th Evening
DJs Robbie Rave, Joey Wall
Flying Hat-Band
Gravy Train
Saturday 16th Evening
DJs Robbie Rave, Joey Wall
Flying Hat Band
Wardog
Sunday 17th Evening
DJ Robbie Rave
Wardog
Monday 18th Evening
DJ Robbie Rave
Parachute
Thursday 21st Evening
DJ Robbie Rave

The Flaming Groovies (from USA)
Bilf Slat
Friday 22nd Evening
DJ Robbie Rave
Argon
Food For Thought
Saturday 23rd Evening
DJ Robbie Rave
Strife
Argon
Sunday 24th Evening
DJ Robbie Rave
Wardog
Monday 25th Evening
DJ Robbie Rave
Confucius
Thursday 28th Evening
DJ Robbie Rave
Strife
Chicken Shack
Friday 29th Evening
DJ Robbie Rave
Highway
Spank
Saturday 30th Evening
DJ Robbie Rave
Highway
Wham Bam Thank You Ma'am

OCTOBER
Sunday 1st Evening
DJ Robbie Rave
Wardog
Monday 2nd Evening
DJ Robbie Rave
Strife
Thursday 5th Evening
DJ Robbie Rave
Rock and Roll All Stars, Singer Mel
  Grey (ex-Wild Angels)
Wardog
Friday 6th Evening
DJ Robbie Rave
Fusion Orchestra
Evolution
Saturday 7th Evening
DJ Robbie Rave
Unicorn
Jerusalem Smith
Sunday 8th Evening
DJ Robbie Rave
Wardog
Monday 9th Evening
DJ Robbie Rave
Strife
Thursday 12th Evening
DJ Robbie Rave
Supertramp
Quadrille

Friday 13th Evening
DJ Robbie Rave
Graphite
Judas Priest
Saturday 14th Evening
DJ Robbie Rave
Graphite
Orphan Harpoon
Sunday 15th Evening
DJ Robbie Rave
Orphan
Monday 16th Evening
Wardog
Thursday 19th Evening
DJ Robbie Rave
Smokey Joe
Budgie (from Wales)
Friday 20th Evening
DJ Robbie Rave
Jericho
Clean Blue Skies
Saturday 21st Evening
DJ Robbie Rave
Strife
Clean Blue Skies
Sunday 22nd Evening
DJ Robbie Rave
Strife
Monday 23rd Evening
DJ Robbie Rave
Confucius
Thursday 26th Evening
DJ Robbie Rave
The Living Dead
Focus (from Holland)
Friday 27th Evening
DJ Robbie Rave
Little Women
Pugmaho
Saturday 28th Evening
DJ Robbie Rave
Wardog
Pugmaho
Sunday 29th Evening
DJ Robbie Rave
Wardog
Monday 30th Evening
DJ Robbie Rave
Harpoon

NOVEMBER
Thursday 2nd Evening
DJ Robbie Rave
Strife
Suzi Quatro (from USA)
Friday 3rd Evening
DJ Robbie Rave
Hackensack
Flash Harry

Saturday 4th Evening
DJ Robbie Rave
Harpoon
The Living Dead
Sunday 5th Evening
DJ Robbie Rave
The Living Dead
Monday 6th Evening
DJ Robbie Rave
Wardog
Thursday 9th Evening
DJ Robbie Rave
Ginhouse
Blackfoot Sue
Friday 10th Evening
DJ Robbie Rave
Quicksand
Unborn Time
Saturday 11th Evening
DJ Robbie Rave
Quicksand
Snakeye
Sunday 12th Evening
DJ Robbie Rave
Wardog
Monday 13th Evening
DJ Robbie Rave
Strife
Thursday 16th Evening
DJ Robbie Rave
Holy Mackerel
Atacama (from South America)
Friday 17th Evening
DJ Robbie Rave
Wardog
Necromandus
Saturday 18th Evening
DJ Robbie Rave
Strife
Necromandus
Sunday 19th Evening
DJ Robbie Rave
Argon
Monday 20th Evening
DJ Robbie Rave
Harpoon
Wednesday 22nd Evening
DJ Robbie Rave
Ro-Do (band formed by John
  Entwhistle of The Who)
Wardog
Bilf Slat
Thursday 23rd Evening
DJ Robbie Rave
Biggies
UFO
Friday 24th Evening
DJ Robbie Rave
Confucius

Victor Brox
Rat
Saturday 25th Evening
DJ Robbie Rave
Victor Brox
Wardog
Sunday 26th Evening
DJ Robbie Rave
Wardog
Monday 27th Evening
DJ Robbie Rave
Strife
Thursday 30th Evening
DJ Robbie Rave
Confucius
Brinsley Schwarz

DECEMBER
Friday 1st Evening
DJ Robbie Rave
Zeus
Steel Peach
Saturday 2nd Evening
DJ Robbie Rave
Zeus
Steel Peach
Sunday 3rd Evening
DJ Robbie Rave
Jerusalem Smith
Monday 4th Evening
DJ Robbie Rave
Wardog
Thursday 7th Evening
DJ Robbie Rave
Amon Duul II (space rock from
  Germany)
Bilf Slat
Friday 8th Evening
DJ Robbie Rave
Bilf Slat
Collusion
Saturday 9th Evening
DJ Robbie Rave
Strife
Confucius
Sunday 10th Evening
DJ Robbie Rave
Strife
Monday 11th Evening
DJ Robbie Rave
The Lettermen
Thursday 14th Evening
DJ Robbie Rave
Patto
Confucius
Friday 15th Evening
DJ Robbie Rave
Fudd
Butch

Saturday 16th Evening
DJ Robbie Rave
Harpoon
Butch
Sunday 17th Evening
DJ Robbie Rave
Strife
Monday 18th Evening
DJ Robbie Rave
Harpoon
Thursday 21st Evening
DJ Robbie Rave
Strife
Friday 22nd Evening
DJs Robbie Rave, Ricky Van Dyke
Possessed
Confucius
Saturday 23rd Evening
DJs Robbie Rave, Ricky Van Dyke
Possessed
Ginhouse
Sunday 24th Evening
DJs Robbie Rave, Ricky Van Dyke
Confucius
Wardog
Tuesday 26th Evening
DJs Robbie Rave, Ricky Van Dyke
Strife
The Blue Mountain Boys
Thursday 28th Evening
DJ Robbie Rave
Amsterdam Lil
Friday 29th Evening
DJ Robbie Rave
The Parlour Band
Jerusalem Smith
Saturday 30th Evening
DJs Robbie Rave, Ricky Van Dyke
Pugmaho
Hiroshima
Sunday 31st Evening
DJs Robbie Rave, Ricky Van Dyke
Strife
Wardog

1973

JANUARY
Thursday 4th Evening
DJ Robbie Rave
Jericho
Saturday 6th Evening
DJs Robbie Rave, Ricky Van Dyke
Mantaray
Orphan
Sunday 7th Evening
Orphan

Monday 8th Evening
Amsterdam Lil
Thursday 11th Evening
Hackensack (Island stars)
Jerusalem Smith
Friday 12th Evening
Fraternity (seventeen-piece rock
   group from Australia)
Shiva
Saturday 13th Evening
Holy Mackerel (CBS stars)
Fraternity
Sunday 14th Evening
The Living Dead
Thursday 18th Evening
Strife
Friday 19th Evening
Wardog
Caliban
Saturday 20th Evening
DJs Robbie Rave, Ricky Van Dyke
Little Women
Blitz
Sunday 21st Evening
Confucius
Monday 22nd Evening
Wardog
Thursday 25th Evening
Geordie (new record 'Don't Do
   That')
Strife
Saturday 27th Evening
Bitter Harvest
Clear Blue Skies
Sunday 28th Evening
Jerusalem Smith
Monday 29th Evening
Bilf Slat
Wednesday 31st Evening
Teeny boppers nights begin – ages
   twelve to sixteen. Top disco

FEBRUARY
Thursday 1st Evening
Glen Comick's Wild Turkey (ex-
   Jethro Tull)
Friday 2nd Evening
White Rabbit
Henry and The Hatchetts
Saturday 3rd Evening
Henry and The Hatchetts
Scapa Flow
Sunday 4th Evening
Wardog
Monday 5th Evening
Amsterdam Lil
Thursday 8th Evening
Babe Ruth
Jerusalem Smith

Friday 9th Evening
Sandgate
Parachute
Saturday 10th Evening
Strife
Hiroshima
Sunday 11th Evening
Zeus
Monday 12th Evening
Zeus
Thursday 15th Evening
Glencoe (epic recording artists from
   Scotland)
Wardog
Friday 16th Evening
Harpoon
Caliban
Saturday 17th Evening
Strife
The Phil Roberts Band
Sunday 18th Evening
Pini
Monday 19th Evening
Wardog
Thursday 22nd Evening
Capability Brown (Charisma
   recording artists)
Friday 23rd Evening
Quadrille
Union
Saturday 24th Evening
Fingers
Amsterdam Lil
Sunday 25th Evening
Amsterdam Lil
Monday 26th Evening
Bulldozer

MARCH
Thursday 1st Evening
Strife
Mojo Hannah (ex-Thunderclap
   Newman)
Friday 2nd Evening
Wardog
Purley King
Saturday 3rd Evening
Jerusalem Smith
Purley King
Sunday 4th Evening
Jerusalem Smith
Monday 5th Evening
Harpoon
Thursday 8th Evening
Solutions (ex-Focus from Holland)
Friday 9th Evening
Fancy Smith
Highway

Saturday 10th Evening
Necromandus
Fancy Smith
Sunday 11th Evening
Harpoon
Monday 12th Evening
Fatgut
Thursday 15th Evening
Alex Harvey Band (first ever
   Liverpool appearance)
Tear Gas
Friday 16th Evening
Bilf Slat
Pugmaho
Saturday 17th Evening
Tasavallan (from Finland)
Presidente
Pugmaho
Sunday 18th Evening
Parachute
Monday 19th Evening
Wardog
Thursday 22nd Evening
Supersister (from Holland)
Friday 23rd Evening
Fingers
Incredible Hog
Saturday 24th Evening
Orphan
Incredible Hog
Sunday 25th Evening
Orphan
Monday 26th Evening
Jerusalem Smith
Thursday 29th Evening
String Driven Thing
Strife
Friday 30th Evening
Wardog
Headstone
Saturday 31st Evening
Graphite
Blackwood

APRIL
Sunday 1st Evening
Fatgut
Monday 2nd Evening
Parachute
Thursday 5th Evening
Saturnalia (New 3D LP)
Friday 6th Evening
Flying Hat Band
Clear Blue Skies
Saturday 7th Evening
Clear Blue Skies
Bilf Slat
Sunday 8th Evening
Bilf Slat

Monday 9th Evening
Amsterdam Lil
Thursday 12th Evening
Bilf Slat
Friday 13th Evening
Zeus
Saturday 14th Evening
Possessed
Zeus
Sunday 15th Evening
Confucius
Monday 16thEvening
Parachute
Thursday 19th Evening
Jonesy (featuring Alan Bown)
Saturday 21st Evening
Supercharge (ex-Confucius)
Sunday 22nd Evening
Harpoon
Monday 23rd Evening
Bullion
Thursday 26th Evening
Parachute
Friday 27th Evening
Al Quin (from Holland)
Jerusalem Smith
Saturday 28th Evening
Bulldozer
Children of God
Sunday 29th Evening
Harpoon
Monday 30th Evening
Fatgut

MAY
Thursday 3rd Evening
Strife (back from America)
Friday 4th Evening
Harpoon
Union
Saturday 5th Evening
Necromandus
Bracken Wood
Sunday 6th Evening
Caliban
Monday 7th Evening
Strife
Thursday 10th Evening
Jonesy with Alan Bown (Dawn
   Records)
Moonstone (CBS Records)
Friday 11th Evening
Harpoon
Bilf Slat
Saturday 12th Evening
Strife
Rondo
Sunday 13th Evening
Supercharge

Monday 14th Evening
Jerusalem Smith
Thursday 17th Evening
Bulldozer
Friday 18th Evening
Gravy Train
Caliban
Saturday 19th Evening
Strife
Gravy Train
Sunday 20th Evening
Strife
Monday 21st Evening
Caliban
Thursday 24th Evening
Incredible Hog
Friday 25th Evening
Orphan
Supercharge
Saturday 26th Evening
Flying Hat Band
Bullion
Sunday 27th Evening
Music Festival 8p.m.–3a.m.
Last Night at the Old Cavern Club.
DJs Robbie Rave, Ricky Van Dyke,
   Billy Butler, Joey Wall, Poser Paul
Hackensack
Supercharge
Strife
Bilf Slat
Harpoon

The Yardleys (from USA)

BIBLIOGRAPHY

Baird, Julia with Geoffrey Guiliano, *John Lennon – My Brother*, Grafton Books, 1988.

Clayton, Peter and Peter Gammond, *The Guinness Jazz A-Z*, Guinness Books, 1986.

Coleman, Ray, *John Lennon,* Futura Publications, 1985.

Davies, Hunter, *The Beatles,* Arrow Books ltd, 1968.

Epstein, Brian, *A Cellarful of Noise*, Hodder and Stoughton, 1964.

Frame, Pete, *The Beatles and Some Other Guys: Rock Family Trees of the Early Sixties,* Omnibus Press, 1997

Godbolt, Jim, *A History of Jazz in Britain, 1950 1970,* Quartet Books, 1989.

Guiliano, Geoffrey, *Dark Horse – the Secret Life of George Harrison,* Pan Books, 1991.

Lewisohn, Mark, *The Beatles Live!* Pavilion Books, 1986.

Marsden, Gerry with Ray Coleman, *I'll Never Walk Alone: An Autobiography,* Bloomsbury, 1993.

Melly, George, *Owning-Up,* Weidenfeld and Nicolson, 1965.

Rogan, Johnny, *Starmakers & Svengalis – The History of British Pop Management,* MacDonald Queen Anne Press, 1988.

Stuckey, David, *The Spinners – Fried Bread and Brandy-o!* Robson Books, 1983.

Tremlett, George, *The John Lennon Story,* Futura Publications Ltd, 1976.

Voce, Steve, Article in *Arts Alive* Merseyside free magazine, March 1972.

Welch, Bruce with Howard Elson, *Rock 'n' Roll I Gave You the Best Years of My Life – A Life in The Shadows,* Viking, 1989.